TRANSATLANTIC FEMINISMS
IN THE
AGE OF REVOLUTIONS

- women's manipulation of religion/rebellion ✳ (agency in)
- women's roles in medicine ← (emphasis on midwifery) ✳
- women disguised as men (physically and in per names) ✳
- women's roles in war/battle
- prostitution/sex work
- homosexuality
- maternity/midwifery ├
- female relationships (homosexual, patronage, organization)

TRANSATLANTIC FEMINISMS IN THE AGE OF REVOLUTIONS

Edited by
Lisa L. Moore,
Joanna Brooks,
and
Caroline Wigginton

OXFORD
UNIVERSITY PRESS

OXFORD
UNIVERSITY PRESS

Oxford University Press, Inc., publishes works that further
Oxford University's objective of excellence
in research, scholarship, and education.

Oxford   New York
Auckland   Cape Town   Dar es Salaam   Hong Kong   Karachi
Kuala Lumpur   Madrid   Melbourne   Mexico City   Nairobi
New Delhi   Shanghai   Taipei   Toronto

With offices in
Argentina   Austria   Brazil   Chile   Czech Republic   France   Greece
Guatemala   Hungary   Italy   Japan   Poland   Portugal   Singapore
South Korea   Switzerland   Thailand   Turkey   Ukraine   Vietnam

Published by Oxford University Press, Inc.
198 Madison Avenue, New York, New York 10016

www.oup.com

Oxford is a registered trademark of Oxford University Press

Library of Congress Cataloging-in-Publication Data
Transatlantic feminisms in the age of revolutions / edited by Joanna Brooks, Lisa L. Moore, and Caroline Wigginton.
p. cm.
Includes bibliographical references.
ISBN 978-0-19-974348-3 (hardcover : acid-free paper)—ISBN 978-0-19-974349-0 (pbk. : acid-free paper)
1. English literature—Women authors. 2. Feminist literature. 3. Women—Literary collections.
4. American literature—Women authors. 5. Feminism in literature. 6. Feminism and literature—English-speaking countries.
7. Women and literature—History—18th century. 8. Women and literature—History—17th century.
I. Brooks, Joanna, 1971– II. Moore, Lisa L. (Lisa Lynne) III. Wigginton, Caroline.
PR113.T73   2011
820.803522—dc22
2011002740

1 3 5 7 9 8 6 4 2

Printed in the United States of America
on acid-free paper

Contents

Acknowledgments

Joanna Brooks: This book is the product of deeply feminist friendships. Lisa Moore became my friend even before I joined the faculty at the University of Texas and our friendship has only deepened through the years. She has been my *comadre* in all things spiritual, intellectual, familial, and practical. Lisa, thank you for inviting me to join you on this project. Caroline Wigginton may have technically been my "student" long ago, but I have always regarded her with admiration as a colleague and a friend. Her contributions to this project have been definitive, and this volume attests to her deep knowledge and incredible effectiveness. I am grateful to Amanda Moulder, who generously shared her expertise and original research in early Cherokee writing. I want to acknowledge as well my teachers and colleagues in early American studies: Michael Colacurcio, Karen Rowe, Richard Yarborough, Meredith Neuman, Lisa Gordis, Bryan Waterman, Hilary Wyss, Kristina Bross, Karen Salt, and many others. Finally, as always, big thanks go to David Kamper, a full partner in feminist aspiration and endeavor, and to my daughters Ella and Rosa who keep me dreaming of feminist futures.

Lisa Moore: My greatest debt is to my two co-editors. Joanna Brooks rescued this project at a crucial moment when I had almost abandoned it. Her wide and deep knowledge of early American writing and capacious sense of the possibilities of global feminisms not only reinvigorated but re-imagined this book. Caroline Wigginton joined our team at an equally delicate moment; her expertise in early women's writing, unflagging energy, and scholarly rigor made it possible to complete the project. With gratitude for their superb colleagueship and feminist solidarity, I thank Joanna and Caroline. Jim Sidbury, Laura Mandell, and George Boulukos, friends and colleagues, talked me through this project with patience and insight, and I appreciate their contributions to this book. I would also like to thank former students who assisted me on this project at various stages: Ashley Shannon, Patrick McKelvey, and Layne Craig. Special thanks to Mary Katherine Matalon, who executed a last-minute, long-distance research task that allowed us to ensure the correctness of our edition of Sarah Pierce's "Verses." Finally, I would like to thank my wife Madge and our children Max and Milo, who never fail to inspire me.

Caroline Wigginton: First and foremost, I would like to thank my co-editors, Joanna Brooks and Lisa Moore, for inviting me to join this project. It has been inspiring to not only read, research, and discuss feminist authors from the Age of Revolutions, but also witness and participate in the feminist practices of these two contemporary scholars, mentors, and friends. I also extend my gratitude to Matt Cohen, Jim Cox, Lydia Wilmeth French, and Alberto Varon, who listened and asked insightful questions as I talked through the complexities of individual chapters. Finally, as always, thank you to Kerry and our children, Luke, Georgia, and Aubrey, for their patience and love.

TRANSATLANTIC FEMINISMS
IN THE
AGE OF REVOLUTIONS

Introduction

LISA L. MOORE AND JOANNA BROOKS

Towards the end of the eighteenth century a change came about which, if I were rewriting history, I should describe more fully and think of greater importance than the Crusades or the Wars of the Roses. The middle-class woman began to write.

—Virginia Woolf, *A Room of One's Own*

"LET YOUR WOMEN HEAR OUR WORDS"

In April 1776, Abigail Adams sat down at her writing desk in her home in Braintree, Massachusetts, to discuss with her friend, the revolutionary playwright Mercy Otis Warren, the possibility that women might gain from the American Revolution. The Revolution was the culmination of a long series of trade, territorial, and political conflicts between England and its colonies in North America that had steadily escalated into warfare. For more than a year, British troops and American militiamen had been skirmishing in New York and Massachusetts, with many major battles fought in Boston, just twelve miles north of the Adams family home. Warren had hosted strategy meetings at her home for the revolutionary group the Sons of Liberty and wrote plays that boldly decried the British Empire. Like many other American revolutionary women, Adams and Warren organized and participated in boycotts of British goods and other political actions. They followed news from battles fought close to home, and read revolutionary pamphlets such as Thomas Paine's influential *Common Sense*, published in

January 1776. They corresponded with revolutionary actors and thinkers of the Atlantic world, men and women in Great Britain and America like John Hancock, George Washington, and Catharine Macaulay. They fully lived their revolutionary moment.

But despite their commitment to the Revolution neither woman was permitted to take a role in the formal political deliberations that would determine its outcomes. Instead, they relied on communication with their husbands John Adams and James Warren and other powerful men to influence the course of revolutionary events. In March 1776, Adams had written to her husband John, who was then in Philadelphia with the Continental Congress, demanding that the Congress "Remember the Ladies" as it framed a "new Code of Laws" to govern the United States of America. In a moment when America was boldly pronouncing its rejection of British tyranny, Abigail Adams called for the end of the tyranny of men over women: "That your Sex are Naturally Tyrannical is a Truth so thoroughly established as to admit of no dispute," she wrote. "We are determined to foment a Rebelion, and will not hold ourselves bound by any Laws in which we have no voice, or Representation." Just as Anglo-American colonists excluded from Parliamentary representation had thrown off the laws of Britain, Abigail Adams raised the specter that the revolutionary moment might lead the unrepresented women of America to rebel against the men who governed their lives. John Adams lovingly but dismissively laughed at Abigail Adams's demands. This did not deter her from continuing serious discussion about the Revolution and the status of women with Warren. "I think I will get you to join me in a petition to Congress," she wrote. Adams specifically hoped to convince the Continental Congress to reform English marriage laws that gave "such unlimited power to the Husband to use his wife Ill" and to correct gender "domination" by "establishing some Laws in favour upon just and Liberal principles." Using the revolutionary discourse of reason, liberty, and justice, Abigail Adams and Mercy Otis Warren seized upon their moment to try and establish a more egalitarian future for Anglo-American women.

A few years later, in July 1781, on the Holston River in Tennessee, another revolutionary woman surrounded by the turmoil of a different war against empire stood up before a crowd of white men to defend the lands and liberties of her people. Her name was Nanye'hi, or Nancy Ward, and she held the powerful office of Beloved Woman of the Cherokee Nation. Responding to the attacks of Anglo-American settlers on Cherokee territory and autonomy, Ward issued a challenge to the United States treaty officials:

> You know Women are always looked upon as nothing; but we are your Mothers; you are our sons. Our cry [is] all for Peace; let it continue because we are Your

Mothers. This Peace must last forever. Let your Womens sons be Ours, and let our sons be yours. Let your Women hear our Words.

Let your Women hear our Words. Within the Cherokee intellectual and political universe, women and men played essential and complementary roles. Women held positions of power like that of Beloved Woman. Women met in their own political councils, as well as within councils with men. Women fought in wars and took part in land and captive negotiations. Women played a full role in maintaining the order and survival of the Cherokee people. To the Cherokee, a nation that did not honor and enfranchise its women was a disorderly nation, a dangerous nation, a nation capable of harm. "Where are your women?" wondered the Cherokee leader Attakullakulla, who led a delegation of Cherokee men and women to negotiate with English colonists in 1759. Attakullakulla was shocked to find no women among the English negotiating party. Nanye'hi also knew from her interactions with white colonial society that Anglo-American women did not enjoy the same rights and powers as Cherokee. She looked upon the gathering of United States Treaty officers, all men, and saw an immature, dangerous political entity. "[W]e are your Mothers; you are our sons," she told them. "Let your Women hear our Words." Nanye'hi demanded that the women of the new United States be consulted in order to arrive at the best possible decision for all concerned.

The words of Nanye'hi and the example of other indigenous American political women did echo around the revolutionary Atlantic world. Seven years later, in 1798, in London, English feminist Mary Robinson also argued for women's political power, and significantly, she did so by invoking the fabled rights of Native American women. Like Anglo-American women in North America, women in Great Britain and Ireland were formally excluded from systems of governance, even as revolutionary news and ideas circulated freely among them by print and word of mouth. No doubt Robinson, for many years the lover of Banaster Tarleton, the feared leader of the British forces in North America and hence the ally of the Mohawk, heard firsthand anecdotes of the status of Mohawk women such as Molly Brant. A contemporary commentator said of Brant, the sister of Chief Joseph Brant: "Miss Molly Brant's influence over [her people] is far Superior to that of all the Chiefs put together."[1] Stories about Nancy Ward and Molly Brant circulated in London, allowing Robinson to observe in her 1799 *Letter to the Women of England,*

---

[1] Sharon Harris, ed., *American Women Writers to 1800* (New York: Oxford University Press, 1996), 279.

Many of the American tribes admit women into their public councils, and allow them the privileges of giving their opinions, *first*, on every subject of deliberation. The ancient Britons allowed the female sex the same right: but in modern Britain women are scarcely allowed to express any opinions at all![2]

Women's political power like that lived by Nanye'hi and advocated by Abigail Adams, Mercy Otis Warren, and Mary Robinson was not achieved during the revolutions of the late eighteenth century. (Suffrage was not achieved until 1917 in Great Britain and 1920 in America. For indigenous women, the moment of suffrage is difficult to pinpoint. Some began voting in national and state elections as early as 1920, others were not enfranchised until the Indian Citizenship Act of 1924, and still others did not realize suffrage until the Civil Rights Era, as was also the case for African-American women.) But the discourse of the revolutionary age inspired women to challenge the tyranny of sex, to discuss passionately the urgent necessity of change in the lives of women, and to devise new ways to live the promises of revolution. *Transatlantic Feminisms in the Age of Revolutions* brings together the voices and writings of seventeenth-and eighteenth-century women around the North Atlantic. In so doing, we seek to tune into a lost historic conversation among English-speaking women, to gain a sense of the many origins of feminist thought, and to create a new history of feminism that abandons national frameworks and instead tracks the revolutionary dreams and words of women as those words traveled around the Atlantic world.

TRANSATLANTICISM, FEMINISM, REVOLUTION: DEFINITIONS

For many, many years, it has been customary to think about literature and culture within national frameworks. Eighteenth-century British literature encompasses a field of its own, while literature written during the same century in English by British-American authors has been treated as an entirely separate field. Scholars who specialize in eighteenth-century British and American literatures have begun only recently to develop a robust conversation comparing these literary cultures, their deep connections, and their telling differences. This new approach to literary study is often called *transatlanticism*: the study of the transnational and intercultural

---

[2] See p. 325, note 4.

networks of literary and cultural movement around the Atlantic world, including Europe, Africa, and the Americas. Scholars of the African diaspora—the network of African and African-descended peoples displaced across Europe and the Americas—have led the transatlanticist movement by encouraging us to think about culture as taking shape along *routes* of movement and exchange rather than as having exclusive *roots* in one homeland. Consequently, transatlantic studies of literature tend to focus on how ideas and words travel, freely and unfreely, in print and in the minds and mouths of people set loose by history, across oceans, through seaports, cities, and across frontiers.

As feminist scholars of eighteenth-century English and American literature, we want to know how transatlantic movements of peoples impacted women's lives, ideas, imaginations, hopes, and fears. In this book, we collect texts, some not published since the eighteenth century, that bear witness to the vibrant English-language discussion of women's status that circulated around the North Atlantic world between Africa, Europe, the Caribbean, and North America. Our focus is on writing by women that appeared in print, but we made a few exceptions where we felt another kind of text (by a man, circulated in manuscript, first published in a language other than English) was too integral a part of this discussion to be left out. Ever since the English-born colonial American poet Anne Bradstreet published her first book of poems *The Tenth Muse Lately Sprung up in America* in London in 1650, books written by Anglophone or English-speaking women have been traveling the North Atlantic. We imagine that the same ships that transported books of poetry by learned and elite women like Bradstreet may have also carried the words of other women—maybe a shipment of religious pamphlets by radical Quaker women like Margaret Fell, or wampum belts and other indigenous forms of nonalphabetic writing created by Native American women and returned to England as souvenirs. If we acknowledge that the cultural circuits of English-language transatlanticism had their foundations in the violent and destructive workings of empire, we must also imagine that the ships that carried poems trafficked unfree, indentured, and enslaved women from Europe and Africa, and in their minds the songs and stories of their original peoples.

We want to know how transatlantic movements and encounters with women from other countries and continents affected the way women thought about themselves in a time of political revolution. The word *feminism*, which we define as consciousness of and opposition to sex- and gender-related oppression, originated in England in the late nineteenth century. Yet we find distinctly *feminist* ideas and writings circulating within Europe as early as the fifteenth century and around the Atlantic world from the sixteenth century onward. The famous *querelle des femmes*—fierce literary debates over the status and character of women—raged among European elites in France, England, and elsewhere from the fifteenth through the eighteenth century. From the sixteenth century, radical elements of the Protestant Reformation, like the Moravians of Germany and the England-based Society of Friends (Quakers), proclaimed the spiritual equality of men and women, and they brought this message to America. Meanwhile, the antifeminism of the Catholic Counter-Reformation deeply impacted independent and educated women who had made their homes within the all-female spaces of the convents, especially brilliant women writers like Sor Juana Ines de la Cruz of seventeenth-century Mexico, who ceased to publish under pressure from her Catholic superiors. Feminism, we find, was alive and well long before there was a name for it.

In fact, when we assemble seventeenth- and eighteenth-century English-language writings about the status of women, most by women but a few key texts by men, we get an exciting new view of the early history of feminism in the English-speaking North Atlantic world. We see that modern feminist literature and thought emerged from many seventeenth-century sources—from elite women defending their ancient right to education, from radical religious women insisting on their unmediated access to divine truth, and from laboring class white women and women of color who told the hard truths of their lives. We also see that in the early eighteenth century, with the rise of the middle class, expanded literacy, and a growing print culture, Anglophone feminism consolidated around the following three major issues: the nature and source of sexual difference, the institutionalized injustice of heterosexual marriage, and women's access to education. Finally, in the late eighteenth century, modern feminism was galvanized by the ideals and the rhetoric of the American, French, and Haitian revolutions both adopting them and applying them to the status of women. While it is true that none of these women would have used the word *feminist* to describe themselves, we call them *feminists* because we recognize in their writings the history that has shaped our twenty-first-century feminist way of seeing and understanding the world.

The third major term in our title that needs definition is the "Age of Revolutions." In 1959, historian R. R. Palmer described the political upheavals of the late eighteenth century in France, America, Haiti, and elsewhere as an "Age of Democratic Revolution." Palmer observed that during this era throughout the Atlantic world societies were rejecting government by monarchy in favor of democratic republics. More recently, Marxist historian Eric Hobsbawm has expanded our concept of the late eighteenth century as an "Age of Revolution" to account not only for the establishment of democratic governments but also the industrial revolution taking place simultaneously. During these same decades, from about 1760 to 1830, slaves were revolting against their masters in North and Latin America and indigenous people were attempting to stop imperial incursions and revitalize their Native nations. We remember, too, religious revolutions that rippled through Europe and America from the sixteenth-century Protestant Reformation through the Second Great Awakening in North America in the early nineteenth century, many of which had significant impacts on the way women understood themselves and their power. Thus, we imagine an *Age of Revolutions* in this most expansive sense, as the culmination of centuries of radical change around the Atlantic world in a concentrated period of organized revolution to advance human freedom.

Between the English Revolution of 1689 and the Irish Rebellion of 1798, the transatlantic world was rocked by political, economic, social, religious, and industrial and political change. The emergence of modern democratic capitalism and democratic rhetorics of equality, liberty, and justice took place against a backdrop of slavery, imperialist violence, and the raping of natural resources, a paradox summed up by the title of David Brion Davis's famous book, *The Problem of Slavery in the Age of Revolution*. Throughout this period, women seized opportunities to argue for an expansion of their roles and rights in the experimental postrevolutionary political systems that were being devised, but repeatedly, revolutionary promises failed to extend to women as citizens. In a famous 1977 essay, the feminist historian Joan Kelly asked, "Did women have a Renaissance?"[3] Kelly observed that the frameworks for understanding history based in institutions and records created by men may not be simply transposable to lives of women. Traditional historical periods developed for a historiography that has typically excluded women's experience may distort our views of women in the past. This leads us to ask, "Did women have an Age of Revolutions?" Given women's exclusion within the new Enlightenment republics established in the eighteenth century, do terms such as "Revolution" and "Enlightenment" obscure more than they reveal? In this volume, we take a middle way between dismissing conventional historical concepts outright and adopting them uncritically. The women's voices collected here, we argue, sometimes participated explicitly and self-consciously in debates about revolution, enlightenment, and liberation, engaging with the major male thinkers and activists of the period as intellectual equals.

---

[3] "Did Women Have a Renaissance?" in *Women, History and Theory: The Essays of Joan Kelly* (Chicago: University of Chicago Press, 1984).

THE AGE OF REVOLUTIONS: HISTORICAL BACKGROUND

Where did this Age of Revolutions come from? What unleashed this great burst of revolutionary energy? The Age of Revolutions was a time in which free and unfree peoples around the Atlantic world were adjusting to massive changes in their traditional ways of life. The end of the feudal era and the rise of capitalism and with it imperialism in the fifteenth and sixteenth centuries caused tremendous loss and upheaval for women living traditional agrarian lifestyles in their ancestral villages in England, Ireland, Wales, Scotland, the indigenous Americas, and West Africa. As societies reorganized themselves around the European imperial drive to control territories, natural resources, and populations in the Americas, Africa, and Asia it became clear that this new historical era would be a time of organized violence on an unprecedented scale, a time of tremendous uncertainty as well as glimmering possibilities.

The rise of imperialism and early capitalism enriched a few wealthy Englishmen and women but uprooted thousands upon thousands of English, Irish, and Scottish commoners. Whole villages were displaced and destroyed by the enclosure of commons and pastures that transformed collective farmlands into private domains for the for-profit raising of sheep and the production of wool for trade and export. The forests common English people relied on for game to feed their families and that were the source of many of their indigenous literary and pre-Christian religious traditions were also destroyed to build legions of war and merchant-adventure ships in the service of imperialism. Common people forced from their ancestral lands fell into disease-ridden cities such as London. Some were successfully recruited to sell themselves as foot soldiers in the colonization of the Americas. Losing their homes, forests, traditional livelihoods, and families to the race for global domination, the hunger to dominate the seas and colonize the New World levied real costs on English, Irish, and Scottish women. With the continuing colonization of Ireland and Scotland by the English, Irish and Scottish women struggled to maintain their lands, languages, and traditional governments; many landless Scots and Irish immigrated to North America. Meanwhile, in the name of global domination, Englishwomen also lost traditional forms of forest-based social government such as the courts called *swainmotes*, and they saw their fathers, brothers, and sons leave home and participate in massive violence (including sexual violence) against and displacement of Irish, Scottish, African, and North American indigenous peoples. Women also shipped themselves to the New World: some went as religious pilgrims, wives and daughters of colonial officers, pirates, prostitutes, or in bondage as indentured servants. Some women sought to preserve or improve their class status by marrying into the elite colonial class and supporting its domination, while others took part in anti-colonial rebellions in the Americas such as Bacon's Rebellion and the Tobacco Cutting riots. Some married into and lived their lives in close relationship with African and indigenous communities in the New World.

Of course, indigenous American women suffered tremendous impacts from European imperialism. Many tribal populations were decimated by epidemic diseases brought by European traders and settlers: it is estimated that European-originated diseases like measles and smallpox killed as many as 6 million indigenous men and women in North America before 1600. Colonial wars and land thefts cut deeply into traditional indigenous territories and caused tremendous upheaval in the economic and political lives of tribal communities and the well-being of their natural environments. The forcible imposition of colonial Christianity also impacted traditionally egalitarian views on gender in many Native communities. Many indigenous thought traditions featured strong female creator figures, such as Grandmother Spider among the Pueblos of the American Southwest, Corn Mother or Selu among the Cherokee, or Changing Woman among the Navajos. Some American indigenous societies such as the Cherokee and the Iroquois vested women with significant political and economic power as holders of land title and determiners of tribal leadership. Women midwives, healers, diplomats, and holy people held positions of public esteem in many indigenous societies. (See, for example, writings by and about Katharine Tegakoüita, Coosaponakeesa/Mary Musgrove Mathews Bosomworth, Mary "Molly" Brant/Tekonwatonti/Konwatsi-Tsiaienni, and Nancy Ward/Nanye'hi anthologized in this volume.) These traditionally egalitarian views on gender were punished by Christian colonial officials and warped under the intense pressures of colonial power struggles. Still, indigenous women found ways to maintain their distinctive cultures, whether by blending them with European forms, adapting new modes of sociocultural leadership, or openly resisting colonization. Despite devastating changes to their populations, territories, and freedoms, women also preserved a sense of their traditional political authority.

In the fifteenth and sixteenth centuries, Africa, too, was a land in turmoil. Regional civil wars rocked the countryside and generated a large internal trade in prisoners of war or slaves. Soon, Portuguese and English traders arrived and exploited Africa's internal conflicts by purchasing prisoners of war to work as slaves on American colonial plantations. Thus began the modern African slave trade. Between 1500 and 1800, approximately 15 million African men, women, and children were bound and taken across the Atlantic under filthy and horrifying conditions. As many as one third died from shipboard diseases, and others attempted or committed suicide on the way. Sexual violence against enslaved African women and men was routine. In addition to these physical atrocities, slaves experienced a form of spiritual and social death in being separated from their homelands, home cultures, and families.

To deal with the spiritual costs of this violently unsettled modern world, many women and men turned to spirituality and religion, which were also undergoing world-shattering changes in the Age of Revolutions. Beginning in the sixteenth century, the Protestant Reformation launched a powerful critique of the Catholic Church and led to the development of new Christian traditions led not by ordained priests but instead by a "priesthood of all believers." Common men and women, newly empowered by the fifteenth-century invention of the printing press and the translation of the Bible out of Latin and into vernacular languages, created their own theologies and developed their own visions for the realization of God's will on earth. The reformation contributed to massive changes in the political landscape of England, such as the English Civil War (1642–1651) between Protestant-identified Parliamentarians and supporters of the Catholic King Charles I. Other English radical reformation sects such as the Ranters and Diggers gleaned from their Bibles millenarian visions in which the poor and laboring classes of England would inherit the earth, while the leveling tendencies of the Society of Friends (Quakers) led them to promote the equality of men and women. (A wonderful example of early Quaker feminist writing by Margaret Fell is included in this volume.) Even moderate English middle-class Protestant movements such as the Separatists (known to us as "Puritans") invested women like Anne Hutchinson (also anthologized here) with a larger sense of their capacity for direct communication with the divine. The Protestant belief that common people could find and make meaning for themselves was a tremendous comfort to people negotiating the turbulent new realities of the modern era.

To protect themselves and their loved ones during these times of genocide, warfare, and enslavement, some Black and indigenous peoples also relied on their own traditional religious practices such as Yoruba or Voudun, while others developed innovatory new forms of religious practice blending African and Christian traditions. In the 1730s and 1740s, the transatlantic evangelical movement described as "the Great Awakening" revived and enhanced the radical and visionary elements of Protestant Christianity, often with a message of mercy, rebirth, and racial and gender inclusiveness that attracted and won significant numbers of Black and indigenous converts (including Damma/Marotta/Magdalena, Phillis Wheatley, and Elizabeth Hart Thwaites, whose writings are included in this volume). To be sure, the Age of Revolutions was an age of rapid change and expansion in religious life around the Atlantic world.

The Age of Revolutions was also a time of contests and conflicts over trade and territory as competing European powers, indigenous nations, and slave populations allied with and against each other to gain power in North America and the Caribbean. Beginning in 1756, the Seven Years War pitted England and its European and indigenous American allies against France and its allies, resulting in a consolidation of British colonial rule in eastern North America in 1763. During the same time period, dozens of slave revolts rippled through North America and the Caribbean as African and African-American slaves strategized for freedom and self-government. Ever since kidnapped Africans had first been enslaved in the Caribbean and North America, they had staged organized revolts against their captors. One important leader, Nanny of the Maroons, horrified by the treatment of female slaves on Jamaican plantations, escaped and founded Nanny Town in 1720, a successful community of formerly enslaved and indigenous people in the Blue Mountains of Jamaica. Nanny and her brothers went on to lead many more slave rebellions. These and other armed conflicts were fueled by a sense that in a time of rapidly changing geopolitical realities, men and women could win new advantages for themselves through armed struggle.

The revolt of British colonies in North America against Great Britain began as a conflict over colonial tax and trade policies. Fueled by a crosscurrent of democratizing movements in Protestant religion, liberal philosophy, and republican political thought, it became a full-scale democratic revolution, a decisive event in the Age of Revolutions and in the turn away from monarchy towards democratic republicanism and middle-class rule. Boycotts of British goods (many of them organized and led by women) and protests against the British government began in the 1760s, while armed battles between British combat troops and American militia began in 1775. Some Anglo-American women participated in the war as soldiers (like the cross-dressing Deborah Sampson Gannett, whose *Addr[e]ss* is included in this volume), spies, and messengers; thousands followed and encamped with the troops as cooks, nurses, laundresses, and sex workers. Many of the most heated battles of the American Revolution took place in the territories of Native American tribes, who suffered disproportionate rates of casualties, home and crop losses, and displacement. African-American women, too, occupied an ambivalent relationship to this revolution, which heralded liberty but made few concrete promises to the enslaved. Thousands of Black women took advantage of a British decree to grant freedom to any slave who defected to the Loyalist cause; records show that single Black mothers with as many as four or five young children ran from their American patriot masters to join the British. By the time the fighting ended in 1783, the new United States of America were on their way to establishing forms of democratic government premised on the recognition of political rights and civil liberties belonging naturally to individual citizens. However, deep contradictions between this ideal of natural rights, the economic dependence of the new nation on slavery, and long-standing customs of gender exclusion were enshrined both in the *Declaration of Independence* (anthologized here) and in the very heart of the United States Constitution (1787), which did not count enslaved Blacks as full persons deserving democratic representation or provide for the enfranchisement of women or African-Americans. (Only in the state of New Jersey did women have the right to vote; it was rescinded in 1807.) For the many American women who deeply supported secession from Britain and drew hopes from revolutionary rhetoric of liberty and equality, the American Revolution proved to be painfully incomplete.

Despite its shortcomings, the American Revolution did set off a chain of democratic revolts around the Atlantic world. In 1789, revolution came to France, where huge national debts, mounting economic woes for the middle and laboring classes, and famine and malnutrition among the poor combined to produce tremendous resentment against the privileges and excesses of King Louis XVI, other royalty, aristocratic clergy, and nobility. In June 1789, representatives of the common people seceded from the monarch-controlled Estates-General to declare themselves a new National Assembly representing the true will of the French people. On July 14, 1789, insurgent Parisians protested monarchical absolutism by storming the Bastille, a prison-fort symbolic of royal despotism. In August 1789, the National Assembly crafted the *Declaration of the Rights of Man and of the Citizen* (anthologized here), one of the most comprehensive and far-reaching statements of the revolutionary ideal of popular sovereignty and equality among men. However, like the chartering documents of the American Revolution, the French Declaration did not correct race slavery nor acknowledge the rights of women, a grave omission French feminists sought to correct with a petition in October 1789 and with political treatises such as *Declaration of the Rights of Women and Citizen* (1791) by Olympe de Gouges and the *Petition to the National Assembly on Women's Rights to Bear Arms* (1791) (both included in this volume). The American Revolution had inspired many English radicals to reconsider the position of women, but the French Revolution struck even closer to home. Mary Wollstonecraft addressed her landmark treatise, *A Vindication of the Rights of Woman* (also included here), to Talleyrand, the minister of education in the new Republican government in the early 1790s, believing that the educational reforms she argued for could be carried out on the brave new world being forged across the channel. When the French Revolution took a dark turn during the Reign of Terror (1792–1794)—a time when tens of thousands of people suspected of counter-revolutionary thought or activity (including central feminist thinkers like Olympe de Gouges) were sent to the guillotine—observers around the Atlantic world were shocked, but many continued to champion the ideals of *liberté, égalité*, and *fraternité* betrayed by Maximilien Robespierre and other Terror extremists.

Thousands of miles across the Atlantic in the French colony of Saint-Domingue (Haiti), African slaves and maroons sought to realize the promises of the French Revolution by taking control of the island into their own hands. Haiti was ripe for revolution: its extremely labor-intensive sugar and coffee industries meant that enslaved Blacks outnumbered free people of color and whites by a ratio of eight to one, and slaves faced high death rates due to extremely difficult living and working conditions. In October 1790, Haitian free people of color seized on the rhetoric of the *Declaration of the Rights of Man* and revolted for civic equality. Haitian slaves followed with their own massive uprising that began in August 1791 with a legendary vodoun ceremony led by Dutty Boukman and an unnamed *mambo*, or priestess, deep in the Haitian woods. Rebel leader Toussaint L'Ouverture produced the Constitution of Haiti in 1801 (the document is included in this volume), and the battles of the Haitian Revolution lasted through 1803, when Haiti defeated an invasion by troops of Napoleon Bonaparte to become (after the United States) the second modern, independent nation in the Western Hemisphere and the first free Black nation in the Americas.

The anti-imperial Irish Rebellion of 1798 swept up Anglo-Irish women writers such as Maria Edgeworth in its path, and was the last attempt until the early twentieth century to establish home rule for Ireland. Under British law, Catholic males could not vote and property and inheritance rights were severely limited. By the end of the eighteenth century there were virtually no Catholic landowners left in Ireland. Many had immigrated to the Americas to try to restore their lost fortunes. Practices of rack-renting (stripping the estate of resources, through the steady raising of rents, by absentee landlords) left peasant families and tenant farmers without livelihood, also fueling immigration. Inspired by American, French, and Haitian revolutionaries, the dissenting Protestants and Catholics of the United Irishmen launched an uprising against British occupiers in the hopes of achieving emancipation for Catholics and political independence from Great Britain. The Rebellion unleashed intensely brutal state-sponsored violence throughout Ireland, including gang rape of Irish women by the British military. Anti-imperial resisters continued to lash out against British rule, even after the end of the Rebellion and the passage of the Act of Union formally joining the Kingdom of Great Britain to the Kingdom of Ireland in 1800.

In addition to experiencing revolutions firsthand, women across the transatlantic experienced them through texts. In writings by and about women, they learned how distant women affected and were affected by these upheavals and how they had sought to realize social and political change. Such writings offered models for how to be women revolutionaries, even in the absence of military violence. For example, many American women began to refer to themselves as *citess* and *citizeness* after observing French women become *citoyennes*. Like their French counterparts, they marched in support of equality, freedom, and sisterhood. Others repudiated abusive husbands and publicly claimed personal freedom, as documented in "On the Marriage of Two Celebrated Widows" (1793) (included in this volume). Some, like Helen Maria Williams and Leonora Sansay (both anthologized here), profited by publishing sensational revolutionary narratives in which they proudly cast women as patriots and heroines who participated in and survived wartime violence.

Around the Atlantic world, from occupied Ireland to the slave plantations of the Caribbean, the Age of Revolutions was a time when women and men, most uprooted from their ancient, agrarian cultures, attempted to sort out all the violent changes of modernization and to determine through struggle what freedom would mean in an unstable modern world. Although the era's democratic revolutions failed to enfranchise women legally, women nonetheless drew from this time of profound economic, religious, political, and social change important resources for their own ongoing feminist struggles.

WOMEN'S LIVES AND FEMINIST STRUGGLES IN THE AGE OF REVOLUTIONS

One of the most important contributions of the Age of Revolutions was the modern concept of the citizen as an individual vested with inalienable rights to life, liberty, happiness, and property. Even though they drew feminist inspiration from this ideal, women did not yet have the rights of citizens, and the hard facts of their daily lives remained unchanged. Women still lived under the weight of thousands of years of customary gender biases institutionalized in common law, theology, and culture. Their struggle to right these biases and achieve greater equality and dignity was compounded by their lack of access to education. Few of the vaunted educational, scientific, or intellectual advances of the Enlightenment addressed basic hardships of women's lives.

Women in the Age of Revolutions, like their male counterparts, could not expect to live into what we would now consider middle age. Average life expectancy for Englishwomen in the period was about 36 years; for men, it was 35. City life was especially harsh: rural landed gentry in England lived anywhere from five to fifteen years longer than their urban counterparts in the period, while laboring-class English people might live as much as twenty-five years longer in the country than the city. Three out of four people died before age 40; one out of two people died under the age of 20. Life expectancy at birth for white women in America was about 40 years; only eighty-two of every hundred infant girls survived to their first birthdays. New immigrants unused to American diseases and climates experienced death rates as much as 70 percent higher during their first years in North America. Mortality rates were even higher among the enslaved Africans who made the treacherous "Middle Passage" from Africa to the Americas: in the late seventeenth and early eighteenth centuries, about one in ten slaves died on the voyage, with shipboard death rates declining to one in twenty slaves by the end of the eighteenth century.[4] Death rates were also astoundingly high—as high as 90 percent—in Native communities encountering new European diseases such as smallpox and measles in the seventeenth century. Even after initial waves of colonization, Native communities remained disproportionately vulnerable to death by warfare, famine, and disease.

Much of a woman's often short lifespan was taken up with marriage and childbearing. With the decline of the feudal order, the hierarchies once maintained through rigid class structures were transferred onto the dichotomy of gender. Marriage bore new weight as a structure of social and economic organization. In seventeenth- and early eighteenth-century England, marriage, especially among the laboring classes, could be carried out by a variety of customary procedures and was less formal than it was to become in the nineteenth century. The average age of first marriage in mid-eighteenth-century England was about 25 years old.[5] Younger women were often involved in relationships of social inequality—as many as 60 percent of such relationships involved older men and younger women, such as masters and servants—leading scholars to conclude that many of these relationships were nonconsenting.[6] In 1753, Parliament passed Lord Hardwicke's Marriage Act, which abolished common-law marriage, required legal marriage ceremonies, and set the age of consent for men at 14 and women at 12. The Act came with mixed consequences for women: it allowed husbands to repudiate their common-law wives, often leaving them in poverty, but it also allowed women to argue in court for their rights to marital property. Some women used the provisions of the Marriage Act to their advantage, but generally the rise of capitalism corresponded with a decline in women's property rights, and by the end of the eighteenth century, women's property legally passed to their husbands upon marriage, thus depriving women of their traditional right to hold property they had possessed before marriage. (Jurist William Blackstone's exposition on the legal

---

[4] Robin Haines and Ralph Shlomowitz, "Explaining the Mortality Decline in the Eighteenth-Century British Slave Trade," *Economic History Review* 53.2 (2000): 263.

[5] Jona Schellekens, "Economic Change and Infant Mortality in England, 1580–1837," *Journal of Interdisciplinary History* 32.1 (Summer 2001): 6.

[6] Cissie Fairchilds, "Female Sexual Attitudes and the Rise of Illegitimacy: A Case Study," *Journal of Interdisciplinary History* 8.4 (Spring 1978): 661.

doctrine of *feme covert* is included in this anthology.) Divorce was possible only by Act of Parliament, which meant that only a Member of Parliament (by legal definition, a male landowner) could initiate such an act. For this reason, there were only one hundred Parliamentary divorces in the eighteenth century. Women had no custody or property rights in the case of divorce, although they were sometimes granted both at the discretion of their ex-husbands.

Marriage was also a crucial determinant of life chances in British North America. Women married for survival, with many practical considerations in mind; for most, the romantic ideal of companionate love was a luxury. Before the American Revolution, women with means married earlier, while those without delayed their marriages until they could afford to support themselves. The average age of marriage among laboring-class people in middle eighteenth-century Virginia was 23 for women and 26 for men. But by the late eighteenth century, most American women married between the ages of 18 and 22. In the seventeenth century men outnumbered women in the colonies; by the Age of Revolutions, women outnumbered men, especially in American seaport cities and Caribbean colonies, where, historians estimate, there were only six or seven men for every ten women.[7] British colonies in the Americas followed English common law, which enforced the dependency of wives and widows. Married women had no control over property and could not write a will, execute an enforceable contract, or initiate a legal action without their husbands' consent or participation. Unlike women in the French and Spanish colonies, who under the Napoleonic codes retained control over their dowries, women in the English colonies saw their property made over to their husbands at marriage; their husbands could then spend or sell the property as they wished. Dowry did not revert to the woman automatically on widowhood, as was the case in the French and Spanish colonies. A woman did have "dower right" to the income from one-third of the husband's property if he died intestate and did not leave her more; but she could not sell or bequeath this property, and her interest in it ended with her death. English common law also favored sons over daughters; if a man died intestate, all his real property passed to his oldest son. Widows, especially middle-aged widows with limited chances of remarriage, faced very difficult economic situations, and a large number survived on public aid or charity. For these reason, many women used their first forays into writing to express their concerns and complaints about the institution of marriage, as did the writers Elizabeth Magawley and the anonymous authors of the poems "Woman's Hard Fate"

---

[7] Elaine Forman Crane, "Sexual Imbalance and Social Development: Eighteenth-Century Bermuda as a Case Study," *Signs* (Winter 1990): 231.

(1733) and "The Lady's Complaint" (1736) (included in this volume). Legal pathways to divorce expanded after the Revolutionary War, especially as many women deserted by their husbands in wartime pressed their cases on new state legislatures. Most women whose marriages dissolved did not seek the costly and time-consuming option of divorce.[8]

Women in communities of color and indigenous communities attempted to maintain traditional bonds of intimacy under the extreme pressures of warfare, colonization, enslavement, and racism. In many indigenous communities, marriage was a path to diplomacy, a tool to foster alliances between communities. This tradition continued even after European colonization, as some Native American women entered into marriages with Europeans and Euro-Americans in an effort to forge diplomatic bonds between their nations and the newcomers. In this spirit, Mohawk diplomat Molly Brant entered into a marital relationship with the English colonial officer William Johnson, and Cherokee Beloved Woman Nancy Ward married the Irish-American trader Bryant Ward. But as the broad consequences of aggressive European colonization became clear, intermarriage increased worries about the fragmentation of traditional societies, loss of cultural memory, and loss of tribal belonging. (See writings by Ward and Brant in this volume.) The system of slavery was extremely destructive to love and family life in African-American communities. Slave marriages were not recognized by law, although they were honored in Black and white churches and, of course, by slaves themselves. Enslaved African-Americans carried on African traditions and developed new ceremonies for solemnizing their own marriages.

For middle-class and elite feminists especially, reforming the spousal relationship was a pressing concern. They believed marriage did not need to be oppressive for women. As an alternative, they advocated companionate marriage founded upon respect and affection. Often, as in the case of Mercy Otis Warren and Abigail Smith Adams who referred to their husbands as friends, their own more equitable experiences of marriage served as evidence that marriage could be fulfilling and elevating. Many, like Mary Wollstonecraft, the anonymous Aspasia, and Annis Boudinot Stockton (all included here), insisted that domestic harmony could only be achieved through women's education. For example, in *Rights of Woman* (included here) Wollstonecraft argues, "[T]he woman who strengthens her body and exercises her mind will, by managing her family and practising various virtues, become the friend, and not the humble dependent of her husband."

---

[8] Deborah Rosen, "Women and Property across Colonial America: A Comparison of Legal Systems in New Mexico and New York," *William and Mary Quarterly* 60.2 (April 2003): 355–381.

A robust tradition of marriage resistance dating from the Middle Ages persisted through the Age of Revolutions and new forms of women's intimacy and women's solitude were shaped by its changes. Sometimes laboring-class women passed as men to gain access to adventure or better-paying work, as did Deborah Sampson Gannett (anthologized here) when she wore men's clothes to fight in the Revolutionary War; sometimes they "passed" to enter into marriages with other women, as did Charlotte Charke in mid-century England when she set up housekeeping with a wealthy widow, "Mrs. Brown." Convents, long a haven for intellectual women and those who chose not to marry, were driven to the Continent by anti-Catholic persecution in eighteenth-century England, but English Catholic women continued to seek out English convents, now located in France and Italy. To provide Protestant women with similar opportunities, Mary Astell suggested in her 1694 *A Serious Proposal to the Ladies* (also included in this volume) the establishment of Protestant religious retreats for those who did not marry, but the Church of England refused to open such retreats on the grounds that they smacked of "Papism." Sarah Scott left her husband after a year in 1752 to join Lady Barbara Scott. The two lived together until Lady Barbara's death, and Scott wrote a novel entitled *Millenium Hall* based on their experiences founding a home for poor women who wished not to marry. Other artistic, scientific, literary, and affectional communities founded by women included those presided over by the Duchess of Portland at her Bulstrode estate and Elizabeth Montagu, "Queen of the Bluestockings," in her London home. Lady Eleanor Butler and Sarah Ponsonby, Irish aristocrats who eloped not once but twice in the 1770s to rescue Ponsonby from an unwanted marriage, became famous as the "Ladies of Llangollen" and were visited by luminaries of the day such as Burke and Wordsworth. (Their relationship is memorialized in the poem "To Miss Ponsonby" by Anna Seward, included in this volume.) Anne Lister, born in 1791 in Yorkshire, kept detailed diaries of her sexual relationships with other women, declaring "I love and only love the fairer sex."[9] When discussing with a lover whether or not the relationship of the Ladies of Llangollen had "always been platonic," Lister wrote, "I look within myself & doubt," suggesting that the relationship was erotic.[10] According to a South Carolina newspaper announcement (included here), the French Revolution inspired two "celebrated widows"—one French, the other American—to renounce their husbands and marry each other in a ceremony presided over by male dignitaries. Genteel women who needed to support themselves financially might become

---

[9] Anne Lister, *I Know My Own Heart: The Diaries of Anne Lister, 1791–1840*, ed. Helena Whitbread (London: Virago, 1988), 210. Reprinted New York University Press, 1992.

[10] ibid., 145.

paid companions to wealthier women, governesses, or commercial writers of journalism, plays, and novels. Mary Wollstonecraft, born to an alcoholic father who dissipated the family's small fortune, hated governessing so much (one of her young charges threw rocks at her while his parents looked on, unconcerned) that she offered a scathing critique of the profession in her famous *Vindication of the Rights of Woman* (1792) (portions of which we include here). Whether as independent single women, sexual adventurers, itinerant laborers, romantic couples, or members of women's intentional communities, then, women continued to find ways to live alone or with each other rather than with men.

Unless they carefully developed such life paths for themselves, however, women could expect to spend the majority of their adult lives bearing children. It is important to note that heterosexual activity was not confined to marital relationships. Indeed, Mary Wollstonecraft refused conventional heterosexual propriety, falling in love first with the married painter Henry Fuseli (and suggesting that she move in with Fuseli and his wife), then with the American adventurer Gilbert Imlay, with whom she had a child, Fanny. Only when pregnant for the second time with the child of the philosopher William Godwin (a baby later to grow up to be Mary Shelley, the author of *Frankenstein*), did she consent to marry for the sake of her children. In eighteenth-century England and America, more than 30 percent of first births occurred less than nine months after marriage, and the average woman gave birth to 7.04 children during her lifetime.[11] In French Canada, women averaged as many as 10 childbirths during their lifetime.[12] Fertility rates were lower in enslaved African-American communities due to malnutrition, forced labor, and ongoing disruption of consensual heterosexual relations[13] as well as covert abortions and contraceptive use. Most enslaved women had their first child at a younger age than their white counterparts. Median age of last birth for all mothers in America was in their late 30s, meaning that women could expect to spend seventeen to twenty years of their life being pregnant or nursing. Women could control their fertility by nursing their children until 1 or 2 years of age, and by tradition many avoided sexual intercourse during the nursing years. Women also sought abortion, a practice known as "taking the trade," which was legal in America before the third month of pregnancy.[14]

---

[11] Cathy Davidson, *Revolution and the Word: The Rise of the Novel in Early America* (New York: Oxford University Press, 1986), 116.

[12] C. Wilson, "Natural Fertility in Pre-Industrial England," *Population Studies* 38.2 (July 1984): 228.

[13] Robert V. Wells, "Demographic Change and the Life Cycle of American Families," *Journal of Interdisciplinary History* 2.2 (Autumn 1971): 273–282.

[14] Cornelia Hughes Dayton, "Taking the Trade: Abortion and Gender Relations in an Eighteenth-Century Village," *William and Mary Quarterly* 48.1 (January 1991): 19–49.

Well into the eighteenth century, especially in rural areas and communities of color, most childbirths were attended by female midwives and other adult females of the community. Carrying on ancient traditions of woman-centered healthcare, many midwives were skilled and respected care providers. Between 1778 and 1812, the now legendary midwife Martha Ballard of Maine delivered more than eight hundred babies with only four recorded fatalities. The shift from midwife home care to hospitals and male medical doctors "trained" by fledgling medical colleges sometimes correlated with an increase in mother mortality. The establishment of "lying-in" hospitals in mid-eighteenth-century urban England led to large outbreaks of puerperal fever, with death rates as high as thirty-four mothers per thousand. One contemporary British observer noted that "a woman has a better chance of recovery after delivery in the meanest, poorest hovel, than in the best-conducted general hospital."[15] (Higher rates of maternal death in hospital than home births were recorded throughout the nineteenth century as the fields of gynecology and obstetrics developed. Early gynecological and obstetric experiments were often carried out through experimentation on enslaved Black women in America.[16]) Between 2 and 3 percent of all births in eighteenth-century America resulted in maternal death by hemorrhage, infection, or other causes. Over the course of their lifetimes—several births—about one in eight women died during or from complications of childbirth.

Death and loss were intimate companions of eighteenth-century women. In England, about one in every five babies died in its first year, and 50 percent of baptized children were dead by their fifth birthdays.[17] The very cheapest burial for a baby cost a week and a half's wages for an English laborer.[18] Anglo-American communities faced similar rates of infant mortality. In eighteenth-century Massachusetts, one in

---

[15] Thomas McKeown and R. G. Brown, "Medical Evidence Related to English Population Changes in the Eighteenth Century," *Population Studies* 9.2 (November 1955): 121; E. A. Wrigley, "Explaining the Rise in Marital Fertility in England in the 'Long' Eighteenth Century," *The Economic History Review* 51.3 (August 1998): 438; Jona Schellekens, "Economic Change and Infant Mortality in England, 1580–1837," *Journal of Interdisciplinary History* 32.1 (Summer 2001): 7.

[16] Marie Jenkins Schwartz, *Birthing a Slave: Motherhood and Medicine in the Antebellum South* (Cambridge: Harvard University Press, 2006).

[17] Thomas McKeown and R. G. Brown, "Medical Evidence Related to English Population Changes in the Eighteenth Century," *Population Studies* 9.2 (November 1955): 119–141; Felicity Nussbaum, "'Savage' Mothers: Narratives of Maternity in the Mid-Eighteenth Century," *Cultural Critique* 20 (Winter 1991–1992): 123–151.

[18] David Coleman and John Salt, *The British Population: Patterns, Trends, and Processes* (New York: Oxford University Press, 1992); Edwin Chadwick, *Report on the Sanitary Conditions of the Labouring Population of Great* Britain (1842), ed. M. W. Flinn (Edinburgh: Edinburgh University Press, 1965).

every six babies died, an increase from seventeenth-century mortality rates.[19] Indigenous and Black infant mortality rates in the eighteenth century were even higher, especially where women lived under conditions of warfare, malnutrition, forced labor, and systematic sexual assault. Upper- and middle-class women in Europe tended not to breastfeed their own children, instead hiring wet nurses from the laboring class. Breastfeeding was common practice among laboring-class Englishwomen, Anglo-American women of all classes, and women of color. Among English and Anglo-American gentry, the Quaker-influenced societies of Pennsylvania, Maryland, Delaware, and New Jersey, and some indigenous American tribes, childhood was viewed protectively as a crucial formative period of innocence and growth. Almost everywhere else, children were expected to work. Children of tenants on English, Irish, and Scottish estates were essentially considered indentured servants of the landowner. Young children in New England were put to work in their family homes and fields or apprenticed out in the service of others. Children of enslaved African-American women inherited their mothers' status. Most were separated from their parents during long working days, and some were sold away from their mothers. One-fifth of all children in America were slaves.[20]

Indeed, most women who traveled across the Atlantic did so under conditions of unfreedom as slaves or indentured servants. English recruiters worked to supply white indentured servants for the Caribbean and American trade; such labor offered plantation owners a cheaper alternative in the short run than the considerable initial cost of lifelong African slaves. Indentured servants transported to the Caribbean faced brutal working conditions and little chance of becoming independent householders once the indenture was fulfilled. About 10 percent of white indentured servants brought to British North American colonies were women, and most arrived under the age of 25. Young women servants, especially those who traveled alone, were extremely vulnerable to exploitative labor practices and physical and sexual violence. Even after completing their terms of servitude, many women remained on the economic margins. Thirty to 40 percent of American city dwellers in the Age of Revolutions were impoverished or on the verge of poverty, and about 2 or 3 percent lived in almshouses or poorhouses.

---

[19] Maris Vinovkis, "Mortality Rates and Trends in Massachusetts before 1860," *Journal of Economic History* 32.1 (March 1972): 198.

[20] Joseph E. Illick, "Childhood in Three Cultures in Early America," *Pennsylvania History* 64 (1997): 308–323; Paula Fass and Mary Ann Mason, eds, *Childhood in America* (New York: New York University Press, 2000).

Across the Atlantic, it is estimated that between 30 and 80 percent of the population of London lived in or near poverty, and 5 to 15 percent received poor relief.[21]

Yet women's basic literacy as well as their opportunities for higher education grew during the eighteenth century, fueled by the rise of middle-class print culture and Protestantism. Indeed, it was important to many of the dissenting sects in England for all people, including women, to read the Bible for themselves, which led to the establishment of Sunday schools for teaching reading. While women were less likely to have formal schooling than men, middle- and upper-class girls were usually taught to read at home, and laboring-class women such as Mary Leapor and Ann Yearsley (whose poems appear in this volume) taught themselves. By the mid-eighteenth century, the rate of signature literacy (the ability to write one's own name) in England was about 60 percent for men and 35 percent for women, while Scottish women's signature literacy rates hovered around 25 percent. In America, New England societies had the highest rates of literacy, with more than 80 percent of men and about 65 percent of women being signature literate on the eve of the Revolution. The lowest rates of literacy among Euro-American men and women were in rural French Canadian colonies, where only 10 percent of women and 15 percent of men could sign their names by the end of the eighteenth century. Among enslaved African Americans, the Great Awakening of the 1730s and 1740s led to widespread teaching of reading, especially by Quakers, Congregationalists, and Anglicans, who saw the conversion of slaves as a religious obligation. On Antigua, Anne and Elizabeth Hart, free women of color who had joined the Methodist mission, established a network of Sunday schools to educate free and enslaved Black Antiguans in literacy and Christianity. (A letter by Elizabeth Hart Thwaites is included here.) On the Dutch island colony St. Thomas, free woman of color Rebecca Protten did similar work with her fellow Moravians. Not until 1831 did it become illegal to teach slaves to read. Literacy rates among Native peoples varied widely by region, class, and religious affiliation, with Christian Natives in the Northeast having the highest literacy rates. One study of Wampanoag people in Massachusetts

---

[21] Peter Solar, "Poor Relief and English Economic Development before the Industrial Revolution," *Economic History Review* 48.1 (1995): 8; Billy G. Smith, "Poverty and Economic Marginality in Eighteenth-Century America," *Proceedings of the American Philosophical Society* 132.1 (1988): 92; Sharon Salinger, *To Serve Well and Faithfully: Labor and Indentured Servants in Pennsylvania, 1682–1800* (Bowie, Md.: Heritage, 2000); David Galenson, *White Servitude in Colonial America: An Economic Analysis* (Cambridge: Cambridge University Press, 1984).

suggests that only one in five Wampanoag women in the early eighteenth century could sign their own names. By 1810, nine out of ten Wampanoag women were signature literate.[22]

Although women's opportunities for formal education were circumscribed throughout the Atlantic world in the eighteenth century, many remarkable women reached high levels of educational achievement. There had been a tradition of the aristocratic learned woman in England ever since the time of Eleanor of Aquitaine in the twelfth century, and the achievements of seventeenth- and eighteenth-century "female philosophers" such as Elizabeth Elstob, Mary Astell (whose 1694 *A Serious Proposal to the Ladies* is included here), Margaret Cavendish (also included here), and the Duchess of Portland were well known. These women contributed to the major debates of their day in linguistics, political philosophy, and natural history, respectively, and were sought out by both male and female scholars as experts. Women at every rank, however, were educated beyond the primary level only at home; they could not be admitted to universities, laboratories, or art academies until well into the nineteenth century. In the United States, the first institution of higher education for women, Sarah Pierce's Litchfield Female Academy, opened in Connecticut as early as 1792. (Read Pierce's beautiful "Verses to Abigail Smith" in this volume.) The Academy became an important incubator for the generation of American women intellectuals who contributed to nineteenth-century reform movements, including Harriet Beecher Stowe and Catherine Beecher. In the Caribbean, free women of color such as Elizabeth and Anne Hart in Antigua wrote letters (one of which is included here) and a famous *History of Methodism* that circulated throughout England and the Americas. Contact between the texts and ideas of women around the Atlantic rim provided new opportunities for knowledge, as did the collision of English, indigenous, Irish, Scottish, and African people brought on by the demographic violence of colonialism. Women's lives—their hardships, adventures, achievements, philosophies, observations, and attempts to better their lots—became the subject matter for an explosion of writing in the period.

---

[22] Joel Perlmann and Dennis Shirley, "When Did New England Women Acquire Literacy?" *William and Mary Quarterly* 48.3 (1991): 1; E. Jennifer Monaghan, *Learning to Read and Write in Colonial America* (Amherst: University of Massachusetts Press, 2005), 385.

RENAMING THE AGE OF REVOLUTION

Returning, then, to the question—did women have an Age of Revolutions?—we find that women did live their revolutionary moment, although they were excluded from realizing some of its most potent emancipatory ideals. Clearly, the Age of Revolutions was not simply an age of democratic citizenship, decolonization, or the triumph of reason over tyranny for women. As feminist literary historiographers, we know it is important to frame our own terms to characterize women's experience.

Displacement in the Age of Revolutions produced an age of unprecedented contact among women from Europe, the Americas, and Africa. It was an age of new female intimacies fraught with dynamics of power, pleasure, ambivalence, inequality, cruelty, love, and possibility. We can imagine that many of these relationships such as those between slave owners and slaves and colonists and indigenous peoples entailed a denial of feminist possibilities for emancipation. But other relationships of mutual respect and acknowledgment enabled women to think comparatively and critically about their place in the modern world. The Age of Revolutions was also a time when friendship assumed new importance as political, artistic, and affective alliance, a bond through which women provided an audience for one another's writings and opinions as well as collaboration in the production of new knowledge.

For women, the Age of Revolutions was an age of mixed political possibilities, an age of opportunity and disappointment, an age of expanding intellectual horizons and social retrenchment. Euro-American women in America experienced the liberatory impulse, rhetoric, and possibility of the establishment of the new Republic, and English feminists cheered the revolution in France. But many of the liberal political forms that emerged from revolutionary movements viewed women as incapable of acting independently as citizens. Women were systematically disfranchised from political and economic participation as voters and property-holders. Postrevolutionary decades saw a rush of conservative social retrenchment as fears for the fate of young democratic nations were projected onto the bodies of women, for example, in the popular new genre of the seduction novel, which depicted young women as being constitutionally incapable of discerning or resisting the designs of men. (At the same time, American feminist Judith Sargent Murray wrote essays on resisting seduction and pursuing education, which are included in this volume.) Especially after the Revolution, Americans became preoccupied with questions of virtuous self-government, and many of these anxieties were deflected onto controlling the sexual lives of women. Men's bodies were generally viewed as more developed, and a woman's as weaker and more vulnerable.

The Age of Revolutions was also the period when the cultural logic of "separate spheres" took hold. The modern liberal political imagination divided the world into two spheres: a public sphere of commerce and politics, imagined as the sphere of men, and a private sphere of the home and family, imagined to be the province of women. The postrevolutionary rhetoric of separate spheres limited women's political influence to the home. For women who had long been working alone or alongside their husbands and other male relatives on ships, docks, farms, and family businesses, this imaginative rendering of "separate spheres" felt very much like a step backwards. It also diminished the political value of their work as mothers, even though idealized images of motherhood were celebrated in the propaganda of the American Revolution.

Similar retrenchments took shape in the sphere of law, where constricting notions of difference led to firmer and more intransigent notions of gender and race. In the later seventeenth and early eighteenth centuries, Anglo-American colonies passed laws criminalizing interracial sex and marriage and formalizing the hereditary quality of slavery. Under these new laws, the children of an unfree white woman were seen as being born free, while the children of an unfree Black woman were destined to slavery. Inequality was codified in ways that privileged white women and disadvantaged women of color. Consolidating new categories of sex and race created a new emphasis on female embodiment, resulting in unprecedented pressure on women to manifest bodily control and new ideals of virtue narrowly defined as sexual chastity. Still, women devised ways to use early national legal frameworks to argue for betterment of their status. In the 1780s, a Massachusetts slave named Belinda successfully petitioned for back wages or reparations from her master's estate. (Her petition is anthologized here.) A freed Black woman of Vermont named Lucy Terry, also a poet, represented herself and her husband in court to defend their land against encroaching neighbors and to petition for her son's admission to Williams College.

In the Age of Revolutions, women around the Atlantic world were telling and hearing stories that changed their understandings of themselves as women. Women shared oral traditions, some of which featured powerful female deities like the Cherokee Selu. The Bible provided new readers and listeners with stories such as Ruth and Naomi, Mary and Martha as models of women who supported one another's spiritual authority. With the popularization of print, women read almanacs, sermons, conversion narratives, hymnals, and miscellanies. They circulated their own writings in manuscript and kept commonplace books. Periodicals, including religious news, were a cheap form of entertainment and communication, and colonial newspapers often published women's poetry both anonymous and signed. Women also read best-sellers such as Richardson's novels, Defoe's *Robinson Crusoe*, both the political philosophy and the novels of Rousseau, and Burke's essays on government.

The second half of the eighteenth century saw the rise of sentimental novels by writers such as Samuel Richardson and Frances Burney, whose style inspired the radical sentimental fiction of the 1790s including that of Elizabeth Inchbald, Charlotte Smith, and Mary Hays in England and Charlotte Rowson and Hannah Foster in America. Just as young women readers of contemporary "chick lit," or popular women's literature, thrill to stories of love lost and found, seductions and escapes, individual victories and traumatic tragedies, young women of the eighteenth century gathered in groups to read best-selling romance novels like Rowson's *Charlotte Temple* and Foster's *The Coquette*. Many sentimental novels focused on the travails of young women victimized by seducers, rakes, and unreliable husbands. Although these novels often exaggerated the susceptibility of women to seduction, they also told hard truths about the starkness of the choices that faced middle-class young women in the early nation, when a woman's social and economic life chances depended tremendously on marriage, and legal codes nullified the rights of married women to act on their own behalf, when marriage meant babies, and for too many women, childbearing meant death. Encouraged by sentimental authors to weep compassionate tears for fallen heroines, young readers of the novel may have been led to believe, as the punitive plotlines of the romances suggested, that young women who made mistakes would never recover: that seduction led inevitably to death. More heartening and emboldening were political treatises by feminist writers like Judith Sargent Murray, an American champion of women's education, and English political theorist Mary Wollstonecraft, whose *Vindication of the Rights of Woman* was read by women around the Atlantic world and in its first year went through four editions in America alone. (Both are anthologized here.)

In the Age of Revolutions, women were writing. We find their words in familiar literary genres such as essays, poems, philosophical treatises, manifestos, and novels. But to do full justice to the range of women's writing in this period, we must train ourselves to listen carefully to genres outside those traditionally considered worthy of study: letters, household account books, legal documents, recipe books, medicinal books, botanical books, gardening and landscape records, sketch books with notes, and commonplace books are treasure troves of women's voices in the Age of Revolutions. With the rise of eighteenth-century middle-class print culture and increased circulation of newspapers and magazines, many women found ways to make their thoughts and writings public. American almanacs regularly featured satirical dialogues between husbands and wives that exposed and contested gender inequities. In newspapers, women assumed pen names and wrote essays and songs about their relationships with men and their status. United by their shared republican political values, the English historian Catharine Macaulay and the Anglo-American author Mercy Otis Warren corresponded across the Atlantic for thirty years; both were respected as political philosophers. Phillis Wheatley, enslaved in Massachusetts in the 1760s, rose in the dark early morning hours so she could write her poetry before beginning her domestic chores for the day. Her poetic career was encouraged and promoted by African-American and Euro-American women she met at literary salons and religious meetings. Women acted as literary patrons to one another, as Hannah Moore did for the laboring-class poet Ann Yearsley. Women not possessed of conventional alphabetic literacy who wanted to express themselves in writing skillfully employed the services of amanuenses, crafting texts that today read as a blend of oration and literature. (All of these women writers are included in this anthology.) Women made their writings public not only through the printing press but through extensive networks of manuscript circulation.

In the Age of Revolutions, women were organizing. Even with a constriction of their public roles, women gathered together in their homes, sewing circles, and at their tea tables to read newspapers, history, philosophy, theology, and literature. They talked about their ideas, feelings, and views of the rapidly changing world around them. They circulated their poems, recorded important ideas in their commonplace books, and exchanged letters with other intellectual women and men around the Atlantic world. Women supported their friends by selling each others' books of poems, forming religious study groups, and creating political action groups outside governmental structures from which they were excluded. Other "weapons of the weak" included political organizing done at salons and tea tables, in work groups such as knitting, sewing, and quilting circles, in public spinning meetings held in revolutionary New England, in informal reading and study groups, and in domestic poetry performances. Women who needed to support themselves and their children financially sometimes became Grub Street hacks, professional journalists whose political efforts and effects were inadvertently organized by the literary marketplace. In addition, women such as Mary Delany and the Duchess of Portland in England; Susanna Wright, Eliza Norris, and Milcah Martha Moore in Pennsylvania; Phillis Wheatley and Obour Tanner in New England; and Sarah Pierce in Connecticut formed intentional artistic communities that solidified bonds among women through visits, letters, poetic tributes, curricula, manuscript circulation, and commonplace books. Among women of color, community activists traveled and listened to other women's stories, then distilled this great oral archive into petitions and diplomatic documents. Laboring women worked together in households, and in agricultural settings, Mary Leapor and Yearsley worked with other women threshers and milkmaids, and chose to tell the stories of working women in their poems. Laboring-class women also knew domestic truths about the elite women in whose homes they worked, and wrote about this elite sphere too.

For women, then, the Age of Revolutions was an age of upheaval, possibility, and retrenchment. As readers, writers, and organizers, feminist women of the transatlantic world in the Age of Revolutions have left us a vibrant archive of feeling, knowledge, and experience, an archive that commemorates their remarkable energy and their remarkable times.

OUR HOPES FOR THIS ANTHOLOGY

Our cover image reflects the complexity of the transatlantic relations between women voiced by our anthology. Women's relationships in the age of revolutions as in all other periods were riven by brutality and violence even when eroticized and romanticized as sisterly bonds, as in the famous 1796 engraving by William Blake on our cover. Entitled "Europe Supported by Africa and America," the image was one of a series created by Blake, a radical printer and poet, to illustrate an important early account of the cruel treatment of slaves in Surinam by John Gabriel Stedman. Blake's illustrations, many of which were grisly depictions of how slaves were tortured and mistreated, were an important visual argument in the emerging abolitionist movement of the late eighteenth century. As such, this idealized image of sisterly bonds both sought to improve conditions for enslaved African and indigenous peoples, and perpetuated the view that an ideal world is one in which the white woman, representing Europe, remains central and "supported" by women representing the peoples of Africa and America, who have a subordinate role to play. The image speaks to the persistence of inequality between women in feminism as in the wider world. It speaks to the ongoing need for a truly inclusive feminism.

Our goal in producing *Transatlantic Feminisms in the Age of Revolutions* is to recapture the excitement of revolutionary times and to give readers an energizing sense of the historical conditions, global movements, collective efforts, and individual actions that make feminist revolution. We hope this book will contribute to the continuing growth of studies of women and gender in the eighteenth century. Feminist scholarship over the last forty years has overthrown the traditional assumption that women writers were rare, infrequent, or silenced in the elite British and American traditions. Many feminist literary scholars have spent decades recovering once-forgotten writings by women, giving us texts such as the monumental *Norton Anthology of Literature by Women*. While we have drawn our inspiration from the Norton Anthology and other works of "second-wave" feminist literary scholarship, we also feel responsible to incorporate a new consciousness of race, class, and imperialism characteristic of "third-wave" feminist studies. For example, we no longer assume that writing in itself is a feminist act: different women experienced different relationships to writing according to their social positions. Some educated, upper-middle-class European and Euro-American women were encouraged to write lyric poems by their families as a demonstration of their privileged status and refinement. For these women, writing may have been an empowering expressive exercise, but it was not the same kind of radical act as it was for imprisoned religious women challenging an oppressive British government or a strategically political act as it was for women of color who drafted petitions and legal memorials. This book places writings by European and Euro-American women side by side with writings by women of color so we can reflect on the ways different groups of women came to writing during the eighteenth century and the different purposes that motivated them. We recognize that there is an imbalance in the materials presented here; far fewer indigenous and African women are represented than white women. We resist, however, reading this inevitable feature of the archive to mean that the voices we *are* able to recover are exceptional. Rather, we have to take the singularity of the writers that remain in view as evidence of a lost archive of experience, challenging ourselves to work that much harder to remember these women's worlds using alternative sources such as oral traditions, public records, and anthropology. Their words were crucial to the Age of Revolutions.

In incorporating writings from a diverse range of traditions, we also hope to open up a new and more complicated sense of the historical origins of feminism. It is often assumed that feminism derives from the political movements of the Age of Revolutions and rests on the modern liberal idea that individuals are vested with natural or God-given rights that cannot be justly infringed upon or denied by other individuals or governments. But this view of feminism ignores the fact that in its conception and application this doctrine of the "Rights of Man" almost always excluded women. It also incorrectly centers the history of feminism around Europe when history shows us that women around the world working from a variety of religious and cultural traditions developed their own ways of thinking about and advancing the status and well-being of women. Looking at the writings presented in this volume, we find that modern Anglophone feminist literature and thought emerged from many seventeenth-century sources—from elite women defending their ancient right to education, from radical religious women insisting on their unmediated access to divine truth, from laboring-class women who told the hard truths of their lives, and from indigenous American women who fought to maintain traditional matrifocal and matrilineal power structures against patriarchal imperialism. The example of indigenous women in particular reminds us that some women come to feminism not to extend European liberal political philosophy of individual rights to include women but rather to defend traditional communal notions of women's authority against European encroachment.

Recognizing the multiple origins of feminism might lead us to open up our definition of feminism to include all women who act consciously as women to defend their communities against economic, political, social, or sexual exploitation, as many feminists of color have suggested.

We have organized the writings presented here in chronological order rather than grouping them by nation, region, language, or other social categories. In doing so, we have hoped to discover how feminist and revolutionary ideas developed in writing over time from the Protestant Reformation through the rise of the middle-class popular press into the Age of Revolutions. We hope our readers can see for themselves how feminist ideas grew and circulated with the circulation of people and print around the Atlantic world. In the early eighteenth century, we observe feminist writing consolidating around three major issues: the nature of sexual difference, the injustice of marriage, and access to education. Later in the century, feminists consistently engaged the ideals and rhetoric of the American, French, and Haitian Revolutions and applied them to the status of women. Reading historically allows us to track how these ideas developed and how women's words traveled across worlds. As we see in the opening examples of Frances Moore Brooke's novel *The History of Emily Montague* (1769) and the letters of Abigail Adams and Mercy Otis Warren, or as in the case of Cherokee orator Nancy Ward, novels about Native communities in Canada or speeches by Cherokee diplomats might reverberate with or inform political letters or philosophical treatises written by Jacobin feminists in ways we can only account for if we work across traditional generic and national boundaries.

Working within the expansive organizing framework of "transatlantic feminisms" not only encourages us to think comparatively across categories of race, ethnicity, and nation but also allows us to bring together writing from a range of literary genres and forms not traditionally considered literary, such as petitions and treaties. We generally reject the notion that writing must meet European and Euro-American aesthetic standards in order to be worthy of study. Through decades of literary scholarship, this standard of judgment has been used to dismiss unfamiliar work by women and non-elite writers from earlier periods. Reading beyond conventional literary standards helps us think more expansively about what writing meant to women from different cultures and the reasons besides the demonstration of individual virtuosity or genius they may have taken up their pens. It also challenges us to develop new terms for conceiving of literary value: for example, recognizing the skillful manipulation of tropes and generic conventions, or powerful first-person testimony, or innovative forms of argumentation. Doing feminist literary historiography, we believe, means being unorthodox and resourceful in the way we use archives and think about what counts as literature. To this end, *Transatlantic Feminisms in the Age of Revolutions* includes poetry, essays, and excerpts from novels, as well as polemic pamphlets, religious tracts, court transcripts, letters, petitions, and speeches.

The Age of Revolutions was a tumultuous and treacherous time for women around the Atlantic world. This was an expansive moment when possibilities emerged for women, many of which were glimpsed in the eighteenth century and still have yet to be realized today. But women created common grounds for the feminist movement. They developed a new (albeit imperfect and sometimes exclusionary) consciousness of women as a global class. They saw that in the revolutionary new world, women would have to define and redefine themselves. Neither a privileged class status inherited from a father nor the centuries-old customs of a tribe could protect them. It was up to them to value themselves, make the most of their lives, and act to protect and enlarge their futures.

What can we learn from them? We can learn the abiding revolutionary power of writing and reading. Transformation begins at the scale of listening, reading, speaking, writing, and publishing. We remember the words of the poet Muriel Rukeyser: "What would happen if one woman told the truth about her life? / The world would split open." In the Age of Revolutions more women than ever before start using writing—in private and public—to tell their truths.

We can also learn from these women the value of affiliating and organizing with other women. Revolutionary women of the eighteenth century dreamed big, but they were not daunted by small beginnings. They wrote even though there was little chance that their writing would reach a mass market beyond their friends and peers. They organized even though they were disenfranchised within major revolutionary movements of their times. From them, we can learn that small or local artistic and political efforts can revolutionize our daily lives, and that this lived form of revolution is richly worth the effort. Even small groups of women talking, thinking, writing, and acting together as students, activists, writers, workers, artists, or mothers can help us build sustaining relationships and develop a better perspective on the injustices of our twenty-first-century world as well as our responsibilities, challenges, and opportunities for emancipation.

Reading early feminist literature from its various beginnings in seventeenth-century England through its consolidation in the classic political treatises of the late eighteenth century, we see that the timeframe of historical change can be long. It was seventy years between the *Declaration of Independence* and the first convention for women's rights in America at Seneca Falls, New York, in 1848; it was seventy years more before American women won the right to vote in 1918. It took thirty-five years from the first organized interracial opposition to the slave trade in the 1780s to its abolition in Great Britain in 1807 and in the United States in 1808; it was twenty-five years more before the legal abolition of slavery in the British empire, and fifty-five years more before the legal abolition of slavery in 1863 in the United States. Women who dreamed of and demanded feminist change in the seventeenth and eighteenth centuries rarely lived to see it on a grand scale. But their daily efforts at thinking, writing, and organizing changed minds and hearts, created infrastructure for future movements, and developed revolutionary ideas and rhetoric. Women in the Age of Revolutions lived fuller, more emancipated lives in their own time because they dared to work for a feminist future.

We are the heirs and beneficiaries of the feminist revolutions of the eighteenth century. We find ourselves in the early twenty-first century having experienced another tidal wave of globalization. Once again, we are face-to-face with an unprecedented diversity of women from around the world who have become newly aware of heartbreaking injustices. Once again, consolidating power structures seem to have little regard for women as a class. In a globalizing world, we can learn from the past that women were always involved in every dimension of imperialism, liberation, and enslavement. They weren't just shuttled around by these great historical forces. They supported them, resisted them, survived them, and negotiated them. Today, remembering the example of European and Euro-American women who asserted the rights for women like themselves but did not challenge racist, classist, or imperialist forms of oppression, we can be aware of how our freedoms are related to the unfreedoms of other women, especially women in economically and politically colonized regions of the globe. Teaching ourselves to hear the words of African and Caribbean, enslaved and indentured, laboring and elite, settler and indigenous women in the Age of Revolutions, we can learn how to listen for underacknowledged women's voices in our world today. We can learn from the past that we must be vigilant against conceding rights that matter most to our daily lives, nor let opportunity for a few come at the expense of many.

The Age of Revolutions is incomplete.

A NOTE ON THE TEXTS

The English-language texts in this anthology have been transcribed from original seventeenth- and eighteenth-century sources (when available). Because English-language spelling and punctuation conventions were not standardized until the late eighteenth century with the introduction of the first dictionaries, many words were spelled differently by different writers and even by the same writer at different times. Thus, variations in spelling are not "incorrect," simply varied. Anthologized texts written originally in French have been modernized through the process of translation and reflect contemporary spelling, punctuation, and grammar conventions.

ONE

Anne Marbury Hutchinson (1591–1643)

*T*HE TREMENDOUS SOCIAL TRANSFORMATIONS IN THE AGE OF REVOLUTIONS INCLUDED THE *Protestant Reformation, which encouraged Christians throughout Europe to question the hierarchies and doctrines of established churches and to create new religious movements directed by the convictions of their members. In England, state repression of dissenting Protestants led the people we now call "Puritans" to seek new homes elsewhere in Europe and in North America. Anne Marbury Hutchinson emigrated from England to Massachusetts with her husband William Hutchinson and fifteen of their children in 1631. Making her home in Boston, Anne Hutchinson held a series of midweek Bible-study classes for women. As many as eighty people attended her study groups, including prominent men such as Massachusetts colony governor Sir Henry Vane.*

Anne Hutchinson's leadership and preaching threatened ministers of Boston churches and challenged conservative theologies that privileged male authority. She believed and taught others the revolutionary idea that the Holy Spirit was entirely responsible for communicating saving grace, faith, and wisdom to believers; she opposed the idea that humans could "prepare" themselves for salvation by doing good works, a position not in keeping with Orthodox Calvinism but quietly espoused by many Puritan ministers. Hutchinson's preaching pointed out fundamental doctrinal disagreements between church-state leaders over the "covenant of works" and the "covenant of grace": the question of whether believers could advance their salvation by their own good works, or whether they were entirely dependent on the grace of Jesus Christ. Leaders themselves would have preferred to ignore that thorny theological question in the interest of closing ranks and consolidating their worldly power as a colony.

Hutchinson was condemned by a conference of ministers in August 1637, tried by the General Court of Massachusetts, found guilty, put under house arrest, and finally banished from the Massachusetts Bay Colony. In her trial, clergy and colonial leaders accused her of dishonoring the "fathers of the commonwealth" and of other behavior "not fitting for [her] sex." They also condemned her claim to have received inspiration directly from God and decried her as an "antinomian" or "familist," terms that connoted sexual licentiousness. Her Puritan inquisitors criticized her association with other radical women of faith like Mary Dyer, who later became a Quaker. Hutchinson was the midwife who helped deliver Mary Dyer of a miscarriage, an event exploited during her trial as a "monstrosity," a physical sign of heresy.

Her trial transcript makes it clear that as a self-educated woman, Hutchinson in fact was better versed in theology than most of her inquisitors. Her bold, witty, brilliant, and spirited challenges to her inquisitors demonstrate that the Puritan movement had the potential to attract many feminist-minded women of faith. However, Hutchinson's fate demonstrates that as the Puritan Revolution became institutionalized in the colonial governments of New England, it sacrificed its revolutionary potential and its prophetic feminists in favor of consolidating patriarchal church-state power.

TRANSCRIPTS FROM THE TRIAL OF ANNE HUTCHINSON (1637)

Mr. Winthrop, governor.   Mrs. Hutchinson, you are called here as one of those that have troubled the peace of the commonwealth and the churches here; you are known to be a woman that hath had a great share in the promoting and divulging of those opinions that are causes of this trouble, and . . . you have spoken divers things as we have been informed very prejudicial to the honour of the churches and ministers thereof, and you have maintained a meeting and an assembly in your house that hath been condemned by the general assembly as a thing not tolerable nor comely in the sight of God nor fitting for your sex . . .

Mrs. H.   What law have I broken?

Gov.   Why the fifth commandment. . . . [1]

Mrs. H.   What breach of law is that Sir?

Gov.   Why dishonouring of parents.

Mrs. H.   But put the case Sir that I do fear the Lord and my parents, may not I entertain them that fear the Lord because my parents will not give me leave?

---

[1] Exodus 20:12: "Honour thy father and thy mother: that thy days may be long upon the land which the Lord thy God giveth thee."

Gov.   If they be the fathers of the commonwealth, and they of another religion, if you entertain them then you dishonour your parents and are justly punishable.

Mrs. H.   If I entertain them, as they have dishonoured their parents I do.

Gov.   No but you by countenancing them above others put honor upon them.

Mrs. H.   I may put honor upon them as the children of God and as they do honor the Lord.

Gov.   We do not mean to discourse with those of your sex but only this; you do adhere unto them and do endeavour to set forward this faction and so you do dishonour us.[2]

Mrs. H.   I do acknowledge no such thing neither do I think that I ever put any dishonour upon you.

Gov.   Why do you keep such a meeting at your house as you do every week upon a set day?

Mrs. H.   It is lawful for me so to do, as it is all your practices and can you find a warrant for yourself and condemn me for the same thing? The ground of my taking it up was, when I first came to this land because I did not go to such meetings as those were, it was presently reported that I did not allow of such meetings but held them unlawful and therefore in that regard they said I was proud and did despise all ordinances, upon that a friend came unto me and told me of it and I to prevent such aspersions took it up, but it was in practice before I came therefore I was not the first.

Gov.   For this, that you appeal to our practice you need no confutation. If your meeting had answered to the former it had not been offensive, but I will say that there was no meeting of women alone, but your meeting is of another sort for there are sometimes men among you.

Mrs. H.   There was never any man with us.

Gov.   Well, admit there was no man at your meeting and that you was sorry for it, there is no warrant for your doings, and by what warrant do you continue such a course?

Mrs. H.   I conceive there lies a clear rule in Titus, that the elder women should instruct the younger[3] and then I must have a time wherein I must do it. . . .

---

[2] The Governor here asserts that the fifth commandment compels Hutchinson to "honour" not only her biological parents but he and other "fathers of the commonwealth."

[3] Titus 2:3–5: "The aged women likewise, that in behavior as becometh holiness, not false accusers, not given to much wine, teachers of good things; That they may teach the young women to be sober, to love their husbands, to love their children; To be discreet, chaste, keepers at home, good, obedient to their own husbands, that the word of God be not blasphemed."

Gov.   But suppose that a hundred men come unto you to be instructed will you forbear to instruct them?

Mrs. H.   As far as I conceive I cross a rule in it.

Gov.   Very well and do you not so here?

Mrs. H.   No Sir for my ground is they are men.

Gov.   Men and women all is one for that, but suppose that a man should come and say Mrs. Hutchinson I hear that you are a woman that God hath given his grace unto and you have knowledge in the word of God I pray instruct me a little, ought you not to instruct this man?

Mrs. H.   I think I may.—Do you think it not lawful for me to teach women and why do you call me to teach the court?

Gov.   We do not call you to teach the court but to lay open yourself. . . . Your course is not to be suffered for, besides that we find such a course as this to be greatly prejudicial to the state, besides the occasion that it is to seduce many honest persons that are called to those meetings and your opinions being known to be different from the word of God may seduce many simple souls that resort unto you, besides that the occasion which hath come of late hath come from none but such as have frequented your meetings, so that now they are flown off from magistrates and ministers and this since they have come to you, and besides that it will not well stand with the commonwealth that families should be neglected for so many neighbours and dames and so much time spent, we see no rule of God for this, we see not that any should have authority to set up any other exercises besides what authority hath already set up and so what hurt comes of this you will be guilty of and we for suffering you.

Mrs. H.   Sir I do not believe that to be so.

Gov.   Well, we see how it is we must therefore put it away from you, or restrain you from maintaining this course.

Mrs. H.   If you have a rule for it from God's word you may.

Gov.   We are your judges, and not you ours and we must compel you to it. . . .

Dep. Gov.   I would go a little higher with Mrs. Hutchinson. About three years ago we were all in peace. Mrs. Hutchinson from that time she came hath made a disturbance, and some that came over with her in the ship did inform me what she was as soon as she was landed. I being then in place dealt with the pastor and teacher of Boston and desired them to enquire of her, and then I was satisfied that she held nothing different from us, but within half a year after, she had vented divers of her strange opinions and had made parties in the country, and at length it comes that Mr. Cotton and Mr. Vane were of her judgment, but Mr. Cotton hath cleared himself that he was not of that mind,[4] but now it appears by this woman's meeting that Mrs. Hutchinson hath so forestalled the minds of many by their resort to her meeting that now she hath a potent party in the country. Now if all these things have endangered us as from that foundation and if she in particular hath disparaged all our ministers in the land that they have preached a covenant of works, and only Mr. Cotton a covenant of grace, why this is not to be suffered, and therefore being driven to the foundation and it being found that Mrs. Hutchinson is she that hath depraved all the ministers and hath been the cause of what is fallen out, why we must take away the foundation and the building will fall . . .

Mrs. H.   If you please to give me leave I shall give you the ground of what I know to be true. Being much troubled to see the falseness of the constitution of the church of England, I had like to have turned separatist; whereupon I kept a day of solemn humiliation and pondering of the thing; this scripture was brought unto me—he that denies Jesus Christ to be come in the flesh is antichrist[5]—this I considered of and in considering found that the papists did not deny him to be come in the flesh nor we did not deny him—who then was antichrist? . . . The Lord knows that I could not open scripture;[6] he must by his prophetical office open it unto me. . . . I bless the Lord, he hath let me see which was the clear ministry and which the wrong. Since that time I confess I have been more choice and he hath let me to distinguish between the voice of my beloved and the voice of Moses, the voice of John Baptist and the voice of antichrist, for all those voices are spoken of in scripture. Now if you do condemn me for speaking what in my conscience I know to be truth I must commit myself unto the Lord.

Mr. Nowell.   How do you know that that was the spirit?

Mrs. H.   How did Abraham know that it was God that bid him offer his son, being a breach of the sixth commandment?

Dep. Gov.   By an immediate voice.

Mrs. H.   So to me by an immediate revelation.

Dep. Gov.   How! an immediate revelation.

---

[4] Cotton, Vane: Reverend John Cotton (1585–1652) was a prominent Puritan minister and the grandfather of Cotton Mather. Like Hutchinson, Cotton believed that men and women could do nothing to achieve their own salvation (a "covenant of works") but must be entirely dependent on the saving grace of Jesus Christ (a "covenant of grace"). He renounced his belief under pressure as the antinominan controversy grew, abandoned Hutchinson, and aligned himself with other male clergy. Sir Henry Vane (1613–1662) was a Puritan statesman who became governor of Massachusetts in 1636.

[5] See 2 John 1:7.

[6] Open scripture: understand the message of the Bible.

Mrs. H.   By the voice of his own spirit to my soul. I will give you another scripture, Jer. 46. 27, 28—out of which the Lord shewed me what he would do for me and the rest of his servants.[7]—But after he was pleased to reveal himself to me . . . Ever since that time I have been confident of what he hath revealed unto me . . . Therefore I desire you to look to it, for you see this scripture fulfilled this day and therefore I desire you that as you tender the Lord and the church and commonwealth to consider and look what you do. You have power over my body but the Lord Jesus hath power over my body and soul, and assure yourselves thus much, you do as much as in you lies to put the Lord Jesus Christ from you, and if you go on in this course you begin you will bring a curse upon you and your posterity, and the mouth of the Lord hath spoken it. . . .

Gov.   The court hath already declared themselves satisfied concerning the things you hear, and concerning the troublesomeness of her spirit and the danger of her course among us, which is not to be suffered. Therefore if it be the mind of the court that Mrs. Hutchinson for these things that appear before us is unfit for our society, and if it be the mind of the court that she shall be banished out of our liberties and imprisoned till she be sent away, let them hold up their hands. . . .

Mrs. Hutchinson, the sentence of the court you hear is that you are banished from out of our jurisdiction as being a woman not fit for our society, and are to be imprisoned till the court shall send you away.

Mrs. H.   I desire to know wherefore I am banished?

Gov.   Say no more, the court knows wherefore and is satisfied.

---

[7] Jeremiah 46:27–28: "But fear not thou, O my servant Jacob, and be not dismayed, O Israel: for, behold, I will save thee from afar off, and thy seed from the land of their captivity; and Jacob shall return, and be in rest and at ease, and none shall make him afraid. Fear thou not, O Jacob my servant, saith the Lord: for I am with thee; for I will make a full end of all the nations whither I have driven thee: but I will not make a full end of thee, but correct thee in measure; yet will I not leave thee wholly unpunished."

TWO

Anne Dudley Bradstreet (ca. 1612–1672)

*I*N 1630, ANNE BRADSTREET—ALONG WITH HER BELOVED HUSBAND, SIMON BRADSTREET, AND *her parents, Thomas and Dorothy Dudley—immigrated to Massachusetts to join the Puritan errand into the wilderness. Raised in England on the Earl of Lincoln's estate where her father's position as steward permitted her virtually unfettered access to the earl's well-stocked library, Bradstreet may have found life in the earliest years of the Massachusetts Bay colony to be coarse and unsettling. There, pervasive violence, malnutrition, and disease would have contrasted sharply with the stability of her childhood in England. Writing may have been a way to negotiate the uncertainty of the colonial frontier as well as to reconnect with the debates—spiritual, social, scientific, political—being circulated in European print and manuscript texts. Puritan women such as Bradstreet's own sister Sarah Dudley Keayne and Anne Hutchinson were both punished by the colony for public speech, which may have been why the 1650 London publication of* The Tenth Muse, Lately Sprung Up in America, *a volume of poems likely based upon a manuscript she had presented to her father, was published by relatives rather than under her own name. Before her death, she corrected and revised some of these poems as well as contributed additional ones to a second edition that did bear her own name,* Several Poems Compiled with Great Variety of Wit and Learning, Full of Delight *(Boston: John Foster, 1678).*

What intrigues many readers about Bradstreet's poetry is how it frequently queries prevailing patriarchal attitudes about gender, marriage, motherhood, and spirituality. Though she typically affirms those attitudes, her irony and rhetorical deftness suggest dissatisfaction with easy resolutions. Her poetry opens a feminist space that cannot be entirely foreclosed at poem's end. Moreover, lyrics such as "The Prologue" and "In Honour of that High and Mighty Princess, Queen Elizabeth of Happy Memory," both included here, suggest that Bradstreet took a skeptical view of those who would limit women's roles to domestic duties and that she was inspired by eminent women in history.

"THE PROLOGUE" (1650)[1]

1.

To sing of Wars, of Captains, and of Kings,
Of Cities founded, Common-wealths begun,
For my mean pen are too superiour things:
Or how they all, or each their dates have run
Let Poets and Historians set these forth,
My obscure Lines shall not so dim their worth.

2.

But when my wondring eyes and envious heart
Great *Bartas*[2] sugar'd lines, do but read o're
Fool I do grudg the Muses[3] did not part
'Twixt him and me that overfluent store;
A *Bartas* can, do what a *Bartas* will
But simple I according to my skill.

3.

From school-boyes tongue no rhet'rick we expect,
Nor yet a sweet Consort[4] from broken strings,
Nor perfect beauty, where's a main defect:
My foolish, broken blemish'd Muse so sings
And this to mend, alas, no Art is able,
'Cause nature, made it so irreparable.

---

[1] The versions of "The Prologue" and "In Honour of that High and Mighty Princess, Queen Elizabeth of Happy Memory" included here are from the 1678 edition of her book. These poems contain some minor revisions and corrections that appear to have been made by the author.

[2] Bartas: Guillaume de Salluste du Bartas (1544–1590) was a French Huguenot poet. His work was translated into English and influenced many poets such as Philip Sidney, also admired by Bradstreet. His most famous work is *La Première Semaine ou La Création du Monde* (1578), an epic poem about the biblical creation story.

[3] Muses: The nine muses of Greek mythology were the daughters of the Titan Mnemosyne (memory) and Zeus. They each patronized a different art, and many poets invoke one or more muses at the beginning of their works, especially in the case of epic poems such as Homer's *The Iliad* and John Milton's *Paradise Lost*.

[4] Consort: Concert.

4.

Nor can I, like that fluent sweet tongu'd Greek,
Who lisp'd at first, in future times speak plain
By Art he gladly found what he did seek
A full requital of his, striving pain.[5]
Art can do much, but this maxime's most sure
A weak or wounded brain admits no cure.

5.

I am obnoxious to each carping tongue
Who says my hand a needle better fits,
A Poets pen all scorn I should thus wrong,
For such despite they cast on Female wits:
If what I do prove well, it won't advance,
They'l[l] say it's stoln, or else it was by chance.

6.

But sure the Antique Greeks were far more mild
Else of our Sexe, why feigned they those Nine
And poesy made, *Calliope*'s own Child;[6]
So 'mongst the rest they placed the Arts Divine:
But this weak knot, they will full soon untie,
The Greeks did nought, but play the fools & lye.

7.

Let Greeks be Greeks, and women what they are
Men have precedency, and still excell.
It is but vain unjustly to wage warre;
Men can do best, and women know it well
Preheminence in all and each is yours;
Yet grant some small acknowledgement of ours.

---

[5] Perhaps a reference to Demosthenes (ca. 384–322 B.C.), the Athenian orator who trained himself to speak clearly by placing pebbles in his mouth and then practicing his speeches.
[6] Calliope: The muse of epic poetry.

8.

And oh ye high flown quills that soar the Skies,

And ever with your prey still catch your praise,

If e'er you daigne these lowly lines your eyes

Give Thyme or Parsley wreath, I ask no bayes.[7]

This mean and unrefinéd [o]re of mine

Will make your glistring gold, but more to shine:

"IN HONOUR OF THAT HIGH AND MIGHTY PRINCESS, QUEEN ELIZABETH OF HAPPY MEMORY" (1650)

The Proeme.

Although great Queen thou now in silence lye

Yet thy loud Herald Fame doth to the sky

Thy wondrous worth proclaim in every Clime,

And so hath vow'd while there is world or time.

So great's thy glory and thine excellence,

The sound thereof rapts every humane sense,

That men account it no impiety,

To say thou wert a fleshly Diety:

Thousands bring offerings (though out of date)

Thy world of honours to accumulate.

'Mongst hundred Hecatombs of roaring verse,

Mine bleating stands before thy royal Herse.

Thou never didst nor canst thou now disdain

T' accept the tribute of a loyal brain.

Thy clemency did yerst esteem as much

The acclamations of the poor as rich,

Which makes me deem my rudeness is no wrong,

Though I resound thy praises 'mongst the throng.

The Poem.

No *Phoenix* Pen, nor *Spencers* poetry,[8]

---

[7] Bayes: Bays, or laurels, symbolize honors (often official) bestowed upon great poets, usually in the form of a crown or wreath.

[8] Phoenix: *The Phoenix Nest* (1593) is a poetry anthology to which authors such as Sir Walter Raleigh and Thomas Lodge contributed. The Phoenix of the title likely refers to Sir Philip Sidney (1554–1586), the subject of a Bradstreet elegy also included in *The Tenth Muse*. Edmund Spenser (ca. 1552–1599) was a poet whose best-known work is *The Faerie Queen*.

No *Speeds* nor *Cambaens* learned History,
Elizahs works, warrs praise, can e're compact,[9]
The World's the Theatre where she did act.
No memoryes nor volumes can contain
The 'leven Olympiads of her happy reign:[10]
Who was so good, so just, so learn'd so wise,
From all the Kings on earth she won the prize
Nor say I more then duly is her due,
Millions will testifie that this is true.
She hath wip'd off th' aspersion of her Sex,
That women wisdome lack to play the Rex:
Spains Monarch sayes not so, not yet his host:
She taught them better manners, to their cost.
The *Salique* law, in force now had not been,[11]
If *France* had ever hop'd for such a Queen.
But can you Doctors now this point dispute,
She's Argument enough to make you mute.
Since first the sun did run, his nere run race,
And earth had once a year, a new old face,
Since time was time, and man unmanly man,
Come shew me such a *Phoenix* if you can?
Was ever people better rul'd then hers?
Was ever land more happy freed from stirrs?
Did ever wealth in *England* more abound?
Her victoryes in forreign Coasts resound,
Ships more invincible then *Spain's* her foe
She wrackt, she sackt, she sunk his Armado:[12]
Her stately Troops advanc'd to *Lisbons* wall
Don Anthony in's right there to install.
She frankly helpt, *Franks* brave distressed King,
The States united now her fame do sing,

---

[9] Speed, Cambaen: John Speed (1551/2–1629) and William Camden (1551–1623) both published histories of Great Britain.

[10] 'leven Olympiads: Forty-four years. Elizabeth I reigned from 1558 to her death in 1603.

[11] Salique law: A strict application of Salique law, here associated with France, barred women from the line of succession and inheritance.

[12] Here and at a number of other points in this section, Bradstreet refers to military, economic, and political successes during Elizabeth's reign, especially ones involving other European powers and English glory.

She their Protectrix was, they well do know

Unto our dread Virago, what they owe.[13]

Her Nobles sacrific'd their noble blood,

Nor men nor Coyn she spar'd to do them good.

The rude untamed *Irish* she did quel.

Before her picture the proud *Tyrone* fell.

Had ever prince such Counsellours as she?

Her self *Minerva* caus'd them so to be.[14]

Such Captains and such souldiers never seen,

As were the Subjects of our *Pallas* Queen.[15]

Her Sea-men through all straights the world did round;

Terra incognita might know the sound.

Her *Drake* came laded home with Spanish gold:

Her *Essex* took *Cades*, their Herculean hold:

But time would fail me, so my tongue would to[o],[16]

To tell of half she did, or she could doe.

Semiramis to her, is but obscure,[17]

More infamy then fame, she did procure.

She built her glory but on *Babels* walls,

Worlds wonder for a while, but yet it falls.

Fierce *Tomris* (*Cyrus* heads-man) *Scythians* queen,

Had put her harness off, had shee but seen

Our Amazon in th' Camp at *Tilbury*,

Judging all valour and all Majesty

Within that Princess to have residence,

And prostrate yielded to her excellence.

Dido first Foundress of proud *Carthage* walls,

(Who living consummates her Funeralls)

A great *Eliza*, but compar'd with ours,

How vanisheth her glory, wealth and powers.

Profuse proud *Cleopatra*, whose wrong name,

---

[13] Virago: A bold and heroic female warrior.

[14] Minerva: A Roman goddess associated with the arts, wisdom, and war. Her Greek equivalent is Athena.

[15] Pallas: Another name for Athena.

[16] The 1650 version has "wit" instead of "tongue."

[17] Semiramis, Tomris, Dido, Cleopatra, and Zenobya: Storied queens of history and mythology. Many of these queens led victorious armies.

Instead of glory, prov'd her Countryes shame:
Of her what worth in Storyes to be seen,
But that she was a rich Egyptian Queen.
Zenobya potent Empress of the East,
And of all these, without compare the best,
Whom none but great *Aurelius* could quel;
Yet for our Queen is no fit Parallel.
She was a Phoenix Queen, so shall she be,
Her ashes not reviv'd, more Phoenix she.
Her personal perfections, who would tell,
Must dip his Pen in th' *Heliconian Well*,[18]
Which I may not, my pride doth but aspire
To read what others write, and so admire.
Now say, have women worth? or have they none?
Or had they some, but with our Queen is't gone?
Nay Masculines, you have thus taxt us long,
But she, though dead, will vindicate our wrong.
Let such as say our Sex is void of Reason,
Know tis a Slander now, but once was Treason.
But happy *England* which had such a Queen;
Yea happy, happy, had those dayes still bean;
But happiness lyes in a higher sphere,
Then wonder not *Eliza* moves not here.
Full fraught with honour, riches and with day[s,]
She sat, she set, like *Titan* in his rayes.
No more shall rise or set so glorious sun
Untill the heavens great revolution.
If then new things their old forms shall retain,
Eliza shall rule *Albion* once again.

HER EPITAPH.

Here sleeps THE Queen, this is the Royal Bed,
Of th' Damask Rose, sprung from the white and red,
Whose sweet perfume fills the all-filling Air:
This Rose is wither'd, once so lovely fair.

---

[18] Heliconian: Refers to Mount Helicon, one of the seats of the Muses.

On neither tree did grow such Rose before,
The greater was our gain, our loss the more.

Another.

Here lyes the pride of Queens, Pattern of Kings:
So blaze it Fame, here's feathers for thy wings.
Here lyes the envi'd, yet unparalleled Prince,
Whose living virtues speak (though dead long since)
If many worlds, as that Fantastick fram'd,
In every one be her great glory fam'd.

"THE AUTHOR TO HER BOOK" (1678)

Thou ill-form'd offspring of my feeble brain,
Who after birth did'st by my side remain,
Till snatcht from thence by friends, less wise then true
Who thee abroad, expos'd to publick view,
Made thee in raggs, halting to th' press to trudg,
Where errors were not lessened (all may judg)
At thy return my blushing was not small,
My rambling brat (in print) should mother call,
I cast thee by as one unfit for light,
Thy visage was so irksome in my sight;
Yet being mine own, at length affection would
Thy blemishes amend, if so I could:
I wash'd thy face, but more defects I saw,
And rubbing off a spot, still made a flaw.
I stretcht thy joynts to make thee even feet,
Yet still thou run'st more hobbling then is meet;
In better dress to trim thee was my mind,
But nought save home-spun Cloth, i' th' house I find
In this array, 'mongst Vulgars may'st thou roam
In Criticks hands, beware thou dost not come;
And take thy way where yet thou art not known,
If for thy Father askt, say, thou hadst none:
And for thy Mother she alas is poor,
Which caus'd her thus to send thee out of door.

THREE

Margaret Cavendish, Duchess of Newcastle (ca. 1623–1674)

*M*ARGARET CAVENDISH WAS BORN MARGARET LUCAS IN ESSEX, ENGLAND AROUND *1623. In 1642, early in the English Civil War, an anti-Royalist mob attacked her aristocratic family's home. Soon after, she fled to Oxford and became attached to the royal court, eventually accompanying Queen Henrietta Marie in exile on the Continent. While in Europe, she met the much older widower William Cavendish, first Marquess of Newcastle. She refused to become his mistress, and they married soon after. The childless couple permanently returned to England in 1660 when Charles II was restored to the throne.*

Though an ardent Royalist, Cavendish took advantage of the interregnum's relaxed censorship rules by publishing her writing. On trips to London on behalf of her husband prior to their 1660 return, she witnessed the period's surge in women's publications, many of them religious. She subsequently became known, even infamous, for her eclectic publications and eccentric dress. Nicknamed "Mad Madge," Cavendish wrote plays, poetry, science fiction, philosophical and scientific essays, and prose romances as well as a biography of her husband and an autobiography. She frequently designed and made her own clothing, and according to anecdote appeared at court and elsewhere in extravagant costumes that at times androgynously combined breeches with elaborate trains.

As a feminist, Cavendish equivocated, at times denigrating women for what she saw as talkativeness and ineloquence and at others envisioning a utopian world deftly ruled by a woman. She delighted in contradiction and paradox, and in Grounds of Natural Philosophy *(1668), she suggests that such intellectual exploration and exhibition of debate was something of a rhetorical philosophy. "Femal Orations," published in 1662 as part of* Orations of Divers Sorts, Accommodated to Divers Places, *exemplifies this playfulness as she approaches women's roles and capabilities. In each oration, the author takes a different point of view in order to create a lively fictional conversation (perhaps based on real-life conversations Cavendish had with other women intellectuals) about women's roles and status at the outset of the Age of Revolutions.*

"FEMAL ORATIONS" (1662)

I.

Ladies, Gentlewomen, and other Inferiours, but not Less Worthy, I have been Industrious to Assemble you together, and wish I were so Fortunate, as to perswade you to make a Frequentation, Association, and Combination amongst our Sex, that we may Unite in Prudent Counsels, to make our Selves as Free, Happy, and Famous as Men; for Men are Happy, and we Women are Miserable, they Possess all the Ease, Rest, Pleasure, Wealth, Power, and Fame, whereas Women are Restless with Labour, Easeless with Pain, Melancholy for want of Pleasures, Helpless for want of Power, and Dye in Oblivion for want of Fame; Nevertheless, Men are so Unconscionable and Cruel against us, as they Indeavour to Barr us of all Sorts or Kinds of Liberty, as not to Suffer us Freely to Associate amongst our Own Sex, but would fain Bury us in their Houses or Beds, as in a Grave; the truth is, we Live like Bats or Owls, Labour like Beasts, and Dye like Worms.

II.

Ladies, Gentlewomen, and other Inferiour Women, The Lady that Spoke to you, hath spoken Wisely and Eloquently in Expressing our Unhappiness, but she hath not Declared a Remedy, or Shew'd us a way to come Out of our Miseries; but if she could or would be our Guide, to lead us out of the Labyrinth Men have put us into, we should not only Praise and Admire her, but Adore and Worship her as our Goddess; but Alas, Men, that are not only our Tyrants, but our Devils, keep us in the Hell of Subjection, from whence I cannot Perceive any Redemption or Getting out; we may Complain, and Bewail our Condition, yet that will not Free us; we may Murmur and Rail against Men, yet they Regard not what we say: In short, our Words to Men are as Empty Sounds, our Sighs as Puffs of Wind, and our Tears as Fruitless Showres, and our Power is so Inconsiderable, as Men Laugh at our Weakness.

III.

Ladies, Gentlewomen, and other more Inferiours, The former *Orations* were Exclamations against Men, Repining at Their Condition, and Mourning for our Own; but we have no Reason to Speak against Men, who are our Admirers, and Lovers; they are our Protectors, Defenders, and Maintainers; they Admire our Beauties, and Love our Persons; they Protect us from Injuries, Defend us from Dangers, are Industrious for our Subsistence, and Provide for our Children; they Swim great Voyages by Sea, Travel long Journies by Land, to Get us Rarities and Curiosities; they Dig to the Centre of the Earth for Gold for us; they Dive to the Bottom of the Sea for Jewels for us; they Build to the Skies Houses for us; they Hunt, Foul, Fish, Plant, and Reap for Food for us; all which we could not do our Selves, and yet we Complain of Men, as if they were our Enemies, when as we could not possibly Live without them: which shews, we are as Ungratefull, as Inconstant; But we have more Reason to Murmur against Nature than against Men, who hath made Men more Ingenious, Witty, and Wise than Women, more Strong, Industrious, and Laborious than Women, for Women are Witless, and Strengthless, and Unprofitable Creatures, did they not Bear Children. Wherefore, let us Love men, Praise men, and Pray for men, for without Men we should be the most Miserable Creatures that Nature Hath, or Could make.

IV.

Noble Ladies, Gentlewomen, and other Inferiour Women, The former Oratoress says, we are Witless, and Strengthless; if so, it is that we Neglect the One, and make no Use of the Other, for Strength is Increased by Exercise, and Wit is Lost for want of Conversation; but to shew Men we are not so Weak and Foolish, as the former Oratoress doth Express us to be, let us Hawk, Hunt, Race, and do the like Exercises as Men have, and let us Converse in Camps, Courts, and Cities, in Schools, Colleges, and Courts of Judicature, in Taverns, Brothels, and Gaming Houses, all which will make our Strength and Wit known, both to Men, and to our own Selves, for we are as Ignorant of our Selves, as Men are of us. And how should we Know our Selves, when as we never made a Trial of our Selves? or how should Men know us, when as they never Put us to the Proof? Wherefore, my Advice is, we should Imitate Men, so will our Bodies and Minds appear more Masculine, and our Power will Increase by our Actions.

V.

Noble, Honourable, and Vertuous Women, The former Oration was to Perswade us to Change the Custom of our Sex, which is a Strange and Unwise Perswasion, since we cannot Change the Nature of our Sex, for we cannot make our selves Men; and to have Femal Bodies, and yet to Act Masculine Parts, will be very Preposterous and Unnatural; In truth, we shall make our Selves like as the Defects of Nature, as to be Hermaphroditical, as neither to be Perfect Women nor Perfect Men, but Corrupt and Imperfect Creatures; Wherefore, let me Perswade you, since we cannot Alter the Nature of our Persons, not to Alter the Course of our Lives, but to Rule our Lives and Behaviours, as to be Acceptable and Pleasing to God and Men, which is to be Modest, Chast, Temperate, Humble, Patient, and Pious; also to be Huswifely,[1] Cleanly, and of few Words, all which will Gain us Praise from Men, and Blessing from Heaven, and Love in this World, and Glory in the Next.

VI.

Worthy Women, The former Oratoress's Oration indeavours to Perswade us, that it would not only be a Reproach and Disgrace, but Unnatural for Women in their Actions and Behaviour to Imitate Men; we may as well say, it will be a Reproach, Disgrace, and Unnatural to Imitate the Gods, which Imitation we are Commanded both by the Gods and their Ministers, and shall we Neglect the Imitation of Men, which is more Easie and Natural than the Imitation of the Gods? for how can Terrestrial Creatures Imitate Celestial Deities? yet one Terrestrial may Imitate an other, although in different sorts of Creatures; Wherefore, since all Terrestrial Imitations ought to Ascend to the Better, and not to Descend to the Worse, Women ought to Imitate Men, as being a Degree in Nature more Perfect, than they Themselves, and all Masculine Women ought to be Praised as Effeminate Men to be Dispraised, for the one Advances to Perfection, the other Sinks to Imperfection, that so by our Industry we may come at last to Equal Men both in Perfection and Power.

VII.

Nobles Ladies, Honourable Gentlewomen, and Worthy Femal Commoners, The former Oratoress's Oration or Speech was to Perswade us Out of our Selves, as to be That which Nature never Intended us to be, to wit Masculine; but why should we

---

[1] Huswifely: Housewifely, meaning skilled and economical in the management of domestic affairs.

Desire to be Masculine, since our Own Sex and Condition is far the Better? for if Men have more Courage, they have more Danger; and if Men have more Strength, they have more Labour than Women have; if Men are more Eloquent in Speech, Women are more Harmonious in Voice; if Men be more Active, Women are more Gracefull; if Men have more Liberty, Women have more Safety; for we never Fight Duels, nor Battels, nor do we go Long Travels or Dangerous Voyages; we Labour not in Building, nor Digging in Mines, Quarries, or Pits, for Metall, Stone, or Coals; neither do we Waste or Shorten our Lives with University or Scholastical Studies, Questions, and Disputes; we Burn not our Faces with Smith Forges, or Chymist Furnaces, and Hundreds of other Actions, which Men are Imployed in; for they would not only Fade the Fresh Beauty, Spoil the Lovely Features, and Decay the Youth of Women, causing them to appear Old, whilst they are Young, but would Break their Small Limbs, and Destroy their Tender Lives. Wherefore, Women have no Reason to Complain against Nature, or the God of Nature, for though the Gifts are not the Same they have given to Men, yet those Gifts they gave given to Women, are much Better; for we Women are much more Favour'd by Nature than Men, in Giving us such Beauties, Features, Shapes, Gracefull Demeanour, and such Insinuating and Inticing Attractives, as Men are Forc'd to Admire us, Love us, and be Desirous of us, in so much as rather than not Have and Injoy us, they will Deliver to our Disposals, their Power, Persons, and Lives, Inslaving Themselves to our Will and Pleasures; also we are their Saints, whom they Adore and Worship, and what can we Desire more, than to be Men's Tyrants, Destinies, and Goddesses?

FOUR

Margaret Askew Fell Fox (1614–1702)

*O*F THE MANY NEW AND REVOLUTIONARY RELIGIOUS MOVEMENTS THAT EMERGED FROM *the Protestant Reformation, none was more empowering of women than the Society of Friends. The Society of Friends were popularly known as "Quakers," a name given in reference to the way some Friends experienced the presence of the Spirit in bodily tremblings.*

Margaret Askew married Thomas Fell in 1632. She first heard the preachings of Quaker founder George Fox in 1652. Her home, Swarthmoor Hall, served as a gathering place and a haven for Quakers. She also used her influence as a member of the English gentry to defend and protect persecuted Quakers. In 1660 and 1662, she petitioned King Charles II for freedom of conscience. She herself was arrested for allowing Quaker meetings to be held at Swarthmoor Hall in 1664, and spent the next four years in jail and lost her property. While in prison, she wrote Women's Speaking Justified. *After her release, in 1669, she married George Fox.*

In Women's Speaking Justified, *Fell strikes a blow at the centuries-old practice of forbidding women's authoritative participation in Christian worship. Christian churches premised their prohibition of women's speaking on two statements by Paul: 1 Corinthians 14:34, "Let your women keep silence in the churches: for it is not permitted unto them to speak," and 1 Timothy 2:11, "Let the woman learn in silence with all subjection." But Fell proves the Quaker doctrine of women's spiritual equality by marshalling many biblical examples of prophetic women, including Mary, Mary Magdalene, Deborah, Hannah, Elizabeth, Esther, and Judith. The end of forbidding women's authority, she announces, is the end of a "Night of Apostacy" and the dawning of a "true Light, clear as Chrystal." Fell exemplifies the important role religion played for women at the leading edge of the Age of Revolutions.*

WOMEN'S SPEAKING JUSTIFIED (1666)

Women's Speaking Justified, Proved, and Allowed of by the Scriptures,
All such as speak by the Spirit and Power of the Lord Jesus. And how
Women were the first that Preached the Tidings of the Resurrection of
Jesus, and were sent by Christ's own Command, before he Ascended
to the Father, John 20. 17.

Whereas it hath been an Objection in the Minds of many, and several times hath been objected by the Clergy, or Ministers and others, against Women's speaking in the Church; and so consequently may be taken, that they are condemned for med[d]-ling in the things of God: The ground of which Objection is taken from the Apostle's Words, which he writ in his first Epistle to the Corinthians, Chap. 14. Vers. 34, 35. And also what he writ to Timothy in the first Epistle, Chap. 2. Vers. 11, 12. But how far they wrong the Apostle's Intentions in these Scriptures, we shall shew clearly when we come to them in their course and order. But first let me lay down how God himself hath manifested his Will and Mind concerning Women, and unto women.

And first, When *God created Man in his own Image, in the Image of God created he them, Male and Female; and God blessed them, and God said unto them, Be fruitful and multiply: And God said, Behold, I have given you of every Herb,* &c. Gen. 1. Here God joyns them together in his own Image, and makes no such Distinctions and Differences as Men do. . . .

It is true, *The Serpent, that was more subtle than any other Beast of the Field,* came unto the Woman with his Temptations, and with a Lye; his Subtlety discerning her to be the weaker Vessel, or more inclinable to hearken to him, when he said, *If ye eat, your Eyes shall be opened*; and the Woman saw *that the Fruit was good to make one wise*: There the Temptation got into her, and *she did eat, and gave to her Husband, and he did eat also,* and so they were both tempted into the Transgression and Disobedience; and therefore God said unto *Adam,* when that he hid himself when he heard his Voice, *Hast thou eaten of the Tree, which I commanded thee that thou should'st not eat?* And *Adam* said, *The Woman which thou gavest me, she gave me of the Tree, and I did eat. And the Lord said unto the Woman, What is this that thou hast done?* And the Woman said, *The Serpent beguiled me, and I did eat.* Here the Woman spoke the Truth unto the Lord. See what the Lord saith, ver. 15. after he had pronounced Sentence on the Serpent; *I will put Enmity between thee and the Woman, and between thy Seed and her Seed; it shall bruise thy Head, and thou shalt bruise his Heel,* Gen. 3.

Let this Word of the Lord, which was from the beginning, stop the Mouths of all that oppose Women's Speaking in the Power of the Lord; for he hath put Enmity between the Woman and the Serpent; and if the Seed of the Woman speak not, the Seed of the Serpent speaks; for God hath put Enmity between the two Seeds; and it is manifest, that those that speak against the Woman and her Seed's Speaking, speak out of the Envy of the old Serpent's Seed. And God hath fulfilled his Word and his Promise, *When the fulness of time was come, he sent forth his Son, made of a Woman, made under the Law, that we might receive the Adoption of Sons*, Gal. 4. 4, 5.

Moreover, the Lord is pleased, when he mentions his Church, to call her by the Name of Woman, by his Prophets, saying, *I have called thee as a Woman forsaken, and grieved in Spirit, and as a Wife of Youth*, Isai. 54. *Again, How long wilt thou go about, thou back-sliding Daughter? For the Lord hath created a new thing in the Earth, a Woman shall compass a Man*, Jer. 31. 22. And *David*, when he was speaking of Christ and his Church, he saith, *The King's Daughter is all glorious within, her Cloathing is of wrought Gold, she shall be brought unto the King; with gladness and rejoycing shall they be brought; they shall enter into the King's Pallace*, Psal. 45. And also King *Solomon* in his Song, where he speaks of Christ and his Church, where she is complaining and calling for Christ, he saith, *If thou knowest not, O thou fairest among Women, go thy way by the Footsteps of the Flock*, Cant. 1. 8. c. 5. 9. And *John*, when he saw the Wonder that was in Heaven, he saw *a Woman cloathed with the Sun, and the Moon under her feet, and upon her Head a Crown of twelve Stars; and there appeared another Wonder in Heaven, a great red Dragon stood ready to devour her Child* here the enmity appears that God put between the Woman and the Dragon, Rev. 12.

Thus much may prove, that the Church of Christ is represented as a Woman; and those that speak against this Woman's speaking, speak against the Church of Christ, and the Seed of the Woman, which Seed is Christ; that is to say, Those that speak against the Power of the Lord, and the Spirit of the Lord speaking in a Woman, simply by reason of her Sex, or because she is a Woman, not regarding the Seed, and Spirit, and Power that speaks in her; such speak against Christ and his Church, and are of the Seed of the Serpent, wherein lodgeth the Enmity. And as God the Father made no such difference in the first Creation, nor never since between the Male and the Female, but alwayes out of his Mercy and loving kindness, had regard unto the Weak. So also his Son, Christ Jesus, confirms the same thing; when the Pharisees came to him, and asked him, if it were lawful for a Man to put away his Wife? He answered and said unto them, Have you not read, *That he that made them in the beginning, made them Male and Female*, and said, *For this Cause shall a Man leave Father and Mother, and shall cleave unto his Wife, and they twain shall be one Flesh; wherefore they are no more twain, but one Flesh; What therefore God hath joyned together, let no Man put asunder,* Mat. 19. . . .

Thus we see that Jesus owned the Love and Grace that appeared in Women, and did not despise it: and by what is recorded in the Scriptures, he received as much love, kindness, compassion, and tender dealing towards him from Women, as he did from any others, both in his life time, and also after they had exercised their cruelty upon him; for *Mary Magdalene*, and *Mary* the Mother of James, beheld where he was laid; *And when the Sabbath was past,* Mary Magdalene, *and* Mary *the Mother of* James, and Salom, *had brought sweet Spices, that they might annoint him: And very early in the Morning, the first Day of the Week, they came unto the Sepulchre at the rising of the Sun; and they said among themselves, Who shall roll us away the Stone from the Door of the Sepulchre? And when they looked the Stone was rolled away, for it was very great,* Mark 16. 1, 2, 3, 4. Luke 24. 1, 2. *and they went down into the Sepulchre,* and as Matthew saith, *The Angel rolled away the Stone, and he said unto the Women, Fear not, I know whom ye seek, Jesus which was Crucified: He is not here, he is risen,* Mat. 28. Now Luke saith thus, *That there stood two Men by them in shining Apparel, and as they were perplexed and afraid, the Men said unto them, He is not here, remember how he said unto you when he was in Galilee, That the Son of Man must be delivered into the Hands of sinful Men, and be Crucified, and the third Day rise again; and they remembered his Words, and return'd from the Sepulchre, and told all these things to the Eleven, and to all the rest.*

It was *Mary Magdalene*, and *Joanna*, and *Mary* the Mother of *James*, and the other Women that were with them, which told these things to the Apostles, *and their Words seemed unto them as Idle Tales, and they believed them not.* Mark this, ye despisers of the Weakness of Women, and look upon your selves to be so wise: But Christ Jesus doth not so; for he makes use of the weak: For when he met the Women after he was risen, he said unto them, *All Hail!* And they came and held him by the Feet, and worshipped him; then said Jesus unto them, *Be not afraid, go tell my Brethren that they go into Galilee, and there they shall see me,* Mat. 28. 10. Mark 16. 9. And John saith, when Mary was weeping at the Sepulchre, that Jesus said unto her, *Woman, why weepest thou? what seekest thou? And when she supposed him to be the Gardner, Jesus said unto her, Mary; she turned her self, and said unto him, Rabboni, which is to say, Master; Jesus saith unto her, Touch me not, for I am not yet ascended to my Father; but go to my Brethren, and say unto them, I ascend unto my Father, and your Father, and to my God, and your God,* John 20. 16, 17.

Mark this, you that despise and oppose the Message of the Lord God that he sends by Women; What had become of the Redemption of the whole Body of Mankind, if they had not cause to believe the Message that the Lord Jesus sent by these Women, of and concerning his Resurrection? And if these Women had not thus, out of their Tenderness, and Bowels of Love, who had received Mercy, and Grace, and

Forgiveness of Sins, and Vertue, and Healing from him; which many Men also had received the like, if their Hearts had not been so united and knit unto him in Love, that they could not depart as the Men did; but sat watching, and waiting, and weeping about the Sepulchre until the time of his Resurrection, and so were ready to carry his Message, as is manifested, else how should his Disciples have known, who were not there? . . .

And how are the Men of this Generation blinded, that bring these Scriptures, and pervert the Apostles Words, and corrupt his Intent in speaking of them? And by these Scriptures, endeavour to stop the Message and Word of the Lord God in Women, by con[d]emning and despising of them. If the Apostle would have had Womens speaking stop'd, and did not allow of them; Why did he intreat his true Yoak-Fellow to help those Women who laboured with him in the Gospel? Phil. 4. 3. And why did the Apostles join together in Prayer and Supplication with the Women, and Mary the Mother of Jesus, and with his Brethren, Acts 1. 14. if they had not allowed, and had Union and Fellowship with the Spirit of God, where-ever it was revealed, in Women as well as others? But all this opposing, and gainsaying of Womens Speaking, hath risen out of the Bottomless Pit, and Spirit of Darkness, that hath spoken for these many Hundred Years together in this Night of Apostacy, since the Revelations have ceased and been hid. And so that Spirit hath limited and bound all up within its Bond and Compass; and so would suffer none to Speak; but such as that Spirit of Darkness approved of, Man or Woman. . . .

FIVE

Bathsua Reginald Makin (1600–ca. 1675)

CELEBRATED IN HER TIME AS "ENGLAND'S MOST LEARNED LADY," BATHSUA MAKIN WAS a formidable proponent of the equal rights of women to receive an education. The daughter of an Anglican schoolmaster, she was educated in classical and modern languages by her father Henry Reginald. Bathsua published her first book of poetry, Musa Virginea, at the age of 16. Married in 1621 to a minor court servant named Richard Makin, Bathsua continued to develop her reputation as a learned woman despite ongoing financial difficulties in the Makin household. She maintained correspondence with intellectual men and women throughout Europe, including the mathematician John Pell and Dutch scholar Anna Maria van Schurman. In the 1640s, Makin served as tutor to Princess Elizabeth (1636–1650), daughter to King Charles I. After the death of her husband Richard Makin in 1659, she tutored Lucy Hastings, Dowager Countess of Huntingdon.

Makin published An Essay to Revive the Antient Education of Gentlewomen in 1673 to encourage noblewomen to challenge custom and avail themselves of learning. Arguing that denial of education to women was only a recent "barbarous" trend and not an "ancient" honorable tradition, she catalogs hundreds of historical examples of women learned in languages, logic, philosophy, arts, oratory, mathematics, and poetry, from the Old Testament prophetess Miriam and the Queen of Sheba, to the ancient Greek philosophers Hsasia and Hypatia, to modern exemplars of learning such as Queen Elizabeth and the Anglo-American poet Anne Bradstreet. After defeating several objections against the education of women, she concludes this pamphlet by announcing the establishment of her own school in London where "Gentlewomen" from the age of 8 years old might be educated in religion, dance, music, writing, Latin, French, Greek, Hebrew, Italian, Spanish, botany, mineralogy, cooking, astronomy, geography, mathematics, history, and philosophy.

AN ESSAY TO REVIVE THE ANTIENT EDUCATION OF GENTLEWOMEN (1673)

An Essay to Revive the Antient Education of Gentlewomen, in Religion, Manners, Arts & Tongues, with An Answer to the Objections against this Way of Education. London Printed by J. D. to be sold by Tho. Parkhurst, at the Bible and Crown at the lower end of Cheapside. 1673.

To all Ingenious and Virtuous Ladies, more especially to her Highness the Lady Mary, eldest Daughter to his Royal Highness the Duke of York.

Custom, when it is inveterate, has a mighty influence: it has the force of Nature it self. The Barbarous custom to breed Women low is grown general amongst us, and hath prevailed so far, that it is verily believed (especially amongst a sort of debauched Sots) that Women are not endued with such Reason, as Men; nor capable of improvement by Education, as they are. It is looked upon as a monstrous thing to pretend the contrary. A Learned Woman is thought to be a Comet, that bodes Mischief, whenever it appears. To offer to the World the liberal Education of Women is to deface the Image of God in Man, it will make Women so high, and men so low like Fire in the House-top, it will set the whole world in a Flame.

These things and worse then these, are commonly talked of, and verily believed by many, who think themselves wise Men: to contradict these is a bold attempt; where the Attempter must expect to meet with much opposition. Therefore, Ladies, I beg the candid Opinion of your Sex, whose Interest I assert. More especially I implore the Favour of your Royal Highness, a Person most Eminent amongst them, whose Patronage alone will be sufficient Protection. What I have written is not out of humour to shew how much may be said of a trivial thing to little purpose. I verily think, Women were formerly Educated in the knowledge of Arts and Tongues, and by their Education, many did rise to a great height in Learning. Were Women thus Educated now, I am confident the advantage would be very great: The Women would have Honour and Pleasure, their Relations Profit, and the whole Nation Advantage. I am very sensible it is an ill time to set on foot this Design: wherein not only Learning but Virtue it self is scorned and neglected, as pedantic things, fit only for the Vulgar. I know no better way to reform these Exorbitancies, than to persuade Women to scorn those Toys and Trifles, they now spend their time about, and to attempt higher things, here offered: This will either reclaim the Men; or make them ashamed to claim the Sovereignty over such as are more Wise and Virtuous than themselves.

Were a competent number of Schools erected to Educate Ladies ingenuously, methinks I see how ashamed Men would be of their Ignorance, and how industrious the next Generation would be to wipe off their Reproach.

I expect to meet with many Scoffes and Taunts from inconsiderate and illiterate Men, that prize their own Lusts and Pleasure more than your Profit and Content. I shall be the less concerned at these, so long as I am in your favour; and this discourse may be a Weapon in your hands to defend your selves, whilst you endeavour to polish your Souls, that you may glorify God, and answer the end of your Creation, to be meet helps to your Husbands. Let not your Ladyships be offended, that I do not (as some have wittily done) plead for Female Preeminence. To ask too much is the way to be denied all. God has made the Man the Head, if you be educated and instructed, as I propose, I am sure you will acknowledge it, and be satisfied that you are helps, that your Husbands do consult and advise with you (which if you be wise they will be glad of) and that your Husbands have the casting Voice, in whose determinations you will acquiesce. That this may be the effect of this Education in all Ladies that shall attempt it, is the desire of Your Servant. . . .

CARE OUGHT TO BE TAKEN BY US TO EDUCATE WOMEN IN LEARNING.

That I may be more distinct in what I intend, I shall distinguish of Women,

Women are of two sorts, $\left\{\begin{array}{l}\text{RICH,}\\ \text{POOR}\end{array}\right\}$ $\left\{\begin{array}{l}\textit{Of good natural Parts.}\\ \textit{Of low Parts.}\end{array}\right\}$

I do not mean, that it is necessary to the *esse[nce]*, to the *subsistence*, or to the Salvation of Women, to be thus educated. Those that are mean in the World, have not an opportunity for this Education: Those that are of low Parts, though they have opportunity, cannot reach this; *Ex quovis ligno non fit Minerva*:[1] My meaning is, Persons that God has blessed with the things of this World, that have competent natural Parts, ought to be educated in Knowledge; That is, it is much better they should spend the time of their Youth, to be competently instructed in those things usually taught to Gentlewoman at Schools, and the overplus of their time to be spent in gaining Arts, and Tongues, and useful Knowledge, rather than to trifle away so many precious minutes merely to polish their Hands and Feet, to curl their Locks, to dress and trim their Bodies; and in the mean time to neglect their Souls, and not at all, or very little to endeavour to know God, Jesus Christ, Themselves, and the things of Nature, Arts, and Tongues, subservient to these. . . . Merely to teach Gentlewomen to

---

[1] *Ex quovis lingo.* . . : Makin here adapts the familiar Latin saying by Horace *ex quovis lingo non fit Mercurius*, meaning "the god Mercury is not to be fashioned from just any piece of wood," to the female example of Minerva, the goddess of wisdom, in order to argue that it is easier to educate women of natural intellectual talents.

Frisk and Dance, to paint their Faces, to curl their Hair, to put on a Whisk,[2] to wear gay Clothes, is not truly to adorn, but to adulterate their Bodies; yea, (what is worse) to defile their Souls. . . . Doubtless this under-breeding of Women began among Heathen and Barbarous People; it continues with the *Indians*, where they make their Women mere slaves, and wear them out in drudgery. It is practiced amongst degenerate and Apostate Christians, upon the same score and now is a part of their Religion; it would therefore be a piece of Reformation to correct it; and it would notably countermine them who fight against us, as Satan against Adam, by seducing our Women, who then easily seduce their Husbands.

Had God intended Women only as a finer sort of Cattle, he would not have made them reasonable bruits, a few degrees higher than Drils[3] or Monkies, (which the *Indians* use to do many Offices) might have better fitted some men's Lust, Pride, and Pleasure; especially those that desire to keep them ignorant to be tyrannized over.

God intended Woman as a help-meet to Man, in his constant conversation, and in the concerns of his Family and Estate, when he should most need, in sickness, weakness, absence, death, &c. Whilst we neglect to fit them for those things, we renounce God's Blessing, he has appointed Women for, are ungrateful to him, cruel to them, and injurious to our selves.

I remember a discourse in *Erasmus*, between an Abbot and a learned Woman.[4] She gives many good Reasons why Women should be learned, that they might know God, their Saviour, understand his Sacred Word, and admire him in his wonderful Works; that they might also better administer their Household Affairs among a multitude of Servants, who would have more reverence towards them, because they were above them in understanding. Further, she found a great content in reading good Authors at spare times. He gives her one Answer to all this, *That Women would never be kept in Subjection if they were learned*; as he found by experience among his Monks, of all things in the World, he hated nothing so much as a learned Monk, who would always be contradicting his Superior, from the Decretals[5] out of *Peter* and *Paul*. He cared not if all his Monks turned into Swine, so long as they would be obedient, and not disturb him in his Pleasures. Doubtless if that generation of Sots[6] (who deny more Polite Learning to Women) would speak out, they would tell you, If Women should be permitted Arts, they would be wiser than themselves (a thing not to be endured) then they

---

[2] Whisk: A fashionable neckerchief.

[3] Dril: Baboon.

[4] Dutch Renaissance humanist and philosopher Desiderius Erasmus published "The Abbot and Learned Woman" in *The Colloquies*, volume 1 (1518).

[5] Decretal: Decree.

[6] Sot: Drunkard, alcoholic.

would never be such tame fools and very slaves as now they make them; therefore it is a wicked mischievous thing to revive the Ancient Custom of Educating them. . . .

Object. No Body means Gentlewomen should be thus educated in manners of sheer vanity; but in practicing their Needle, in knowing and doing those things that concern good House wifery, which is Women's particular qualification.

Answ. I know not what may be meant, but I see what is generally done. In most Schools for educating this Sex, little more is proposed by the Undertakers, or expected by the Parents. As far as I can observe, the less any thing of solidity is taught, the more such places are frequented. I do acknowledge, in the state of the Question, that Women should be accomplished in all those things that concern them as Women. My meaning is, The over-plus time may be imployed in polishing their minds with the knowledge of such things as may be honourable, pleasant and profitable to them, and their Relations afterwards.

Before I proceed further to Answer the remaining Objections, I desire this may be taken notice of, That whatever is said against this manner of Educating Women, may commonly be urged against the Education of Men.

Object. If we bring up our Daughters to Learning, no Persons will adventure to marry them.

Answ. 1. Many men, silly enough, (God knows) think themselves wise, and will not dare to marry a wise Woman, lest they should be over-topt.

2. As some Husbands, debauched themselves, desire their Wives should be chast[e], their Children virtuous: So some men, sensible of their own want, (caused by their Parents neglect) will choose a learned Woman, in whom they may glory, and by whose prudence their defect may be supplied.

3. Learned men, to be sure, will choose such the rather, because they are suitable. Some Men marrying Wives of good natural parts, have improved themselves in Arts and Tongues, the more to fit them for their converse.

4. Many Women formerly have been preferred for this very thing. *Aihenais*, Daughter to Leontius the Philosopher, left destitute by him, was entertained by his Sister *Placida* for her Learning, and was after married to the emperor *Theodosius*, charmed by her worth, being fitted by her education for that high place; she is recorded for an excellent Empress. Upon her being baptized, she was called Eudocea.

Constantine married *Helena* the Daughter of *Lois*, more for the Learning, than any other accomplishments.

We may probably imagine *Hortensia, Terentia, Tullia*, and divers others, had never been married to such brave men, had not their Education preferred them. If this way of educating Gentlewomen should now be set on foot, there will not be so great a number bred; but (as degenerate as times are) there would be found learned men enough, to whom they may be preferred for their Education.

Object. It is against custom to Educate Gentlewomen thus.

Answ. Bad customs ought to be broken, or else many good things would never come into use. I have showed this is a Heathenish Custom, or a worse, continued among us upon very bad ground. . . .

Object. Women are of ill natures, and will abuse their Education: They will be proud, and not obey their Husbands; they will be pragmatic, and boast of their Parts and Improvements. The ill nature that is in them, will become more wicked, the more wit you furnish them with.

Answ. This is the killing Objection, and every thick skulled Fellow that babbles this out, thinks no *Billingsgate* Woman[7] can Answer it. I shall take the Objection in pieces.

1. *They will abuse Learning.* So do men; he is egregiously simple, that argues against the use of a necessary or very convenient thing from the abuse of it. By this Argument no men should be liberally brought up; strong Drinks should never be used any more in the World, and a hundred such like things.

2. *They are of ill natures.* This is an impudent calumny; as if the whole Sex of Women, or the greatest part of them, had that malice infused into their verity Natures and Constitutions, that they are ordinarily made worse by that Education that makes Men generally better.

Ingenuas didicisse fideliter artes
Emollit mores, nec sinit esse feros.[8]

The Heathen found, that Arts wrought upon Men, the rougher Sex. Surely it is want of fidelity in the Instructor, if it have not the like effect upon softer and finer materials.

3. *They will be proud, and not obey their Husbands.* To this I Answer; What is said of Philosophy, is true of Knowledge; a little Philosophy carries a Man from God, but a great deal brings him back again; a little knowledge, like Ballast in a Ship, settles down, and makes a person move more even in his station; 'tis not knowing too much, but too little that causes the irregularity. This same Argument may be turned upon Men; what-ever they answer for themselves, will defend Woman.

Those that desire Answer, let them peruse *Erasmus* his Dialogue, of the *Ignorant Abbot* and the *Learned Woman*. An ignorant Magistrate, or Minister, may as well

---

[7] Billingsgate Woman: Billingsgate was an area of London known for its fish-market and populated by famously vulgar and foul-mouthed "fishwives."

[8] *Emollit mores* . . . : Latin saying, from Ovid, "Learning makes gentle the character and does not allow it to be unrefined."

plead against improvement of Knowledge in all below them, lest they should be wiser than themselves, and to deride them. Do not deny Women their due, which is to be as well instructed as they can, but let Men do this duty, to be wiser than they are. If this does not please, let silly Men let wise Women alone; the rule is, All should be (as near as they can) equally yoked.

Object. *Women do not desire Learning. . . .*

Answ. Neither do many Boys, (as Schools are now ordered) yet I suppose you do not intend to lay Fallow all Children that will not bring forth Fruit of themselves, to forbear to instruct those which at present do not thank you for it.

But I have said, there is in all innate desire of knowing, in Women as well as Men: if the ways to the Temple of Pallas[9] be so tedious and intricate, that they confound or tire her Servants; or, if you dress up Learning in such an ugly and monstrous shape, that you affright Children; I have nothing to say to such, but that they should reform their Schools, or else we will think they have no desire any, either Male or Female, should be instructed. . . .

I hope I shall by this Discourse persuade some Parents to be more careful for the future of the Breeding of their Daughters. You cark[10] and care to get great Portions for them, which sometimes occasions their ruin. Here is a sure Portion, an easy way to make them excellent. How many born to good Fortunes, when their Wealth has been wasted, have supported themselves and Families too by their Wisdom?

I hope some of these Considerations will at least move some of this abused Sex to set a right value upon themselves, according to the dignity of their Creation, that they might, with an honest pride and magnanimity, scorn to be bowed down and made to stoop to such Follies and Vanities, Trifles and Nothings, so far below them, and unproportionable to their noble Souls, nothing inferior to those of Men, and equally precious to God in Christ, in whom there is neither Male nor Female.

Let a generous resolution possess your minds, seeing Men in this Age have invaded Women's Vices, in a noble revenge, reassume those Virtues, which Men sometimes unjustly usurped to themselves, but ought to have left them in common to both Sexes.

---

[9] Temple of Pallas: Pallas Athena is the Greek goddess of wisdom.
[10] Cark: To fret or vex.

SIX

Aphra Behn (1640–1689)

*W*HILE SOME WOMEN FOUND EMPOWERMENT THROUGH RELIGION, OTHERS TOOK REVOLU-*tionary inspiration from the new imaginative horizons of libertinism. Libertine, dramatist, royalist, world-traveler, and spy, Aphra Behn is celebrated as one of the first English women to make her living by writing. Virginia Woolf declared, "All women together, ought to let flowers fall upon the grave of Aphra Behn . . . for it was she who earned them the right to speak their minds." Little is known about her early life. She was born near Canterbury and raised in the company of the wealthy Colepeper family. Some scholars believe she was the illegitimate daughter of Lady Willoughby, and some believe she was the daughter of a local butcher and nurse. In 1663, she traveled to Suriname, in South America, which was then an English colony. This experience formed the basis for one of her most famous works, the novella* Oroonooko: or, the Royal Slave. A True History *(1688).*

After returning to England, Behn established herself in courtly circles and was recruited as a spy by King Charles II during the Second Anglo-Dutch War (1665–1667). It is reported that Behn used her powers of sexual persuasion to obtain strategic secrets from Dutch royalty. However, her service was not rewarded financially, and she ended up in debtor's prison in 1669. In 1670, she began her professional writing career, producing eighteen plays including The Forced Marriage *(1670),* The Dutch Lover *(1673),* The Rover *(1677; 1681), and* The Widdow Ranter *(1690). As part of a libertine culture tolerant of sexual diversity, Behn explored in her writing women's erotic desires for both men and women. Many of her poems use the traditional English pastoral setting as a venue for frank, humorous, and liberatory explorations of the pleasures and problems of sexual love, including male impotence. Behn wanted to free sexuality from the domain of modesty, virtue, and custom and treat it as a basic form of human expression. First published in 1688, "To* the Fair Clarinda" uses pastoral conventions—Clarinda being a common shepherdess name in the genre—to celebrate the erotic pleasures of love between women.

"TO THE FAIR CLARINDA WHO MADE LOVE TO ME, IMAGIN'D MORE THAN WOMAN" (1688)

Fair lovely Maid, or if that Title be
Too weak, too Feminine for Nobler thee,
Permit a Name that more Approaches Truth:
And let me call thee, Lovely Charming Youth.
This last will justifie my soft complaint,
While that may serve to lessen my constraint;
And without Blushes I the Youth persue,
When so much beauteous Woman is in view.
Against thy Charms we struggle but in vain
With thy deluding Form thou giv'st us pain,
While the bright Nymph[1] betrays us to the Swain.[2]
In pity to our Sex sure thou wer't sent,
That we might Love, and yet be Innocent:
For sure no Crime with thee we can commit;
Or if we shou'd—thy Form excuses it.
For who, that gathers fairest Flowers believes
A Snake lies hid beneath the Fragrant Leaves.

Though beauteous Wonder of a different kind,
Soft *Cloris* with the dear *Alexis* join'd;[3]
When e'er the Manly part of thee, wou'd plead
Though tempts us with the Image of the Maid,
While we the noblest Passions do extend
The Love to *Hermes*, *Aphrodite* the Friend.

---

[1] Nymph: Minor nature goddess in Greek mythology.
[2] Swain: Rustic male lover.
[3] Cloris, Alexis: Common female and male names in the pastoral tradition.

SEVEN

Mary Astell (1663–1731)

*M*ARY ASTELL WAS A POLITICAL PHILOSOPHER, RELIGIOUS WRITER, AND ADVOCATE OF *women's education. Part of a well-regarded circle of High Church Anglican women intellectuals living in the Chelsea section of London at the turn of the eighteenth century, Astell has been called a "conservative" or "Tory" feminist by many commentators, who note her support for monarchy rather than republicanism, her repeated statement that women should have no official role in public life, and her religious views, those of the orthodox Church of England rather than the newly influential radical Protestant dissenting sects. But Astell believed that women were actually better off being governed by just one king rather than by the many masters—male heads of household, male clergy, male political officers— empowered by the Republican Protestantism. "If all Men are born Free," she asked, "why are all Women born Slaves?"*

First published in 1694, A Serious Proposal to the Ladies, for the Advancement of Their True and Greatest Interest, by a Lover of her Sex *builds on Bathsua Makin's argument that differences between the sexes are not natural but cultural—the consequence of unenlightened custom, especially the denial of education for women—and presses for the establishment of modern women's institutions of secular and religious learning. Astell published* A Serious Proposal, Part II, *in 1697, dedicating the book to Princess Anne of Denmark, who would ascend to the throne as Queen Anne in 1702. Engaging and debating prominent philosophers such as Descartes and Locke, Astell admonished women to look to their personal growth—both their intellectual training and their spiritual development—instead of to marriage, fashion, and family ties. During England's great surge of imperial expansion, Astell advises women to avoid the fate of the Roman emperor Domitian, "catching Flies when you should be busied in obtaining Empires." Her proposal for an institution in which women could live together, pursuing scholarly and spiritual pursuits without having to negotiate the marriage market, critiques the inequality of an English revolutionary world in which women's traditional economic power was falling away and citizenship was being described as both public and male. Mary Astell died of breast cancer in 1731.*

A SERIOUS PROPOSAL TO THE LADIES (1694)

LADIES, . . .

Pardon me the seeming rudeness of this Proposal, which goes upon a supposition that there is something amiss in you, which it is intended to amend. My design is not to expose, but to rectify Your Failures. To be exempt from mistake, is a privilege few can pretend to, greatest is to be past Conviction, and too obstinate to reform. Even the *Men*, as exact as they wou'd seem, and as much as they divert themselves with our Miscarriages, are very often guilty of greater faults, and such as considering the advantages they enjoy, are much more inexcusable. But I will not pretend to correct their Errors, who either are, or at least think themselves too wise to receive Instruction from a Womans Pen. My earnest desire is, that you Ladies, would be as perfect and happy as 'tis possible to be in this imperfect state, for I Love you too well to endure a spot upon your Beauties, if I can by any means remove and wipe it off. I would have you live up to the dignity of your Nature, and express your thankfulness to GOD for the benefits you enjoy by a due improvement of them. . . . Hither, Ladies, I desire you wou'd aspire, 'tis a noble and becoming Ambition, and to remove such Obstacles as lye in your way is the design of this Paper. We will therefore enquire what it is that stops your flight, that keeps you groveling here below, like *Domitian*[1] catching Flies when you should be busied in obtaining Empires? . . .

The Cause therefore of the defects we labour under, is, if not wholly, yet at least in the first place, to be ascribed to the mistakes of our Education; which like an Error in the first Concoction,[2] spreads its ill Influence through all our Lives. . . . When a poor Young Lady is taught to value her self on nothing but her Cloaths,[3] and to think she's very fine when well accoutred.[4] When she hears say that 'tis Wisdom enough for her to know how to dress her self, that she may become amiable in his eyes; to whom it appertains to be knowing and learned; who can blame her if she lay out her Industry and Money on such

---

[1] Domitian: Titus Flavius Domitianus (51–96), Roman Emperor who reigned from 81–96. Viewed as a self-indulgent tyrant, Domitian is said to have spent most of his days catching and killing flies.

[2] An error in the First concoction: Digestion of a poison or bad food.

[3] Cloaths: Clothes.

[4] Accoutred: Dressed.

Accomplishments, and sometimes extends it farther than her misinformer desires she should? When she sees the vain and the gay, making Parade in the World and attended with the Courtship and admiration of all about them, no wonder that her tender Eyes are dazled with the Pageantry; and wanting Judgement to pass a due Estimate on them and their Admirers, longs to be such a fine and celebrated thing as they! What tho' she be sometimes told of another World, she has however a more lively perception of this, and may well think, that if her Instructors were in earnest when they tell her of *hereafter*, they would not be so busied and concerned about what happens *here*. . . .

Now as to the Proposal it is to erect a *Monastery*, or if you win (to avoid giving offence to the scrupulous and injudicious, by names which tho' innocent in themselves, have been abus'd by superstitious Practices,) we will call it a *Religious Retirement*,[5] and such as shall have a double aspect, being not only a Retreat from the World for those who desire that advantage, but likewise, an institution and previous discipline, to fit us to do the greatest good in it; such an institution as this (if I do not mightily deceive my self,) would be the most probable method to amend the present and improve the future Age. For here, those who are convinc'd of the emptiness of earthly Enjoyments, who are sick of the vanity of the world, and its empertinencies may find more substantial and satisfying entertainments, and need not be confin'd to what they justly loath. Those who are desirous to know and fortify their weak side, first do good to themselves, that hereafter they may be capable of doing more good to others; or for their greater security are willing to avoid *temptation*, may get out of that danger which a continual stay in view of the Enemy and the familiarity and unwearied application of the Temptation may expose them to; and gain an opportunity to look into themselves, to be acquainted at home and no longer the greatest strangers to their own hearts. Such as are willing in a more peculiar and undisturb'd manner, to attend the great business they came into the world about, the service of GOD and improvement of their own Minds, may find a convenient and blissful recess from the noise and hurry of the World. A world so cumbersome, so infectious, that altho' thro' the grace of GOD and their own strict watchfulness, they are kept from sinking down into its corruptions, 'twill however damp their flight to heav'n, hinder them from attaining any eminent pitch of Vertue.

You are therefore Ladies, invited into a place, where you shall suffer no other confinement, but to be kept out of the road of Sin: You shall not be depriv'd of your grandeur, but only exchange the vain Pomps and Pageantry of the world, empty Titles

---

[5] Anglican Church leaders had criticized previous proposals for women's academies for appearing too much like Catholic nunneries.

and Forms of State, for the true and solid Greatness of being able to despise them. You will only quit the Chat of insignificant people for an ingenious Conversation; the froth of flashy Wit for real Wisdom; idle tales for instructive discourses. The deceitful Flatteries of those who under pretence of loving and admiring you, really served their *own* base ends, for the seasonable Reproofs and wholsom Counsels of your hearty well-wishers and affectionate Friends, which will procure you those perfections your feigned lovers pretended you had, and kept you from obtaining. No uneasy task will be enjoyn'd[6] you, all your labour being only to prepare for the highest degrees of that Glory, the very lowest of which is more than at present you are able to conceive, and the prospect of it sufficient to out-weigh all the Pains of Religion, were there any in it, as really there is none. All that is requir'd of you, is only to be as Happy as possibly you can, and to make sure of a Felicity that will fill all the capacities of your Souls! A happiness, which when once you have tasted, you'l be fully convinc'd, you cou'd never do too much to obtain it; nor be too solicitous to adorn your Souls, with such tempers and dispositions, as will at present make you in some measure such holy and Heavenly Creatures, as you one day hope to be in a more perfect manner; without which Qualifications you can neither reasonably expect, nor are capable of enjoying the Happiness of the Life to come. Happy Retreat! which will be the introducing you into such a Paradise as your Mother Eve forfeited, where you shall feast on Pleasures, that do not like those of the World, disappoint your expectations, pall your Appetites, and by the disgust they give you, put you on the fruitless search after new Delights, which when obtain'd are as empty as the former; but such as will make you truly happy now, and prepare you to be *perfectly* so hereafter. Here are no Serpents to deceive you, whilst you entertain your selves in these delicious Gardens. No Provocations will be given in this Amicable Society, but to Love and to good Works, which will afford such an entertaining employment, that you'll have as little inclination as leisure to pursue those Follies which in the time of your ignorance pass'd with you under the name of love; altho' there is not in nature two more different things, than true Love and that brutish Passion which pretends to ape it. Here will be no Rivalling but for the Love of GOD, no Ambition but to procure his Favour, to which nothing will more effectually recommend you, than a great and dear affection to each other. Envy, that Canker, will not here disturb your Breasts; for how can she repine[7] at an-others welfare, who reckons it the greatest part of her own? No Covetousness will gain admittance in this blest abode, but to amass huge Treasures of good Works, and

---

[6] Enjoyn'd: Imposed upon.

[7] Repine: Complain against.

to procure one of the brightest Crowns of Glory. You will not be solicitous to encrease your Fortunes, but enlarge your Minds; esteeming no Grandeur like being conformable to the meek and humble JESUS. So that you only withdraw from the noise and trouble, the folly and temptation of the world, that you may more peaceably enjoy your selves, and all the innocent Pleasures it is able to afford you, and particularly that which is worth all the rest, noble Vertuous and Disinteress'd[8] Friendship. And to compleat all, that *acme* of delight which the devout Seraphic Soul enjoys, when dead to the World, she devotes her self entirely to the Contemplation and Fruition of her Beloved; when having disengag'd her self from all those Lets[9] which hindered her from without, she moves in a direct and vigorous motion towards her true and only Good, whom now she embraces and acquiesces in, with such an unspeakable pleasure, as is only intelligible to those who have tried and felt it, which we can no more describe to the dark and sensual part of Mankind, than we can the beauty of Colours and harmony of Sounds to the Blind and Deaf. In fine, the place to which you are invited is a Type[10] and Antepast[11] of Heav'n, where your Employment will be as there, to magnify GOD, to love one another, and to communicate that useful *knowledge*, which by the due improvement of your time in Study and Contemplation you will obtain; and which when obtain'd, will afford you a much sweeter and more durable delight, than all those pitiful diversions, those revellings and amusements, which now thro your ignorance of better, appear the only grateful and relishing Entertainments.

But because we were not made for our selves, nor can by any means so effectually glorify GOD, and do good to our own Souls, as by doing Offices of Charity and Beneficence to others; and to the intent, that every Vertue, and the highest degrees of every Vertue may be exercis'd and promoted the most that may be; your Retreat shall be so manag'd as not to exclude the good Works of an *Active*, from the pleasure and serenity of a contemplative Life, but by a due mixture of both retain all the advantages and avoid the inconveniences that attend either. It shall not so cut you off from the world as to hinder you from bettering and improving it; but rather qualify you to do it the greatest Good, and be a Seminary to stock the Kingdom with pious and prudent Ladies; whose good Example it is to be hop'd, will so influence the rest of their Sex, that Women may no longer pass for those little useless and impertinent Animals, which the ill conduct of too many has caus'd them to be mistaken for. . . . [O]ne great end of this institution, shall be to expel that cloud of Ignorance, which

---

[8] Disinteress'd: Disinterested, selfless.
[9] Lets: Impediments.
[10] Type: Symbol, figure.
[11] Antepast: Foretaste.

Custom has involv'd us in, to furnish our minds with a stock of solid and useful
Knowledge, that the Souls of women may no longer be the only unadorn'd and
neglected things. It is not intended that our Religious[12] shou'd waste their time, and
trouble their heads about such unconcerning matters, as the vogue of the world has
turn'd up for Learning, the impertinency of which has been excellently expos'd by an
ingenious pen[13] but busy themselves in a serious enquiry after necessary and perfec-
tive truths, something which it concerns them to know, and which tends to their real
interest and perfection, and what that is the excellent Author just now mention'd, will
sufficiently inform them, such a course of Study will neither be too troublesome nor
out of the reach of a Female Virtuoso[14] . . . Nor need she trouble her self in turning
over a great number of Books, but take care to understand and digest a few well chosen and good ones. Let her but obtain right Ideas, and be truly acquainted with the
nature of those Objects that present themselves to her mind, and then no matter
whether or no she be able to tell what fanciful people have said about them: And
thoroughly to understand Christianity as profess'd by the Church of England, will be
sufficient to confirm her in the truth, tho' she have not a Catalogue of those particular
errors which oppose it. . . .

For since GOD has given Women as well as Men intelligent Souls, why should
they be forbidden to improve them? Since he has not denied us the faculty of Thinking,
why shou'd we not (at least in gratitude to him) employ our Thoughts on himself their
noblest Object, and not unworthily bestow them on Trifles and Gaities and secular
Affairs? Being the Soul was created for the contemplation of Truth as well as for the
fruition of Good, is it not as cruel and unjust to preclude Women from the knowledge
of the one, as well as from the enjoyment of the other? Especially since the Will is
blind, and cannot chuse but by the direction of the Understanding; or to speak more
properly, since the Soul always *Wills* according as she *Understands*, so that if she
Understands amiss, she *Wills* amiss. And as Exercise enlarges and exalts any Faculty,
so thro' want of using, it becomes crampt and lessened; if therefore we make little or
no use of our Understandings we shall shortly have none to use; and the more contracted,[15] and unemploy'd the deliberating and directive Power is, the more liable is the
elective to[16] unworthy and mischievous options. What is it but the want of an ingenious

---

[12] Religious: Members of a religious order.

[13] Astell's marginal note: "Mr. Nor Conduct of Human Life." She refers to John Norris, *Reflections
upon the Conduct of Human Life: with reference to the Study of Learning and Knowledge. In a Letter to the Excellent Lady, the Lady Masham* (1690), an argument that education for women should
be in "necessary" rather than "contingent" or superfluous ideas and truths.

[14] Virtuoso: Savant, expert, scholar.

[15] Contracted: Narrowed, limited, confined.

[16] Elective to: Choice of.

Education that renders the generality of Feminine Conversations so insipid and foolish and their solitude so *insupportable*? Learning is therefore necessary to render them more agreeable and useful in company, and to furnish them with becoming entertainments when alone, that so they may not be driven to those miserable shifts,[17] which too many make use of to put off their time, that precious Talent that never lies on the hands of a judicious Person. And since our Happiness in the next World, depends so far on those dispositions which we carry along with us out of this, that without a right habitude and temper of mind we are not capable of Felicity; and seeing our Beatitude[18] consists in the contemplation of the divine Truth and Beauty, as well as in the fruition of his Goodness, can Ignorance be a fit preparative for Heaven? Is't likely that she whose Understanding has been busied about nothing but froth and trifles, shou'd be capable of delighting her self in noble and sublime Truths? . . .

And let us also acquire a true Practical Knowledge, such as will convince us of the absolute necessity of *Holy Living* as well as of *Right Believing*, and that no Heresy is more dangerous, than that of an ungodly and wicked Life. And since the *French Tongue* is understood by most Ladies, methinks they may much better improve it by the study of Philosophy (as I hear the French Ladies do) *Des Cartes*,[19] *Malebranch*[20] and others, than by reading idle *Novels and Romances*. 'Tis strange we shou'd be so forward to imitate their Fashions and Fopperies, and have no regard to what is really imitable in them! And why shall it not be thought as genteel to understand *French Philosophy*, as to be accoutred in a *French Mode*? . . .

The Ladies, I'm sure, have no reason to dislike this Proposal, but I know not how the Men will resent it, to have their enclosure broke down, and Women invited to tast[e] of that Tree of Knowledge they have so long unjustly *monopoliz'd*. But they must excuse me, if I be as partial to my own Sex as they are to theirs, and think Women as capable of Learning as Men are, and that it becomes them as well. . . .

And as this institution will strictly enjoyn all pious and profitable Employments, so does it not only permit but recommend harmless and ingenious Diversions, Musick particularly, and such as may refresh the Body without enervating the Mind. They do a disservice to Religion who make it an enemy to innocent Nature, and injure the Almighty when they represent him as imposing burdens that are not to be

---

[17] Driven to those miserable shifts: Forced to extremities.

[18] Beatitude: Blessedness.

[19] Des Cartes: Rene Descartes (1596–1650), influential French philosopher and mathematician, often called the "Father of Modern Philosophy."

[20] Malebranch: Father Nicolas Malebranche (1638–1715), French philosopher of the Cartesian school and mathematician.

born.[21] Neither GOD nor Wise men will like us the better for an affected severity and waspish sourness. . . .

As to *Lodging*, *Habit* and *Diet*, they may be quickly resolv'd on by the Ladies who shall subscribe; who I doubt not will make choice of what is most plain and decent, what Nature, not Luxury requires. And since neither Meat nor Cloaths commend us unto GOD, they'l content themselves with such things as are fit and convenient, without occasioning scruple to themselves or giving any trouble or offence to others. She who considers to how much better account that Money will turn which is bestow'd on the Poor, then that which is laid out in unnecessary Expences on her self, needs no Admonitions against superfluities. She who truly loves her self, will never waste that Money on a decaying Carkass, which if prudently disburs'd, wou'd procure her an eternal Mansion. She will never think her self so fine, as when the backs of the Poor do bless her; and never feast so luxuriously as when she treats an hungry person. No perfume will be thought so grateful as the Odour of Good Works; nor any Wash so Beautifying as her own tears. For her Heroick Soul is too great to ambition any Empire but that of her own Breast, or to regard any other Conquest than the rescuing poor unhappy Souls from the slavery of Sin and Satan, those only unsupportable Tyrants; and therefore what Decays[22] she observes in her Face will be very unconcerning[23] but she will with greatest speed and accuracy rectify the least Spot that may prejudice the beauty of her lovely Soul.

In a word, this happy Society will be but one Body, whose Soul is love, animating and informing it, and perpetually breathing forth it self in flames of holy desires after GOD, and acts of Benevolence to each other. . . . And that every one who comes under this holy Roof, may be such an amiable, such a charming Creature, what faults they bring with them shall be corrected by sweetness not severity; by friendly Admonitions, not magisterial Reproofs; Piety shall not be roughly impos'd, but wisely insinuated by a perpetual Display of the Beauties of Religion in an exemplary Conversation, the continual and most powerful Sermon of an holy Life. And since Inclination can't be forc'd, (and nothing makes people more uneasy than the fettering themselves with unnecessary Bonds) there shall be no Vows or irrevocable Obligations, not so much as the fear of Reproach to keep our Ladies here any longer than they desire. No: Ev'ry act of our Religious Votary shall be voluntary and free, and no other tye but the Pleasure, the Glory and Advantage of this blessed Retirement, to confine her to it. . . .

---

[21] Astell criticizes Puritan prohibitions against arts and music.
[22] Decays: Flaws, blemishes.
[23] Unconcerning: Irrelevant.

EIGHT

Pierre Cholenec, S.J. (1641–1723)

*T*HE AGE OF REVOLUTIONS WAS ALSO AN AGE OF IMPERIAL EXPANSION THAT PUT EUROPEAN *peoples, cultures, and beliefs into contact with indigenous Americans, often with destructive or unpredictable results. Pierre Cholenec was a Jesuit missionary at the Mission of Saint Francis Xavier of the Sault in New France (now Sault Ste. Marie, Ontario). There, he was the spiritual advisor and confessor of Katharine Tegakoüita (1656–1680), a young Iroquois woman. He composed a biography of her in 1695, and this document, along with others, became the basis for her canonization by the Roman Catholic Church in the twentieth century.[1]*

Tegakoüita was born in 1656 to a Mohawk father and an Algonquin mother, and spent her childhood in a village near what is present day Auriesville, New York. She was baptized at the age of 20, and not long after she ran away from her village (abetted by her priest) to join other pious Catholic Indians at the Sault Mission, about two hundred miles away in present-day Canada. On her journey, she encountered nuns for the first time and determined that their lives of chastity, female companionship, and seclusion accorded with her own vision of worship. The Jesuit missionaries denied her request to take similar vows and establish a convent-like community with several like-minded pious Native women. She continued to refuse to marry despite immense pressure from her adopted relatives. Still quietly insistent about directing her own spiritual practice, Tegakoüita daily performed penances from a repertoire that included fasting, beating herself with switches, burning the bottoms of her feet with hot coals, sleeping on a bed of thorns, and standing barefoot

---

[1] Tegakoüita has alternate spellings, including Tekakwitha and Degagwitha. Katharine can also be spelled multiple ways. Kateri, another name sometimes used, was actually the result of a nineteenth-century attempt to "Indianize" her name.

in the snow for long stretches of time. Though Cholenec maintains that Tegakoüita was motivated by a holy hatred of her body, this mortification of her flesh and her vows of chastity escape such an explanation; ecstasy colors Cholenec's descriptions of her "great thirst" for "suffering," and her secretive acts of penance and vows of chastity elude Jesuit and Iroquois authority alike, often disturbingly. After her death Tegakoüita was soon renowned for her chastity and piety. Native and French Catholics prayed to her, visited her grave, sought her relics, and performed similar penances in imitation of her piety. Her miraculous intervention is credited with the preservation of the Sault mission during a violent conflict between Iroquois and French forces and with curing the sick.

Although this account was neither written nor dictated by Tegakoüita herself, it is included here as one of the few accounts we have of Native women's lives, words, and relationships early in the Age of Revolutions. Tegakoüita's powerful personality, impressive discipline, and love for her female companions leap off the page in Cholenec's account.

FROM *THE LIFE OF KATHARINE TEGAKOÜITA, FIRST IROQUOIS VIRGIN* (1696)[2]

"Her Religious Fervor"

Katharine was not satisfied with an ordinary life; driven by this insatiable desire for good and by her extreme fervor to undertake and accomplish much, she began by embracing what was most perfect. She took for her principal, or rather her only maxim, to search in all things for what would be most pleasing to God, not to reserve anything from Him and to make it a rule to give Him everything that depended on her, without any respect for creatures and without any return for herself. So holy a maxim had as its foundation the exalted idea that she was made to the likeness of God, and the extreme gratefulness she felt and retained during her entire life for the great grace God had bestowed on her in choosing her among so many others whom He left in darkness, to see the Light at the Mission of the Sault.

With such beautiful principles, with such powerful and such efficacious motives to inspire her, the first thing our virtuous savage did was to attach herself to the holy place and to make the church her dearest and most habitual refuge, certain of

---

[2] From The Sacred Congregation of Rites, ed., *Katharine Tekakwitha: The Lily of the Mohawks.* Used with permission of Fordham University Press.

always finding Him to whom she had already consecrated her heart and all her affections. In order to converse with Him far from all noise and without any distractions from creatures, she would go there every morning as early as four o'clock, even during the severest winter weather. She heard the first Mass at the break of day and the Mass for the Indians at sunrise. She returned often during the day, interrupting her work to satisfy devotion. Finally, her work done, she returned again in the evening, and left only late at night: the first in the morning to enter, and last every night to leave.

As for Sundays and feast days, it may be said that Katharine spent them entirely in church, since she scarcely ever left it on those days except to take refreshment.

This fervor which filled her in church, shone forth even more in her prayers; she learned with marvelous diligence those which were said in common. She prayed very little with her lips, but a great deal with her eyes and her heart; her eyes were always filled with tears, while she sighed deeply from her heart. She appeared immobile and closed up within herself. Through such eagerness to unite herself to God in her prayers, she attained, without any other teacher than the Holy Ghost, a sublime gift of prayer, together with such heavenly sweetness, that she often passed several hours at a time in these intimate communications with her God. [. . .]

Her devotion was all the more admirable since it was not one of those idle devotions, where usually there is only self-love, nor was Katharine one of those obstinate devotees, who are in church when they should be at home. In attaching herself to God she attached herself to work, as to a very proper means of being united with Him, as well as in order to preserve during the entire day the good inspirations she had received in the morning at the foot of the altar. For this reason she formed a great friendship with the good Anastasia of whom we have spoken;[3] she made it a rule to avoid all other company and to go with her alone, whether to the woods or to the fields.

They went together, therefore, and since they had only one purpose, namely, to seek for God, they not only offered Him their work, but they also held pious conversations while performing their tasks, Anastasia speaking to Katharine only of God, of the means of pleasing Him and advancing His service, of the life and habits of the good Christians, of the fervor of the Saints, of their hatred for sin, and of the harsh penances they performed for the atonement of those they had committed.

---

[3] Anastasia: Anastasia Tegonhatsihongo was an older Native woman who served as Tegakoüita's Christian instructor or mentor. Tegakoüita lived in her home at the Sault along with others, including an adopted sister.

Thus Katharine sanctified her work by spiritual conferences. So holy a conversation, together with her zeal for the things of God, had the result that she always came away with new desires to give herself entirely to Him and to put into practice what she had just heard. She found God everywhere, whether she was in church, in the wood or in the fields. Lest she live a moment that was not spent for Him, she might be observed coming and going with a rosary in her hand, which led her instructress [Anastasia] to say that Katharine never lost sight of her God, but that she always walked in His presence. If rain or extreme cold prevented her from working, she passed almost all her time before the Blessed Sacrament,[4] or she made small objects of mat work, but she did not spend her time visiting other girls in order to play or seek amusement, as those of her age are apt to do on similar occasions.

Weeks so well utilized were indeed weeks filled, that is to say, in the sense of the Holy Scriptures, with virtue and merit. Katharine nevertheless ended each week with a severe discussion in which she gave account to herself of all that had happened; then she had her sins taken away in the Sacrament of Penance,[5] for she went to confession every Saturday evening. But she did so in an extraordinary manner, one that could have been inspired by the Holy Ghost alone, who Himself guided her, and who first had given her a love of suffering and, as we shall see later, a hatred of her body.[6]

In order to prepare herself for these confessions, she began with the last part, I mean the penance. She would go into the woods and tear her shoulders open with large osiers.[7] From there she went to the church and passed a long time weeping for her sins. She confessed them, interrupting her words with sighs and sobs, believing herself to be the greatest sinner alive, although she was of angelic innocence. Not only the desire to be always united with God, and not to be distracted by the people, made her love solitude so much and flee society, but also her desire to preserve herself in innocence, her horror of sin, and the fear of displeasing God. [. . .]

---

[4] Blessed Sacrament: A reference to bread (or Host) and wine, already consecrated in the Catholic Eucharist. Catholics believe in transubstantiation: that the consecrated Host and wine are the actual body and blood of Christ. Some Catholic churches place the Blessed Sacrament on display for devotional purposes.

[5] Sacrament of Penance: One of the seven Christian sacraments. In the seventeenth century, penitents usually confessed their sins, received absolution, and then performed a (light) penance. Here, Cholenec describes how Tegakoüita altered the order of these steps.

[6] Probably a reference to a description of the many penances Tegakoüita inflicted upon herself.

[7] Osier: A flexible branch from one of several kinds of tough, pliant willows, often used in basketwork.

"The Story of Katharine's Companion"

In the spring of 1678, God gave a companion to Katharine who aided her greatly in her progress, and from whom we have learned several important things concerning her, since this girl was the only one who really had her confidence, and to whom she communicated her most intimate thoughts and actions from the first they met one another. Katharine, it is true, until that time had never wished to attach herself to any one except the good Anastasia, whose authority, since she had taken her mother's place, and frequent exhortation in the capacity of instructress, had greatly aided Katharine in taking the right course of action she now pursued. But this good Anastasia was advanced in age and could not increase the fervor of her pupil, who had already surpassed her and who performed actions of which the older woman was not capable. She needed a companion more of her own age, one who had the same resolution of giving herself entirely to God, and who was capable of leading the same kind of austere life that she herself had embraced. God, therefore, let her find such a companion in the person of a young woman. [. . .][8]

"Spiritual Friendship"

[. . .] [I]n 1678, [Tegakoüita] became acquainted with her companion in the following manner. The first chapel of the Sault was then under construction. One day Katharine walked around this building merely to see how the work progressed, as did the Christian of whom we speak. But God had planned this unexpected meeting for His glory and the good of these two souls. They greeted and spoke to each other for the first time. Katharine asked where the women would sit in the new church; and the other, in reply, showed her where she thought their place would be. Katharine replied that a chapel of wood was not what God asked most of us, but that He longed rather for our souls, that He might dwell therein and make His temple in them, and that she did not deserve to enter this material chapel, for she had so often driven God from her heart, and merited rather to be put out with the dogs.

These sentiments of profound humility, uttered with tears and with words of grace, touched the other all the more because she did not expect them, and, indeed, were for her words of life, grace, and salvation. Moved by remorse, she soon

---

[8] Tegakoüita's companion was Mary Teresa Tegaiaguenta. She was a baptized Christian and a member of either the Onondanga or Oneida tribe. The Onondangas, Oneidas, and Mohawks were all members of the Iroquois confederacy.

resolved to carry out the principal part of the promise she had made while on the hunt.[9] She was of a fiery temperament and went to extremes in good or evil; was possessed of great energy, and was also in the prime of her life, that is to say, about twenty-eight or thirty years of age. She gradually became enlightened while listening to Katharine, believing that what she said came from God, and that He had sent this holy girl, of whom so much good was spoken, to help her change her life, as she had promised.

Then she told Katharine her ideas, and they found that both their hearts and their plans were in perfect accord. They became friends during this first interview, and one word leading on to another, they then communicated their most secret thoughts to each other. In order to talk more easily, they seated themselves at the foot of a cross near the bank of the river.[10] They told each other of their past lives, and resolved to unite themselves in order to do penance. As I was their spiritual director, they spoke to me of this union and asked for my approval, which I gladly gave, seeing that it would be good for both.

From this time forward they became one in heart and soul, and were inseparable until Katharine's death, after which she was always in her companion's mind. Although Katharine did not neglect Anastasia, and still occasionally visited with her, she nevertheless devoted herself entirely to this second companion, who was more zealous, and able to help her more in her devotions. They could be seen going to the woods, fields, and everywhere together, avoiding meeting other girls and women. This they did not only to avoid the trivial affairs of the village, but also in order not to swerve from their devotions. They spoke only of God and of things pertaining to Him. Their conversations were as so many spiritual conferences, in which they disclosed to each other their lives, their desires, and their slightest trials, in order to encourage each other to remain firm under all conditions and to suffer something for Our Lord. Several times during the week they went deep into the woods and there chastised their shoulders with rods, as Katharine had been doing by herself for a long time. [. . .]

---

[9] In the previous section, Cholenec relates Mary Teresa Tegaiaguenta's story, telling how she participated in an Iroquois hunting party that was plagued by snow, sickness, and starvation. The group eventually resorted to cannibalism to survive. In the wake of the incident, Mary Teresa promised to go to confession, reform her life, and do penance. Two years later, at the time of her first encounter with Tegakoüita, she had only fulfilled the first of her three promises.

[10] The Sault Mission was on the St. Lawrence River near Montreal (near what is present-day Ville Sainte-Catherine). Sault is another word for waterfall or rapid.

"Vow of Chastity"

Among the Fathers of the Church, disputing with holy zeal to discover which of Our Lady's[11] virtues rendered her most pleasing in the eyes of God and worthy of being His mother, there are some who think with reason that it is her virginity. They think that by being the greatest among all pure creatures, who by an express desire raised the divine standard of virginity in the world, she surpassed all the grace, perfection, and sanctity of all the other saints together. I say the same regarding an act so heroic as that done by this young virgin in following the example of the Queen of Virgins. It was her greatest glory before God, and considering her from that aspect alone, it is not surprising that she deserved to receive so many graces during her lifetime, and to bring about such miracles after her death. God had preserved her for this even among the Iroquois for more than twenty years in angelic purity of soul and body in the midst of corruption. She herself aided in this preparation by renouncing marriage,[12] contrary to the custom of the other girls, and by generously rising above the persecutions which she suffered on this occasion in her country.

Almost as soon as she arrived at the Sault, Katharine resolved to lead a life of virginity; she kept this a secret until, again being persecuted, she was obliged to disclose her decision. After Katharine had declared herself, she would have preferred to accomplish her purpose without further delay, so much did she wish to belong wholly to Our Lord, and as soon as possible to make Him the entire sacrifice of her person by an irrevocable pledge. The thing was so unusual, however, and appeared so incompatible with the life of the Indians, that I thought it best not to precipitate matters, so as to give her plenty of time to weigh a matter of such consequence. I tried her, therefore, for some time, and after I had noted the great progress she made in every kind of virtue, and above all with what profusion God communed with His Servant, it seemed to me that Katharine's design could come from no other source than from Him. Thereupon, I at last gave her permission to carry it out. It would be hard to put in words the joy she felt and the fervor with which she prepared for so great an act. But when this day, so longed for, the happiest and most beautiful of her life, at last arrived, she made one more effort to offer her sacrifice to the Lord with all the devotion and ardor she could command.

---

[11] Our Lady: The Virgin Mary

[12] In an earlier chapter, Cholenec relates how Tegakoüita and her companion, Mary Teresa Tegaiaguenta, had secretly vowed never to marry: "After considering all things well, Katharine and her companion agreed never to marry, the one to dedicate to God her virginity, and the other her perpetual widowhood. They kept this decision a secret, and resolved not to speak of it unless absolutely necessary." Cholenec and others learned of the vow when Tegakoüita's adopted sister pressed her to marry and she refused.

It was the Feast of the Annunciation,[13] March 25, 1679, at eight o'clock in the morning when, a moment after Jesus Christ gave Himself to her in Communion, Katharine Tegakoüita wholly gave herself to Him, and renouncing marriage forever, promised Him perpetual virginity. With a heart aglow with love she implored Him to be her only Spouse, and to accept her as His bride. She prayed Our Lady, for whom she had a tender devotion, to present her to her Divine Son; then, wishing to make a double consecration in one single act, she offered herself entirely to Mary at the same time that she dedicated herself to Jesus Christ, earnestly begging her to be her mother and to accept her as her daughter.

It was in this manner that the great act took place, by which no doubt much joy was caused in heaven, and Katharine's greatest desire was achieved. After her heroic sacrifice had been made, she no longer seemed of this world; her conversation was of heaven alone, her soul already tasted of its sweetness, while she mortified her body by her new austerities, which, joined to her intense striving to be constantly united to God, finally exhausted her forces, so that she fell dangerously ill the same summer and narrowly escaped death. She retained a great pain in her stomach, accompanied by frequent vomitings, and a low fever, which, gradually undermining her, reduced her to a state of languor from which she was unable to rouse herself.

It took a courage such as hers to retain, in spite of her infirmities, all the fervor of a devotion which never slackened until she died. On the contrary, her spirit seemed to take new strength at the expense of her body, and she sought new means by which to sanctify herself in the little time she had left to live. The just are admirable in their ways, the more they realize their end is near, the more rapidly they advance in perfection. They are holy misers, who are never content with what they have given to God, but always wish to give Him more, so as to receive more from Him in return, and thus to amass greater riches for eternity. Our chaste maiden without doubt stored up a large number during the two years and a half she lived at the Sault, not only by the remarkable things she accomplished there and of which we have made note here, but even more by the constant practice of Christian virtues, which, I may say, she possessed in such an eminent degree that it would be difficult to judge which one shone forth most.

---

[13] Feast of the Annunciation: A Catholic feast day celebrating the angel Gabriel's announcement to Mary of the incarnation and the conception of Christ in her womb.

NINE

Sarah Fyge Egerton (1670–1723)

*I*F MARY ASTELL VOICED CONCERN THAT REPUBLICAN PROTESTANTISM EMPOWERED EVERY *man to exercise dominion over women, other English feminists drew authority from the democratizing energies of this revolution. When she was just 14 years old, London-born Sarah Fyge wrote a long polemical defense of women in response to the poet Robert Gould's anti-feminist satire* Love Given O're *(1682). Fyge's* The Female Advocate *was published in 1686, upsetting her father so badly that he banished her from the household. She was 16 years old. Within a few years, he arranged for Sarah Fyge to be married against her will to Edward Field. After his death, she entered into a spectacularly unhappy marriage with her second cousin Thomas Egerton, an Anglican rector. In 1703, Thomas Egerton filed suit for divorce. That same year, over the objections of her husband, Sarah Fyge Egerton published* Poems on Several Occasions, *which contained several love poems to her paramour Henry Pierce as well as fierce critiques of gender inequality, such as "The Emulation." Observing critically that "in every State" woman is a "Slave," Egerton, like many feminist writers of her time, is careful to credit inequality to unjust "custom" rather than to any natural or essential hierarchy of the sexes. She condemns the institution of heterosexual marriage as a male-devised conspiracy to keep women in subjection. Egerton also seizes on the revolutionary spirit of the Protestant Reformation that has empowered "every man" to "explain the Will of Heaven," asking "shall we Women now sit tamely by, / Make no excursions in Philosophy, / Or grace our Thoughts in tuneful Poetry?"*

"THE EMULATION" (1703)

Say, Tyrant Custom, why must we obey,

The impositions of thy haughty Sway;

From the first dawn of Life, unto the Grave,

Poor Womankind's in every State, a Slave.

The Nurse, the Mistress, Parent and the Swain,

For Love she must, there's none escape that Pain;

Then comes the last, the fatal Slavery,

The Husband with insulting Tyranny

Can have ill Manners justify'd by Law;

For Men all join to keep the Wife in awe.

Moses who first our Freedom did rebuke,

Was Marry'd when he writ the Pentateuch;[1]

They're Wise to keep us Slaves, for well they know,

If we were loose, we soon should make them, so.

We yield like vanquish'd Kings whom Fetters bind,

When chance of War is to Usurpers kind;

Submit in Form; but they'd our Thoughts controul,

And lay restraints on the impassive Soul:

They fear we should excel their sluggish Parts,

Should we attempt the Sciences and Arts.

Pretend they were design'd for them alone,

So keep us Fools to raise their own Renown;

Thus Priests of old their Grandeur to maintain,

Cry'd vulgar Eyes would sacred Laws Profane.

So kept the Mysteries behind a Screen,

There Homage and the Name were lost had they been seen:

But in this blessed Age, such Freedom's given,

That every Man explains the Will of Heaven;

And shall we Women now sit tamely by,

Make no excursions in Philosophy,

Or grace our Thoughts in tuneful Poetry?

We will our Rights in Learning's World maintain,

---

[1] Pentateuch: First five books of the Old Testament. Egerton here criticizes Moses, who was at the time presumed to be the author of the Pentateuch, for codifying laws in Exodus 21 that treated women as property.

Wit's Empire, now, shall know a Female Reign;
Come all ye Fair, the great Attempt improve,
Divinely imitate the Realms above:
There's ten celestial Females govern Wit,[2]
And but two Gods[3] that dare pretend to it;
And shall these finite Males reverse their Rules,
No, we'll be Wits, and then Men must be Fools.

---

[2] Ten celestial females: The goddess of memory, Mnemosyne, and the nine muses Calliope (epic poetry), Euterpe (lyric poetry), Erato (erotic poetry), Polyhynia (divine poetry), Terpsichore (choral song and dance), Clio (history), Melpomene (tragedy), Urania (astronomy), and Thalia (comedy).

[3] Two Gods: the Two gods associated with wit in the Greek pantheon are Apollo (truth) and Hermes (cleverness). Athena is usually considered the goddess of wisdom.

TEN

Martha Fowke Sansom (1689–1736)

GROWING UP IN LONDON, THE DAUGHTER OF A LIBERTINE FATHER, YOUNG MARTHA FOWKE *delighted in seventeenth-century French novels that celebrated the fashionable ideal of Platonic love: the notion that love between two partners might be passionate, affectionate, absorbing, spiritual, and yet sexually chaste. Her own first literary efforts were love poems to her father's mistresses. Taking Clio, the Greek muse of history, as her pen name, Fowke published several of these early poems in English magazines and miscellanies beginning in 1711. Her* Epistles of Clio and Strephon, *a romantic poetic correspondence with a man named William Bond, was published in 1720, securing her fame with English audiences, admiring comparisons to the ancient Greek lyric poet Sappho, and the adoration of a circle of fashionable friends. Unapologetic about her several public affairs of the heart and extremely reticent to enter into the constraints of conventional marriage, in 1720, she was pressured by friends to enter into what would be an unhappy marriage with the lawyer Arnold Sansom. Marriage, however, did not deter Martha Fowke from romance or from writing. In 1723, at the age of 34, she wrote her autobiography,* Clio: or, a Secret History of the Life and Amours of the Late Celebrated Mrs. S-n—m. Written by Herself, in a Letter to Hillarius, *a romantic chronicle of her upbringing, her early writing career, and her love affairs, dedicated to her paramour Aaron Hill.* (Clio *was published in 1752.)*

Forty of Sansom's love poems were published by Samuel Keimer (now known as the one-time employer of Benjamin Franklin) in Keimer's newspaper the Barbados Gazette *(1732–1735) and later collected in his two-volume miscellany* Caribbeana *(1741). Although Sansom lived in London, many of her poems were addressed to her lover Nicholas Hope who lived in the English sugar colony of Barbados; Keimer recruited her poems both for their local interest to Anglo-Barbadian audiences as well as for the prestige of their London origins. Keimer praised Sansom's poetry for its "fire and ease." Sansom too viewed herself as belonging to a distinctly Sapphic tradition of passionate autobiographical writing, as she describes in these lines from one of her poems: "Angry, the scrawling Side I turn, / I write and blot, and write and burn." In "On being charged with Writing incorrectly," written when she was 19 years old, Sansom defends her spontaneous, seductive, and fearless mode of writing. "My freeborn Thoughts I'll not confine," she declares, rejecting in art as in love the constraints of propriety and custom.*

"ON BEING CHARGED WITH WRITING INCORRECTLY" (1710)

I'm incorrect, the Learned say,
That *I write well, but not their way.*
For this to every Star I bend;
From their dull Method Heaven defend;
Who labour up the Hill of Fame,
And pant and struggle for a Name;
My freeborn Thoughts I'll not confine,
Tho' all *Parnassus*[1] could be mine.
No, let my Genius have its Way,
My Genius I will still obey;
Nor, with their stupid Rules, controul
The sacred Pulse that beats within my Soul.
I, from my very Heart, despise
These mighty dull, these mighty wise,
Who were the Slaves of *Busby's* Nod,[2]
And learn'd their Methods from his Rod.
Shall bright *Apollo*[3] drudge at School,
And whimper till he grows a Fool?
Apollo, to the Learned coy,
In Nouns and Verbs find little Joy;
The tuneful Sisters[4] still he leads

---

[1] Parnassus: In Greek mythology, a sacred mountain, home to the Muses.
[2] Busby: The Rev. Dr. Richard Busby (1606–1695), revered (albeit cruel) headmaster of Westminster School and teacher of some of England's most noted intellectuals including John Dryden and John Locke.
[3] Apollo: Greek god of light, truth, and the arts.
[4] Tuneful sisters: The muses.

To Silver Streams and flow'ry Meads;
He glories in an artless Breast,
And loves the Goddess Nature best.
Let *Dennis*[5] hunt me with his Spite,
Let me read *Dennis* every Night,
Or any Punishment sustain,
To 'scape the Labour of the Brain.
Let the Dull think, or let 'em mend
The trifling Errors they pretend;
Writing's my Pleasure, which my Muse
Wou'd not for all their Glory lose:
With Transport I the Pen employ,
And every Line reveals my Joy:
No Pangs of Thought I undergo,
My Words descend, my Numbers flow;
Tho' disallow'd, my Friend, I'd swear,
I wou'd not think, I wou'd not care,
If I a Pleasure can impart,
Or to my own, or thy dear Heart;
If I thy gentle Passions move;
'Tis all I ask of Fame, or Love.
This to the very learned say;
If they are angry,—why they may;
I, for my very Soul, despise
These mighty dull, these mighty wise.

---

[5] Dennis: John Dennis (1657–1737), Cambridge-educated English literary critic, author of *The Advancement and Reformation of Modern Poetry* (1701).

ELEVEN

Anne Kingsmill Finch, Countess of Winchilsea (1661–1720)

*T*HE DAUGHTER OF A LANDED, ESTABLISHED FAMILY, ANNE KINGSMILL BECAME A MAID OF *honor to Princess Mary of Modena in 1682 and thus took a front seat to the social and literary escapades of the Restoration court wits, a group of gentleman-poets such as John Wilmot, the earl of Rochester, notorious for their free-thinking and libertinism. This context inspired Finch herself to begin writing poems, which she did in secret for many years. In 1684, she married Heneage Finch, another promising member of the royal court, but the revolution of 1688 and the ouster of King James II forced the couple out of royal circles and into a lifetime as political outcasts. Anne Finch continued to write pastorals, occasional poems, love poems, drama, and fables, with her husband acting as her editor and supporter. She began to publish her own poems in 1691, but did so anonymously, until her own collection* Miscellany Poems on Several Occasions *appeared in 1713, winning praise from Jonathan Swift and Alexander Pope. "The Unequal Fetters" presents a witty and knowing critique of the institution of heterosexual marriage. Observing that marriage makes women "close Pris'ners" to their husbands, while husbands often go out to "seek" "new Faces" when their wives grow older, Finch's poetic persona forswears marriage, promising to stay as "Free" as nature made her. In an ironic concluding twist, she celebrates her freedom from marriage by depicting men who constantly seek female attention and companionship as the "larger Slaves."*

"THE UNEQUAL FETTERS" (1713)

Cou'd we stop the time that's flying
    Or recall itt when 'tis past
Put far off the day of Dying
    Or make Youth for ever last
To Love wou'd then be worth our cost.

But since we must loose those Graces
    Which at first your hearts have wonne
And you seek for in new Faces
    When our Spring of Life is done
It wou'd but urge our ruine on

Free as Nature's first intention
    Was to make us, I'll be found
Nor by subtle Man's invention
    Yield to be in Fetters bound
By one that walks a freer round.

Mariage does but slightly tye Men
    Whil'st close Pris'ners we remain
They the larger Slaves of Hymen
    Still are begging Love again
At the full length of all their chain.

TWELVE

Anonymous

*T*HE PRINTING PRESS WAS A KEY IMPLEMENT OF THE AGE OF REVOLUTIONS, GIVING WOMEN *and men (especially the middle classes) unprecedented access to reading, writing, and publication and thus democratizing the circulation of ideas. Magazines emerged in the early eighteenth century to entertain a growing population of middle-class readers, including women. They quickly became an important venue for popular poetry indicting inequalities of sex and foibles of sexuality. A pointed critique of heterosexual relations, "Cloe to Artemisa" was published in a London magazine in 1720. "Cloe" describes the role of a legitimate wife as being "worse" than that of a mistress, and refers to men as "monsters," unnatural and "vulgar" creatures beneath the notice of women. But perhaps most radical is the suggestion, in lines 5–8, that women of a "nicer taste" turn for pleasure not to men, whom they "despise," but to "ourselves"—which could have been read in the 1720s as a reference to masturbation or even to sexual love between women. The type-names in the title further this suggestion, as Cloe is a conventional name for a nymph and "nymphae" is the French and Latin term for the labia, while Artemisa refers to Artemis, the Greek goddess famous for her refusal to marry and her masculine pursuits of hunting and outdoor sports, as well as for the group of beautiful nymphs who followed her in refusing heterosexual love.*

"CLOE TO ARTEMISA" (1720)

WHILE vulgar souls their vulgar love pursue,
And in the common way themselves undo;
Impairing Health, and Fame, and risqu'ing Life,
To be a Mistress, or what's worse, a Wife,

We, whom a nicer taste has rais'd above
The dangerous follies of such slavish Love;
Despise the Sex,[1] and in our selves we find
Pleasures for their gross senses too refin'd,
Let brutish Men, made by our weakness vain,
Boast of the easy Conquest they obtain.
Let the poor loving Wretch do all she can,
And all won't please th' ungrateful Tyrant Man;
We'll scorn the Monster and his Mistress too,
And show the World what Women ought to Do.

---

[1] The poet refers to men as "the sex," a term usually used derisively, in imitation of the French "la sexe," to mean women.

THIRTEEN

Elizabeth Magawley

*A*S *MAGAZINES AND NEWSPAPERS BECAME VENUES FOR PUBLIC QUARRELS BETWEEN THE sexes, women like Elizabeth Magawley leaped into authorship to defend "women of sense" like herself. This letter to the editor of the* Philadelphia American Weekly Mercury *published in January 1730–31 is Magawley's first known published piece of writing. Writing under the pseudonym "Generosa," she responds to the misogynistic satires on women frequently published in the* Mercury *by the male "wits" of Philadelphia. Against the charge that women prefer "Fools and Coxcombs," Magawley replies that "women of sense" do in fact toy with foolish men because "men of sense" are so "scarce." The* Mercury *subsequently published three replies to "Generosa" authored by men who in turn offered her marriage, defended male "coxcombs," and accused her of being a sour old maid.*

LETTER TO THE EDITOR OF THE *PHILADELPHIA AMERICAN WEEKLY MERCURY* (1730/31)

Semper ego Auditor tantum? Juv.[1]

To the Author of the American-Mercury.

Sir,

I have observ'd of late, that our unfortunate Sex have been the Subject of almost all the Satyr[2] that has dropt from your Pen for some Months past; I do assure you notwithstanding, that as I am your constant Reader, so I am your hearty Well-wisher;

---

[1] *Semper ego Auditor tantum?*: Roman saying, from Juvenal: Must I always be only a listener?
[2] Satyr: Satire.

I am not sorry to find Vice or even Fooleries put in odious Colours; nor more angry to see ill Women expos'd, than a Valiant Soldier would be to see a Cowardly one call'd Coward. But as there is an Insinuation in one of your Papers, which I think is entirely groundless: I hope you will pardon me the Freedom of telling you it is! The Sum of the Charge is, *That Fools and Coxcombs[3] are most acceptable to the Ladies*. The Word Ladies is an ambiguous Term, to which no single Idea can be affix'd; as in your Sex there are the several Classes of Men of Sense, Rakes, Fops, Coxcombs and downright Fools, so I hope, without straining your Complaisance, you will allow there are some Women of Sense comparatively, as well as Coquets, Romps, Prudes and Idiots. If you had said Fools and Coxcombs are most acceptable to Coquets and Romps I readily grant it: Men of Sense value themselves too much to be used as Tools, they cannot stoop to the little Fooleries impos'd on them by their imaginary Goddesses, and their Resentments are too strong to bear Contempt and Insults. As to the Women of Sense, (if you will allow any to be so) you will also own THEY are more delighted with the Conversation of Men of Sense, than with that of Coxcombs or Fools, since the contrary takes away their Character of Sense. But Men of Sense are scarce Sir, very scarce indeed, and those few that are, are too proud or think their Time ill bestow'd, in the Conversation of the Ladies. They very often think for Want of Trial, that what I argue against is true; the Vulgar Error has impos'd even upon them. This is our lamentable Case, and what must we do? Must we resolve never to Converse with the opposite Sex, or go under the Reproach of favouring Coxcombs? It may be said we love Fops and Fools, because we play with them, and so we do with Parrots, Monkeys and Owls; and if we cannot procure Objects of Admiration and Esteem, we divert our selves with those of Ridicule and Contempt: But, Oh, Sir, if you knew the exquisite Pleasure that we Women receive from the Conversation of a Man of Sense; what Raptures we conceive upon the least Imagination of being belov'd by him, you will confess with me, that Coxcombs are only indulged out of meer Necessity; and the ill Success of Men of Sense, is owing to their Want of Courage.

I am, Sir, with the greatest Respect,

Yours,

GENEROSA.

---

[3] Coxcomb: A conceited, foolish man.

FOURTEEN

Anonymous

*I*N A MALE-HEADED OR PATRIARCHAL HOUSEHOLD, WHAT COULD WOMEN EXPECT BUT TYRANNY: *to be handed from the "stern command" of her father to the domination of a "tyrant husband"? This is the sharp lament of the unnamed author of this poem, who uses metaphors of sovereignty and slavery to depict relations between women and men. In the final line, the speaker wishes for "a slavish mind" that would inure her to the "slave's fetters" she wears as a woman in a man's world—betraying the common eighteenth-century assumption that some people suffer more than others under slavery. First published in the London* Gentleman's Magazine *in July 1733, this poem struck such a strong chord with readers that it traveled across the Atlantic and was republished consistently in American newspapers and magazines from Massachusetts to South Carolina in the eighteenth and nineteenth centuries.*

"WOMAN'S HARD FATE" (1733)

How wretched is a *woman's* fate,
    No happy change her Fortune knows;
Subject to man in every state,
    How can she then be free from woes?

In youth, a *father's* stern command
    And jealous eyes controul her will;
A lordly *brother* watchful stands
    To keep her closer captive still.

The tyrant *husband* next appears,
    With awful and contracted brow;
No more a *lover's* form he wears,
    Her *slave's* become her *sov'reign* now.

If from this fatal bondage free,
    And not by marriage chains confin'd,
But blest with single life, can see
    A *parent* fond, a *brother* kind;

Yet *love* usurps her tender breast,
    And paints a *phoenix* to her eyes,
Some darling youth disturbs her rest,
    And painful sighs in secret rise.

Oh cruel pow'rs, since you've design'd
    That man, *vain* man! should bear the sway,
To a *slave's* fetters add a *slavish* mind,
    That I may cheerfully your will obey.

FIFTEEN

Anonymous

*T*HIS SHORT, RAZOR-SHARP POEM WAS FIRST PUBLISHED IN THE **VIRGINIA** GAZETTE *ON OCTO-ber 22, 1736, and reprinted many times in colonial papers throughout the eighteenth century. The poem uses ballad meter (a four-line stanza in which the first and third lines are in iambic tetrameter and the second and fourth in iambic trimeter), setting us up to expect a traditional ballad story of a mourning woman forsaken by her lover. And indeed the poem starts with the complaint of a lovelorn woman in the first stanza, but then begins a stealthy movement through a philosophical critique of the way custom represses women's thoughts and "truth," to an economic argument in stanza three, and finally to an explicit call for legal reform ("equal laws let custom find") in the final stanza. Of course, this argument for improving the legal status of women is treated with typical neoclassical satirical wit in the suggestion of the final couplet, that if readers object to giving women "more freedom," the alternative would be to give men "less." This image of reducing the power of men is a fresh and startling one that gives readers the opportunity to see the relations between the sexes in a new light, far from the cliché terms of heterosexual romance with which the poem opens, and which it ultimately ironizes.*

"THE LADY'S COMPLAINT" (1736)[1]

Custom, alas! doth partial prove,
Nor give us even measure;
A pain it is to maids in love,
But 'tis to men a pleasure.

---

[1] "The Lady's Complaint" first appeared in the *Virginia Gazette* in 1736. The version of the poem reprinted here appeared in the *Vermont Journal and Universal Advertiser* (February 16, 1789), 3.

They freely can their tho'ts disclose,
    But ours must burn within:
We have got eyes and tongues, in vain,
    And truth from us is sin.

Men to new joys and conquests fly,
    And yet no hazard run:
Poor we are left, if we deny,
    And if we yield—undone.

Then equal laws let custom find,
    Nor thus the sex oppress,[2]
More freedom grant to womankind,
    Or give to mankind less.

---

[2] The sex: Women.

SIXTEEN

Katherine Garret (Pequot; ?–1738)

*W*HILE ENGLISH AND ANGLO-AMERICAN WOMEN DEBATED THE OPPRESSIONS OF MARRIAGE, *indigenous American women grappled to wrest control over their lives and their families from the devastating forces of colonization. In 1738, Katherine Garret, a member of New England's Pequot nation, was executed for the murder of her newborn son. As a servant in the Connecticut household of Reverend William Worthington, the unmarried Garret had hidden her pregnancy. According to the testimony of Temperance Worthington, on the day of the child's birth Garret complained of illness, retired, and later emerged from the barn. The baby was found under a pile of hay later that day; nearby was a bloody wooden block. Garret reportedly confessed to striking the newborn (though not to intentionally killing him) but later pled not guilty. When a jury convicted her of murder and sentenced her to hang, "she was thrown into the utmost Confusion & Distress," and made "Expressions" that were "rash and unguarded." During the six months between her conviction and execution, she converted to Christianity and was baptized by Congregationalist minister Eliphalet Adams. Adams preached the sermon at her execution, and the following* Confession and Dying Narrative *was published as an appendix to the sermon along with an account of her life and death, probably written by Adams. Execution narratives, including those involving infanticide, were a popular genre, and about twelve examples by or about Native persons have been identified.*

Garret's execution was a spectacle, attracting a "Vast Circle of people, more Numerous, perhaps, than Ever was gathered together before, On any Occasion, in this Colony." Before the mostly white crowd, Garret read her Confession and Dying Warning *and made "many Other Warnings and Counsels by word of mouth." Though inescapably shaped by Adams, this document testifies to Garret's role in defining her narrative as well. It follows genre conventions by casting sin as a slippery slope, limiting sensationalist details, using her story as an example to warn readers, and advocating Christian morality and salvation. Yet it also unexpectedly addresses "Parents and Masters" directly and subtly accuses her executioners of subjecting her to a "Violent Death."[1] Moreover, she emphasizes the active and communal nature of her conversion (a process that also delayed her execution and allowed her some measure of freedom while she was imprisoned). Thus, this text is ambiguous, offering a glimpse into how one poor Pequot woman sought to survive, and calling attention to the range of ways——some hopeful, some horrific——that women used reproduction and fertility to control their lives and bodies in the face of colonization and poverty.*

THE CONFESSION AND DYING WARNING OF *KATHERINE GARRET* (1738)

I *Katherine Garret*, being Condemned to Die for the Crying Sin of Murder, Do Own the Justice of GOD in suffering me to die this Violent Death; and also Acknowledge the Justice of the Court who has Sentenced me to die this Death; and I thank them who have Lengthned the Time to me, whereby I have had great Opportunity to prepare for my Death: I thank those also who have taken pains with me for my Soul; so that since I have been in Prison, I have had opportunity to seek after Baptism & the Supper of the Lord & have obtained both. I Confess my self to have been a great Sinner; a sinner by Nature, also guilty of many Actual Transgressions, Particularly of Pride and Lying, as well as of the Sin of destroying the Fruit of my own Body, for which latter, I am now to Die. I thank God that I was learn'd to Read in my Childhood, which has been much my Exercise since I have been in Prison, and especially since my Condemnation. The Bible has been a precious Book to me. There I read, *That JESUS CHRIST came into the world to Save Sinners*, Even the *Chief of Sinners*: And that *all manner of Sins shall be forgiven, One only Excepted;*[2] *For His Blood Cleanseth from all Sin*. And other good Books I have been favoured with, by peoples giving and lending them to me, which has been blessed to me.

I would Warn all Young People against Sinning against their own Consciences; For there is a *GOD* that Knows all things. Oh! Beware of all Sin, Especially of Fornication; for that has led me to Murder. Remember the Sabbath-day to keep it Holy. Be Sober and wise. Redeem your Time, and Improve it well.

---

[1] In his execution sermon, Adams repeatedly emphasizes Proverbs 28:17: "A Man that doth Violence to the blood of any person, shall flee to the Pit, Let no man stay him."

[2] Only one excepted: According to Protestant theology, only the "original sin" of Adam's fall from innocence.

Little Children I would Warn you to take heed of Sinning against God. Be Dutiful to your Parents; For *the Eye that Mocks at his Father and despiseth to Obey his Mother, the Ravens of the Valley shall pick it out, and the Young Eagles shall eat it.*[3] Little Children, Learn to Pray to God; Sit still on the Lord's Day, and Love your Books.

I would also Warn Servants, Either *Whites* or *Blacks*, to be Obedient to your Masters & Mistresses. Be Faithful in your places and diligent: Above all Fear God; fear to Sin against Him: He is our Great Master.

I would also Intreat Parents and Masters to set a good Example before their Children and Servants, for You also must give an Account to God how you carry it to them.

I desire the Prayers of all God's People for me, Private Christians, as well as Ministers of the Gospel, that I may while I have Life Improve it aright; May have all my Sins Pardoned and may be Accepted through *CHRIST JESUS*. Amen.

New London, May 3, 1738

Katherine Garret

---

[3] See Proverbs 30:17.

SEVENTEEN

Mary Collier (b. 1679)

*A*LTHOUGH MARY COLLIER WAS BORN TO POOR LABORING-CLASS PARENTS, THEY FOUND THE *resources to teach her to read. She composed her first known poem,* The Woman's Labour, *in response to Stephen Duck, another laboring-class phenomenon, known as the "Thresher Poet," who had published his poem* The Thresher's Labour *in 1730. Duck dismisses the "little Work" of women laborers in his poem, asserting that they are more idle than men. Collier challenges this, arguing that women actually work much harder than men, not only for their employers but then for their families at home, and for less pay ("Six-pence or Eight-pence pays us off at last"). She was overheard by her employers reciting it as she went about her work as a washerwoman. They encouraged her to write more and helped make her work known, securing her reputation as the "Washerwoman Poet." Collier published* The Woman's Labour *at her own expense in 1739; it went through three editions but she never saw a profit from it. She continued to work as a washerwoman and then housekeeper to support herself as she wrote more poetry. In 1762, she published* Poems on Several Occasions, *a collection of her own poetry. Toward the end of her life she refused a request to write a poem about disappointed old maids, claiming she had never known any. She worked as a washerwoman until she was 63, retired from labor altogether at 70, and died shortly thereafter.*

In The Woman's Labour, *Collier refers to women as "slaves," but in the context of Collier's detailed description of the physical toil ("Not only sweat, but blood runs trickling down/Our wrists and fingers") and mental strain ("With heavy hearts we often view the Sun/Fearing he'll set before our work is done") experienced by women who must work as haymakers, gleaners, laundresses, scullery maids, and more while also caring for their own families, her use of the term is much less metaphorical than in the writing of genteel women. But in her references to the mute slaves of the "Turks," Collier draws on a more familiar Orientalist image of women as slaves to male despotism, using it to counter the assumption that she should refrain from criticizing Duck on account of her sex. Her poem is both a documentary account of the often hidden world of women's labor, and a bold assertion of the necessity of women speaking out about their conditions.*

THE WOMAN'S LABOUR (1739)

IMMORTAL Bard! thou Favrite of the Nine!
Enrich'd by Peers, advanc'd by CAROLINE![1]
Deign to look down on One that's poor and low
Remembering you yourself was lately so;
Accept these Lines: Alas! what can you have
From her, who ever was, and's still a Slave?
No Learning ever was bestow'd on me;
My Life was always spent in Drudgery:
And not alone; alas! with Grief I find,
It is the Portion of poor Woman-kind.
Oft have I thought as on my Bed I lay,
Eas'd from the tiresome Labours of the Day,
Our first Extraction from a Mass refin'd,
Could never be for Slavery design'd;
Till Time and Custom by degrees destroy'd
That happy State our Sex at first enjoy'd.
When Men had us'd their utmost Care and Toil,
Their Recompence was but a Female Smile;
When they by Arts or Arms were render'd Great,
They laid their Trophies at a Woman's Feet;
They, in those Days, unto our Sex did bring
Their Hearts, their All, a Free-will Offering;
And as from us their Being they derive,
They back again should all due Homage give.

---

[1] Caroline: Caroline of Brandenburg-Ansbach (1683–1737), German-born Queen of England (1727–1737).

JOVE[2] once descending from the Clouds, did drop
In Show'rs of Gold on lovely *Danae*'s[3] Lap;
The sweet-tongu'd Poets, in those generous Days,
Unto our Shrine still offer'd up their Lays:
But now, alas! that Golden Age is past,
We are the Objects of your Scorn at last.
And you, great DUCK, upon whose happy Brow
The Muses seem to fix the Garland now,
In your late *Poem* boldly did declare
Alcides'[4] Labours can't with your's compare;
And of your annual Task have much to Say,
Of Threshing, Reaping, Mowing Corn and Hay;
Boasting your daily Toil, and nightly Dream,
But can't conclude your never-dying Theme,
And let our hapless Sex in Silence lie
Forgotten, and in dark Oblivion die;
But on our abject State you throw your Scorn
And Women wrong, your Verses to adorn.
You of Hay-making speak a Word or two,
As if our Sex but little Work could do:
This makes the honest Farmer smiling say,
He'll seek for Women still to make his Hay;
For if his Back be turn'd, their Work they mind
As well as Men, as far as he can find.
For my own Part, I many a *Summer*'s Day
Have spent in throwing, turning, making Hay;
But ne'er could see, what you have lately found,
Our Wages paid for sitting on the Ground.
'Tis true, that when our Morning's Work is done,
And all our Grass expos'd unto the Sun,
While that his scorching Beams do on it shine,
As well as you, we have a Time to dine:

[2] Jove: English name for the Greek god Zeus, counterpart of the Roman god Jupiter, patron of laws and government.
[3] Danae: In Greek mythology, mother of Perseus by Zeus. Legend relates that Zeus impregnated her with a golden rain.
[4] Alcides: Original name of the Greek hero Heracles, son of Zeus.

I hope, that since we freely toil and sweat
To earn our Bread, you'll give us Time to eat.
That over, soon we must get up again,
And nimbly turn our Hay upon the Plain;
Nay, rake and row it in, the Case is clear;
Or how should *Cocks*[5] *in equal Rows appear?*
But if you'd have what you have wrote believ'd,
I find, that you to hear us talk are griev'd:
In this, I hope, you do not speak your Mind,
For none but *Turks*, that ever I could find,
Have Mutes to serve them, or did e'er deny
Their Slaves, at Work to chat it merrily.
Since you have Liberty to speak your Mind,
And are to talk, as well as we, inclin'd
Why should you thus repine, because that we,
Like you, enjoy that pleasing Liberty?
What! would you Lord it quite, and take away
The only Privilege our Sex enjoy? . . .

[W]e, alas! but little Sleep can have,
Because our froward[6] Children cry and rave;
Yet, without fail, soon as Day-light doth spring,
We in the Field again our Work begin
And there, with all our Strength, our Toil renew,
Till *Titan*'s[7] golden Rays have dry'd the Dew;
Then home we go unto our Children dear,
Dress, feed, and bring them to the Field with care.
Were this your Case, you justly might complain
That Day nor Night you are secure from Pain;
Those mighty Troubles which perplex your Mind,
(*Thistles* before, and *Females* come behind)
Would vanish soon, and quickly disappear,
Were you, like us, encumber'd thus with Care.
What you would have of us we do not know:

---

[5] Cocks: Haycocks, stacks of cut hay left in the field to dry.
[6] Froward: Difficult, obstinate.
[7] Titan: The Greek sun-god, also known as Helios.

We oft take up the Corn that you do mow;
We cut the Peas, and always ready are
In every Work to take our proper Share;
And from the Time that Harvest doth begin,
Until the Corn be cut and carry'd in,
Our Toil and Labour's daily so extreme,
That we have hardly ever *Time to dream*.

The Harvest ended, Respite none we find;
The hardest of our Toil is still behind:
Hard Labour we most chearfully pursue,
And out, abroad, a Chairing[8] often go:
Of which I now will briefly tell in part,
What fully to declare is past my Art;
So many Hardships daily we go through,
I boldly say, the like *you* never knew.

When bright *Orion* glitters in the Skies
In *Winter* Nights, then early we must rise;
The Weather ne'er so bad, Wind, Rain, or Snow,
Our Work appointed, we must rise and go;
While you on easy Beds may lie and sleep,
Till Light does thro' your Chamber Windows peep.
When to the House we come where we should go,
How to get in, alas! we do not know:
The Maid quite tir'd with Work the Day before,
O'ercome with Sleep; we standing at the Door
Oppress'd with Cold, and often call in vain,
E're to our Work we can Admittance gain:
But when from Wind and Weather we get in,
Briskly with Courage we our Work begin;
Heaps of fine Linen we before us view,
Whereon to lay our Strength and Patience too;
Cambricks and Muslins, which our Ladies wear,
Laces and Edgings, costly, fine, and rare,

---

[8] Chairing: To go "a charing" is to seek odd jobs, like housework.

Which must be wash'd with utmost Skill and Care;
With Holland Shirts, Ruffles and Fringes too,
Fashions which our Fore-fathers never knew.
For several Hours here we work and slave,
Before we can one Glimpse of Day-light have;
We labour hard before the Morning's past,
Because we fear the Time runs on too fast.

At length bright *Sol* illuminates the Skies,
And summons drowsy Mortals to arise;
Then comes our Mistress to us without fail,
And in her Hand, *perhaps*, a Mug of Ale
To cheer our Hearts, and also to inform
Herself, what Work is done that very Morn;
Lays her Commands upon us, that we mind
Her Linen well, nor *leave the Dirt behind:*
Not this alone, but also to take Care
We don't her Cambricks nor her Ruffles tear;
And *these* most strictly does of us require,
To save her Soap, and sparing be of Fire;
Tells us her Charge is great, nay furthermore,
Her Cloaths are fewer than the Time before.
Now we drive on, resolv'd our Strength to try,
And what we can, we do most willingly;
Until with Heat and Work, 'tis often known,
Not only Sweat, but Blood runs trickling down
Our Wrists and Fingers; still our Work demands
The constant Action of our lab'ring Hands.

Now Night comes on, from whence you have Relief,
But that, alas! does but increase our Grief;
With heavy Hearts we often view the Sun,
Fearing he'll set before our Work is done;
For either in the Morning, or at Night,
We piece the *Summer*'s Day with Candle-light.
Tho' we all Day with Care our Work attend,
Such is our Fate, we know not when 'twill end:
When Evening's come, you homeward take your Way,

We, till our Work is done, are forc'd to stay;
And after all our Toil and Labour past,
Six-pence or *Eight-pence* pays us off at last;
For all our Pains, no Prospect can we see
Attend us, but *Old Age* and *Poverty.*

The *Washing* is not all we have to do:
We oft change Work for Work as well as you.
Our Mistress of her Pewter doth complain,
And 'tis our Part to make it clean again.
This Work, tho' very hard and tiresome too,
Is not the worst we hapless Females do:
When Night comes on, and we quite weary are,
We scarce can count what falls unto our Share;
Pots, Kettles, Sauce-pans, Skillets, we may see,
Skimmers and Ladles, and such Trumpery,
Brought in to make complete our Slavery. . . .

But to rehearse all Labour is in vain,
Of which we very justly might complain;
For us, you see, but little Rest is found;
Our Toil increases as the Year runs round.
While you to *Sisyphus*[9] yourselves compare,
With *Danaus' Daughters*[10] we may claim a Share;
For while *he* labours hard against the Hill,
Bottomless Tubs of Water *they* must fill.

So the industrious Bees do hourly strive
To bring their Loads of Honey to the Hive;
Their sordid Owners always reap the Gains,
And poorly recompense their Toil and Pains.

---

[9] Sisyphus: In Greek mythology, a king cursed to roll a boulder up a hill, and then watch it roll down again, for eternity.

[10] Danaus' Daughters: According to Greek mythology, the fifty daughters of King Danaus were punished for killing their bridegrooms by being cursed to carry water in jugs that were actually sieves.

EIGHTEEN

Damma/Marotta/Magdalena

*J*UST AS IT HAD BEEN FOR ANNE HUTCHINSON AND MARGARET FELL, FOR MANY WOMEN OF AFRICAN *descent in the Americas, the practice of religion—even European-identified religions like Christianity—served as a powerful tool for social organizing and political empowerment. Among the Christian faiths most welcoming of Black women's membership and leadership were the Moravians, an evangelical Protestant faith known for its worldwide missionary program as well as its emphasis on personal faithfulness and communal living, and led in the eighteenth century by Count Nicholas Zinzendorf (1700–1760).*

The Danish sugar colony of St. Thomas in the Caribbean was home to one of the strongest Afro-Moravian communities in the Americas. One of the leaders of this community was a woman named Marotta, who by her own account was born at Popo on the west coast of Africa in what might be present-day Benin. On St. Thomas, Marotta continued to practice traditional African religious rites by making burnt sacrifices of goats and lambs, until she converted to Moravianism and was christened and renamed "Magdalena" after the New Testament figure Mary Magdalene. She came to be regarded, historian Jon Sensbach writes, as the St. Thomas Moravian congregation's "venerated evangelical elder." Magdalena's son Domingo Gesu, or "Mingo," a literate slave fluent in both Dutch and German, also helped lead the Moravian mission in St. Thomas, as well as traveling the Atlantic world on business for his master.

In 1739, a group of thirty Danish sugar planters petitioned the governor of St. Thomas to end the Moravian mission on the island and throw out the Moravians, complaining that religious observances were distracting their slaves from work and perhaps also spurring them to hope, pray, and plan for their deliverance from

voortgaan te leeren den Heere Jefus. Ons
ftaan vaft tot noch tœ, als het God den
Heere gelieft, fchon ons feer gedrukt wörd
van all, en komen ons flagen en kappen,
as ons by den Heyland leert, en Bœk ver-
branden, en doop Honde Doop nœmen, en
Brœders Beeften, en Negér mœt niet zaalig
worden, een gedoopt Neger is Brandhout
in de Hell. En hebben ons Brœders, fon-
derlyk Bas Martinus, die God aan ons al
had gebrúikt, en die van twentig Brœders
overgebleven is, (die geftorven zyn,) met
fyn Brœders, over drie Maant op de Fort ge-
fett, en wil fy van de land bannen. All
beriepen fich nú op S. Majefteits, en fegge
Gy heeft verboden, dat Negers niet mo-
gen de Heiland leere kennen, en Gy fult
Bas Martinus haft weg yagen. Maar we &c.
&c. en bidden U. laat ons den Heere leeren
kennen, en by de Brœder-kerke blyven:
Want wy willen met haar tot den Hey-
landt gaan. Ons wil ons Meefters in all
ding gehoorfam zyn, enkel ons fiel na de
Hemel by den Heer Jefus ftúuren. Want
ons heeft ons Heere geftoolen, Maron ge-
loopen, na Porto Rico gegaan, vlaw ge-
weft, en de Heeren an d'leftogd bedrogen;
en nú is dat all anders by ons, fo de meefters wool weeten. Menig Neger heeft
overhed quad ftandfaftig vœten en handen
fin laten afkappen. Wy fullen grac onfen
kop voor de Gemeente onder het buil leg-
gen,

gen, voor den Heere Jefús, als ons Mee-
fters ons dooden, foo als fy feggen.
God den Heere fegne ons Genaadigfte
Koning duifendmaal. Gefchreven in St.
Thomas, ten 15. Febr. 1739.

Op naam van over de feshondert en
vyftig fwarte fcholieren van Jefus
Chriftus, die Bas Martinus leert,
vornaamlyk van alle degeen die
Hy al gedoopt heeft,

> PIETER.
> MINGO.
> ANDRIES.
> ABRAHAM.
> MADLENA.
> RÉBECCA, MALATTINEM.
> ANNA MARIA.

XII.

Der Aelteftin der Gemeine der
Negros in St. Thomas Schreiben an die
Königin von Dännemarck.
An. 1739.

Ne acadda.

Cabe my le ad ga Tome minge bruhu
mau, mi wago voltomé. Gewoma
Hh 3   dihé,

dihé, na mangi Bruhu Ajuba malle na mado
wi tu ma gagni na mu, quaffi nangi netto
dy a Wo Du Gowo maja powo Dn. Poppo
leofi, Mia meyji diké bowo dn. mille dikbe
migeé Meacadda nadak be no vo Dn Mau
e na dak bena Anibà daffi fala Martinus na
doclio na mi naffé na mi angé vo Dn. na
coffi de tami, denikó Do Batrœ Mau lé
Mau mé agnisà ne a cadda.

*Minzu Gnonù en bo
ma poppo!*

Damma.

Uberfetzung ins Cariolifche.

Groote Koniginne.

Die tyd mi a wes na Poppo op Africa,
doen mi a dint die Heer Mau, nu ko-
me na blanco land, mi no wilt gu dín de
Heere. Mi no ha di grond vor tú dien díe
Heere; mi ben bedrœv na min herte, voor
dat Negrinne no kan dien die Heere Jefus in
Thomas, die Blanke no wil dien die Heere.
Lat fo as fili wil, maar foo de povre fwarte
Brœders en fufters wil dien de Heer Jefus,
fo mœt zilli dœn, as fi bin maron volk. As
Neacanda belyv, gy mœt bidde de Heere Je-
fus voor ons, en bidd ook A Niba, voor-lá
                                                    ftan

ftan Bas Martinus prek de Heere woord,
voor ons mœ leer voor kenn de Heere, en
voor Doop ons Negers, op Naam des Va-
ders, Sons en Hilig Geeft. Die Heer be-
waar finder, en feegene finder, fon en doch-
terfen, heel Familie, en mi fal bid den Heer
Jefus voor finder.

Ob naam van over Tweehondert en
Vyftig Negersfen Zrouwen, die
den Heere Jefus beminnen, gefchreven door

Marotta
nú
Madlena
van Poppo uyt Africa.

XIII.

Declaration wegen des Auff=
wands bey der Heyden=Be=
kehrung.

Es find einige Urfachen vorhanden, war-
um wir eine Sache, die wir noch fer-
ner, wie fchon in die 7: Jahre gefche-
hen, in der gröften Stille zu bewahren wünfch-
ten, in etwas bekannt machen müffen: Es be-
Hh 4   trifft

FIGURE 18.1: **Letter from Damma/Marotta/Magdalena to the Queen of Denmark,** **published in** *Büdingische Sammlung* **(Leipzig, Germany, 1741).** *Marotta or Magdalena was an Afro-Moravian woman who lived on the Caribbean island of St. Thomas, a Danish colony. Count Nikolaus Ludwig von Zinzendorf, the charismatic and wealthy head of the Moravian church, included Magdalena's petition to Queen Sophia Magdalena in his multivolume* Büdingische Sammlung, *a collection of tracts, letters, and diaries. He reproduced two versions, one in a West African language (perhaps Fon) and another in Dutch Creole. The English translation included in this volume is of the Dutch Creole text. Image courtesy of Pitts Theological Library, Candler School of Theology, Emory University.*

slavery. Magdalena, Mingo, an important Afro-Moravian missionary named Rebecca Protten, and four other Afro-Moravian men and women wrote a response on February 15, 1739, on behalf of more than six hundred Afro-Moravians expressing their determination to continue in their faith. Planters later punished Afro-Moravians with beatings, curfews, and other acts of intimidation and repression.

Drawing on her stature as an elder in the community, Magdalena wrote a second letter under her own name in her native African language and in Dutch Creole, addressed to the Queen of Denmark requesting that Baas *Friedrich Martin, the leader of the Moravian St. Thomas mission, be allowed to continue his work and that Black women in particular be allowed to continue their religious observances. These letters first appeared in 1744 in a German collection of Moravian religious writings and were shortly thereafter republished in English in* The Christian Monthly History, *an evangelical Christian journal based in Scotland. Magdalena's letter may be the first by a woman of African descent to appear and circulate the Atlantic world in print. It is a historic and powerful document of the determination of women of the African diaspora to claim and defend the spiritual sources of their survival.*

PETITION TO QUEEN SOPHIA MAGDALENE OF DENMARK (1739)[1]

Great Queen!

At the time when I lived in Papaa [Popo], in Africa, I served the Lord Masu. Now I have come into the land of the Whites, and they will not allow me to serve the Lord Jesus. Previously, I did not have any reason to serve Him, but now I do. I am very sad in my heart that the Negro women on St. Thomas are not allowed to serve the Lord Jesus. The Whites do not want to obey Him. Let them do as they wish. But when the poor black Brethren and Sisters want to serve the Lord Jesus, they are looked upon as maroons.[2] If the Queen thinks it fitting, please pray to the Lord Jesus for us and let

---

[1] Translation of the salutation and body from Jon Sensbach, *Rebecca's Revival: Creating Black Christianity in the Atlantic World*. Used with permission of Harvard University Press.

[2] Maroons: A term for fugitives from slavery who established separatist communities. In the Caribbean, maroon villages were usually in the islands' mountainous interiors.

her intercede with the King to allow *Baas Martinus*[3] to preach the Lord's word, so that we can come to know the Lord and so that he can baptize us[4] in the name of the Father, the Son, and the Holy Spirit.

In the name of about two hundred and fifty Negro women,

who love the Lord Jesus,

written by

Marotta

now

Madlena

of Poppo in Africa

---

[3] *Baas Martinus*: Friedrich Martin (1704–1750) was the white German Moravian who led the St. Thomas mission.

[4] Us: The original published Dutch letter has "*ons Negers*" or "us Negroes."

NINETEEN

Coosaponakeesa/Mary Musgrove Mathews Bosomworth (Creek; ca. 1700–1767)

W*HEN ENGLISH COLONISTS FIRST ARRIVED IN GEORGIA, COOSAPONAKEESA WAS READY for them. The daughter of a white trader and a Creek woman and the oper-ator of her own trading post, Coosaponakeesa was ideally situated to profit from and influence the colony's success or failure. Georgia's governor, James Oglethorpe, quickly came to depend on her as an interpreter and diplomat, and she helped guide him as he negotiated first with the local Yamacraw Indians and then with the Creeks, a group that would become Georgia's primary military and economic partners in the region. After Oglethorpe's departure, other colonial administrators——both from Georgia and South Carolina——continued to employ her skills, though with more reluctance. Creek women, like their English counterparts, had little official political power, so Coosaponakeesa used the establishment of Georgia as an opportunity to push the quotidian limits of gender roles—Creek and English——and advance her personal interests even as she sought the economic advancement of her nation through alliance.*

Yet Coosaponakeesa's relationship with Georgia soured after officials—many of them in England and dismissive of the contributions of an Indian woman—refused to adequately compensate her for her services and expenses. In response, she unapolo-getically waged a legal war that lasted over a decade and at times appeared to be leading towards a military war with the Creeks. Writing petitions and filing memo-rials and affidavits in support of the facts, she relied upon a flexible and active language of kinship to describe her relationships to Creeks and Anglo-Georgians alike. The source of this kinship language is distinctively Creek, as her words repeat-edly highlight the matrilineal origins of her influence and cast affiliation (including political) as an ongoing process of exchange and mutual obligation. In her letters (as in the letters of Mary Brant included in this volume), we see early evidence of how indigenous American women asserted themselves and used writing to hold ground against colonial domination.

MEMORIAL (1747)[1]

TO the Honourable Lieutenant Collonel Alexander Heron[2] Commander in Chief of his Majestys Forces in the Province of Georgia the Memorial and Representation of Mary Bosomworth[3] of the Said Province.

HUMBLY SHEWETH

That your Memorialist was born at the Cowetaw Town on the Oakmulgee River which is a branch of the Alatamaha, and the Chief Town of the Creek Indian Nation.[4]

That She is by Descent on the Mothers Side, (who was Sister to the Old Emperor) of the Same Blood of the Present Mico's and Chief's now in that Nation, and by their Laws, and the Voice of the Whole Nation is esteemed their Rightfull and Natural Princess.[5]

That her Ancesstors, Tho under the Appellation of Savages, or Barbarions, were a brave and free born people, who never owed Allegiance, to or Acknowledged the sovereignty of any Crowned Head whatever, but have always maintained their own Possessions and Independency, Against all Opposers by Warr, at the Expence of their Blood; as they Can shew by the many Troophies of Victory, and Relicts of their Enimies slain in Defence of their Natural Rights.

---

[1] This memorial, or a statement of facts in support of a petition, is the first of many memorials that Coosaponakeesa wrote to various officials in Georgia and England. For each successive memorial, she revised the last version instead of starting anew and altered it to meet the shifting rhetorical situation.

[2] Heron: Lieutenant Colonel Alexander Heron took over command of a Georgian military regiment in 1747. Having relied upon Coosaponakeesa's assistance, he was sympathetic to her claims, if powerless to fulfill them. Per her request, he did write on her behalf to the Duke of Newcastle (via a deputy secretary) and described her as a "most usefull person" who could be of "Infinite Service."

[3] Having married three times, Coosaponakeesa was also known by her English names, which were (in order) Mary Musgrove, Mary Mathews, and Mary Bosomworth. Towards the end of her life, she returned to signing documents with her Creek name.

[4] Oakmulgee: Ocmulgee River. Coweta was a chief *talwa*, or town, of the Lower Creek confederacy.

[5] In the eighteenth century, Creeks were matrilineal, meaning the lines of descent occurred through mothers instead of fathers. Therefore, this statement proclaims Coosaponakeesa's direct descendance from past and present Creek *micos*, or leaders. Her use of the word "Princess" is a rhetorical move. Elsewhere, she also referred to herself as "Empress and Queen of the Upper and Lower Creeks" and, at one point, "King."

That they have entered into Several Treaties of Peace, Friendship and Commerce, with Persons properly impowered, in behalf of the Crown of Great Britain.

That they Have made Concessions of Several Portions of Land, (their Natural Right by Ancient Possession) in behalf of his Majesty; and have for several Years past on their parts, Strictly and faithfully Observed the Treaty of Friendship and Alliance entered into with the Honourable Major General Oglethorpe[6] in behalf of his Brittanick Majesty. And have on all Occasions been ready to fight Against his Majestys Enimies which they Have very much Annoyed.

That both the french and Spaniards well know by Dear Experience how terrible they are to their Enemies in war. They are so highly Sensible of the Vast Importance of the Friendship and Alliance of the Creek Nation to the British Interest; (and the only Barrier to hinder them from gaining the Utmost of their Wishes upon the Continent of America) That they Have for some time past, and are at this Juncture, Labouring by all the Artifices Imaginable to seduce that Nation from their Alliance with his Majestys Subjects, which will certainly be a great Addition and Increase of Territory Strength and Power to his Majestys Enimies; and the Dangerous Consequence May be the Utmost Hazard of the safety of his Majestys Southern Frontiers Carolina and Georgia.[7]

That your Memorialist hath by her Interest since the First Settlement of the Colony of Georgia for the Space of 14 Years continued that Important Nation Steady and Steadfast in their Friendship and Alliance with his Majestys subjects at the Expence of her own private Fortune to the Utter Ruin of her self and Fam[i]ly as will evidently Appear by a plain Narrative of Incontestable Matters of Fact.

That Whereas your Memorialist by the Laws of Great Britain is a Subject of that Crown, and has given many Signal Proofs of her Zeal and Loyalty as such; amongst the many Blessings and Previlidges she hopes to enjoy under his Majestys Just Government a Right of Complaining of the Hardships and Grievances which she at Present Labours under (which are now become too great for her any Longer to bear) and the hopes of Redress, she Esteems none of the Least.

---

[6] Oglethorpe: James Oglethorpe (1696–1785) was the founder and first governor of Georgia. During his tenure, Oglethorpe relied heavily upon Coosaponakeesa as an interpreter and diplomat.

[7] His Majestys Southern Frontiers: The Spanish colony of Florida, the French colony of Louisiana, and the uncolonized lands in possession of the various Indian nations, many of which had alliances with Spain and France. Georgia was chartered partially to provide a colonial buffer between South Carolina—an important commercial colony—and Native and European forces located to the south and west that were hostile to British interests. The Creeks had been invaluable allies for the Georgian colonists and, in part through Coosaponakeesa's influence, had fought with the British against Spain in the War of Jenkins' Ear (1739–1742).

Your Memorialist therefore humbly begs Leave to Represent unto you a State of her Deplorable Case which she hopes will Appear to be such, that the Justice and Compassion of a British Parliament will be extended to the Relief of her Present Grievances; upon a Representation of the Cause thereof, and of her services performed in Georgia, th[at] Others have Assumed the Merit and shared His Majestys most Royal Favour.

If a faithfull Account of the Whole should Derogate any thing from the Character of any Gentleman, it has been her Misfortune, that its in her Power to Doe it with Justice, and not in her Power to Omitt it without Injustice to her self; and to His Majestys Service as her Case is such as has Some Connection with the Generall Peace and Tranquility of the Colony.

That your Memorialist about the Age of 7 Years, was brought Down by her Father[8] from the Indian Nation, to Pomponne in south Carolina; There baptized, Educated and bred up in the Principles of Christianity.

That She was in south Carolina when the Indian War broke out in the year 1715;[9] that the Cause thereof was owing to the repeated Acts of Injustice which the Indians had Received from time to time from the Traders; as She has been informed by Old Chickilli her Mothers Brother;[10] who at the Head of 600 Creek Indians at that time Advanced as far as Stono River.[11]

That in the Year 1716 Collonel John Musgrove[12] (your Memorialists Father in Law) was sent into the Nation Agent from the Government of South Carolina; who entered into a Treaty of Friendship and Commerce, with the Creek Indian Nation in behalf of the Government; the Conditions of which were, that Traders should be sent up Amongst them etc. that none of his Majestys subjects should Live, hold any Lands, or claim any Right or Title to any Cattle etc. to the southward of the River Savannah, which was to be the Boundary between the Creek Indian Nation, and his Majestys Subjects of that Province.

That after She was Married to Mr. John Musgrove[13] she was Settled in Carolina upwards of Seven Years till June 1732 at which time She and her then Husband (at

---

[8] Her father was Edward Griffin, a white trader. Her mother was an unnamed Creek woman from Tuckabatchee.

[9] The Yamasee War (1715–1718) was a violent and expensive colonial war primarily between South Carolina colonists and the Yamasee Indians. Some have linked white fathers' removal of mixed-blood children from Indian towns to the outbreak of hostilities.

[10] Old Chickilli: Chigelley was the Coweta *mico* and thus a powerful and influential Creek leader. Chigelley was probably not "her mother's brother" as she claims.

[11] "Stono River": A South Carolina river southwest of Charleston.

[12] Col. John Musgrove: Colonel John Musgrove was an Indian trader who also negotiated with the Creeks on behalf of South Carolina.

[13] John Musgrove: Johnny Musgrove was the mixed-blood son of Colonel John Musgrove. He died in 1735.

the Request of the Creek Nation, and with the Consent and Approbation of His Excellency Governor Johnston[14]) Moved all their Goods Cattle, and Other Effects to the southward of the River Savannah, and settled a Trading House at Yamacraw[15] near the place where The Town Savannah now stands, where they took from the Indians very Large Quantities of Deer Skins, and had Large Credit and Supplies of Goods to carry on that Traffick from Merchants in Charles Town.

That upon the Arrival of James Oglethorpe Esqr. with the first Imbarkation for the settlement of the Colony of Georgia the Indians that were then settled at Yamacraw, were very uneasy, and Threatned to take up Arms Against them, (which they certainly would have Done as they looked upon all white peoples settling there as a Breach of the Treaty of Peace, entered into with the Government of Carolina,) had not your Memorialist used the Utmost of her Intrest and Influence, to Perswade them from it, and to bring About a Treaty betwixt Mr. Oglethorpe in behalf of his Majesty and the Indians that were then there, in behalf of the Creek Nation, which Treaty was Provisionary till the Consent of the Nation could be Obtained which Also, was with the Greatest Difficulty effected by your Memorialist's Intrest and Influence.

That her then Husband Mr. John Musgrove brought, Considirable Effects into Georgia, as Horses, Cattle etc; that as there was at that time no Other House or Settlement in the Colony, they supplyed the first settlers, and Other Persons employed on publick service in their greatest Wants and Necessities with every Necessary their Plantation Afforded or that they Could purchase on their own Creditt from Merchants In Charles Town.

THAT she and her then Husbands having at that time had but Little Experience of the World, and the fraudulent Designs of Bad people have greatly suffered by giving Large Creditt to sundry Inhabitants and Other Persons on publick service in the Collony of Georgia, and out of mere Compassion, Relieving them in their greatest Necessities thinking thereby to enable them to continue and improve their New settlements most of which are either Dead, have Left the Colony or not in Circumstances to pay her.

She further Declareth that in the years 1733 and 1734 she took from the Indians near 12000 Weight of Deer Skins, each year as she can make Appear by Remittances made to Charles Town, and that the Trade would have very Much encreased; as great

---

[14] Governor Johnson: Robert Johnson (1682–1735) was governor of South Carolina from 1717 to 1719 and 1729 to 1735.

[15] The Yamacraws were a band of Indians composed largely of exiled Creeks living near what became Georgia's first settlement, Savannah. The Yamacraws and their leader, Tomochichi, likely saw the arrival of the colonists as an opportunity to regain standing with the Creeks.

Number of Indians were Daily coming down from the Nation to trade with her by which Traffick alone she Could soon have made a very Large Fortune and prevented those Calamities which are now fallen upon her, had she persued the same Methods that the Rest of the Traders did in perswading the Indians to keep Constantly out a hunting for Deer, which she had Interest and Influence enough to have Done.

But as at that time there was no Other Defence and Protection for this Infant Colony, and the Southern Parts of Carolina, which lay exposed to the Incursions of the spaniards and Indians in Amity with them; but the Friendship and Alliance of the Creek Indians. She so far prefered the Lives and Properties of his Majestys subjects, to her own private Interest that she not only employed her own Interest to continue the Creek Indians steady in their Friendship and Alliance with his Majestys subjects, but constantly supported at her own Expence, great Numbers of her Friends, and Other War Indians, who were always ready to go Against his Majestys Enimies at her Command, by which Means her Trade Daily decreased and almost intirely went to Ruin. The Indians who were her Hunters being most frequently employed on some Expedition for the Publick Service, and thereby rendered incapable to pay the Debts they had before Contracted which Amounts to several Thousand's Weight of Leather, which remains unpaid to this Day, some being Dead, and Others killed in his Majestys service Particularly her own Brother and Other Near Relations at the Seige of Augustine in the Year 1740.[16]

That in the year 1736; 1737 when Mr. Oglethorpe thought Proper to strengthen the southern Parts of the Province by a Settlement at the Island of St. Simons and on the Alatamaha, The Assistance of the Creek Indians became much more Necessary, as there were then Advices that the spaniards were then Making preparations to Dislodge this Colony.

That she was then Sent for on all Occasions to Frederica[17] (above a Hundred Miles Distant from her own settlement) when ever any Indians came there, (as they Did not Chuse to talk of any Affairs of Consequence unless she was present,) which has often, Occasioned her being absent from Home for several Months at a time by Which means her own Private Affairs and Improvements on her Lands, at and near Savannah, Daily went to Ruin, being in her Absence on publick service entirely Left to the Care and Management of Servants.

---

[16] Seige of Augustine: A conflict led by Oglethorpe against the Spanish fort of St. Augustine during the War of Jenkins' Ear. The siege was unsuccessful.

[17] Frederica: Fort Frederica was on St. Simon's Island, south of Savannah along Georgia's coast and at the mouth of the Altahama River. In 1742, at the end of the War of Jenkins' Ear, the British led by Oglethorpe crucially defeated the Spanish at Fort Frederica.

That as these Frontier Settlements lay Exposed to the Ravages of the Enemy Indians; bouyed up by the Extensive Promises and great Rewards so signal a service would Merit; at the Request of his Excellency General Oglethorpe she settled a Trading house on the south side of the Alatamaha River about Sixty Miles up the Country; the Intention of which was, that the Creek Indians that would be Constantly with them there, would be an out Guard to prevent any Incursions of the Indians in Friendship with the Spaniards on the out settlements of Georgia, and be alway[s] Ready at Hand when his Majestys Service Required their Assistance, which Answered the Intentions of the Publick but was a heavy Burthen to your Memorialist.

That after the War with Spain the services of the Indians were so frequently required that no Advantage could Possably be made by the Trade there; that she Constantly employed her Interest to bring Down her Friends and Relations from the Nation to fight against his Majestys Enemies which since the War they have so much Annoyed that they have been a strong Barrier and Defence of the Country against the Designs of the Spaniards as must be universally Allowed by every Unprejudiced Person.

That by hers, and her then Husbands[18] Absence at their settlement on the Alatamaha, all their Affairs at Savannah, stock of Cattle, Buildings, Improvements upon the Lands etc. which were very considerable; intirely went to Ruin.

That in the Year 1742 her then Husband Jacob Mathews being taken very sick at his settlement on the Alatamaha was brought from thence to Savannah and there soon After Died; that her Affairs on Account of his Death being in great Confusion, Occasioned her stay there Longer than she Expected, the Indians that were then at Her settlement on the Alatamaha being very uneasy that she Did not Return: on that Account Left the place which the Yamasee Indians taking the Advantage of came in a partey, committed several barbarous Murthers; and entirely burnt and Distroyed her settlement there, by which she greatly suffered.

That in the Year 1743 when His Excellency General Oglethorpe was going for England he then paid her £180 which with £20 before Received made £200; which was the totall Sum Received for her services from the first settlement of the Colony in 1732 till that time. Whereas Notwithstanding the great Trouble and Fatigue she has undergone, in frequently Travelling on all Occassions Several Hundred miles by Water in Open Boats; exposed to the Inclemencies of the Weather both heat and Cold and no other Covering but the Cannopy of the Heavens, The Losses sustained in her own private

---

[18] Jacob Mathews was a white ranger assigned to the Altamaha outpost and a former indentured servant. They were married from 1737 until Mathews died in 1742. She married her third and final husband, Thomas Bosomworth, in 1744. Bosomworth was an ordained Anglican minister, and likely advised Coosaponakeesa in her legal petitions.

Affairs, by the Neglect thereof on his Majestys service from the first settlement of the Collony, will upon the Most Moderate Computation Amount to Five Thousand Seven Hundred and Fourteen Pounds Seventeen shillings and Eleven pence sterling.

That As she has hitherto in vain relyed on and confided in Generall Oglethorpes Promises to make her Restitution for all her Losses Sustained in his Majestys service to sollicit Redress for those Grievances which are now become, intolerable, and to Obtain from the Government at Home such Rewards for her past services as were adequate to the Consequence thereof; As you Sir have the Deserved Honour to Command his Majestys Forces in this Province, and may have Personal Knowledge, of the Truth of several Facts herein Contained Viz. The merit of your Memorialist's past services, the Necessity of a Strict friendship and Alliance with the Creek Indian Nation; the Dangers that at present seem to threaten the General Peace and Tranquility of both the Provinces of Georgia and Carolina, from the Loss of that friendship: the Causes thereof, and the Consequence of her present Interest (if She is not Deprived of the means of using it for the Good of his Majestys Service). She therefore Humbly Begs that you would be Pleased to make a Representation of those things to the Government at Home in such a Light as you shall think Most Conducive to the Welfare of the Colony and His Majestys Service.

THAT whereas His Majesty in the Preamble of the Royal Charter to the Honourable the Trustees for Establishing the Colony of the Georgia, bearing Date the 9th Day of June 1732 has been graciously pleased to Declare that the Intention of the Settlement of Said Colony was partly as a Protection to his Majestys Subjects of South Carolina, whose Southern Frontiers continued unsettled and Lay exposed to the frequent Ravages of Enimy Indians etc. which Signal Instance of his Majestys peculiar Care for the Protection of that Province, is Most gratefully Acknowledged by a Memorial sent to his Majesty from the Governor and Council of the Said Province Dated the 9th April 1734.

And whereas, his Majestys Gracious Intentions in the Settlement of the Colony of Georgia, have been so far Answered: that no out Settlements have been cutt off; Boats taken; nor men killed; since that time (which used before frequently to happen,) your Memorialist therefore humbly hopes that upon a Representation of her Case to his Majestys Governor and Council of the Province of South Carolina; How far his Majestys Subjects of that Province have been enabled to Improve the southern parts of that Province (which Before Lay Waste) by your Memorialist's Interest in Continuing the Indians in friendship and Alliance with his Majestys Subjects: THAT, That Government would be induced to make her some Restitution for her past services and Losses sustained in his Majestys service as she is Now indebted several Considerable sums of Money to Merchants in Charles Town, and Other Persons in south Carolina: and Destitute of Credit to Carry on her Affairs (which take away the Very Means of her having it in her Power to Do Justice to her Creditors in the Province) and Whatever the Government shall think her Worthy o[f], she Desires may be Applied to that end.

AND Lastly your Memorialist cannot Help repeating with an equal Mixture of a Real Grief of Heart, and Indignation; that her Injuries and Oppressions have been such, as she believes; have been scarce paralleled under a British Government. Language is too Weak to Represent her present Deplorable Case; She at present Labours under every sence of Injury; and Circumstance of Distress; Destitute of even the Common Necessaries of Life, being Insulted, Abused, contemned[19] and Dispised by those ungratefull People who are indebted to her for the Blessings they Injoy.

The Only Returns she has met with for her past Services, Generosity, and Maternal Affection (she has at all times shewn for the whole Colony) has been injust Loads of Infamy and Reproach; Branded and Stigmatized with the Odious Name of Traytor, for Making any Pretensions to those Rights she is Justly entitled to by the Laws of God and Nature (as her ancestors were the Natural born Heirs Sole Owners and Proprietors of every Foot of Land which is now his Majestys Colony of Georgia,) tho she has in Vain made Application for a Grant from the Crown, and is Desireous and Willing to hold What Posesions she is there entitled to by the Laws of Nature and Nations, as a Subject of great Britain.

It is with the greatest Reluctancy, that your Memorialist is Drove to the Necessity to declare; That the Collony of Georgia was settled by her Interest with the Creek Indians: that it has in a Great Measure been supported by it, (as she can make Appeare by Authentick Letters and Testimonies,) and that she has at this Day Interest enough to command a Thousand fighting men to stand in the face of his Majestys Enemies; and to Countermine every intended Design of both the french and spaniards in alienating the Creeks Nation of Indians from the British Interest; If Suitable Encouragements are given her, to prevent her being Drove to the Necessity of Flying to her Indian Friends for Bread which will Greatly Confirm the Jealousies and uneasiness which his Majestys Enimies have so Industriously fomented and Spirited up Amongst them.

The French Emissaries in particular are at this Day Assuming all shapes, and trying every scheme to Debauch their faith to the English. They Magnify the Power and Grande[u]r of France; and are Loading them with presents.

They Study to Render the English Diminitive and Contemptable which is greatly Confirmed by your not being able to give them Presents as Usual. Your Memorialist

---

[19] Contemn: To treat with contemptuous disregard, disdain, or scorn.

therefore humbly begs Leave to Represent unto you, that the Expence of our safety on this Occasion must Certainly be very Considerable if you think the friendship and Alliance of that Nation Worth preserving. These ends cannot be Affected by any Other Means but by Extraordinary Presents being Allowed them [and] a Proper Person being Sent Amongst them in Whom the[y] Repose Fa[i]th and Confidence who can gain an Ascendancy in their Councils to Remove every Insinuation of His Majestys Enimies.[20]

THAT Whereas your Memorialist is highly sensible that it is not in your Power to Redress her Grievances, and of the Great Difficulties you Labour under at this Juncture, in not being allowed any fund for continuing the Creek Indians in Friendship and Alliance with his Majestys Subjects and how far his Majestys service and Interest may Suffer thereby, she therefore Humbly begs that you would be Pleased to Lay this Memorial before his Grace the Duke of Newcastle[21] one of His Majestys Principal Secretarys of State for His Graces Consideration with this Assurance, that if the Government should think proper to allow a Certain Sum per Annum to be applyed for maintaining his Majestys Peace and Authority Amongst the Indians that she on her Part would engage by her Interest Amongst them, to Doe every Duty that ever was Done by Rangers etc. in Georgia which have Cost the Government so many Thoussands, of Pounds, and With the Regiment under your Honours Command, and her Interest with the Creek Indians she believes that every Foot of his Majestys Possessions, and this Important Frontier could be maintained Against all his Majestys Enimies.

All Which is Humbly Submitted to your Consideration by your Memorialist this
10th Day August 1747.
Mary Bosomworth

---

[20] Presents were a crucial component of Creek diplomacy. Presents were necessary not only to negotiate treaties, but also to maintain them as Creeks saw the alliances created through treaties with Britain as temporary rather than perpetual. Moreover, as the Creek Nation was a confederacy of many *talwas*, negotiation occurred with multiple leaders who sought consensus, but who might also enter into separate treaties with the English. This passage also reflects the importance of the English rivalry with the French for holdings in eastern North America, which Coosaponakeesa alludes to in order to influence her readers.

[21] The Duke of New Castle: Thomas Pelham-Holles, Duke of Newcastle (1693–1768), served as Secretary of State during this period and was largely responsible for colonial affairs.

TWENTY

Mary Leapor (1722–1746)

*I*N ENGLAND, LABORING-CLASS WOMEN FOLLOWING IN THE FOOTSTEPS OF MARY COLLIER *continued to make literary inroads as the Age of Revolutions advanced. Born in 1722, at Marston St. Lawrence, Northamptonshire, the daughter of Ann and Philip Leapor, Mary Leapor worked as a kitchen maid and, after the death of her mother in 1742, kept house for her father, who at that time kept a nursery garden at Brackley and worked for the local gentry. Her parents were literate and taught her to read and write, and to their chagrin she became enamored of books, especially poetry. Contemporaries describe her neglecting her work in order to read and write. Her verse circulated locally and Leapor gained the patronage of Bridget Fremantle (called "Artemisia" in Leapor's poems), a local clergyman's daughter, who sent one of Leapor's plays to a London producer. Although the play was rejected, Freemantle's plans to bring out a volume of Leapor's verse were successful, but sadly the project came to fruition only after Leapor's early death at the age of 24. There were 600 subscribers to the first edition of Leapor's poems, which attracted the attention of the novelist Samuel Richardson. Richardson edited a second edition with many well-known writers listed as subscribers, although the list numbered only 300. Her* Poems on Several Occasions *was published in 1748, with all profits accruing to her indigent father. It was reviewed in* The Monthly Review *in 1749.* Poems *was reissued and again reviewed by* The Monthly Review *in 1751.*

In "Man the Monarch," Leapor envisions an alternative creation story which came down to her through a female tradition, from Mother Nature to the Muse and hence to the poet. In this story, Adam ("our Grandsire"), "Greedy of Power," is unable to control the animals and so decides to deny power to Woman, whom Nature had "design'd a Queen" with gifts of beauty and grace. This theme of the impotence of beauty is continued in "An Essay on Woman," in which Leapor argues that women's charms and even wealth are no match for the inequalities of the institution of marriage ("mighty Hymen"). Leapor lists many women known to her and the poem's addressee, "Artemisia" (Bridget Fremantle), describing how Nature's gifts of beauty, wealth, and even intelligence only make women experience "Superior Woe," more pain than otherwise. Significantly, Leapor turns to colonial and Orientalist imagery to emphasize the charms of English women: their fair skin makes snow seem to "turn a Negro" by comparison, and wherever they tread, sweet perfumes of "Arabian odours" rise up from the ground. Leapor's uncritical adoption of this imagery suggests how widespread and common the language of colonial travel and the slave trade was becoming in the period, achieving the status of cliché by the time these poems were published in 1748.

"MAN THE MONARCH" (1748)

AMAZED we read of Nature's early throes,
How the fair heavens and ponderous earth arose;
How blooming trees unplanted first began;
And beasts submissive to their tyrant, man:
To man, invested with despotic sway,
While his mute brethren tremble and obey;
Till heaven beheld him insolently vain,
And checked the limits of his haughty reign.
Then from their lord the rude deserters fly,
And, grinning back, his fruitless rage defy;
Pards,[1] tigers, wolves to gloomy shades retire,
And mountain-goats in purer gales respire.
To humble valleys, where soft flowers blow,
And fattening streams in chrystal mazes flow,
Full of new life, the untamed coursers run,
And roll and wanton in the cheerful sun;
Round their gay hearts in dancing spirits rise,
And rouse the lightnings in their rolling eyes:
To craggy rocks destructive serpents glide,
Whose mossy crannies hide their speckled pride;

---

[1] Pard: Panther.

And monstrous whales on foamy billows ride.
Then joyful birds ascend their native sky:
But where! ah, where shall helpless woman fly?

Here smiling Nature brought her choicest stores,
And roseate beauty on her favourite pours:
Pleased with her labour, the officious dame
Withheld no grace would deck the rising frame.
Then viewed her work, and viewed and smiled again,
And kindly whispered, "Daughter, live and reign."
But now the matron mourns her latest care,
And sees the sorrows of her darling fair;
Beholds a wretch, whom she designed a queen,
And weeps that e'er she formed the weak machine.
In vain she boasts her lip of scarlet dyes,
Cheeks like the morning, and far-beaming eyes;
Her neck refulgent, fair and feeble arms—
A set of useless and neglected charms.
She suffers hardship with afflictive moans:
Small tasks of labour suit her slender bones.
Beneath a load her weary shoulders yield,
Nor can her fingers grasp the sounding shield;
She sees and trembles at approaching harms,
And fear and grief destroy her fading charms.
Then her pale lips no pearly teeth disclose,
And time's rude sickle cuts the yielding rose.
Thus wretched woman's shortlived merit dies:
In vain to Wisdom's sacred help she flies,
Or sparkling Wit but lends a feeble aid:
'Tis all delirium from a wrinkled maid.

A tattling dame, no matter where or who—
Me it concerns not, and it need not you—
Once told this story to the listening Muse,
Which we, as now it serves our turn, shall use.

When our grandsire[2] named the feathered kind,
Pondering their natures in his careful mind,

---

[2] Our grandsire: Adam.

'Twas then, if on our author we rely,
He viewed his consort with an envious eye;
Greedy of power, he hugged the tottering throne,
Pleased with the homage, and would reign alone;
And, better to secure his doubtful rule,
Rolled his wise eyeballs, and pronounced her *fool*.
The regal blood to distant ages runs:
Sires, brothers, husbands, and commanding sons,
The sceptre claim; and every cottage brings
A long succession of domestic kings.

"AN ESSAY ON WOMAN" (1748)

WOMAN, a pleasing but a short-lived flower,
Too soft for business and too weak for power:
A wife in bondage, or neglected maid;
Despised, if ugly; if she's fair, betrayed.
'Tis wealth alone inspires every grace,
And calls the raptures to her plenteous face.
What numbers for those charming features pine,
If blooming acres round her temples twine!
Her lip the strawberry, and her eyes more bright
Than sparkling Venus in a frosty night;
Pale lilies fade and, when the fair appears,
Snow turns a negro and dissolves in tears,
And, where the charmer treads her magic toe,
On English ground Arabian odours grow;
Till mighty Hymen[3] lifts his sceptred rod,
And sinks her glories with a fatal nod,
Dissolves her triumphs, sweeps her charms away,
And turns the goddess to her native clay.

But, Artemisia,[4] let your servant sing
What small advantage wealth and beauties bring.

---

[3] Hymen: Greek god of marriage.
[4] Artemisia: Greek goddess of nature and the hunt.

Who would be wise, that knew Pamphilia's[5] fate?
Or who be fair, and joined to Sylvia's mate?
Sylvia, whose cheeks are fresh as early day,
As evening mild, and sweet as spicy May:
And yet that face her partial husband tires,
And those bright eyes, that all the world admires.
Pamphilia's wit who does not strive to shun,
Like death's infection or a dog-day's sun?
The damsels view her with malignant eyes,
The men are vexed to find a nymph so wise:
And wisdom only serves to make her know
The keen sensation of superior woe.
The secret whisper and the listening ear,
The scornful eyebrow and the hated sneer,
The giddy censures of her babbling kind,
With thousand ills that grate a gentle mind,
By her are tasted in the first degree,
Though overlooked by Simplicus[6] and me.
Does thirst of gold a virgin's heart inspire,
Instilled by nature or a careful sire?
Then let her quit extravagance and play,
The brisk companion and expensive tea,
To feast with Cordia in her filthy sty
On stewed potatoes or on mouldy pie;
Whose eager eyes stare ghastly at the poor,
And fright the beggars from her hated door;
In greasy clouts[7] she wraps her smoky chin,
And holds that pride's a never-pardoned sin.

If this be wealth, no matter where it falls;
But save, ye Muses, save your Mira's[8] walls:

---

[5] Pamphilia: Heroine of a prose romance *The Countesse of Mountgomeries Urania* and a sonnet cycle *Pamphilia to Amphilanthus* published in 1621 by Englishwoman Lady Mary Wroth; Pamphilia was celebrated for her constant faithfulness to her lover Amphilanthus despite his own failings in virtue.

[6] Simplicus: Conventional name for a rustic or simple man.

[7] Clouts: Cloths.

[8] Mira: Leapor's poetic identity.

Still give me pleasing indolence and ease,
A fire to warm me and a friend to please.

  Since, whether sunk in avarice or pride,
A wanton virgin or a starving bride,
Or wondering crowds attend her charming tongue,
Or, deemed an idiot, ever speaks the wrong;
Though nature armed us for the growing ill
With fraudful cunning and a headstrong will;
Yet, with ten thousand follies to her charge,
Unhappy woman's but a slave at large.

TWENTY-ONE

Susanna Wright (1697–1784)

*A*N HEIR TO THE GENDER-EGALITARIAN QUAKER LEGACY OF MARGARET FELL (WHOSE WRITINGS *are included in this volume), English-born Susanna Wright migrated to Pennsylvania with her Quaker parents in 1714. When her mother died in 1722, Susanna assumed charge of the family household, but still developed an impressive reputation as a poet and intellectual. She never married. Her family's home at a busy crossroads on the Pennsylvania frontier put her in contact with many of the leading intellectuals of eighteenth-century Philadelphia including Benjamin Rush and Benjamin Franklin. Like these other Enlightenment-era thinkers, Wright pursued a range of scientific and intellectual interests, including herbal medicine, silkworm cultivation, and local history. She also wrote poetry and participated in an important Philadelphia-area network of women poets, including Hannah Griffitts, Deborah Logan, and Milcah Martha Moore, who exchanged poetry with each other in manuscript. Raised with Quaker ideals of gender equality like those articulated so powerfully by Fell, these women began to achieve the kind of mutually enriching female intellectual community dreamed of by Mary Astell and so many other early Anglo-feminist writers. In "To Eliza Norris—at Fairhill," Wright addresses her friend Elizabeth Norris (1704–1779), member of a prominent Philadelphia Quaker family; Fairhill was the Norris family estate and served as a retreat space for Norris's circle of women friends, intellectuals, and writers. Celebrating the independent lives of intellectual fulfillment she and her friend have managed to achieve, Wright encourages all "womankind" to "call reason to their aid" in order to challenge the unjust customary rule of men. "Reason governs all the mighty frame," Wright proclaims; "Reason rules in every one the same,/No right has man his equal to control,/Since all agree, there is no sex in soul." Wright's poem is noteworthy for its unapologetic declaration of the essential equality of men and women and its visionary celebration of self-made women.*

"TO ELIZA NORRIS—AT FAIRHILL" (1750)

Since Adam, by our first fair Mother won
To share her fate, to taste, & be undone,
And that great law, whence no appeal must lie,
Pronounc'd a doom, that she should rule & die,
The partial race, rejoicing to fulfill
This pleasing dictate of almighty will
(With no superior virtue in their mind),
Assert their right to govern womankind.
But womankind call reason to their aid,
And question when or where that law was made,
That law divine (a plausible pretence)
Oft urg'd with none, & oft with little sense,
From wisdom's source no origin could draw,
That form'd the man to keep the sex in awe;
Say Reason governs all the mighty frame,
And Reason rules in every one the same,
No right has man his equal to control,
Since, all agree, there is no sex in soul;
Weak woman, thus in agreement grown strong,
Shakes off the yoke her parents wore too long;
But he, who arguments in vain had tried,
Hopes still for conquest from the yielding side,
Soft soothing flattery & persuasion tries,
And by a feign'd submission seeks to rise,
Steals, unperceiv'd, to the unguarded heart,
   And there reigns tyrant—
But you, whom no seducing tales can gain
To yield obedience, or to wear the chain,
But set a queen, & in your freedom reign
O'er your own thoughts, of your own heart secure,
You see what joys each erring sex allure,
Look round the most intelligent—how few
But passions sway, or childish joys pursue;
Then bless that choice which led your bloom of youth
From forms & shadows to enlight'ning truth,
best found when leisure & retirement reign,

Far from the proud, the busy & the vain,

Where rural views soft gentle joys impart,

Enlarge the thought, & elevate the heart,

Each changing scene adorns gay Nature's face,

Ev'n winter wants not its peculiar grace,

Hoar frosts & dews, & pale & summer suns.

Paint each revolving season as it runs,

The showery bow delights your wond'ring eyes,

Its spacious arch, & variegated dyes,

[You] watch the transient colours as they fade,

Till, by degrees, they settle into shade,

Then calm reflect, so regular & fine,

Now seen no more, a fate will soon be mine,

When life's warm stream, chill'd by death's fey[1] hand,

Within these veins a frozen current stands

Tho' conscious of desert superior far,

Till then, my friend, the righteous claim forbear—

Indulge man in his darling vice of sway,

He only rules those who of choice obey;

When strip'd of power, & plac'd in equal light,

Angels shall judge who had the better right,

All you can do is but to let him see

That woman still shall sure his equal be,

By your example shake his ancient law,

And shine yourself, the finish'd piece you draw.

---

[1] Fey: Fated, doomed to death. This word is only partly legible in the original manuscript so scholars are not certain what Wright wrote here.

TWENTY-TWO

William Blackstone (1723–1780)

WHAT WAS THE LEGAL STATUS OF WOMEN IN THE ENGLISH-SPEAKING WORLD IN THE AGE *of Revolutions? These passages from Sir William Blackstone's* Commentaries on the Laws of England *(1765–1769) represent a defining modern articulation of the legal doctrine of coverture or* feme covert *(literally meaning "covered woman"). As stated here by Blackstone, an English judge and law professor,* feme covert *means that a married woman has no legal personhood: no independent standing before the law. Single women had the right to make their own contracts and own their own property; upon marriage, those rights effectively passed to their husbands. A married woman was not empowered under common law to make contracts, own property, or sign legal documents. The wages of married, working women were considered the property of their husbands. In these pages, Blackstone also legally authorizes husbands to discipline their wives as though they were "servants" or "children."*

The doctrine of feme covert *did not begin with Blackstone: it had its roots in medieval English common law, but it did assume new formality and force in the late eighteenth century after the Oxford-educated Blackstone synthesized and systematized the common law in his* Commentaries. *The* Commentaries *were first published in America in 1771 and are still considered the definitive representation of British and Anglo-American common law in the era of revolutions.*

It was Blackstone who defined property rights as the "sole and despotic dominion which one man claims and exercises over the external things of the world, in total exclusion of the right of any other individual in the universe." The doctrine of feme covert *may reflect in part the impossibility of squaring this notion of individual legal sovereignty in matters of property with the nonsingularity of the marital relationship. But the doctrine of* feme covert *also speaks to a basic tension concerning the political status of women in the Age of Revolutions. If married women did not have legal personhood, should they have political personhood independent of their husbands? Should they count as citizens? Should they vote?*

For their part, women responded to the idea of feme covert *by expressing increasing anxiety about their status in marriage and the costs poor marital choices exacted on women's lives. We see this anxiety especially in sentimental novels like Susana Rowson's* Charlotte Temple *(1791) that depict the vulnerability of girls and young women to exploitation by rakes who game the marital bond to their own purposes. Blackstone's* Commentaries *remind us that what twenty-first-century women understand as the ideal of companioniate marriage—marriage as the willingly entered partnership of two independent equals on the basis of a mutual love—was not available under the law to women in the eighteenth century.*

"OF HUSBAND AND WIFE" (1765)

[. . .] By marriage, the husband and wife are one person in law: that is, the very being or legal existence of the woman is suspended during the marriage, or at least is incorporated and consolidated into that of the husband: under whose wing, protection and *cover*, she performs every thing; and is therefore called in our law-french[1] a *feme-covert*; is said to be *covert-baron*, or under the protection and influence of her husband, her *baron* or lord; and her condition during her marriage is called her *coverture*. Upon this principle, of an union of person in husband and wife, depend almost all the legal rights, duties, and disabilities that either of them acquire by the marriage. I speak not at present of the rights of property, but of such as are merely *personal*. For this reason, a man cannot grant any thing to his wife, or enter into covenant with her: for the grant would be to suppose her separate existence; and to covenant with her, would be only to covenant with himself: and therefore it is also generally true, that all compacts made between husband and wife, when single, are voided by the intermarriage. A woman indeed may be attorney for her husband; for that implies no separation from, but is rather a representation of, her lord. And a husband may also bequeath any thing to his wife by will; for that cannot take effect till the coverture is determined by his death. The husband is bound to provide his wife with necessaries by law, as much as himself; and if she contracts debts for them, he is obliged to pay them: but for any thing besides necessaries, he is not chargeable. Also if a wife

---

[1] Law-french: An archaic Norman variant of the French language, utilized in English law from the time of the 1066 Norman Conquest through the seventeenth century. To this day, many legal noun phrases in English retain the syntax of Law French.

elopes, and lives with another man, the husband is not chargeable even for necessaries; at least if the person, who furnishes them, is sufficiently apprized of her elopement. If the wife be indebted before marriage, the husband is bound afterwards to pay the debt; for he has adopted her and her circumstances together. If the wife be injured in her person or her property, she can bring no action for redress without her husband's concurrence, and in his name, as well as her own: neither can she be sued, without making the husband a defendant. There is indeed one case where the wife shall sue and be sued as a *feme sole*,[2] viz. where the husband has abjured the realm, or is banished: for then he is dead in law; and the husband being thus disabled to sue for or defend the wife, it would be most unreasonable if she had no remedy, or could make no defence at all. In criminal prosecutions, it is true, the wife may be indicted and punished separately; for the union is only a civil union. But, in trials of any sort they are not allowed to be evidence for, or against, each other: partly because it is impossible their testimony should be indifferent; but principally because of the union of person: and therefore, if they were admitted to be witnesses *for* each other, they would contradict one maxim of law, "*nemo in propria causa testis esse debet*;["][3] and if *against* each other, they would contradict another maxim, "*nemo tenetur seipsum accusare.*"[4] But where the offence is directly against the person of the wife, this rule has been usually dispensed with: and therefore, by statute 3 Hen. VII. c. 2.[5] in case a woman be forcibly taken away, and married, she may be a witness against such her husband, in order to convict him of felony. For in this case she can with no propriety be reckoned his wife; because a main ingredient, her consent, was wanting to the contract: and also there is another maxim of law, that no man shall take advantage of his own wrong; which the ravisher here would do, if by forcibly marrying a woman, he could prevent her from being a witness, who is perhaps the only witness to that very fact.

IN the civil law the husband and wife are considered as two distinct persons; and may have separate estates, contracts, debts, and injuries: and therefore, in our ecclesiastical courts, a woman may sue and be sued without her husband.

BUT, though our law in general considers man and wife as one person, yet there are some instances in which she is separately considered; as inferior to him, and acting by his compulsion. And therefore all deeds executed, and acts done, by her, during her coverture, are void, or at least voidable; except it be a fine, or the like

---

[2] *feme-sole*: In law French, a solitary female.

[3] *nemo in propria causa testis esse debet:* A Latin phrase meaning "no one can be a witness in his own case."

[4] *nemo tenetur seipsum accusare:* A Latin phrase meaning "no one is bound to accuse himself."

[5] 3 Hen. VII. c. 2: nominates a legal statute passed during the reign of King Henry VII (1452–1509).

matter of record, in which case she must be solely and secretly examined, to learn if her act be voluntary. She cannot by will devise lands to her husband, unless under special circumstances; for at the time of making it she is supposed to be under his coercion. And in some felonies, and other inferior crimes, committed by her, through constraint of her husband, the law excuses her: but this extends not to treason or murder.

THE husband also (by the old law) might give his wife moderate correction. For, as he is to answer for her misbehaviour, the law thought it reasonable to intrust him with this power of restraining her, by domestic chastisement, in the same moderation that a man is allowed to correct his servants or children; for whom the master or parent is also liable in some cases to answer. But this power of correction was confined within reasonable bounds; and the husband was prohibited to use any violence to his wife, *aliter quam ad virum, ex causa regiminis et castigationis uxoris suae, licite et rationabiliter pertinet*.[6] The civil law gave the husband the same, or a larger, authority over his wife; allowing him, for some misdemeanors, *flagellis et fustibus acriter verberare uxorem*;[7] for others, only *modicam castigationem adbibere*.[8] But, with us, in the politer reign of Charles the second,[9] this power of correction began to be doubted: and a wife may now have security of the peace against her husband; or, in return, a husband against his wife. Yet the lower rank of people, who were always fond of the old common law, still claim and exert their antient privilege: and the courts of law will still permit a husband to restrain a wife of her liberty, in case of any gross misbehaviour.

THESE are the chief legal effects of marriage during the coverture; upon which we may observe, that even the disabilities, which the wife lies under, are for the most part intended for her protection and benefit. So great a favourite is the female sex of the laws of England.

---

[6] *aliter quam ad virum, ex causa regiminis et castigationis uxoris suae, licite et rationabiliter pertinet*: A Latin phrase meaning "other than what is reasonably necessary to the discipline and correction of the wife."

[7] *flagellis et fustibus acriter verberare uxorem*: A Latin phrase meaning "to wound his wife severely with whips and fists."

[8] *modicam castigationem adbibere:* A Latin phrase meaning "to apply modest corrective punishment."

[9] King Charles II (1630–1685), who succeeded his father, the deposed and executed King Charles I (1600–1649), at the close of the Interregnum and the restoration of the monarchy in 1660.

TWENTY-THREE

Hannah Griffitts (1727–1817)

*H*ANNAH GRIFFITTS WAS A CLOSE FRIEND TO SUSANNAH WRIGHT; IN FACT, WRIGHT'S POEM *"To Eliza Norris—at Fairhill," included in this anthology, survives only in Griffitts's handwriting. Both women belonged to an important eighteenth-century network of women writers centered on Philadelphia. Both women were Quakers, raised in a tradition of gender egalitarianism; both opted for lives of intellectual pursuit and bonds with other women rather than traditional marriage. For more than a decade, Hannah Griffitts lived with her friend Mary Norris at the Norris family's Fairhill estate, an important site for social and intellectual exchange for Quaker women. Wright closely followed and engaged in the debates and controversies surrounding the American Revolution. As a Quaker pacifist, she celebrated the revolutionary cause while mourning the war's impacts on her pacifist and Loyalist friends and family members and rejecting extremist elements of the American Independence movement. Her poem "The Female Patriots," published in the* Pennsylvania Chronicle *and recorded also in the commonplace book of Milcah Martha Moore, encourages other women to exercise their political agency and participate in boycotts protesting the Sugar Act (1764), Stamp Act (1765), and Townshend Duties (1767), which imposed heavy taxes on commodities needed by British colonists in North America.*

"THE FEMALE PATRIOTS. ADDRESS'D TO THE DAUGHTERS OF LIBERTY IN AMERICA" (1768)

Since the men, from a party or fear of a frown,
Are kept by a sugar-plum quietly down,
Supinely asleep,—and depriv'd of their Sight,
Are strip'd of their Freedom, and rob'd of their Right;

If the sons, so degenerate! the blessings despise,

Let the Daughters of Liberty nobly arise;

And tho' we've no Voice but a negative here,

The use of the Taxables, let us forbear:—

(Then merchants import till yr. Stores are all full,

May the buyers be few, and yr. traffick be dull!)

Stand firmly resolv'd, and bid Grenville[1] to see,

That rather than freedom we'll part with our tea,

And well as we love the dear draught when adry,

As American Patriots,—our taste we deny,

Sylvania's gay Meadows can richly afford

To pamper our Fancy or furnish our Board.

And Paper sufficient (at home) still we have,

To assure the Wise-acre, we will not sign Slave;

When this Homespun shall fail, to remonstrate our Grief,

We can speak with the Tongue or scratch on a Leaf;

Refuse all their Colours, though richest of Dye,

The juice of a berry—our paint can supply,

To humor our fancy—and as for our Houses,

They'll do without painting as well as our Spouses;

While to keep out the Cold of a keen winter Morn,

We can screen the Northwest with a well polish'd Horn;

And trust Me a Woman, by honest Invention,

Might give this State Doctor a Dose of Prevention.

Join mutual in this, and but small as it seems,

We may jostle a Grenville, and puzzle his Schemes;

But a motive more worthy our patriot Pen,

Thus acting—we point out their Duty to Me;

And should the bound Pensioners, tell us to hush,

We can throw back the Satire by biding them blush.

---

[1] George Grenville (1712–1770), Prime Minister of Great Britain (1763–1765).

TWENTY-FOUR

Frances Moore Brooke (1725–1789)

*B*RITISH COLONISTS IN NORTH AMERICA OBSERVED THAT MANY NATIVE-AMERICAN SOCIETIES *enjoyed a decidedly different politics of gender than their own. Women were central to the cultural practices, cosmologies, diplomacies, and internal politics of many indigenous peoples. The* Gayanashagowa *or "Great Binding Law" of the Iroquois Confederacy—the Oneida, Seneca, Mohawk, Onandaga, Cayuga, and Tuscarora tribes of Northeastern North America—vested women with land rights and with the power to select tribal chiefs. (By comparison, according to English law, women were not permitted to own land except as widows.) Although many Anglo-colonial writers misunderstood the power and responsibility held by Native women and stereotyped them as "drudges," others saw in indigenous American communities an example of gender egalitarianism, as in this excerpt from* The History of Emily Montague *(1769), the first English-language novel to be published in Canada.*

Author Frances Brooke left her family home in Lincolnshire, England, at the age of 24 to become a writer. She moved to London, where she established herself among the leading literary circles of the day, produced plays, poems, essays, and translations, and published her own weekly magazine, The Old Maid *(1755–1756). In 1756, she married Rev. John Brooke, who soon deployed to Canada to serve as a chaplain to British armies at Quebec, then the capital city of New France. In 1763, following the end of the Seven Years' War between Britain and France and the signing of the Treaty of Paris, Quebec, Acadia, the Hudson Bay and Newfoundland all became British territories. Frances Brooke followed her husband to Canada in the tumultuous year of 1763, and there she wrote* The History of Emily Montague, *an epistolary novel relating an account of life in Quebec, including a description of its native Huron people, excerpted below. Brooke was one of the first in a long line of Anglo-American women to look to exemplary instances of the gender equality among North*

America's indigenous peoples. This part of the novel consists of a letter from a young Englishman stationed in Quebec to his sweetheart back in London.

FROM *THE HISTORY OF EMILY MONTAGUE* (1769)

Letter 11

To Miss Rivers, Clarges Street.

Quebec, Sept. 10.

But to my savages: other nations talk of liberty, they possess it; nothing can be more astonishing than to see a little village of about thirty or forty families, the small remains of the Hurons,[1] almost exterminated by long and continual war with the Iroquoise,[2] preserve their independence in the midst of an European colony consisting of seventy thousand inhabitants; yet the fact is true of the savages of Lorette;[3] they assert and they maintain that independence with a spirit truly noble. One of our company having said something which an Indian understood as a supposition that they had been subjects of France, his eyes struck fire, he stop'd him abruptly, contrary to their respectful and sensible custom of never interrupting the person who speaks, "You mistake, brother," said he; "we are subjects to no prince; a savage is free all over the world." And he spoke only truth; they are not only free as a people, but every individual is perfectly so. Lord of himself, at once subject and master, a savage knows no superior, a circumstance which has a striking effect on his behaviour; unawed by rank or riches, distinctions unknown amongst his own nation, he would enter as unconcerned, would possess all his powers as freely in the palace of an oriental monarch, as in the cottage of the meanest peasant: 'tis the species, 'tis man, 'tis his equal he respects, without regarding the gaudy trappings, the accidental advantages, to which polished nations pay homage.

I have taken some pains to develop their present, as well as past, religious sentiments, because the Jesuit missionaries have boasted so much of their conversion; and find they have rather engrafted a few of the most plain and simple truths of Christianity on their ancient superstitions, than exchanged one faith for another; they are baptized, and even submit to what they themselves call the yoke of confession, and worship according to the outward forms of the Romish church, the drapery of which

---

[1] Hurons: An indigenous nation, also known as Wendat or Wyandot, based originally in what are now the Canadian provinces of Ontario and Quebec.

[2] Iroquoise: The Iroquois Confederacy, comprised the Seneca, Mohawk, Cayuga, Onandaga, Oneida, and Tuscarora tribes, with home territories in upstate New York and central Canada.

[3] Lorette: Huron village near Quebec City.

cannot but strike minds unused to splendor; but their belief is very little changed, except that the women seem to pay great reverence to the Virgin, perhaps because flattering to the sex. They anciently believed in one God, the ruler and creator of the universe, whom they called the Great Spirit and the Master of Life; in the sun as his image and representative; in a multitude of inferior spirits and demons; and in a future state of rewards and punishments, or, to use their own phrase, in a country of souls. They reverenced the spirits of their departed heroes, but it does not appear that they paid them an religious adoration. Their morals were more pure, their manners more simple, than those of polished nations, except in what regarded the intercourse of the sexes: the young women before marriage were indulged in great libertinism, hid however under the most reserved and decent exterior. They held adultery in abhorrence, and with the more reason as their marriages were dissolvable at pleasure. The missionaries are said to have found no difficulty so great in gaining them to Christianity, as that of persuading them to marry for life: they regarded the Christian system of marriage as contrary to the laws of nature and reason; and asserted that, as the Great Spirit formed us to be happy, it was opposing his will, to continue together when otherwise.

The sex we have so unjustly excluded from power in Europe have a great share in the Huron government; the chief is chose by the matrons from amongst the nearest male relations, by the female line, of him he is to succeed; and is generally an aunt's or sister's son; a custom which, if we examine strictly into the principle on which it is founded, seems a little to contradict what we are told of the extreme chastity of the married ladies.

The power of the chief is extremely limited; he seems rather to advise his people as a father than command them as a master: yet, as his commands are always reasonable, and for the general good, no prince in the world is so well obeyed. They have a supreme council of ancients, into which every man enters of course at an age fixed, and another of assistants to the chief on common occasions, the members of which are like him elected by the matrons: I am pleased with this last regulation, as women are, beyond all doubt, the best judges of the merit of men; and I should be extremely pleased to see it adopted in England: canvassing for elections would then be the most agreeable thing in the world, and I am sure the ladies would give their votes on much more generous principles than we do. In the true sense of the word, we are the savages, who so impolitely deprive you of the common rights of citizenship, and leave you no power but that of which we cannot deprive you, the resistless power of your charms. By the way, I don't think you are obliged in conscience to obey laws you have had no share in making; your plea would certainly be at least as good as that of the Americans, about which we every day hear so much.

The Hurons have no positive laws; yet being a people not numerous, with a strong sense of honor, and in that state of equality which gives no food to the most tormenting passions of the human heart, and the council of ancients having a power to punish atrocious crimes, which power however they very seldom find occasion to use, they live together in a tranquillity and order which appears to us surprizing.

TWENTY-FIVE

Aspasia

*A*S MIDDLE-CLASS READERSHIPS GREW IN ENGLAND AND NORTH AMERICA, MAGAZINES *continued to serve as a forum for essays and dialogues on sexual politics. In 1768, the* Pennsylvania Magazine; or, American Monthly Museum, *published a series of essays written under the pen name "The Visitant" that offered observations and advice on the proper education and conduct of women: too much education, the anonymous author averred, would spoil women and unfit them for marriage. The series drew attention from leading figures in the flourishing women's intellectual circles of Philadelphia, including Annis Boudinot Stockton, who argued that a lack of education not the fact of their sex made women "so oft appear puerile and blind." Another woman responded to the Visitant under the pen name "Aspasia"; Aspasia (470 BCE–400 BCE) was an influential and highly regarded Athenian philosopher, consort of the ruler Pericles. Philadelphia's eighteenth-century Aspasia argued that bold, learned, and resourceful women made better wives and that, conversely, men who sought timid, ill-educated wives revealed weakness in their own character. One scholar has suggested that "Aspasia" was Elizabeth Graeme Ferguson (1737–1801), a Philadelphia writer and intellectual, famed for her learning and her intellectual salons. The exchange was reprinted in the* American Museum *in 1789.*

REPLY TO "THE VISITANT," NUMBER XI (1769)

Mr. Visitant,

The candid and kind manner, in which you treat both the errors and perfections of the female sex, must make every woman, who reads your paper with as good a heart, as you appear to have, when you write it, your admirer and friend. [. . .]

You endeavour to shew, what are the steps [for women] to attain esteem, and what to attain admiration. As far as I am a judge, the means are well calculated to gain their respective ends. But, sir, you must correct some faults in your own sex, before you can brighten the shades of ours. The ways you have pointed out, will, as I have just observed, secure us esteem; but at esteem we shall always stop.

When a worthy young woman, not without a share of sensibility in her composition, has attentively cultivated the virtues of the mind, and has improved herself in the several branches of education, with much resolution, and, on many occasions, with much self-denial—when, thus accomplished, she enters upon life, and mixes in a polite circle of both sexes—must it not give her a sensible mortification, to see a girl of sprightly levity, whose understanding, if she is pretty, is thought brilliant; whose tartness is styled elegant repartee; and rises only to what Pope calls "the pert low dialogue, scarce a degree above Swift's polite conversation"[1]—must it not mortify her to see such a one singled out, and draw the attention of men of merit, while she is passed by without notice? As for the *moths* of the season, that are always buzzing about, their neglect gives no uneasiness.

The men are extremely confined in their notions of our sex. It is true, they do not all express themselves in the coarse, inelegant, trite saying, "give me a wife, that can make a shirt, and a pudding;" but, indeed, Mr. Visitant, if you will be as candid as you have hitherto been, you will own, that this sentiment runs through the major part of the lordly race.

One would think, that they were throwing sarcasms on their own sex, when they draw the following conclusions—-that the more a woman's understanding is improved, the more apt she will be to despise her husband—that the strengthening of her reason will weaken her affection—that the duties of tenderness and attention, and all the social train, will be disregarded, in proportion as her knowledge is increased—that, to teach her God and nature, will, in the end, destroy all order, and domestic comfort. Good heavens! What subversions of truths are all these assertions! Does not the enlargement of the understanding point out the relative duties? And is not subordination to a husband, one of them? Does not reason as frequently rouse, as damp the affections?—Does not knowledge dilate and expand the finer feelings of the mind, and make it thrill in a thousand vibrations, unknown to the savage and untutored soul?—Do not God and nature lead us to a course of tender affections and

---

[1] "Pert low dialogue": A phrase from Pope's poem "Imitations of Horace", in which he criticizes the compositions of dramatist George Farquhar (1678–1707); Jonathan Swift published *Polite Conversation*, a satire on British manners posing as a social manual, in 1738.

pleasing duties, which can be practised only by one, whose mind is touched with ardent piety, and who can observe, with refined delight, the regular and beautiful order of the universe.

However, in gratitude to the generous few, that have condescended to treat us as reasonable beings, let us never forget that an Addison,[2] a Richardson,[3] and a Fordyce,[4] have not thought it beneath them, to point out, what is, and what is not, female excellence.

Hard, indeed, is that medium to be observed, which you mention in your ninth paper; and it only falls to the lot of a happy few, to answer the poet's elegant picture:

Favours to none, to all she smiles extends:

Oft she rejects; but never once offends.[5]

Howsoever pleasing timidity and implicit submission in us may be to your sex, yet what lord Halifax[6] observed, is very true; "that a woman who has not too much spirit on some occasions, will run the risque of having too little on others." As maids, as wives, and as widows, we meet with a thousand occasions in life, where fortitude and resolution are absolutely necessary. I would not wish a lady be a Camilla or a Thalestris;[7] but steadiness, to a degree of perseverance, is absolutely requisite in us. Before marriage, it is necessary, in the important point of dismissing or accepting lovers; for you know, sir, that is all a single woman has to do. After marriage, it is necessary in the education of children, and in regulating the more subordinate members of a family; for, as to a husband, it is a virtue, which must never peep out, where his lordly prerogative is concerned. And surely equally essential is it, in the lonely widowed state, where we have to act in so many different capacities.—In which of these classes the writer of this is, cannot be material; let it suffice, that, in your public character of Visitant, she is much your admirer.

ASPASIA.

---

[2] Joseph Addison (1672–1719): English essayist, author of the influential tragedy *Cato* (1712), and cofounder of the *Spectator* magazine.

[3] Samuel Richardson (1689–1761): English author of popular epistolary novels *Pamela: Or, Virtue Rewarded* (1740) and *Clarissa: Or, the History of a Young Lady* (1748).

[4] James Fordyce (1720–1796): British clergyman, author of *Sermons for Young Women* (1766).

[5] Lines from Alexander Pope, *Rape of the Lock* (1712), Canto 2, lines 11–12.

[6] Charles Montague, Earl of Halifax (1661–1715), English statesman and poet.

[7] Camilla and Thalestris are both warrior figures from classical mythology: Camilla was a servant of Diana; Thalestris was a leader of the Amazons and consort of Alexander the Great.

TWENTY-SIX

Phillis Wheatley (1753?–1784)

*N*O ONE KNOWS EXACTLY WHEN OR WHERE PHILLIS WHEATLEY WAS BORN, BUT WHEN SHE *arrived in Boston on July 11, 1761, on the decks of the slaveship* Phillis, *a small child slave wearing only a scrap of dirty carpet, her purchaser, John Wheatley, surmised that she was probably 6 or 7 years old because she was missing her two front teeth. Young Phillis was raised by the Wheatleys and soon taught to read and write. Within a few years, she was renowned in Boston for her ability to read the Bible and Greek and Latin classics, as well as for her knowledge of literature, geography, history, and astronomy. After publishing her first poem in a Newport, Rhode Island, newspaper in 1767, at the age of 12, Phillis became an active contributor to women's literary circles in Boston, giving domestic performances of her poems, and enlisting the support of white and Black women who commissioned, purchased, published, sold, and celebrated her poems. She published* Poems on Various Subjects, Religious and Moral, *a collection of thirty-nine poems, in London in 1773. It was the first volume of poetry ever published by an African-American woman. She traveled to London in support of her publication in 1773, and there managed to secure her own manumission, thanks to Lord Mansfield's ruling in the* Somerset *case of 1772, which declared that no slave brought to England from the British colonies could be compelled to return to the colonies a slave. After the death of her mistress Susannah Wheatley in 1774, Phillis for a time made a living from her writings. She married John Peters, a free Black man, in 1778, bore three children, none of whom survived, and died in childbirth in 1784.*

Many of Wheatley's poems focus on themes of loss and consolation. A few directly address issues of race and slavery, sometimes launching pointed criticisms of white privilege in coded and subtle ways. Her poem addressed "To the Right Honourable William, Earl of Dartmouth," partakes in the spirit of the American

Revolution, with Wheatley declaring a love of freedom rooted in her own experience as a slave. William Legge, Second Earl of Dartmouth (1731–1801), was Secretary of State for the British North American colonies (1772–1775); he also belonged to a network of evangelical Christians who supported Wheatley in her poetic career. We gain an even better understanding of Wheatley's views on slavery in her eloquent letter to the Reverend Samson Occom, a Native American Mohegan author, ordained Presbyterian minister, and friend of the Wheatley family, first published in the New London, Connecticut, Gazette *on March 11, 1774, and reprinted frequently thereafter in colonial newspapers. Wheatley also maintained a lengthy correspondence with Obour Tanner, an African-American woman in Newport, Rhode Island, forming what some scholars have called the first African-American women's writing community.*

"TO THE RIGHT HONOURABLE WILLIAM, EARL OF DARTMOUTH, HIS MAJESTY'S PRINCIPAL SECRETARY OF STATE FOR NORTH-AMERICA" (1773)

Hail, happy day, when, smiling like the morn,
Fair *Freedom* rose *New-England* to adorn:
The northern clime beneath her genial ray,
Dartmouth, congratulates thy blissful sway:
Elate with hope her race no longer mourns,
Each soul expands, each grateful bosom burns,
While in thine hand with pleasure we behold
The silken reins, and *Freedom's* charms unfold.
Long lost to realms beneath the northern skies
She shines supreme, while hated *faction* dies:
Soon as appear'd the *Goddess* long desir'd,
Sick at the view, she lanquish'd and expir'd;
Thus from the splendors of the morning light
The owl in sadness seeks the caves of night.

No more, *America*, in mournful strain
Of wrongs, and grievance unredress'd complain,
No longer shalt thou dread the iron chain,
Which wanton *Tyranny* with lawless hand
Had made, and with it meant t' enslave the land.

Should you, my lord, while you peruse my song,
Wonder from whence my love of *Freedom* sprung,
Whence flow these wishes for the common good,

By feeling hearts alone best understood,
I, young in life, by seeming cruel fate
Was snatch'd from *Afric's* fancy'd happy seat:
What pangs excruciating must molest,
What sorrows labour in my parent's breast?
Steel'd was that son and by no misery mov'd
That from a father seiz'd his babe belov'd:
Such, such my case. And can I then but pray
Others may never feel tyrannic sway?

For favours past, great Sir, our thanks are due,
And thee we ask thy favors to renew,
Since in thy pow'r, as in thy will before,
To sooth the griefs, which thou did'st once deplore.
May heav'nly race the sacred sanction give
To all thy works, and thou for ever live
Not only on the wings of fleeting *Fame*,
Though praise immortal crowns the patriot's name,
But to conduct to heav'ns refulgent fane,[1]
May fiery coursers sweep th' ethereal plain,
And bear thee upwards to that blest abode,
Where, like the prophet, thou shalt find thy God.

LETTER TO SAMSON OCCOM (1774)

Feb. 11, 1774

Reverend and honoured Sir,

I have this day received your obliging kind epistle, and am greatly satisfied with your reasons respecting the negroes, and think highly reasonable what you offer in vindication of their natural rights: Those that invade them cannot be insensible that the divine light is chasing away the thick darkness which broods over the land of Africa; and the chaos which has reigned so long, is converting into beautiful order, and reveals more and more clearly the glorious dispensation of civil and religious liberty, which are so inseparably united, that there is little or no enjoyment of one without the other: Otherwise, perhaps, the Israelites had been less solicitous for their

---

[1] Fane: Temple or shrine.

freedom from Egyptian slavery; I do not say they would have been contented without it, by no means; for in every human breast God has implanted a principle which we call love of freedom; it is impatient of oppression, and pants for deliverance; and by the leave of our modern Egyptians I will assert, that the same principle lives in us. God grant deliverance in his own way and time, and get him honour upon all those whose avarice impels them to countenance and help forward the calamities of their fellow creatures. This I desire not for their hurt, but to convince them of the strange absurdity of their conduct, whose words and actions are so diametrically opposite. How well the cry for liberty, and the reverse disposition for the exercise of oppressive power over others agree—I humbly think not require the penetration of a philosopher to determine.

TWENTY-SEVEN

Mercy Otis Warren (1728–1814)

*L*IKE PHILLIS WHEATLEY, MERCY OTIS WARREN LIVED IN BOSTON DURING THE HEIGHT OF *the American Revolution and witnessed the city's occupation by British forces. As a white woman born into a socially connected family, she had the privilege of moving among intellectual and political leaders of the Revolution. Born in West Barnstable, Massachusetts, she received no formal education but was tutored, along with her brother James Otis (later a leader in the agitation against the Stamp Act) at the home of the local pastor. She participated actively in revolutionary causes alongside her brother and her husband, James Warren, a member of the Massachusetts House of Representatives. An acclaimed epistolary author, she also exchanged letters with both Abigail and John Adams and a coterie of elite American women.*

The correspondence between Mercy Otis Warren and Catharine Macaulay (whose writing also appears in this anthology) began in 1773, and liberty, the American Revolution, and their shared view of Britain's government as corrupt and oppressive were frequent topics. Otis Warren, an admirer of Macaulay's multivolume History of England, *initiated their relationship with something akin to a fan letter. Herself a published author of political plays, she saw much to emulate in this woman whom she addressed as an "incomparable female patriot." Otis Warren's 1788 pamphlet, "Observations on the New Constitution," was an influence on the design and adoption of the Bill of Rights. In 1805, Otis Warren published her own history, titled* History of the Rise, Progress, and Termination of the American Revolution, *thus placing her name among the transatlantic ranks of women historians and helping to confirm women as patriots.*

LETTER TO CATHARINE SAWBRIDGE MACAULAY (1774)[1]

Plimouth N.E. December 29 1774

Dear Madame

Your kind Notice of my last Emboldens me again to Interrupt your more important pursuits by offering my Warmest acknowledgments for the Expressions of personal Regard contained in your agreable Favour of Sept 11th as well as for your Generous Attention to the publick Calamities of my Country.

Though I never imagined that while you were Researching the Records of time & by your Elegant pen Exhibiting to the World the most striking traits of former Tyrants, you was inattentive to the living Agents of a Corrupt Court: who have been long forming a system of Despotism that should Reach beyond the Atlantic & involve this Extensive Continent in the same Thralldom that Awaits the Miserable Asiatic.

But how Absurd will the plans of modern policy appear when the faithful Historian shall transmit to posterity the late Manoeuvres of a British Administration: when they shall Behold them plunging the Nation still deeper in an immense debte, Equiping her Fleets to Harrass the Coasts, & her armies to insult & subjugate these loyal & populous Colonies, who (from the first settlement of this once dreary Wilderness to the mad project of shuting up the port of Boston,) have been Voluntarily pouring their treasures into the Lap of Britain.

Will not succeeding generations be Astonished when told that this Maritime City was Blokaded at a period when her Commercial interests were closely interwoven with those of Britain, when the Tracts of Cultivated Lands on this Continent, acknowledging the sceptre of Brunswick were almost immeasurable, & when at the same time they boasted their united Millions Ready to pour out the Warm Blood as a Libation at the shrine of Freedom ere they would submit to become the slaves of Arbitrary power?

But tho America stands Armed with Resolution and Virtue, she still Recoils at the thought of Drawing the sword against the state from whence she derived her Origen, tho that state like an unnatural parent has plung'd her dagger into the Bosom of her affectionate offspring.

But may I not hope to hear from you Madam, who can easily Delineate their Characters that the New parliment principly Consists of men of more conciliating tempers, of men who inherit the glorious spirit which distinguished their Noble Ancestors: & stimulated them to stand forth as the Barriers of English Liberty in the most perilous seasons: yet such is the prevailing Luxury & Dissipation of the times,

---

[1] GLC 01800.01 Courtesy of The Gilder Lehrman Collection, The Gilder Lehrman Institute of American History. Not to be reproduced without written permission.

such the undue influence of the Crown from the tribes of placemen, Pensioners, & Dependants (Backed with a large standing army, that Nursery of slavery & Vice, that Bane of Every free state) that I fear there is little Reason to Expect it.

But if the Majority of the Commons still continue the Dupes of Venality and Corruption, they will soon see the Genius which once Animated their Hambdens, Haringtons, & Pyms,[2] has taken up her Residence on these Distant shores.

The seeds of Empire are sown in this new World, the Ball Rolls Westward fast,[3] and though daily threatned with the incursion of savages: & the Depredations of foreign auxilliries, yet each City from Nova Scotia to Georgia has her Decii & her Fabii:[4] Ready to Sacrifice their Devoted Lives to preserve inviolate & to convey to their Children the inherent Rights of Men, confered on all by the God of Nature, and the priviledges of English men claimed by Americans from the sacred sanctions of Compacts.

It is not possible for me Madam to give you an Adequate Idea of the situation of this Country, 'tho doubtless it will be done by some more able pen.

The Boston port Bill ocasions such A stagnation of commerce as is felt in Every Villa of the Massachusets. The Bill for altering the Constitution has Reduced the province to a state of Nature. The Legislative Body is prevented meeting, the Executive officers Rendered incapable of acting, & the Courts of justice shut up. Nothing but the Virtue of this people prevents our Daily feeling the Dreadful Consequences of Anarchy in the Exstream.[5]

---

[2] John Hampden (1594–1643) was Oliver Cromwell's cousin and a parliamentary army officer. James Harrington (1611–1677) wrote *The Commonwealth of Oceana* (1656) and other political works, all of which advocate a republican form of government. John Pym (1584–1643) led the opposition against Charles I and the organization of the parliamentary army.

[3] Here, Warren seems to be referencing the theory of *translatio imperii*, which interprets the history of empires as a series of successions in which power and divine favor move westward. Almost simultaneously with the composition of this letter, Macaulay published the pamphlet *An Address to the People of England, Scotland and Ireland on the Present Important Crisis of Affairs* and warned her audience that a "civil war" with the colonies would result in a shifting of prosperity and liberty to America.

[4] Her Decii & her Fabii: The Roman consuls Publius Decius Mus and Fabius Maximus Rullianus, Quintus, heroes of the 295 BCE Battle of Sentium. Decius supposedly sacrificed himself by charging the enemy. "Decii" and "Fabii" are thus individuals willing to serve the public good, even at great personal cost.

[5] In this paragraph, Warren is discussing the Intolerable Acts of 1774. They were passed in response to the Boston Tea Party, and were intended to isolate that region's rebelliousness. They included the Boston Port Act, which temporarily closed the Boston port, and the Massachusetts Government Act, which created a crown-appointed council to replace the one elected by colonists. For Warren, these acts were especially intolerable, since she feared her husband James Warren, a politician who had helped formulate plans for the Continental Congress, was being sought as a traitor by British officials under the authority of these acts.

Heaven only knows how long we can continue in this state. But such is the Ferocity of Human Nature that it is not to be expected society can subsist long without some Government which may finally drive us to assume such a form as is most consistent with the taste & genius of a free people.

Ere this Reaches your Hand you will doubtless have seen the Resolves of the provincial & the result of the Continental Congress. Perhaps there never was any Human Law to which Mankind so Religiously & So generally Adhered as the Americans do to the Resolutions of those Assemblys.[6]

And now a firm, undaunted, persevering people, (with the sword half Drawn from the scabard) are patiently waiting the Effects of those measures.

The Vigorous spirit that universally Reigns, the Determined oppo[s]ition to the strides of Wanton power, & the unshaken union of the American Colonies is so Remarkable that I think we must Ascribe it to the Divine Agency of a superintending providence. But what are the grand designs of the Almighty Governour of the universe, or what the important Events, the present Comotions will produce time only can only disclose, but if pacific Measures do not soon take place, none can wonder that a timid Woman should tremble for the consequences, more especially one who is connected by the tenderest tie to a Gentleman whose principles & conduct in this province may Expose him to fall an Early Victim, either in the day of Battle, or by the Vindictive Hand of Lawless power.

Will you pardon me Madam if I own that my Apprehensions are sometimes Awake least Britain should be infatuated enough to push the unhappy Americans to the last appeal. I behold the civil sword Brandish'd over our Heads & an innocent Land Drenched in Blood. I see the inhabitants of our plundered cities quitting the Elegancies of life, possesing nothing but their Freedom, taking refuge in the Forests. I Behold Faction & Discard tearing up an Island we once held dear as our own inheritance, and A Mighty Empire (long the dread of distant Nations) tottering to the very Foundation.

Forgive dear Madam & I draw a Veil over the painful Revire.

It gives me particular pleasure to hear that your Worthy Brother is reelected a Member of parliment. Mr Sawbridge[7] has been often Mentioned with Respect & Gratitude at the social Boards of the American patriots, & when assured by his good sister that he will still continue an Advocate to the injured, we thank her for the communication,

---

[6] In response to the Intolerable Acts, the colonies formed the Continental Congress and resolved to boycott British goods.

[7] John Sawbridge (1732–1795) was Macaulay's brother and a member of the British Parliament who supported the American cause.

And ardently wish that his Laudable Example might fire the Breasts of a certain August Assembly to do that justice, which not only the Colonies Wish but Every Honest Man in Europe must Expect.

I am Exstreamly obliged by your kind Remembrance of an unhappy man[8] once the pride of his numerous friends & a principle supporter of the invaded Rights of his Country. But Heaven who bestows superior intelects has a right to limit the Duration, and so inscrutable are the ways of providence that the Vilest instruments are often permited to work the Ruin of the individual to undermine the Happiness of the State. The truth of the first I feel in an instance too painful to mention, & the tears of all America Witness the Last: traduced & misrepresented as she has been by men that were Bound by all the ties of Honour, Gratitude, and Humanity to Defend her.

Were not the peculiar Circumstances of the times some Apology, yet from your Candor Madam I should Expect a pardon for the length of this Letter, & as a proof therof may I hope for the indulgence of a few more of your Excellent Sentiments & judicious observations in the next I am favoured with from you, but whatever Cause may prevent or postpone me that pleasure, may your want of Health be the Last. Heaven grant you the confirmation & long continuance [of] that invaluable Blessing with the Addition of every other Felicity that life can Boast.

And if the lowering Cloud which now darkens the American Hemisphere should pass over & a more Bright and Tranquil prospect appear, May you be able to gladen with A visit your Admiring Friends in this quarter of the Globe.

Among which there is no one who [can] subscribe

With More Respect & Affe[ction] than your

very Humble [serv]ant,

Mercy Warren

---

[8] An unhappy man: James Otis, Jr. (1725–1783), Warren's brother. Though in the 1760s he was a prominent Republican voice, he had lost his influence by 1774 due to mental illness and public instability.

TWENTY-EIGHT

Thomas Paine (1737–1809)

*T*HE WRITINGS OF THE GREAT ENGLISH RADICAL PAMPHLETEER AND REVOLUTIONARY *Thomas Paine radiated influence around the Atlantic world during the Age of Revolutions. Paine himself exemplified transatlantic radicalism, as he emigrated from England to America on the eve of the American Revolution, in 1774, and to France just after the Revolution there in 1791. His tremendously influential pamphlet* Common Sense *(1776), which was after the Bible the best-selling book in eighteenth-century America, advocated American independence from Great Britain; his treatise* The Rights of Man *(1791) influenced the French Revolution and helped win Paine a seat at the French National Convention in 1792. An opponent of slavery and monarchy, a deist, freethinker, and republican, Paine distilled from Enlightenment thought a political view that liberty was the natural right of all human beings. His concern extended to the situation of women, addressed here in this "Occasional Letter on the Female Sex," published anonymously under Paine's editorship in the* Pennsylvania Magazine *in August 1775. (Some scholars have argued that the "Occasional Letter" was not written by Paine himself but instead is a translation of* Essai sur le Caractere, les Mouers, et l'Esprit des Femmes dans les Differens Siecles, *by the French author M. Antoine Leonard Thomas, published in Paris in 1772 and translated and republished in Philadelphia in 1774.) Citing "data" gathered worldwide by colonial historians, philosophers, and scientists, the "Letter" argues that the oppression of women is universal: "Over three quarters of the globe nature has placed them between contempt and misery." Despite Paine's cosmopolitanism, several of the observations made here partake in what were by the 1770s well-established colonialist stereotypes of indigenous North American women as "drudges" and Asian women as inmates of the "seraglio." As was also conventional in the emerging field of anthropology in the late eighteenth century, the author of the "Letter" attempts to ascribe*

the treatment of women in various parts of the globe to differences in climate and
their effects on the human temperament and passions. Articulate in its plea for the
better treatment of women, the "Letter" notably does not recommend expanded
access to education as a remedy for inequality, a mainstay of feminist argument since
the early seventeenth century.

"AN OCCASIONAL LETTER ON THE FEMALE SEX" (1775)

"O Woman! lovely Woman!
Nature made thee to temper man,
We had been Brutes without you."

—Otway[1]

If we take a survey of ages and of countries, we shall find the women, almost—
without exception—at all times and in all places, adored and oppressed. Man, who
has never neglected an opportunity of exerting his power, in paying homage to their
beauty, has always availed himself of their weakness. He has been at once their
tyrant and their slave.

Nature herself, in forming beings so susceptible and tender, appears to have been
more attentive to their charms than to their happiness. Continually surrounded with
griefs and fears, the women more than share all our miseries, and are besides subjected
to ills which are peculiarly their own. They cannot be the means of life without ex-
posing themselves to the loss of it; every revolution which they undergo, alters their
health, and threatens their existence. Cruel distempers attack their beauty—and the
hour, which confirms their release from those, is perhaps the most melancholy of their
lives. It robs them of the most essential characteristic of their sex. They can then only
hope for protection from the humiliating claims of pity, or the feeble voice of gratitude.

Society, instead of alleviating their condition, is to them the source of new miseries. More than one half of the globe is covered with savages; and among all these
people women are completely wretched. Man, in a state of barbarity, equally cruel
and indolent, active by necessity, but naturally inclined to repose, is acquainted with
little more than the physical effects of love; and, having none of those moral ideas
which only can soften the empire of force, he is led to consider it as his supreme law,
subjecting to his despotism those whom reason had made his equal, but whose

---

[1] Thomas Otway (1652–1685): English Restoration dramatist; these lines are from his play *Venice*
Preserved (1682).

imbecility betrayed them to his strength. "Nothing" (says Professor Miller, speaking of the women of barbarous nations) "can exceed the dependence and subjection in which they are kept, or the toll and drudgery which they are obliged to undergo.—The husband, when he is not engaged in some warlike exercise, indulges himself in idleness, and devolves upon his wife the whole burden of his domestic affairs. He disdains to assist her in any of those servile employments. She sleeps in a different bed, and is seldom permitted to have any conversation or correspondence with him."

The women among the Indians of America are what the Helots were among the Spartans, a vanquished people, obliged to toil for their conquerors. Hence on the banks of the Oroonoko[2], we have seen mothers slaying their daughters out of compassion, and smothering them in the hour of their birth. They consider this barbarous pity as a virtue.

"The men (says Commodore Byron,[3] in his account of the inhabitants of South-America) exercise a most despotic authority over their wives, whom they consider in the same view they do any other part of their property, and dispose of them accordingly: Even their common treatment of them is cruel; for though the toll and hazard of procuring food lies entirely on the women, yet they are not suffered to touch any part of it till the husband is satisfied; and then he assigns them their portion, which is generally very scanty, and such as he has not a stomach for himself."

Among the nations of the East we find another kind of despotism and dominion prevail—the Seraglio,[4] and the domestic servitude of woman, authorised by the manners and established by the laws. In Turkey, in Persia, in India, in Japan, arid over the vast empire of China, one half of the human species is oppressed by the other.

The excess of oppression in those countries springs from the excess of love.

All Asia is covered with prisons, where beauty in bondage waits the caprices of master. The multitude of women there assembled have no will, no inclinations but his: Their triumphs are only for a moment; and their rivalry, their hate, and their animosities, continue till death. There the lovely sex are obliged to repay even their servitude with the most tender affections; or, what is still more mortifying, with the counterfeit of an affection, which they do not feel: There the most gloomy tyranny has subjected them to creatures, who, being of neither sex, are a dishonour to both:

---

[2] Oroonoko: The Orinoco is a major river in South America and the site of frequent exploration by European colonists; the word came to signify any foreign place or person deemed exotic, as when Aphra Behn used it as the name of the West African protagonist in her novel *Oroonoko: or, The Royal Slave* (1688).

[3] John Byron (1723–1786), author of *An Account of a Voyage Round the World* (1778).

[4] Seraglio: A harem, or living quarters for wives and concubines. See p.265, note 2

There, in short, their education tends only to debase them; their virtues are forced; their very pleasures are involuntary and joyless; and after an existence of a few years—till the bloom of youth is over—their period of neglect commences, which is long and dreadful. In the temperate latitude where the climates, giving less ardour to passion, leave more confidence in virtue, the women have not been deprived of their liberty, but a severe legislation has, at all times, kept them in a state of dependence. One while, they were confined to their own apartments, and debarred at once from business and amusement; at other times, a tedious guardianship defrauded their hearts, and insulted their understandings. Affronted in one country by polygamy, which gives them their rivals for their inseparable companions; inslaved in another by indissoluble ties, which often join the gentle to the rude, and sensibility to brutality: Even in countries where they may be esteemed most happy, constrained in their desires in the disposal of their goods, robbed of freedom of will by the laws, the slaves of opinion, which rules them with absolute sway, and construes the slightest appearances into guilt; surrounded on all sides by judges, who are at once tyrants and their seducers, and who, after having prepared their faults, punish every lapse with dishonour—nay, usurp the right of degrading them on suspicion! Who does not feel for the tender sex? Yet such, I am sorry to say, is the lot of woman over the whole earth. Man with regard to them, in all climates, and in all ages, has been either an insensible husband or an oppressor; but they have sometimes experienced the cold and deliberate oppression of pride, and sometimes the violent and terrible tyranny of jealousy. When they are not beloved they are nothing; and, when they are, they are tormented. They have almost equal cause to be afraid of indifference and of love. Over three quarters of the globe nature has placed them between contempt and misery.

"The melting desires, or the fiery passions," says Professor Ferguson, "which in one climate take place between the sexes, are, in another, changed into a sober consideration, or a patience of mutual disgust. This change is remarked in crossing the Mediterranean, in following the course of the Mississippi, in ascending the mountains of Caucasus, and in passing from the Alps and the Pyrenees to the shores of the Baltic.

"The burning ardours and torturing jealousies of the Seraglio and Harem, which have reigned so long in Asia and Africa, and which, in the southern parts of Europe, have scarcely given way to the differences of religion and civil establishments, are found, however, with an abatement of heat in the climate, to be more easily changed, in one latitude, into a temporary passion, which engrosses the mind without infeebling it, and which excites to romantic achievements. By a farther progress to the north it is changed into a spirit of gallantry, which employs the wit and fancy more than the heart, which prefers intrigue to enjoyment, and substitutes affection and vanity where sentiment and desire have failed. As it departs from the sun, the same passion is farther, composed into a habit of domestic connection, or frozen into a state of insensibility, under which the sexes at freedom scarcely choose to unite their society."

Even among people where beauty received the highest homage, we find men who would deprive the sex of every kind of reputation: "The most virtuous woman," says a celebrated Greek, "is she who is least talked of." That morose man, while he imposes duties upon women, would deprive them of the sweets of public esteem, and in exacting virtues from them, would make it a crime to aspire at honour.

If a woman were to defend the cause of her sex, she might address him in the following manner:

"How great is your injustice? If we have an equal right with you to virtue, who should we not have an equal right to praise? The public esteem ought to wait upon merit. Our duties are different from yours, but they are not therefore less difficult to fulfil, or of less consequence to society: They are the fountains of your felicity, and the sweetness of life. We are wives and mothers. 'Tis we who form the union and the cordiality of families: 'Tis we who soften that savage rudeness which considers everything as due to force, and which would involve man with man in eternal war. We cultivate in you that humanity which makes you feel for the misfortunes of others, and our tears forewarn you of your own danger. Nay, you cannot be ignorant that we have need of courage not less than you: More feeble in ourselves, we have perhaps more trials to encounter. Nature assails us with sorrow, law and custom press us with constraint, and sensibility and virtue alarm us with their continual conflict. Sometimes also the name of citizen demands from us the tribute of fortitude. When you offer your blood to the State think that it is ours. In giving it our sons and our husbands we give more than ourselves. You can only die on the field of battle, but we have the misfortune to survive those whom we love most. Alas! while your ambitious vanity is unceasingly labouring to cover the earth with statues, with monuments, and with inscriptions to eternize, if possible, your names, and give yourselves an existence, when this body is no more, why must we be condemned to live and to die unknown? Would that the grave and eternal forgetfulness should be our lot. Be not our tyrants in all: Permit our names to be sometimes pronounced beyond the narrow circle in which we live: Permit friendship, or at least love, to inscribe its emblems on the tomb where our ashes repose; and deny us not that public esteem which, after the esteem of one's self, is the sweetest reward of well doing."

All men, however, it must be owned, have not been equally unjust to their fair companions. In some countries public honours have been paid to women. Art has erected them monuments. Eloquence has celebrated their virtues, and History has collected whatever could adorn their character.

TWENTY-NINE

Thomas Jefferson (1743–1826)

*I*N 1776, OVER A YEAR AFTER THE OUTBREAK OF MILITARY CONFLICT IN THE AMERICAN *Revolution, Thomas Jefferson drafted the Declaration of Independence at the behest of the Continental Congress and in collaboration with several others, including Benjamin Franklin and John Adams. On July 4, Congress made some revisions, including the deletion of a condemnation of slavery, and approved the Declaration. Within days, it appeard in newspapers such as the* Pennsylvania Evening Post *(whose version is included here) and was read aloud in a variety of venues to the cheers of soldiers and citizens alike. The document famously declares that "all men are created equal" and that they are "endowed, by their Creator" with the "unalienable rights" of "life, liberty and the pursuit of happiness." The concrete meanings of these words, including the potentially universal "men," remained undefined. This perhaps purposeful vagueness stirred not only elite white male patriots but also those marginalized on the basis of gender, class, race, sexuality, and religion to engage in audacious imaginings about the possibilities of their own liberty and equality. Indeed, although the* Declaration *failed to take up issues of slavery and women's rights and included language disparaging of American Indians, its inspiring rhetoric would be claimed by all of these groups as their revolutionary struggles continued through the nineteenth and twentieth centuries.*

DECLARATION OF INDEPENDENCE (1776)

In CONGRESS, July 4, 1776.

A Declaration by the Representatives of the United States of America, in General Congress assembled.

WHEN, in the course of human events, it becomes necessary for one people to dissolve the political bands which have connected them with another, and to assume, among the powers of the earth, the separate and equal station to which the laws of nature and of nature's God intitle them, a decent respect to the opinions of mankind requires that they should declare the causes which impel them to the separation.

We hold these truths to be self-evident, That all men are created equal; that they are endowed, by their Creator, with certain unalienable rights; that among these are life, liberty and the pursuit of happiness. That to secure these rights, governments are instituted among men, deriving their just powers from the consent of the governed; that whenever any form of government becomes destructive of these ends, it is the right of the people to alter or to abolish it, and to institute new government, laying its foundation on such principles, and organizing its powers in such form, as to them shall seem most likely to effect their safety and happiness. Prudence, indeed, will dictate that governments long established should not be changed for light and transient causes; and accordingly all experience hath shewn, that mankind are more disposed to suffer, while evils are sufferable, than to right themselves by abolishing the forms to which they are accustomed. But when a long train of abuses and usurpations, pursuing invariably the same object, evinces a design to reduce them under absolute despotism, it is their right, it is their duty, to throw off such government, and to provide new guards for their future security. Such has been the patient sufferance of these colonies, and such is now the necessity which constrains them to alter their former systems of government. The history of the present King of Great Britain is a history of repeated injuries and usurpations, all having in direct object the establishment of an absolute tyranny over these states. To prove this, let facts be submitted to a candid world.

He has refused his assent to laws, the most wholesome and necessary for the public good.

He has forbidden his Governors to pass laws of immediate and pressing importance, unless suspended in their operation till his assent should be obtained; and, when so suspended, he has utterly neglected to attend to them.

He has refused to pass other laws for the accommodation of large districts of people, unless those people would relinquish the right of representation in the legislature, a right inestimable to them, and formidable to tyrants only.

He has called together legislative bodies at places unusual, uncomfortable, and distant from the depository of their public records, for the sole purpose of fatiguing them into compliance with his measures.

He has dissolved Representative Houses repeatedly, for opposing with manly firmness his invasions on the rights of the people.

He has refused for a long time, after such dissolutions, to cause others to be elected; whereby the legislative powers, incapable of annihilation, have returned to the people at large for their exercise; the state remaining in the mean time exposed to all the dangers of invasion from without, and convulsions within.

He has endeavoured to prevent the population of these states; for that purpose obstructing the laws for naturalization of foreigners; refusing to pass others to encourage their migrations hither, and raising the conditions of new appropriations of lands.

He has obstructed the administration of justice, by refusing his assent to laws for establishing judiciary powers.

He has made Judges dependant on his will alone, for the tenure of their offices, and the amount and payment of their salaries.

He has erected a multitude of new offices, and sent hither swarms of officers to harass our people, and eat out their substance.

He has kept among us, in times of peace, standing armies, without the consent of our legislatures.

He has affected to render the military independant of and superior to the civil power.

He has combined with others to subject us to a jurisdiction foreign to our constitution, and unacknowledged by our laws; giving his assent to their acts of pretended legislation:

For quartering large bodies of armed troops among us:

For protecting them, by a mock trial, from punishment for any murders which they should commit on the inhabitants of these states:

For cutting off our trade with all parts of the world:

For imposing taxes on us without our consent:

For depriving us, in many cases, of the benefits of trial by jury:

For transporting us beyond seas to be tried for pretended offences:

For abolishing the free system of English laws in a neighbouring province, establishing therein an arbitrary government, and enlarging its boundaries, so as to render it at once an example and fit instrument for introducing the same absolute rule into these Colonies

For taking away our charters, abolishing our most valuable laws, and altering fundamentally the forms of our governments:

For suspending our own legislatures, and declaring themselves invested with power to legislate for us in all cases whatsoever.

He has abdicated government here by declaring us out of his protection and waging war against us.

He has plundered our seas, ravaged our coasts, burnt our towns, and destroyed the lives of our people.

He is, at this time, transporting large armies of foreign mercenaries to complete the works of death, desolation, and tyranny, already begun with circumstances of cruelty and perfidy scarcely paralleled in the most barbarous ages, and totally unworthy the head of a civilized nation.

He has constrained our fellow citizens taken captive on the high seas to bear arms against their country, to become the executioners of their friends and brethren, or to fall themselves by their hands.

He has excited domestic insurrections amongst us, and has endeavoured to bring on the inhabitants of our frontiers the merciless Indian Savages, whose known rule of warfare is an undistinguished destruction of all ages, sexes and conditions.

In every stage of these oppressions we have petitioned for redress in the most humble terms: Our repeated petitions have been answered only by repeated injury. A Prince, whose character is thus marked by every act which may define a tyrant, is unfit to be the ruler of a free people.

Nor have we been wanting in attentions to our British brethren. We have warned them from time to time of attempts by their legislature to extend an unwarrantable jurisdiction over us. We have reminded them of the circumstances of our emigration and settlement here. We have appealed to their native justice and magnanimity, and we have conjured them by the ties of our common kindred to disavow these usurpations, which would inevitably interrupt our connexions and correspondence. They too have been deaf to the voice of justice and of consanguinity. We must, therefore, acquiesce in the necessity, which denounces our separation, and hold them, as we hold the rest of mankind, enemies in war, in peace, friends.

We, therefore, the Representatives of the UNITED STATES OF AMERICA, in GENERAL CONGRESS assembled, appealing to the Supreme Judge of the world for the rectitude of our intentions, do, in the name, and by authority of the good people of these colonies, solemnly publish and declare, that these United Colonies are, and of right ought to be, FREE AND INDEPENDANT STATES; that they are absolved from all allegiance to the British Crown, and that all political connexion between them and the state of Great-Britain is and ought to be totally dissolved; and that, as FREE AND INDEPENDANT STATES, they have full power to levy war, conclude peace, contract alliances, establish commerce, and to do all other acts and things which INDEPENDANT STATES may of right do. And for the support of this declaration, with a firm reliance on the protection of Divine Providence, we mutually pledge to each other our lives, our fortunes, and our sacred honor.

THIRTY

Abigail Smith Adams (1744–1818)

*H*OW DOES IT FEEL TO BE AT THE FOREFRONT OF A REVOLUTION THAT DOES NOT RECOGNIZE *or honor your rights as a female citizen? The letters of the diplomat and political thinker Abigail Smith Adams of Massachusetts and her husband, the American statesman John Adams (1735–1826), reveal how the deep gender contradictions of the American Revolution were lived at their most personal level. Born into a prominent family of liberal Congregationalist clergy in Massachusetts, Abigail Smith was educated at home and in her family's private libraries. She met Harvard-educated lawyer John Adams in 1759, and the two were married in 1764. Both John and Abigail were deeply involved in the boycotts, organizing, and other activities leading up to the American Revolution. John represented Massachusetts at the Continental Congresses held in the 1770s to coordinate strategy among the rebelling British North American colonies and hammer out the political foundations of a new nation. Throughout this time, as the letters show, John and Abigail wrote each other frequently, engaging in a frank, confident exchange of political ideas and strategically sensitive information. (Over the course of their courtship and marriage, the two wrote more than 1,100 letters to one another.) The spirit of the Adams marriage was deeply egalitarian. John valued Abigail's perspectives and ideas, even as he responded with chiding humor to her demand that the male framers of American nationhood abandon the "Natural Tyranny" of their sex and "Remember the Ladies" as full partners in American nationalism. For her part, Abigail did not allow the egalitarianism she enjoyed at home to dull her own sharp critical awareness of the unequal status of women generally in revolutionary America. Abigail discussed the question of women's political rights in the new republic with her friend Mercy Otis Warren (whose writings are also included in this anthology) in letters she signed "Portia," a reference to the wise judge in Shakespeare's* The Merchant of Venice. *We* include one of those letters below. After the Revolution, John Adams served as president of the United States (1797–1801); the couple's son, John Quincy Adams, also served as president (1825–1829).

LETTER TO JOHN ADAMS, MARCH 31, 1776

. . . I long to hear that you have declared an independancy—and by the way in the new Code of Laws which I suppose it will be necessary for you to make I desire you would Remember the Ladies, and be more generous and favourable to them than your ancestors. Do not put such unlimited power into the hands of the Husbands. Remember all Men would be tyrants if they could. If perticuliar care and attention is not paid to the Ladies we are determined to foment a Rebelion, and will not hold ourselves bound by any Laws in which we have no voice, or Representation. That your Sex are Naturally Tyrannical is a Truth so thoroughly established as to admit of no dispute, but such of you as wish to be happy willingly give up the harsh title of Master for the more tender and endearing one of Friend. Why then, not put it out of the power of the vicious and the Lawless to use us with cruelty and indignity with impunity. Men of Sense in all Ages abhor those customs which treat us only as the vassals of your Sex. Regard us then as Beings placed by providence under your protection and in immitation of the Supreem Being make use of that power only for our happiness.

LETTER FROM JOHN ADAMS TO ABIGAIL ADAMS, APRIL 14, 1776

As to Declarations of Independency, be patient. Read our Privateering Laws, and our Commercial Laws. What signifies a Word. As to your extraordinary Code of Laws, I cannot but laugh. We have been told that our Struggle has loosened the bands of Government every where. That Children and Apprentices were disobedient—that schools and Colledges were grown turbulent—that Indians slighted their Guardians and Negroes grew insolent to their Masters. But your Letter was the first Intimation that another Tribe more numerous and powerfull than all the rest were grown discontented.—This is rather too coarse a Compliment but you are so saucy, I wont blot it out.

Depend upon it, We know better than to repeal our Masculine systems. Altho they are in full Force, you know they are little more than Theory. We dare not exert our Power in its full Latitude. We are obliged to go fair, and softly, and in Practice you know We are the subjects. We have only the Name of Masters, and rather than give up this, which would compleatly subject Us to the Despotism of the Peticoat, I hope

General Washington,[1] and all our brave Heroes would fight. I am sure every good Politician would plot, as long as he would against Despotism, Empire, Monarchy, Aristocracy, Oligarchy, or Ochlocracy.[2]—A fine Story indeed. I begin to think the Ministry[3] as deep as they are wicked. After stirring up Tories, Landjobbers,[4] Trimmers,[5] Bigots, Canadians, Indians, Negroes, Hanoverians, Hessians, Russians, Irish Roman Catholicks, Scotch Renegadoes, at last they have stimulated the [women] to demand new Priviledges and threaten to rebell.

LETTER TO MERCY OTIS WARREN, APRIL 27, 1776

Braintree. *April 27, 1776*

I set myself down to comply with my Friend's request who I think seems rather low spirited.

I did write last week, but not meeting with an early conveyance I thought the Letter of but little importance and tossed it away. I acknowledge my Thanks due to my Friend for the entertainment she so kindly afforded me in the Characters drawn in her Last Letter, and if coveting my Neighbour's Goods was not prohibited by the Sacred Law, I should be most certainly tempted to envy her the happy talent she possesses above the rest of her Sex, by adorning with her pen even trivial occurances, as well as Dignifying the most important.[6] Cannot you communicate some of those Graces to your Friend and suffer her to pass them upon the World for her own, that she may feel a Little more upon an Equality with you? 'Tis true I often receive large packages from P[hiladelphi]a. They contain, as I said before, more Newspapers than Letters. Tho they are not forgotten, it would be hard indeed if absence had not some alleviations.

I dare say he writes to no one unless to Portia oftener than to your Friend, because I know there is no one besides in whom he has an equal confidence.[7] His letters to me have been generally short; but he pleads in Excuse the critical State of Affairs and the

---

[1] George Washington (1732–1799): Commander in chief of American Revolutionary forces and first president of the United States (1789–1797).

[2] Oclochracy: Government by mob.

[3] "The ministry": The government of the British prime minister George Grenville.

[4] "Land-jobbers": Land speculators.

[5] "Trimmers": Political moderates.

[6] In a April 17, 1776, letter, Warren describes a journey during which she visited with Martha Washington and made other new acquaintances as well as toured Charleston, Massachusetts, the site of recent battles.

[7] "he," "Portia," "your Friend": "He" refers to Adams's husband, John Adams. Portia is Adams's epistolary pseudonym in her correspondence with Warren. "Your Friend" is Warren's husband, James Warren. Both James Warren and Mercy Otis Warren corresponded with John Adams.

Multiplicity of avocations and says further that he has been very Busy, and writ near ten sheets of paper about some affairs which he does not chuse to Mention for fear of accident. He is very saucy to me in return for a List of Female Grievances which I transmitted to him. I think I will get you to join me in a petition to Congress. I thought it was very probable our wise Statesmen would erect a New Government and form a New Code of Laws. I ventured to speak a Word in behalf of our Sex who are rather hardly Dealt with by the Laws of England, which gives such unlimited power to the Husband to use his Wife Ill. I requested that our Legislators would consider our case, and as all Men of Delicacy and Sentiment are averse to exercising the power they possess, yet as there is a Natural propensity in Humane Nature to domination, I thought the most Generous plan was to put it out of the power of the Arbitrary and tyrannick to injure us with impunity by establishing some Laws in our favour upon just and Liberal principals.

I believe I even threatned fomenting a Rebellion in case we were not considerd, and assured him we would not hold ourselves bound by any Laws in which we had neither a voice nor representation.

In return he tells me he cannot but Laugh at my Extraordinary Code of Laws; that he had heard their Struggle had loosned the bonds of Government; that children and apprentices were disobedient; that Schools and Colledges were grown turbulent; that Indians slighted their Guardians, and Negroes grew insolent to their Masters. But my Letter was the first intimation that another Tribe more Numerous and powerfull than all the rest were grown discontented. This is rather too coarse a compliment, he adds, but that I am so sausy he won't blot it out.

So I have helpd the Sex abundantly; but I will tell him I have only been making trial of the disinterestedness of his Virtue and when weighd in the balance have found it wanting.

It would be bad policy to grant us greater power, say they, since under all the disadvantages we labour we have the assendancy over their Hearts.

And charm by accepting, by submitting sway.[8]

I wonder Apollo and the Muses could not have indulged me with a poetical Genious. I have always been a votary to her charms, but never could ascend Parnassus myself.[9]

---

[8] From "Epistle II, To a Lady: On the Characters of Women" by Alexander Pope (1688–1744). The section of the poem describes the ideal lady: "She, who ne'er answers till a Husband cools,/Or, if she rules him, never shows she rules;/Charms by accepting, by submitting sways,/Yet has her humour most, when she obeys[.]"

[9] Parnassus: A mountain in central Greece, said to be sacred to Apollo and the Muses.

I am very sorry to hear of the indisposition of your Friend. I am afraid it will hasten his return and I do not think he can be spaired.

> Though certain pains attend the cares of State
> A Good Man owes his Country to be great
> Should act abroad the high distinguished part
> Or shew at least the purpose of his heart.[10]

Good Night, my Friend, you will be so good as to remember me to our Worthy Friend, Mrs. W[inthrop]e[11] when you see her, and write soon to your

PORTIA

LETTER TO JOHN ADAMS, JUNE 30, 1778

Now I know you are Safe [in France] I wish myself with you. Whenever you entertain such a wish recollect that I would have willingly hazarded all dangers to have been your companion, but as that was not permitted you must console me in your absence by a Recital of all your adventures, tho methinks I would not have them in all respects too similar to those related of your venerable Colleigue [Benjamin Franklin],[12] Whose Mentor like appeerence, age and philosiphy must certainly lead the polite scientifick Ladies of France to suppose they are embraceing the God of Wisdom, in a Humane Form, but I who own that I never yet wish'd an Angle[13] whom I loved a Man,[14] l shall be full as content if those divine Honours are omitted. The whole Heart of my Friend is in the Bosom of his partner, more than half a score of years has so riveted [it] there that the fabrick which contains it must crumble into Dust e'er the particles can be seperated. I can hear of the Brilliant accomplishment[s] of any of my Sex with pleasure and rejoice in that Liberality of Sentiment which acknowledges them. At the same time I regret the trifling narrow contracted Education of the Females of my own country. I have entertaind a superiour opinion of the

---

[10] From "An Epistle to the Earl of Burlington" by Lady Mary Wortley Montagu (1689–1762).

[11] "Mrs. W[inthrop]e": Hannah Fayerweather Winthrop (ca. 1727–1790) corresponded with both Adams and Warren. She was married to John Winthrop (1714–1779), a noted astronomer and a professor at Harvard University.

[12] Benjamin Franklin (1706–1790): Iconic American politician, scientist, writer, diplomat, and printer.

[13] Angle: Angel.

[14] Adams here quotes the line "Nor wish'd an Angel whom I lov'd a Man" from Alexander Pope, *Eloisa to Abelard* (1717).

accomplishments of the French Ladies ever since I read the Letters of Dr. Sherbear,[15] who professes that he had rather take the opinion of an accomplished Lady in matters of polite writing than the first wits of Italy and should think himself safer with her approbation than of a long List of Literati, and he give[s] this reason for it that Women have in general more delicate Sensations than Men, what touches them is for the most part true in Nature, whereas men warpt by Education, judge amiss from previous prejudice and refering all things to the model of the ancients, condemn that by comparison where no true Similitud ought to be expected.

But in this country you need not be told how much female Education is neglected, nor how fashonable it has been to ridicule Female learning, tho I acknowled[ge] it my happiness to be connected with a person of a more generous mind and liberal Sentiments.

---

[15] John Shebbeare (1709–1788): English physician and satirist.

THIRTY-ONE

Mary "Molly" Brant/Tekonwatonti/ Konwatsi-Tsiaienni (Mohawk; 1735/6–1796)

*S*TEPDAUGHTER OF THE POWERFUL MOHAWK SACHEM CHIEF BRANT CANAGARA DUNCKA AND *wife of the British Superintendent of Indian Affairs Sir William Johnson, Mary Brant was well positioned to influence relationships between her own politically powerful Mohawk family and the British colonial administration at a pivotal point in the American Revolution. Mohawk traditions of kinship and matrilineal inheritance assured her an automatic role in land negotiations and political alliances as a Clan Mother, while her daily access to Johnson as the mother of his nine children gave her valuable insight into the customs and assumptions of the British. After Johnson's death in 1774, Mary Brant became an ally to the British in the Revolutionary War, passing information to a mixed Mohawk and British loyalist force led by her brother Joseph that resulted in a military defeat for the Americans at Oriskany, New York. Forced to flee with her family to escape the revenge of American patriots, she settled in Cataraqui (now Kingston, Ontario), where the British built her a house and gave her an income of 100 pounds a year. A statue of Mary Brant still stands in Kingston, and she is a national heroine in Canada. (The Mohawk Nation does not formally recognize the national border between the United States and Canada, which cuts through their own sovereign nation.)*

The letters below were dictated to an amanuensis, and they show Mary Brant's role in passing on military information and her determination to take care of her own and her family's material needs. In the second letter, she takes the role of political advisor to Judge Daniel Claus without apology, as a powerful Mohawk woman would expect to do in the period. Her family had built kinship relations with Claus when he stayed with them in 1750 to study Native languages. Claus married Ann

(Nancy) Johnson, Mary Brant's sister-in-law, in 1760. He became Superintendent of Indian Affairs in Canada after William Johnson's death, and the letters below date from this period, one in which the loyalties of the Seven Nations of Canada, allied with the French for generations, were sought by the British.

LETTERS TO JUDGE DANIEL
CLAUS (1778–1779)[1]

Niagara, 23 June 1778

Dear Sir

I have been favor'd with Yours and the Trunk & parcels by Mr. Street: everything mentioned in the Invoice You sent me has come safe, except the pair of gold Earrings which I have not been able to find.

We have a report of Joseph having had a brush with the Rebels, but do not know at what place. A Cayuga[2] Chief is said to be Wounded, and Schohary Indian (Jacob) killed,[3] & one missing since when it's reported that Col⁰ Butler, & Joseph have Joined;[4] Every hour we look for a confirmation of this news.

I am much obliged to You for the care, & attention in sending me up those very necessary articles, & should be very glad if you have any accounts from New York that you would let me know them, as well as of the health of George, & Peggy, whom I hope are agreably settled: My Children are all in good health, & desire their loves to You, Mrs. Claus, Lady, & Sir John Johnson. I hope the Time is very near, when we shall all return to our habitations on the Mohawk River.

> I am Dr Sir ever
> affectionately Your
> Mary Brandt

---

[1] The manuscripts of these letters are located in the Library and Archives of Canada. These transcriptions are from Sharon Harris, ed., *American Women Writers to 1800* and are used by permission of Oxford University Press.

[2] Cayuga: One of the six Iroquois or Haudenosaunee Nations.

[3] Schohary: During the Revolution, New York's Schoharie Valley was an important source of grain for the American troops. In 1780, Sir John Johnson and British forces would pillage and burn much of the valley.

[4] Colonel John Butler (1717–1782) and his son Walter Butler led the region's Butler's Rangers, a group of loyalists fighting for the British who were supposed to fight alongside their Native allies. They were quite brutal, scalping the dead and torturing the wounded.

Carleton Island, 5th October 1779

Sir

We arrived here the 29th last month after Tedaous and dissagreable Voyage; where we remain and by all Appearance may for the winter I have rote to Col° Butler and my brother Acquainting them of my Situation, desireing there advice, as I was left no Directions Concerning my self or family. Only when a Vessel Arraived, I Could get a passage to Niagara–I have been promised by Col° Johnson at Montreal that I Should hear from the Genl [Haldimand][5] and have his directions & order to be provided at whatever place my little service should be wanted which you know I am always ready to do, Should you think proper to speak to the Genl on that head will be much Oblidged to You. the Indians are a Good deele dissatisfied on acc^t of the Col°.s hasty temper which I hope he will soon drop Otherwise it may be Dissadvantageous I need not tell You whatever is promised or told them it ought to be perform'd—

Those from Canada are much Dissatisfied on Account of his taking more Notice of those that are suspected than them that are known to be Loyal, I tell this only to you that you advise him on that head——Meantime beg leave to be remembered to all Your family from Sir—

Your wellwisher

Mary Brant

---

[5] In 1778, Sir Frederick Haldimand (1718–1791) was sent to North America to replace the former Quebec governor Guy Carleton. To secure the loyalty of Indian allies, he spent massive amounts on presents and arms.

THIRTY-TWO

Esther de Berdt Reed (1747–1780)

*E*NGLISH-BORN ESTHER DE BERDT MARRIED JOHN REED, AN AMERICAN LAW STUDENT, IN *London in 1770. Soon after, she and her mother moved with Reed to Philadelphia, where the family joined the movement for American independence. Her husband served as secretary and aide to General George Washington, and then acting governor of Pennsylvania. In May 1780, Esther learned that revolutionary forces suffered desperately from shortages of clothes, rations, and pay. Just weeks after the birth of her sixth child, George Washington Reed, she organized three dozen women to go door to door in Philadelphia collecting funds to support the Revolution. The fund drive organized by Reed with the collaboration of Martha Washington served as a model for other women's collective efforts in Virginia, New Jersey, and Maryland. Her statement* The Sentiments of an American Woman *not only maps out practical logistics for organizing women and girls throughout the colonies, but also delivers a rousing argument that women can and should undertake revolutionary action beyond the customary confines of the domestic sphere.*

THE SENTIMENTS OF AN AMERICAN WOMAN (1780)

On the commencement of actual[1] war, the Women of America manifested a firm resolution to contribute as much as could depend on them, to the deliverance of their country. Animated by the purest patriotism, they are sensible of sorrow at this day, in not offering more than barren wishes for the success of so glorious a Revolution. They aspire to render themselves more really useful; and this sentiment is universal from the north to the south of the Thirteen United States. Our ambition is kindled by the fame of those heroines of antiquity, who have rendered their sex illustrious, and

---

[1] Actual: Current.

have proved to the universe, that, if the weakness of our Constitution, if opinion and manners did not forbid us to march to glory by the same paths as the Men, we should at least equal, and sometimes surpass them in our love for the public good. I glory in all that which my sex has done great and commendable. I call to mind with enthusiasm and with admiration, all those acts of courage, of constancy and patriotism, which history has transmitted to us: The people favoured by Heaven preserved from destruction by the virtues, the zeal and the resolution of Deborah, of Judith, of Esther![2] The fortitude of the mother of the Macchabees,[3] in giving up her sons to die before her eyes: Rome saved from the fury of a victorious enemy by the efforts of Volumnia,[4] and other Roman Ladies: So many famous sieges where the Women have been seen forgetting the weakness of their sex, building new walls, digging trenches with their feeble hands, furnishing arms to their defenders, they themselves darting the missile weapons on the enemy, resigning the ornaments of their apparel, and their fortune, to fill the public treasury, and to hasten the deliverance of their country; burying themselves under its ruins; throwing themselves into the flames rather than submit to the disgrace of humiliation before a proud enemy.

Born for liberty, disdaining to bear the irons of a tyrannic Government, we associate ourselves to the grandeur of those Sovereigns, cherished and revered, who have held with so much splendour the scepter of the greatest States, the Matildas, the Elizabeths, the Maries, the Catharines,[5] who have extended the empire of liberty, and contented to reign by sweetness and justice, have broken the chains of slavery, forged by tyrants in the times of ignorance and barbarity. The Spanish Women, do they not make, at this moment, the most patriotic sacrifices, to encrease the means of victory in the hands of their Sovereign. He is a friend to the French Nation. They are our allies. We call to mind, doubly interested, that it was a French Maid who kindled up amongst her fellow-citizens, the flame of patriotism buried under long misfortunes: It was the Maid of Orleans[6] who drove from the kingdom of France the ancestors of those same British, whose odious yoke we have just shaken off; and whom it is necessary that we drive from this Continent.

---

[2] "Deborah . . . Judith . . . Esther": Female heroines from the Old Testament; Deborah was a judge and prophetess (Judges 4–5), Judith a warrior, and Esther a diplomat.

[3] Macchabees: Jewish anti-imperialist and liberation movement in Israel (167–160 BCE).

[4] Volumnia: Patriotic Roman matron, mother of Coriolanus, celebrated in Plutarch's *Lives* and Shakespeare's play *Coriolanus*.

[5] The Matildas, the Elizabeths, the Maries, the Catharines: A catalog of European queens and empresses, including Queen Matilda of England (1031–1083), Empress Matilda (1102–1167) of the Holy Roman Empire, Queen Elizabeth I of England (1533–1603), and Russian Empress Catherine the Great (1729–1796).

[6] Maid of Orleans: French national heroine Joan of Arc (1412–1431), warrior and saint.

But I must limit myself to the recollection of this small number of achievements. Who knows if persons disposed to censure, and sometimes too severely with regard to us, may not disapprove our appearing acquainted even with the actions of which our sex boasts? We are at least certain, that he cannot be a good citizen who will not applaud our efforts for the relief of the armies which defend our lives, our possessions, our liberty? The situation of our soldiery has been represented to me; the evils inseparable from war, and the firm and generous spirit which has enabled them to support these. But it has been said, that they may apprehend, that, in the course of a long war, the view of their distresses may be lost, and their services be forgotten. Forgotten! never; I can answer in the name of all my sex. Brave Americans, your disinterestedness, your courage, and your constancy will always be dear to America, as long as she shall preserve her virtue.

We know that at a distance from the theatre of war, if we enjoy any tranquility, it is the fruit of your watchings, your labours, your dangers. If I live happy in the midst of my family; if my husband cultivates his field, and reaps his harvest in peace; if, surrounded with my children, I myself nourish the youngest, and press it to my bosom, without being affraid of seeing myself separated from it, by a ferocious enemy; if the house in which we dwell, if our barns, our orchards are safe at the present time from the hands of those incendiaries, it is to you that we owe it. And shall we hesitate to evidence to you our gratitude? Shall we hesitate to wear a cloathing more simple; hair dressed less elegant, while at the price of this small privation, we shall deserve your benedictions. Who, amongst us, will not renounce with the highest pleasure, these vain ornaments, when she shall consider that the valiant defenders of America will be able to draw some advantage from the money which she may have laid out in these, that they will be better defended from the rigours of the seasons, that after their painful toils, they will receive some extraordinary and unexpected relief; that these presents will perhaps be valued by them at a greater price, when they will have it in their power to say: This is the offering of the Ladies. The time is arrived to display the same sentiments which animated us at the beginning of the Revolution, when we renounced the use of teas, however agreeable to our taste, rather than receive them from our persecutors; when we made it appear to them that we placed former necessaries in the rank of superfluities, when our liberty was interested; when our republican and laborious hands spun the flax, prepared the linen intended for the use of our soldiers; when exiles and fugitives we supported with courage all the evils which are concomitants of war. Let us not lose a moment; let us be engaged to offer the homage of our gratitude at the altar of military valour, and you, our brave deliverers, while mercenary slaves combat to cause you to share with them, the irons with which they are loaded, receive with a free hand our offering, the purest which can be presented to your virtue.

By An AMERICAN WOMAN.

IDEAS, relative to the manner of forwarding to the American Soldiers, the presents of the American Women.

ALL plans are eligible, when doing good is the object; there is however one more preferable; and when the operation is extensive, we cannot give it too much uniformity. On the other side, the wants of our army do not permit the slowness of an ordinary path. It is not in one month, nor in eight days, that we would relieve our soldiery. It is immediately; and our impatience does not permit us to proceed by the long circuity of collectors, receivers and treasurers. As my idea with regard to this, have been approved by some Ladies of my friends, I will explain them here, every other person will not be less at liberty to prepare to adopt a different plan.

1st. All Women and Girls will be received without exception, to present their patriotic offering; and, as it is absolutely voluntary, every one will regulate it according to her ability, and her disposition. The shilling offered by the Widow or the young Girl, will be received as well as the most considerable sums presented by the Women who have the happiness to join to their patriotism, greater means to be useful.

2d. A Lady chosen by the others in each county, shall be the Treasuress; and to render her task more simple, and more easy, she will not receive but determinate sums, in a round number, from twenty hard dollars to any greater sum. The exchange forty dollars in paper for one dollar in specie.

3d. The Women who shall not be in a condition to send twenty dollars in specie, or above, will join in as great a number as will be necessary to make this or any greater sum, and one amongst them will carry it, or cause it to be sent to the Treasuress.

4th. The Treasuress of the county will receive the money, and will keep a register, writing the sums in her book, and causing it to be signed at the side of the whole by the person who has presented it.

5th. When several Women shall join together to make a total sum of twenty dollars, or more, she amongst them who shall have the charge to carry it to the Treasuress, will make mention of all their names on the register, if her associates shall have so directed her; those whose choice it shall be, will have the liberty to remain unknown.

6th. As soon as the Treasuress of the county shall judge, that the sums which she shall have received, deserve to be sent to their destination, she will cause them to be presented with the lists, to the wife of the Governor or President of the State, who will be the Treasuress-General of the State; and she will cause it to be set down in her register, and have it sent to Mistress Washington. If the Governor or President are unmarried, all will address themselves to the wife of the Vice-President, if there is one, or of the Chief-Justice, &c.

7th. Women settled in the distant parts of the country, and not chusing for any particular reason as for the sake of greater expedition, to remit their Capital to the Treasuress, may send it directly to the wife of the Governor, or President, &c. or to Mistress Washington who, if she shall judge necessary, will in a short answer to the sender, acquaint her with the reception of it.

8th. As Mrs. Washington may be absent from the camp when the greater part of the bank shall be sent there, the American Women considering, that General Washington is Father and Friend of the Soldiery; that he is himself, the first Soldier of the Republic, and that their offering will be received at its destination, as soon as it shall have come to his hands, they will pray him, to take the charge of receiving it, in the absence of Mrs. Washington.

9th. General Washington will dispose of this fund in the manner that he shall judge most advantageous to the Soldiery. The American Women desire only that it may not be considered as to be employed, to procure the army, the objects of subsistence, arms or cloathing, which are due to them by the Continent. It is an extraordinary bounty intended to render the condition of the Soldier more pleasant, and not to hold place of the things which they ought to receive from the Congress, or from the States.

10th. If the General judges necessary, he will publish at the end of a certain time, an amount of that which shall have been received from each particular State.

11th. The Women who shall send their offerings, will have in their choice to conceal or to give their names; and if it shall be thought proper, on a fit occasion, to publish one day the lists, they only, who shall consent, shall be named; when with regard to the sums sent, there will be no mention made, if they so desire it.

THIRTY-THREE

Nancy Ward/Nanye'hi (Cherokee; 1738?–1824) and Cherokee Women

*A*S THE LARGE AND POWERFUL CHEROKEE NATION FACED THE CHALLENGES OF MAINTAINING *its sovereignty, culture, and vast territory against the continuing encroachments of white settlers in the eighteenth century, it relied upon the authority, courage, and intelligence of Cherokee women. In traditionally matriarchal Cherokee society, women anchored their families, oversaw the use of the land, and held political offices like* Ghighua, *or Beloved Woman. They participated fully in the political life of their nation.*

Four documented speeches from the 1780s reprinted in this selection demonstrate how in addressing Euro-American colonists Cherokee women diplomats consistently drew from a powerful rhetorical tradition that established motherhood as the grounds for political authority and judgment. The first document in our selection is a speech made by a group of Cherokee women to a diplomatic commission organized by General Nathanael Greene (1742–1786), a major general of the Continental Army during the Revolutionary War. In this speech, the Cherokee women assert their authority as women and "mothers" over the male Euro-American diplomats whom they characterize as "sons," and they remind their Euro-American auditors of the great rates of intermarriage between Cherokee and European-descended peoples in the South, underscoring their common stake in peace and reconciliation.

Anthologized in its entirety for the first time in this volume, the second document in this selection is a speech by Nanye'hi/Nancy Ward. Born around the year

1738 into a politically powerful family of the Wolf Clan, at Chota, a Cherokee city traditionally designated as a "Mother Town," "Peace Town," or place of refuge, the Cherokee warrior and diplomat Nanye'hi married a Cherokee man named Tsu-la, or Kingfisher, in 1751. Tsu-la and Nanye'hi fought side by side during a conflict between the Cherokee and Creek nations; when Tsu-la was shot, Nanye'hi picked up his rifle and helped lead the Cherokee to victory. For her valor, she was selected to hold the traditional office of Ghighua, *or Beloved Woman. (Nanye'hi became known as Nancy Ward after marrying Bryant Ward, an Irish trader, in the 1750s. Some historians have viewed their marriage as a conscious act of international diplomacy to foster peace and trade. Under the matrilineal Cherokee system, Bryant Ward married into Nanye'hi's clan and family, benefiting from* her *political status.)*

As a Beloved Woman, Nanye'hi held a voting position on the Cherokee General Council, served as the leader of the Cherokee Women's Council, and acted as a diplomat and negotiator. During her tenure, the vast Cherokee Territory—encompassing parts of Tennessee, Kentucky, Virginia, North Carolina, South Carolina, Alabama, and Georgia—was under constant threat from white settlers. In July 1781, at a treaty negotiation on the Holston River in Tennessee, Ward called for peace and demanded that U.S. Treaty Commissioners "let [their] Women hear our Words." Her words echo those of her mother's brother Chief Attakullakulla, who once demanded of white negotiators, "Where are your women?" To Cherokee people accustomed to matrilineal social structures and women's political participation, the political voicelessness of women in the United States was symptomatic of the imbalance, disorder, and violence of white colonial society. In her speech to United States Commissioners at the negotiation of the Treaty of Hopewell (1785), the third document in this selection, Nanye'hi used the rhetoric of motherhood to counter Anglo-American rhetorical conventions that positioned whites as "fathers" or "elder brothers" to Native people, to establish her moral and political authority as a mother figure to both Native peoples and whites, and to indicate that kinship is the proper framework for diplomatic relations. A fourth document by Cherokee women diplomats marshals the same powerful rhetoric of political motherhood to address Benjamin Franklin, then governor of Pennsylvania. Some scholars believe that this document, which was endorsed by at least three Cherokee women, was authored by Nancy Ward. Others, including Cherokee scholars Daniel Heath Justice and Virginia Carney, suggest that "Katteuha" may have been the name of another Beloved Woman of Chota or a collective of lesser-known Beloved Women.

SPEECH OF CHEROKEE WOMEN TO GENERAL GREENE'S COMMISSION, JULY 26–AUGUST 2, 1781[1]

Beloved Men and Warriors

We the Women of the Cherokee Nation now speak to you. We are Mothers, and have many sons, some of them Warriors, an[d] beloved Men. We call you also our sons: We have a right to call you so, because you are the sons of Mothers, and all descended from the same Woman at first. We say you are our Sons, because by Women, you were brought forth into this World, nursed, suckled, and raised up to be men befo[re] you reached your present Greatness. You are our Son[s.] Why should there be any Difference amongst us, we liv[e] on the same Land with you, and ou[r] Peo[ple] [ar]e mixed with white Blood: one third of our [people are] mixed with white Bl[oo]d: why will you ga[*text missing*] for us. Here is wha [*text missing*]indled. I placed our elder Brother Col. [Martin] here to take care of it for us. There has been a little [disturb]ance betwixt you and us, and so has it been, [betwixt] [you a]nd your Fathers over the great Water: but a[ll is w]ell again. Col. Martin our elder Brother will take care of it for us. We hope although there has been a sho[w?] [of] [d]isturbance between us that our elder Brothers will not [thin]k of taking away this beloved spot reserved to hold g[ran]d Talks on.

NANCY WARD SPEECH TO THE U.S. TREATY COMMISSIONERS (1781)[2]

We did never concern in the [for]mer Treaty, which has been broken, but we do in this, and on our account, who are your Mothers, let it never [be] broken. You know Women are always looked upon as nothing; but we are your Mothers; you are our sons. Our cry [is] all for Peace; let it continue because we are Your Mothers. This Peace must last forever. Let your Womens sons be Ours, and let our sons be yours. Let your Women hear our Words.

---

[1] The speech is from *Report of Proceedings of a Commission Appointed by General Nathanael Greene on 26 February 1781 to Conduct Talks with the Cherokees*, Nathanael Greene Papers, 1775–1785, folder 5, Library of Congress.

[2] The speech is from *Report of Proceedings of a Commission Appointed by General Nathanael Greene on 26 February 1781 to Conduct Talks with the Cherokees*, Nathanael Greene Papers, 1775–1785, folder 5, Library of Congress.

SPEECH TO THE U.S. TREATY COMMISSIONERS (1785)

I am fond of hearing that there is a peace, and I hope you have now taken us by the hand in real friendship. I have a pipe and a little tobacco to give the commissioners to smoke in friendship. I look on you and the red people as my children. Your having determined on peace is most pleasing to me, for I have seen much trouble during the late war. I am old, but I hope yet to bear children, who will grow up and people our nation, as we are now to be under the protection of Congress, and shall have no more disturbance.—[A string, little old pipe, and some tobacco.[3]]

The talk I have given, is from the young warriors I have raised in my town as well as myself. They rejoice that we have peace, and we hope the chain of friendship will never more be broke.—[A string of beads.[4]]

CHEROKEE WOMEN TO GOVERNOR BENJAMIN FRANKLIN (SEPTEMBER 8, 1787)

Brother,

I am in hopes my Brothers & the Beloved men near the water side will heare from me. This day I filled the pipes that they smoaked in piece, and I am in hopes the smoake has Reached up to the skies above. I here send you a piece of the same To-bacco, and am in hopes you & your Beloved men will smoake it in Friendship—and I am glad in my heart that I am the mother of men that will smoak it in piece.

Brother,

I am in hopes if you Rightly consider it that woman is the mother of All—and that woman Does not pull Children out of Trees or Stumps nor out of old Logs, but out of their Bodies, so that they ought to mind what a woman says, and look upon her as a mother—and I have Taken the privelage to Speak to you as my own Children, & the same as if you had sucked my Breast—and I am in hopes you have a beloved woman amongst you who will help to put her Children Right if they do wrong, as I shall do the same—the great men have all promised to Keep the path clear & straight, as my Children shall Keep the path clear & white so that the Messengers shall go & come in safety Between us—the old people is never done Talking to their Children—which makes me say so much as I do. The Talk you sent to me was to talk to my Children,

---

[3] A string, little old pipe, and some tobacco: This list indicates wampum, a traditional implement of indigenous diplomacy, and other ceremonial items presented by Nanye'hi during her speech.

[4] A string of beads: Wampum.

which I have done this day, and they all liked my Talk well, which I am in hopes you will heare from me Every now & then that I keep my Children in piece—tho' I am a woman giving you this Talk, I am in hopes that you and all the Beloved men in Congress will pay particular Attention to it, as I am Delivering it to you from the Bottom of my heart, that they will Lay this on the white stool in Congress, wishing them all well & success in all their undertakings—I hold fast the good Talk I Received from you my Brother, & thanks you kindly for your good Talks, & your presents, & the kind usage you gave to my son.

From KATTEUHA, The Beloved woman of Chota.[5]

[Indorsed by Kaattahee, Scolecutta, and Kaattahee, Cherokee Indian Women.]

---

[5] Scholars believe that Katteuha was either a mistranscription of Nanye'hi's title Ghighua, the name of the Cherokee Women's Council, or the name of another Cherokee woman who authored this document.

THIRTY-FOUR

Women of Wilmington

*A*T THE END OF THE AMERICAN REVOLUTIONARY WAR, TENS OF THOUSANDS OF TORIES LOYAL *to the British government and its cause fled the new United States of America for England, Nova Scotia, and other destinations within the British Empire. On December 25, 1782, North Carolina Governor Alexander Martin issued an order that all Tories be evacuated immediately from the state of North Carolina. The edict fell hard on women and children abandoned by Loyalist husbands and fathers who had already fled the state. Still, Martin and his allies vindictively accused these families of "nursing up serpents in our own bosoms for our own destruction," and ordered their departure. Twenty-one women in Wilmington, North Carolina, a town occupied by British forces in 1781, composed this petition to interject a note of compassion and sensibility into the postwar Patriot fervor. Although these women were pro-revolutionary Patriots, they organized on behalf of their Loyalist friends, demanding that Governor Martin allow Loyalist women to remain in their homes. Minimizing their own losses during the British occupation of Wilmington, knowing intimately the special impacts of the Revolutionary War on all women and families, the women of Wilmington called on the state of North Carolina to rescind its evacuation order and end the state's "war with women and children."*

PETITION TO HIS EXCELLENCY GOV. ALEXANDER MARTIN AND THE MEMBERS OF THE HONORABLE COUNCIL (1782)

We, the subscribers, inhabitants of the town of Wilmington, warmly attached to the State of North Carolina, and strenuously devoted to our best wishes and endeavours to the achievement of its independence, feeling for the honor of, and desirous that our Enemies should not have the smallest pretext to brand them as cruel or precipitate, that the dignity of our public characters may not be degraded to the imitation of examples of inhumanity exhibited by our Enemies.

Humbly shew to His Excellency, the Governor, and the honorable the council, that we have been informed that orders have issued from your honorable board that the wives and children of Absentees should depart the State with a small part of their property in forty eight hours after notice given them. It is not the province of our sex to reason deeply upon the policy of the order, but as it must affect the helpless and innocent, it wounds us with the most sincere distress and prompts our earnest supplication that the order may be arrested, and the officers forbid to carry it into execution. If it is intended as retaliation for the expulsion of some of us, the subscribers, by the British from the Town of Wilmington, and to gratify a resentment which such inhumanity to us may be supposed to have excited, its object is greatly mistaken.

Those whom your proclamation holds forth as marks of public vengeance, neither prompted the British order nor aided the execution of it. On the contrary, they expressed the greatest indignation at it, and with all their power strove to mitigate our sufferings. Still some instances attended which made the execution of it less distressing to us than yours must be to those upon whom it is intended to operate. We were ordered without the British Lines and then our friends were ready to receive us. They received us with a cordial welcome, and ministered to our wants with generosity and politeness. With pleasure we bear this public testimony. But our Town women now ordered out must be exposed to the extreme of human wretchedness. Their friends are in Charles Town;[1] they have neither carriages nor horses to remove them by land, nor vessels to transport them by water, and the small pittance allotted them of their property, could they be procured, would be scarce equal to the purchase of them. It is beneath the character of the independent State of North Carolina to war with women and children. The authors of our ill treatment are the proper subjects of our own and the resentment of the public. Does their barbarity strike us with abhorrence? Let us blush to imitate it; not justify by our own practice what we so justly condemn in others. To Major Craig[2], and him alone, is to be imputed the inhuman edicts, for even the British Soldiers were shocked at it.

If we may be allowed to claim any merit with the public for our steady adherence to the Whig principles of America; if our sufferings induced by that attachment have given us favor and esteem with your honorable body, we beg leave to assure you that

---

[1] Charles Town: Charleston, South Carolina, home to a large Loyalist community.
[2] James Henry Craig (1748–1812): British army officer who oversaw the occupation of Wilmington, North Carolina.

we shall hold it as a very signal mark of your respect for us if you will condescend to suffer to remain amongst us our old friends and acquaintances whose husbands, though estranged from us in political opinions, have left wives and children much endeared to us, and who may live to be an honor to the State and to Society if permitted to continue here.

The safety of this State, we trust in God, is now secured beyond the most powerful exertions of our Enemies, and it would be a system of abject weakness to fear the feeble efforts of women and children.

And as in Duty bound we shall ever pray.

Anne Hooper, Ann Towkes, Mary Allen, M. Hand, Sarah Nash, S. Wilkings, Mary Nash, M. Lord, Mary Moore, Isabella Read, E. Nash, Sally Read, Sarah Moore, Mary Granger, M. Loyd, Jane Ward, Catharine Young, Hannah Ward, J. M. Drayton, Kitty Ward, E. Wilkings.

THIRTY-FIVE

Belinda (born about 1713)

*W*HILE ANGLO-AMERICAN COLONISTS REVOLTED AGAINST THE BRITISH EMPIRE, HUNDREDS *of thousands of African-American slaves pursued their own freedom cause. The British promised freedom to slaves who fled their masters and fought for the British; many thousands of Black Loyalists, including single mothers fleeing slavery with their small children, sought freedom behind British lines and evacuated at the war's end to new communities in Nova Scotia and other Loyalist settlements. Other African-Americans identified with the American or Patriot cause and remained in the new United States of America, to claim a share in the new nation their military service and unwaged labor helped build. Born in Ghana, Belinda was brought forcibly to America as a young girl and served Isaac Royall (1719?–1781), a wealthy British slave merchant, for more than fifty years. At the outbreak of the Revolutionary War, in 1775, Royall fled his home in Medford, Massachusetts, for England; Massachusetts seized his property and manumitted his slaves, including Belinda. Struggling to provide for themselves, without a steady means of income, Belinda and her daughter, Prine, made their way to Boston, home to a significant and politically active free Black community. In February 1782, aided perhaps by the charismatic and astute Black community leader Prince Hall, Belinda drafted a petition to the Massachusetts state legislature to demand back pay or reparations from the estate of Isaac Royall. In so doing, she joined many other Native and African-Americans who tested the use of the petition and the legal systems of the new United States as an avenue for redress and justice-seeking. Her narrative of her capture in Africa and her transport to the United States is one of the first accounts of the Middle Passage from Africa to America originated by an African-American woman. Belinda was awarded an annual income of 15 pounds and 12 shillings, but she received it only twice: in 1783, and after a second petition (which appears below) in 1787. Her 1782 petition* *was published in an English magazine,* The Weekly Entertainer, *in September 1783, and again in the Philadelphia magazine* American Museum *in June 1787.*

PETITION OF 1782

To the honourable the senate and house of representatives, in general court assembled: The petition of Belinda, an African,

 Humbly shews,

 That seventy years have rolled away, since she, on the banks of the Rio de Valta,[1] received her existence. The mountains, covered with spicy forests—the vallies; loaded with the richest fruits, spontaneously produced—joined to that happy temperature of air, which excludes excess, would have yielded her the most complete felicity, had not her mind received early impressions of the cruelty of men, whose faces were like the moon, and whose bows and arrows were like the thunder and the lightning of the clouds. The idea of these, the most dreadful of all enemies, filled her infant slumbers with horror, and her noon-tide moments with cruel apprehensions! But her affrighted imagination, in its most alarming extension, never represented distresses equal to what she has since really experienced: for before she had twelve years enjoyed the fragrance of her native groves, and ere she realized that Europeans placed their happiness in the yellow dust,[2] which she carelessly marked with her infant foot-steps—even when she, in a sacred grove, with each hand in that of a tender parent, was paying her devotion to the great Orisa,[3] who made all things, an armed band of white men, driving many of her countrymen in chains, rushed into the hallowed shades! Could the tears, the sighs, and supplications, bursted from the tortured parental affection, have blunted the keen edge of avarice, she might have been rescued from agony, which many of her country's children have felt, but which none have ever described. In vain she lifted her supplicating voice to an insulted father, and her guiltless hands to a dishonoured deity! She was ravished from the bosom of her country, from the arms of her friends, while the advanced age of her parents, rendering them unfit for servitude, cruelly separated her from them for ever.

---

[1] Rio de Valta: The Volta River of Ghana.

[2] Yellow dust: A reference to gold. The modern nation of Ghana was known as the Gold Coast until independence in 1957, because of the rich gold deposits in the soil, which had attracted European traders since the fifteenth century. Belinda refers to Isaac Royall's wealth using the same term later in her petition.

[3] Orisa: Orisha, a class of deities in the Yoruba religion of West Africa and the African diaspora.

Scenes which her imagination had never conceived of, a floating world, the sporting monsters of the deep, and the familiar meetings of billows and clouds, strove, but in vain, to divert her attention from three hundred Africans in chains, suffering the most excruciating torment; and some of them rejoicing that the pangs of death came like a balm to their wounds.

Once more her eyes were blest with a continent: but alas! how unlike the land where she received her being! How all things appeared unpropitious. She learned to catch the ideas, marked by the sounds of language, only to know that her doom was slavery, from which death alone was to emancipate her. What did it avail her, that the walls of her lord were hung with splendor, and the dust trodden under foot in her native country, crouded his gates with sordid worshippers! The laws rendered her incapable of receiving property: and though she was a free moral agent, accountable for her own actions, yet never had she a moment at her own disposal! Fifty years her faithful hands have been compelled to ignoble servitude for the benefit of an Isaac Royall, until, as if nations must be agitated, and the world convulsed, for the preservation of that freedom, which the Almighty Father intended for all the human race, the present war commenced. The terrors of men, armed in the cause of freedom, compelled her master to fly, and to breathe away his life in a land, where lawless dominion sits enthroned, pouring blood and vengeance on all who dare to be free.

The face of your petitioner is now marked with the furrows of time, and her frame feebly bending under the oppression of years, while she, by the laws of the land, is denied the enjoyment of one morsel of that immense wealth, a part whereof hath been accumulated by her own industry, and the whole augmented by her servitude.

Wherefore, casting herself at the feet of your honours, as to a body of men, formed for the extirpation of vassalage, for the reward of virtue, and the just returns of honest industry—she prays that such allowance may be made her, out of the estate of colonel Royall, as will prevent her, and her more infirm daughter, from misery in the greatest extreme, and scatter comfort over the short and downward path of their lives: and she will ever pray.

BELINDA.

Boston, February, 1782.

PETITION OF 1787

The Memorial of Belinda, an African, formerly a Servant to the late Isaac Royal Esq an Absentee[4]

Humbly sheweth

---

[4] Absentee: A term for a British Loyalist who has fled America.

That in the year 1783 she petitioned the General Court for a maintenance out of the income of the Said Royall Estate, she being thro' age & infirmity unable to Support

Herself, & that the Hon. Court were pleased to pass the following Resolve in her favour,

Date Feb. 19. 1783

"Resolved that there be paid out of the Treasury of this Commonwealth, out of the Rents & Profits arising from the estate of the late Isaac Royal Esq an absentee Fifteen pounds twelve Shillings per annum to Belinda an aged Servant to the late Isaac Royal Esq an Absentee, until the further Order of the Gen. Court, for the reasons set forth in the said Belinda's petition."

That your Memorialist afterwards received out of the Treasury £15.12s for one year's allowance, & no more & that she never could obtain any more to this day tho she often applied to the Governour & Council to grant her an Order upon the Treasurer for the same.

She is now advised to lay her distressed Case before your honrs, and she humbly prays that Y.r Honrs would be pleased to take her case into consideration & to grant that she may receive the annual pension made unto her as above mentioned, & your Memorialist as in duty bound shall ever pray her

Belinda X Mark[5]

Witness

Willis Hall

Nath Hall

---

[5] By legal custom, petitioners who could not write their own names signed documents with a mark, typically an "X."

THIRTY-SIX

Judith Sargent Murray (1751–1820)

*A*S IT BECAME CLEAR THAT THE GAINS OF THE AMERICAN REVOLUTION WOULD NOT SUB-*stantially change the status of women, feminists reissued the call for improved female education. Massachusetts-born Judith Sargent was raised in a household where she was taught to honor and improve her own estimable intellect. Educated alongside her brother, who was preparing for study at Harvard, Judith learned Greek, Latin, literature, and science, receiving a far superior education to that of most women. She put her advantages to work on behalf of all women when she argued in her widely published essays that access to education should not be restricted by sex. After her first husband died in 1786, Judith Sargent married John Murray, a leading figure in Universalism, a progressive Christian movement that held that all human beings are eligible for divine love and will be redeemed. The couple enjoyed an equitable and mutually supportive intellectual and spiritual companionship.*

One of her earliest essays, "Desultory Thoughts upon the Utility of encouraging a degree of Self-Complacency, especially in Female Bosoms," was published under the pen name "Constantia" in The Gentleman and Lady's Town and Country Magazine *in October 1784. Murray denounced as "melancholy" the prevalent imagery of helpless, seduced young women found in the popular novels of her era. She argued that properly educated young women who were encouraged to develop a rational understanding of themselves and a reverence for their own intellectual capacity would be less susceptible to flattery and seduction. Flattering young girls, focusing only on their beauty and charm, she insisted, diminished the quality of their life chances. Murray extends this argument in "On the Equality of the Sexes," which appeared in* The Massachusetts Magazine, or, Monthly Museum of Knowledge and Rational Entertainment *in March 1790. Continuing a long tradition of feminist* argumentation begun in the seventeenth century, Murray insists that differences between the sexes are the result of differential access to education: "custom" has "taken the place of nature." She demands that women's lives are hobbled without equal opportunity for intellectual accomplishment, asking, "Is it reasonable, that a candidate for immortality, for the joys of heaven, an intelligent being, who is to spend an eternity in contemplating the works of Deity, should at present be so degraded, as to be allowed no other ideas, than those which are suggested by the mechanism of a pudding, or the sewing of the seams of a garment?" If women exchange customarily frivolous pursuits for "the flowery paths of science" and the "refined and sentimental pleasures of contemplation," Murray argues, the result will be more satisfying lives, happier marriages, and more harmonious families.

DESULTORY THOUGHTS UPON THE UTILITY OF ENCOURAGING A DEGREE OF SELF-COMPLACENCY, ESPECIALLY IN FEMALE BOSOMS (1784)

Self-estimation, kept within due bounds,
However oddly the assertion sounds,
May, of the fairest efforts be the root,
May yield the embow'ring shade—the mellow fruit;
May stimulate to most exalted deeds,
Direct the soul where blooming honor leads;
May give her there, to act a noble part,
To virtuous pleasures yield the willing heart.
Self-estimation will debasement shun,
And, in the path of wisdom, joy to run;
An unbecoming act in fears to do,
And still, its exaltation keeps in view.
"To rev'rence self," a Bard long since directed,
And, on each moral truth HE well reflected;
But, lost to conscious worth, to decent pride,
Compass nor helm there is, our course to guide:
Nor may we anchor cast, for rudely tost
In an unfathom'd sea, each motive's lost,
Wildly amid contending waves we're beat,
And rocks and quick sands, shoals and depths we meet;
'Till, dash'd in pieces, or, till found'ring, we
One common wreck of all our prospects see!

> Nor, do we mourn, for we were lost to fame,
> And never hap'd to reach a tow'ring name;
> Ne'er taught to "rev'rence self," or to aspire,
> Our bosoms never caught ambition's fire;
> An indolence of virtue still prevail'd,
> Nor the sweet gale of praise was e'er inhal'd;
> Rous'd by a new stimulus, no kindling glow.
> No soothing emulations gentle flow,
> We judg'd that nature, not to us inclin'd,
> In narrow bounds our progress had confin'd,
> And, that our forms, to say the very best,
> Only, not frightful, were by all confest.

I think, to teach young minds to aspire, ought to be the ground work of education: many a laudable achievement is lost, from a persuasion that our efforts are unequal to the arduous attainment. Ambition is a noble principle, which properly directed, may be productive of the most valuable consequences. It is amazing to what heights the mind by exertion may tow'r: I would, therefore, have my pupils believe, that every thing in the compass of mortality, was placed within their grasp, and that, the avidity of application, the intenseness of study, were only requisite to endow them with every external grace, and mental accomplishment. Thus I should impel them to progress on, if I could not lead them to the heights I would wish them to attain. It is too common with parents to expatiate in their hearing, upon all the foibles of their children, and to let their virtues pass, in appearance, unregarded: this they do, least they should, (were they to commend) swell their little hearts to pride, and implant in their tender minds, undue conceptions of their own importance. Those, for example, who have the care of a beautiful female, they assiduously guard every avenue, they arrest the stream of due admiration, and endeavour to divest her of all idea of the bounties of nature: what is the consequence? She grows up, and of course mixes with those who are less interested: strangers will be sincere; she encounters the tongue of the flatterer, he will exaggerate, she finds herself possessed of accomplishments which have been studiously concealed from her, she throws the reins upon the neck of fancy, and gives every encomiast full credit for his most extravagant eulogy. Her natural connexions, her home is rendered disagreeable, and she hastes to the scenes, whence arise the sweet perfume of adulation, and when she can obtain the regard due to a merit, which she supposes altogether uncommon. Those who have made her acquainted with the dear secret, she considers as her best friends; and it is more than probable, that she will soon fall a sacrifice to some worthless character, whose interest may lead him to the most hyperbolical lengths in the round of flattery. Now, I should be solicitous that my daughter should possess for me the fondest love, as well as that respect which gives birth to duty; in order to promote this wish of my soul, from my lips she should be accustomed to hear the most pleasing truths, and, as in the course of my instructions, I should doubtless find myself but too often impelled to wound the delicacy of youthful sensibility. I would therefore, be careful to avail myself of this exuberating balance: I would, from the early dawn of reason, address her as a rational being; hence, I apprehend, the most valuable consequences would result: in some such language as this, she might from time to time be accosted. A pleasing form is undoubtedly advantageous, nature, my dear, hath furnished you with an agreeable person, your glass, was I to be silent, would inform you that you are pretty, your appearance will sufficiently recommend you to a stranger, the flatterer will give a more than mortal finishing to every feature; but, it must be your part, my sweet girl, to render yourself worthy respect from higher motives: you must learn "to reverence yourself," that is, your intellectual existence; you must join my efforts, in endeavouring to adorn your mind, for, it is from the proper furnishing of that, you will become indeed a valuable person, you will, as I said, give birth to the most favorable impressions at first sight: but, how mortifying should this be all, if, upon a more extensive knowledge you should be discovered to possess no one mental charm, to be fit only at best, to be hung up as a pleasing picture among the paintings of some spacious hall. The FLATTERER, indeed, will still pursue you, but it will be from interested views, and he will smile at your undoing! Now, then, my best Love, is the time for you to lay in such a fund of useful knowledge, as shall continue, and judgment every kind sentiment in regard to you, as shall set you above the snares of the artful betrayer.

Thus, that sweet form, shall serve but as a polished casket, which will contain a most beautiful gem, highly finished, and calculated for advantage, as well as ornament. Was she, I say, habituated thus to reflect, she would be taught to aspire; she would learn to estimate every accomplishment, according to its proper value; and, when the voice of adulation should assail her ear, as she had early been initiated into its true meaning, and from youth been accustomed to the language of praise; her attention would not be captivated, the Siren's song would not borrow the aid of novelty, her young mind would not be enervated or intoxicated, by a delicious surprise, she would possess her soul in serenity, and by that means, rise superior to the deep-laid schemes which, too commonly, encompass the steps of beauty.

Neither should those to whom nature had been parsimonious, be tortured by me with degrading comparisons; every advantage I would expatiate upon, and there are few who possess not some personal charms; I would teach them to gloss over their imperfections, inasmuch is, I do think, an agreeable form, a very necessary introduction to society, and of course it behooves us to render our appearance as pleasing as possible: I would, I must repeat, by all means guard them against a low estimation of self. I would leave no charm undiscovered or unmarked, for the penetrating eye of the pretended admirer, to make unto himself a merit by holding up to her view; thus, I would destroy the weapons of flattery, or render them useless, by leaving not the least room for their operation.

A young lady, growing up with the idea, that she possesses few, or no personal attractions, and that her mental abilities are of an inferior kind, imbibing at the same time, a most melancholly idea of a female, descending down the vale of life in an unprotected state; taught also to regard her character ridiculously contemptible, will, too probably, throw herself away upon the first who approaches her with tenders of love, however indifferent may be her chance for happiness, least if she omits the present day of grace, she may never be so happy as to meet a second offer, and must then inevitably be stigmatized with that dreaded title, an Old Maid, must rank with a class whom she has been accustomed to regard as burthens upon society, and objects whom she might with impunity turn into ridicule! Certainly love, friendship and esteem, ought to take place of marriage, but, the woman thus circumstanced, will seldom regard these previous requisites to felicity, if she can but insure the honors, which she, in idea, associates with a matrimonial connection—to prevent which great evil, I would early impress under proper regulations, a reverence of self; I would endeavour to rear to worth, and a consciousness thereof. I would be solicitous to inspire the glow of virtue, with that elevation of soul, that dignity, which is ever attendant upon self-approbation, arising from the genuine source of innate rectitude. I must be excused for thus insisting upon my hypothesis, as I am, from observation, persuaded, that many have suffered materially all their life long, from a depression of soul, early inculcated, in compliance to a false maxim, which hath supposed pride would thereby be eradicated. I know there is a contrary extreme, and I would, in almost all cases, prefer the happy medium. However, if these fugitive hints may induce some abler pen to improve thereon, the exemplification will give pleasure to the heart of

CONSTANTIA.
October 22, 1784

"ON THE EQUALITY OF THE SEXES" (1790)

That minds are not alike, full well I know,
This truth each day's experience will show;
To heights surprising some great spirits soar,
With inborn strength mysterious depths explore;

Their eager gaze surveys the path of light,
Confest it stood to Newton's piercing sight.

  Deep science, like a bashful maid retires,
And but the ardent breast her worth inspires;
By perseverance the coy fair is won.
And Genius, led by Study, wears the crown.

  But some there are who wish not to improve,
Who never can the path of knowledge love,
Whose souls almost with the dull body one,
With anxious care each mental pleasure shun;
Weak is the level'd, enervated mind,
And but while here to vegetate design'd.
The torpid spirit mingling with its clod,
Can scarcely boast its origin from God;
Stupidly dull they move progressing on
They eat, and drink, and all their work is done.
While others, emulous of sweet applause,
Industrious seek for each event a cause,
Tracing the hidden springs whence knowledge flows,
Which nature all in beauteous order shows.

  Yet cannot I their sentiments imbibe,
Who this distinction to the sex ascribe,
As if a woman's form must needs enrol,
A weak, a servile, an inferiour soul;
And that the guise of man must still proclaim,
Greatness of mind, and him, to be the same:
Yet as the hours revolve fair proofs arise,
Which the bright wreath of growing fame supplies;
And in past times some men have sunk so low,
That female records nothing less can show.
But imbecility is still confin'd,
And by the lordly sex to us consign'd;
They rob us of the power t'improve,
And then declare we only trifles love;
Yet haste the era, when the world shall know,
That such distinctions only dwell below;
The soul unfetter'd, to no sex confin'd,
Was for the abodes of cloudless day design'd.

Mean time we emulate their manly fires,
Though erudition all their thoughts inspires,
Yet nature with equality imparts,
And noble passions, swell e'en female hearts.

Is it upon mature consideration we adopt the idea, that nature is thus partial in her distributions? Is it indeed a fact, that she hath yielded to one half of the human species so unquestionable a mental superiority? I know that to both sexes elevated understandings, and the reverse, are common. But, suffer me to ask, in what the minds of females are so notoriously deficient, or unequal. May not the intellectual powers be ranged under these four heads—imagination, reason, memory and judgment. The province of imagination hath long since been surrendered up to us, and we have been crowned undoubted sovereigns of the regions of fancy. Invention is perhaps the most arduous effort of the mind; this branch of imagination hath been particularly ceded to us, and we have been time out of mind invested with that creative faculty. Observe the variety of fashions (here I bar the contemptuous smile) which distinguish and adorn the female world; how continually are they changing, insomuch that they almost render the wise man's assertion problematical, and we are ready to say, there is something new under the sun. Now what a playfulness, what an exuberance of fancy, what strength of inventive imagination, doth this continual variation discover? Again, it hath been observed, that if the turpitude of the conduct of our sex, hath been ever so enormous, so extremely ready are we, that the very first thought presents us with an apology, so plausible, as to produce our actions even in an amiable light. Another instance of our creative powers, is our talent for slander; how ingenious are we at inventive scandal? what a formidable story can we in a moment fabricate merely from the force of a prolifick imagination? how many reputations, in the fertile brain of a female, have been utterly despoiled? how industrious are we at improving a hint? suspicion how easily do we convert into conviction, and conviction, embellished by the power of eloquence, stalks abroad to the surprise and confusion of unsuspecting innocence. Perhaps it will be asked if I furnish these facts as instances of excellency in our sex. Certainly not; but as proofs of a creative faculty, of a lively imagination. Assuredly great activity of mind is thereby discovered, and was this activity properly directed, what beneficial effects would follow. Is the needle and kitchen sufficient to employ the operations of a soul thus organized? I should conceive not. Nay, it is a truth that those very departments leave the intelligent principle vacant, and at liberty for speculation. Are we deficient in reason? we can only reason from what we know, and if an opportunity of acquiring knowledge hath been denied us, the inferiority of our sex cannot fairly be deduced from thence. Memory, I believe, will be allowed us in common, since every one's experience must testify, that a loquacious old woman is as frequently met with, as a communicative old man; their subjects are alike drawn from the fund of other times, and the transactions of their youth, or of maturer life, entertain, or perhaps fatigue you, in the evening of their lives. "But our judgment is not so strong—we do not distinguish so well."—Yet it may be questioned, from what doth this superiority, in this determining faculty of the soul, proceed. May we not trace its source in the difference of education, and continued advantages? Will it be said that the judgment of a male of two years old, is more sage than that of a female's of the same age? I believe the reverse is generally observed to be true. But from that period what partiality! how is the one exalted, and the other depressed, by the contrary modes of education which are adopted! the one is taught to aspire, and the other is early confined and limited. As their years increase, the sister must be wholly domesticated, while the brother is led by the hand through all the flowery paths of science. Grant that their minds are by nature equal, yet who shall wonder at the *apparent* superiority, if indeed custom becomes *second nature*; nay if it taketh place of nature, and that it doth the experience of each day will evince. At length arrived at womanhood, the uncultivated fair one feels a void, which the employments allotted her are by no means capable of filling. What can she do? to books she may not apply; or if she doth, *to those only of the novel kind*, lest she merit the appellation of a *learned lady*; and what ideas have been affixed to this term, the observation of many can testify. Fashion, scandal, and sometimes what is still more reprehensible, are then called in to her relief; and who can say to what lengths the liberties she takes may proceed. Meantime she herself is most unhappy; she feels the want of a cultivated mind. Is she single, she in vain seeks to fill up time from sexual employments or amusements.[1] Is she united to a person whose soul nature made equal to her own, education hath set him so far above her, that in those entertainments which are productive of such rational felicity, she is not qualified to accompany him. She experiences a mortifying consciousness of inferiority, which embitters every enjoyment. Doth the person to whom her adverse fate hath consigned her, possess a mind incapable of improvement, she is equally wretched, in being so closely connected with an individual whom she cannot but despise. Now, was she permitted the same instructors as her brother, (with an eye however to their particular departments) for the employment of a rational mind an ample field would be opened. In astronomy she might catch a glimpse of the immensity of the Deity, and thence she would form amazing conceptions of the august and supreme Intelligence. In geography she would admire Jehovah in the

---

[1] Sexual employments or amusements: Those considered appropriate for one sex or the other, such as needlework for women or hunting for men.

midst of his benevolence; thus adapting this globe to the various wants and amusements of its inhabitants. In natural philosophy she would adore the infinite majesty of heaven, clothed in condescension; and as she traversed the reptile world, she would hail the goodness of a creating God. A mind, thus filled, would have little room for the trifles with which our sex are, with too much justice, accused of amusing themselves, and they would thus be rendered fit companions for those, who should one day wear them as their crown. Fashions, in their variety, would then give place to conjectures, which might perhaps conduce to the improvement of the literary world; and there would be no leisure for slander or detraction. Reputation would not then be blasted, but serious speculations would occupy the lively imaginations of the sex. Unnecessary visits would be precluded, and that custom would only be indulged by way of relaxation, or to answer the demands of consanguinity and friendship. Females would become discreet, their judgments would be invigorated, and their partners for life being circumspectly chosen, an unhappy Hymen[2] would then be as rare, as is now the reverse.

Will it be urged that those acquirements would supersede our domestick duties? I answer that every requisite in female economy is easily attained; and, with truth I can add, that when once attained, they require no further *mental attention*. Nay, while we are pursuing the needle, or the superintendency of the family, I repeat, that our minds are at full liberty for reflection; that imagination may exert itself in full vigor; and that if a just foundation is early laid, our ideas will then be worthy of rational beings. If we were industrious we might easily find time to arrange them upon paper, or should avocations press too hard for such an indulgence, the hours allotted for conversation would at least become more refined and rational. Should it still be vociferated, "Your domestick employments are sufficient"—I would calmly ask, is it reasonable, that a candidate for immortality, for the joys of heaven, an intelligent being, who is to spend an eternity in contemplating the works of Deity, should at present be so degraded, as to be allowed no other ideas, than those which are suggested by the mechanism of a pudding, or the sewing the seams of a garment? Pity that all such censurers of female improvement do not go one step further, and deny their future existence; to be consistent they surely ought.

Yes, ye lordly, ye haughty sex, our souls are by nature equal to yours; the same breath of God animates, enlivens, and invigorates us; and that we are not fallen lower than yourselves, let those witness who have greatly towered above the various discouragements by which they have been so heavily oppressed; and though I am

---

[2] Hymen: God of marriage.

unacquainted with the list of celebrated characters on either side, yet from the observations I have made in the contracted circle in which I have moved, I dare confidently believe, that from the commencement of time to the present day, there hath been as many females, as males, who, by the *mere force of natural powers*, have merited the crown of applause; who, *thus unassisted*, have seized the wreath of fame. I know there are who assert, that as the animal powers of the one sex are superiour, of course their mental faculties also must be stronger; thus attributing strength of mind to the transient organization of this earth born tenement. But if this reasoning is just, man must be content to yield the palm to many of the brute creation, since by not a few of his brethren of the field, he is far surpassed in bodily strength. Moreover, was this argument admitted, it would prove too much, for ocular demonstration evinceth, that there are many robust masculine ladies, and effeminate gentlemen. Yet I fancy that Mr. Pope,[3] though clogged with an enervated body, and distinguished by a diminutive stature, could nevertheless lay claim to greatness of soul; and perhaps there are many other instances which might be adduced to combat so unphilosophical an opinion. Do we not often see, that when the clay built tabernacle is well nigh dissolved, when it is just ready to mingle with the parent soil, the immortal inhabitant aspires to, and even attaineth heights the most sublime, and which were before wholly unexplored. Besides, were we to grant that animal strength proved any thing, taking into consideration the accustomed impartiality of nature, we should be induced to imagine, that she had invested the female mind with superiour strength as an equivalent for the bodily powers of man. But waving this however palpable advantage, for *equality only*, we wish to contend.

I am aware that there are many passages in the sacred oracles which seem to give the advantage to the other sex; but I consider all these as wholly metaphorical. Thus David was a man after God's own heart, yet see him enervated by his licentious passions! behold him following Uriah to the death,[4] and shew me wherein could consist the immaculate Being's complacency. Listen to the curses which Job bestoweth upon the day of his nativity, and tell me where is his perfection, where his patience— *literally* it existed not.[5] David and Job were types of him who was to come; and the superiority of man, as exhibited in scripture, being also emblematical, all arguments deduced from thence, of course fall to the ground. The exquisite delicacy of the female mind proclaimeth the exactness of its texture, while its nice sense of honour

---

[3] Alexander Pope (1688–1744): Famed English poet and essayist, author of *The Rape of the Lock* (1712) and the *Dunciad* (1728).
[4] David, Uriah: According to 2 Samuel 11–12 in the Bible, the legendary King David fell in love with Bathsheba, the wife of his soldier Uriah, and ordered Uriah's murder.
[5] Job is the long-suffering and much afflicted protagonist of the Old Testament book of Job.

announceth its innate, its native grandeur. And indeed, in one respect, the preeminence seems to be tacitly allowed us, for after an education which limits and confines, and employments and recreations which naturally tend to enervate the body, and debilitate the mind; after we have from early youth been adorned with ribbons, and other gewgaws, dressed out like the ancient victims previous to a sacrifice, being taught by the care of our parents in collecting the most showy materials that the ornamenting our exteriour ought to be the principal object of our attention; after, I say, fifteen years thus spent, we are introduced into the world, amid the united adulation of every beholder. Praise is sweet to the soul; we are immediately intoxicated by large draughts of flattery, which being plentifully administered, is to the pride of our hearts the most acceptable incense. It is expected that with the other sex we should commence immediate war, and that we should triumph over the machinations of the most artful. We must be constantly upon our guard; prudence and discretion must be our characteristicks; and we must rise superiour to, and obtain a complete victory over those who have been long adding to the native strength of their minds, by an unremitted study of men and books, and who have, moreover, conceived from the loose characters which they have seen portrayed in the extensive variety of their reading, a most contemptible opinion of the sex. Thus unequal, we are, notwithstanding, forced to the combat, and the infamy which is consequent upon the smallest deviation in our conduct, proclaims the high idea which was formed of our native strength; and thus, indirectly at least, is the preference acknowledged to be our due. And if we are allowed an equality of acquirement, let serious studies equally employ our minds, and we will bid our souls arise to equal strength. We will meet upon even ground, the despot man; we will rush with alacrity to the combat, and, crowned by success, we shall then answer the exalted expectations which are formed. Though sensibility, soft compassion, and gentle commiseration, are inmates in the female bosom, yet against every deep laid art, altogether fearless of the event, we will set them in array; for assuredly the wreath of victory will encircle the spotless brow. If we meet an equal, a sensible friend, we will reward him with the hand of amity, and through life we will be assiduous to promote his happiness; but from every deep laid scheme for our ruin, retiring into ourselves, amid the flowery paths of science, we will indulge in all the refined and sentimental pleasures of contemplation. And should it still be urged, that the studies thus insisted upon would interfere with our more peculiar department, I must further reply, that *early hours*, and close application, will do wonders; and to her who is from the first dawn of reason taught to fill up time rationally, both the requisites will be easy. I grant that niggard fortune is too generally unfriendly to the mind; and that much of that valuable treasure, time, is necessarily expended upon the wants of the body; but it should be remembered, that in embarrassed circumstances our companions have as little leisure for literary improvement, as is afforded to us; for most certainly their provident care is at least as requisite as our exertions. Nay, we have even more leisure for sedentary pleasures, as our avocations are more retired, much less laborious, and, as hath been observed, by no means require that avidity of attention which is proper to the employments of the other sex. In high life, or, in other words, where the parties are in possession of affluence, the objection respecting time is wholly obviated, and of course falls to the ground; and it may also be repeated, that many of those hours which are at present swallowed up in fashion and scandal, might be redeemed, were we habituated to useful reflections. But in one respect, O ye arbiters of our fate! we confess that the superiority is indubitably yours; you are by nature formed for our protectors; we pretend not to vie with you in bodily strength; upon this point we will never contend for victory. Shield us then, we beseech you, from external evils, and in return we will transact *your* domestick affairs. Yes, *your*, for are you not equally interested in those matters with ourselves? Is not the elegancy of neatness as agreeable to your sight as to ours; is not the well favoured viand equally delightful to your taste; and doth not your sense of hearing suffer as much, from the discordant sounds prevalent in an ill regulated family, produced by the voices of children and many *et ceteras*?

CONSTANTIA.

By way of supplement to the foregoing pages, I subjoin the following extract from a letter, wrote to a friend in the December of 1780.

And now assist me, O thou genius of my sex, while I undertake the arduous task of endeavouring to combat that vulgar, that almost universal errour, which hath, it seems, enlisted even Mr. P—under its banners. The superiority of your sex hath, I grant, been time out of mind esteemed a truth incontrovertible; in consequence of which persuasion, every plan of education hath been calculated to establish this favourite tenet. Not long since; weak and presuming as I was, I amused myself with selecting some arguments from nature, reason, and experience, against this so generally received idea. I confess that to sacred testimonies I had not recourse. I held them to be merely metaphorical, and thus regarding them, I could not persuade myself that there was any propriety in bringing them to decide in this *very important debate*. However, as you, sir, confine yourself entirely to the sacred oracles, I mean to bend the whole of my artillery against those supposed proofs, which you have from thence provided, and from which you have formed an intrenchment *apparently* so invulnerable. And first, to begin with our great progenitors; but here, suffer me to premise, that it is for mental strength I mean to contend, for with respect to animal powers, I yield them undisputed to that sex, which enjoys them in common with the lion, the tyger, and many other beasts of prey; therefore your observations respecting the *rib under the arm, at a distance from the head, &c. &c.* in no sort militate against my view. Well, but the woman was first in the transgression.[6] Strange how blind *self love* renders you men; were you not wholly absorbed in a partial admiration of your own abilities, you would long since have acknowledged the force of what I am now going to urge. It is true some ignoramuses have absurdly enough informed us, that the beauteous fair of paradise, was seduced from her obedience, by a malignant demon, *in the guise of a baleful serpent*; but we, who are better informed, know that the fallen spirit presented himself to her view, *a shining angel still*; for thus, saith the criticks in the Hebrew tongue, ought the word to be rendered.[7] Let us examine her motive—Hark! the seraph declares that she shall attain a perfection of knowledge; for is there aught which is not comprehended under one or other of the terms good and evil. It doth not appear that she was governed by any one sensual appetite; but merely by a desire of adorning her mind; a laudable ambition fired her soul, and a thirst for knowledge impelled the predilection so fatal in its consequences. Adam could not plead the same deception; assuredly he was not deceived; nor ought we to admire his superiour strength, or wonder at his sagacity, when we so often confess that example is much more influential than precept. His gentle partner stood before him, a melancholy instance of the direful effects of disobedience; he saw her not possessed of that wisdom which she had fondly hoped to obtain, but he beheld the once blooming female, disrobed of that innocence, which had heretofore rendered her so lovely. To him then deception became impossible, as he had proof positive of the fallacy of the argument, which the deceiver had suggested. What then could be his inducement to burst the barriers, and to fly directly in the face of that command, which *immediately* from the mouth of deity *he* had received, since, I say, he could not plead that fascinating stimulous, the accumulation of knowledge, as indisputable conviction was so visibly portrayed before him. What mighty cause impelled him to sacrifice myriads of beings yet unborn, and by one impious act, which *he saw* would be productive of such fatal effects, entail undistinguished ruin upon a race of beings, which he was yet to produce. Blush, ye vaunters of fortitude; ye boasters of resolution; ye haughty lords of the creation; blush when ye remember, that he was influenced by no other motive than a bare pusillanimous attachment to a woman! by sentiments so exquisitely soft, that all his sons have, from that period, when they have designed to degrade them, described as highly feminine. Thus it should seem, that all the arts of the grand

---

[6] A reference to the Biblical Eve, who ate first from the Tree of Knowledge, against God's command.

[7] Murray here indicates a disagreement among Biblical scholars over the translation of the Hebrew word *nachash*, used in Genesis 3:1 to describe the serpent that tempts Eve. That Murray opts to view the serpent as a "shining angel" presages her defense of Eve's decision to eat the fruit of the Tree of Knowledge.

deceiver (since means adequate to the purpose are, I conceive, invariably pursued) were requisite to mislead our general mother, while the father of mankind forfeited his own, and relinquished the happiness of posterity, merely in compliance with the blandishments of a female. The subsequent subjection the apostle Paul explains as a figure; after enlarging upon the subject, he adds, *"This is a great mystery; but I speak concerning Christ and the church."'* Now we know with what consummate wisdom the unerring father of eternity hath formed his plans; all the lie types which he hath displayed, he hath permitted *materially* to fail, in the very virtue for which *they* were famed. The reason for this is obvious, we might otherwise mistake his economy, and render that honour to the creature, which is due only to the creator. I know that Adam was a figure of him who was to come. The grace contained in this figure, is the reason of my rejoicing, and while I am very far from prostrating before the shadow, I yield joyfully in all things the preeminence to the second federal head. Confiding faith is prefigured by Abraham, yet he exhibits a contrast to affiance,[8] when he says of his fair companion, she is my sister. Gentleness was the characteristick of Moses, yet he hesitated not to reply to Jehovah himself, with unsaintlike tongue he murmured. It the waters of strife, and with rash hands he break the tables, which were inscribed by the finger of divinity. David, dignified with the title of the man after God's own heart, and yet how stained was his life. Solomon was celebrated for wisdom, but folly is wrote in legible characters upon his almost every action. Lastly, let us turn our eyes to man in the aggregate. He is manifested as the figure of strength, but that we may not regard him as any thing more than a figure, his soul is formed in no sort superiour, but every way equal to the mind of her, who is the emblem of weakness, and whom he hails the gentle companion of his better days.

---

[8] Affiance: Faithfulness.

THIRTY-SEVEN

Anonymous

*W*OMEN *IN REVOLUTIONARY TIMES ADOPTED POLITICAL TOOLS SUCH AS PETITIONS TO address even intimate concerns. For young women in the new American nation, marriage was a source of intense anxiety and concern. Young women knew that their social and economic opportunities depended heavily if unjustly upon their ability to marry, but the Revolutionary War and transatlantic population movements hurt their access to prospective husbands, creating a great population "disproportion" between the sexes. To draw attention to this imbalance, a network of young women up and down the Atlantic shore of the United States, from Maine to South Carolina, organized this satirical petition demanding that Congress rotate its meeting place among the metropolitan cities of the new United States of America in order to bring large groups of men to each city according to a fair rotation. (From 1774 to 1800, Congress met in numerous locations including New York, Baltimore, and Philadelphia, before settling permanently in Washington D.C.) A playful way of both demonstrating the authors' familiarity with political discourse and venting anxiety about a genuine social problem, the petition appeared in the Philadelphia magazine* American Museum *in April 1787.*

PETITION OF THE YOUNG LADIES (1787)

To the honourable the Delegates of the United States in Congress assembled.

The petition of the young ladies of Portsmouth, Boston, Newport, New-London. Amboy, New-Castle, Williamsburgh, Wilmington, Charleston and Savannah,

Most ardently sheweth,

That your petitioners possess the qualities of youth, health and beauty, in an eminent degree.

That notwithstanding these advantages, they see with great pain but little prospect of getting good husbands, owing to the passion the pretty fellows have of going abroad and marrying in other countries, thereby leaving a great disproportion between the sexes at home.

That population is the true source of national wealth and power.

That in all countries, population increases, in proportion as marriages are frequent.

That without marriage, even the object of the Almighty, in creating them, must be defeated, and his first and great command disobeyed.

That your petitioners have been informed of the many marriages that have taken place in New-York, since your residence in that city, and that even some of your own members have to their great honour, become husbands.

That delegates in congress ought to be all bachelors, and a new election ordered in consequence of marriage, domestic duty being a good excuse from public service.

That with due deference to their New-York sisters, they cannot allow them any just preference in the requisite qualities to make the married state happy.

That as the first motive for appointing a congress was, to promote the welfare of humanity, they presume the daughters, as well as the sons of America, have an equal right to a participation of the blessings arising therefrom.

That for these reasons, your petitioners earnestly request you would annually remove the seat of federal government into the metropolis of each state, in due rotation; leaving Maryland, Pennsylvania and New-York the three last upon the list, you having already resided in each of their capitals.

That if your petitioners' request be granted, they hope, from the number of foreigners and other fine fellows, who keep themselves in the sunshine of preferment, as well as from your own body, to have at least a chance of bringing their accomplishments and good qualities into their destined use, and of thereby improving as well as augmenting society.

THIRTY-EIGHT

Benjamin Rush (1746–1813)

*T*HE INFLUENTIAL PHILADELPHIA PHYSICIAN BENJAMIN RUSH, A SIGNER OF THE DECLARATION *of Independence and an educational reform activist, delivered his* Thoughts on Female Education *(1787) as a speech to visitors at the Young Ladies' Academy in Philadelphia. In it, Rush justifies education for women as a patriotic necessity. Along with such figures as Judith Sargent Murray and Susanna Haswell Rowson, Rush advanced the middle-class ideal of "republican motherhood," which acknowledged women to be intelligent and capable people who deserved education beyond reading the Bible so that they could properly raise good citizens and thus assure the stability and health of the Republic. This notion of republican motherhood, then, more resolutely aligned women with the domestic sphere even as it broadened their right to education. Rush's speech was published in Philadelphia and republished in Boston in 1787.*

FROM *THOUGHTS UPON FEMALE EDUCATION* (1787)

GENTLEMEN,

I HAVE yielded with diffidence to the solicitations of the Principal of the Academy, in undertaking to express my regard for the prosperity of this Seminary of Learning, by submitting to your candor, a few Thoughts upon Female Education.

The first remark that I shall make upon this subject, is, that female education should be accommodated to the state of society, manners, and government of the country, in which it is conducted.

This remark leads me at once to add, that the education of young ladies, in this country, should be conducted upon principles very different from what it is in Great

Britain, and in some respects different from what it was when we were part of a monarchical empire.

There are several circumstances in the situation, employments, and duties of women, in America, which require a peculiar mode of education.

I. The early marriages of our women, by contracting the time allowed for education, renders it necessary to contract its plan, and to confine it chiefly to the more useful branches of literature.

II. The state of property, in America, renders it necessary for the greatest part of our citizens to employ themselves, in different occupations, for the advancement of their fortunes. This cannot be done without the assistance of the female members of the community. They must be the stewards, and guardians of their husbands' property. That education, therefore, will be most proper for our women, which teaches them to discharge the duties of those offices with the most success and reputation.

III. From the numerous avocations to which a professional life exposes gentlemen in America from their families, a principal share of the instruction of children naturally devolves upon the women. It becomes us therefore to prepare them by a suitable education, for the discharge of this most important duty of mothers.

IV. The equal share that every citizen has in the liberty, and the possible share he may have in the government of our country, make it necessary that our ladies should be qualified to a certain degree by a peculiar and suitable education, to concur in instructing their sons in the principles of liberty and government.

V. In Great Britain the business of servants is a regular occupation; but in America this humble station is the usual retreat of unexpected indigence; hence the servants in this country possess less knowledge and subordination than are required from them; and hence, our ladies are obliged to attend more to the private affairs of their families, than ladies generally do, of the same rank in Great Britain. "They are good servants (said an American lady[1] of distinguished merit in a letter to a favorite daughter) who will do well with good looking after." This circumstance should have great influence upon the nature and extent of female education in America. [. . .]

It should not surprise us that British customs, with respect to female education, have been transplanted into our American schools and families. We see marks of the same incongruity, of time and place, in many other things. We behold our houses accommodated to the climate of Great Britain, by eastern and western directions. We behold our ladies panting in a heat of ninety degrees, under a hat and cushion, which

---

[1] The text notes that this woman is "Mrs. Graeme." Mrs. Graeme was likely Anne Diggs Graeme, the mother of Elizabeth Graeme Fergusson (1737–1801). Graeme Fergusson was a well-respected intellectual who held a literary salon in her home, Graeme Park, in which Rush participated.

were calculated for the temperature of a British summer. We behold our citizens condemned and punished by a criminal law, which was copied from a country where maturity in corruption renders public executions a part of the amusements of the nation. It is high time to awake from this servility—to study our own character—to examine the age of our country—and to adopt manners in every thing, that shall be accommodated to our state of society, and to the forms of our government. In particular it is incumbent upon us to make ornamental accomplishments, yield to principles and knowledge, in the education of our women.

A philosopher once said "let me make all the ballads of a country and I care not who makes its laws."[2] He might with more propriety have said, let the ladies of a country be educated properly, and they will not only make and administer its laws, but form its manners and character. It would require a lively imagination to describe, or even to comprehend, the happiness of a country, where knowledge and virtue, were generally diffused among the female sex. Our young men would then be restrained from vice by the terror of being banished from their company. The loud laugh, and the malignant smile, at the expence of innocence, or of personal infirmities—the feats of successful mimickry—and the low priced wit, which is borrowed from a misapplication of scripture phrases, would no more be considered as recommendations to the society of the ladies. A double entendre, in their presence, would then exclude a gentleman forever from the company of both sexes, and probably oblige him to seek an asylum from contempt, in a foreign country. The influence of female education would be still more extensive and useful in domestic life. The obligations of gentlemen to qualify themselves by knowledge and industry to discharge the duties of benevolence, would be encreased by marriage; and the patriot—the hero—and the legislator, would find the sweetest reward of their toils, in the approbation and applause of their wives. Children would discover the marks of maternal prudence and wisdom in every station of life; for it has been remarked that there have been few great or good men who have not been blessed with wise and prudent mothers. Cyrus was taught to revere the gods, by his mother Mandane[3]—Samuel was devoted to his prophetic office before he was born, by his mother Hannah[4]—Constantine was rescued from paganism by his mother Constantia[5]—and Edward the sixth inherited those great and excellent qualities which made him the delight of the age in which he lived, from his mother, lady

---

[2] This quote is from *The Political Works of Andrew Fletcher* (London, 1732).

[3] Cyrus the Great (559–529 BC) was the founder of the Persian empire.

[4] Samuel is an Old Testament prophet. The childless Hannah prayed for his birth and promised to dedicate her child to God if she conceived. See 1 Samuel 1.

[5] Probably Constantine the Great. Constantine (306–337) was the first Christian Roman emperor. Constantia (ca. 292–ca. 329) was his half-sister, not his mother.

Jane Seymour.[6] Many other instances might be mentioned, if necessary, from ancient and modern history, to establish the truth of this proposition.

I am not enthusiastical[7] upon the subject of education. In the ordinary course of human affairs, we shall probably too soon follow the footsteps of the nations of Europe in manners and vices. The first marks we shall perceive of our declension, will appear among our women. Their idleness, ignorance and profligacy will be the harbingers of our ruin. Then will the character and performance of a buffoon on the theatre, be the subject of more conversation and praise, than the patriot or the minister of the gospel;—then will our language and pronunciation be enfeebled and corrupted by a flood of French and Italian words;—then will the history of romantic amours, be preferred to the immortal writings of Addison, Hawkesworth and Johnson;[8]—then will our churches be neglected, and the name of the supreme being never be called upon, but in profane exclamations;—then will our Sundays be appropriated, only to feasts and concerts;—and then will begin all that train of domestic and political calamities.—But, I forbear. The prospect is so painful, that I cannot help, silently, imploring the great arbiter of human affairs, to interpose his almighty goodness, and to deliver us from these evils, that, at least one spot of the earth may be reserved as a monument of the effects of good education, in order to shew in some degree, what our species was, before the fall, and what it shall be, after its restoration.—

Thus, gentlemen, have I briefly finished what I proposed. If I am wrong in those opinions in which I have taken the liberty of departing from general and fashionable habits of thinking, I am sure you will discover, and pardon my mistakes. But, if I am right, I am equally sure you will adopt my opinions; for to enlightened minds truth is alike acceptable, whether it comes from the lips of age, or the hand of antiquity, or whether it be obtruded by a person, who has no other claim to attention, than a desire of adding to the stock of human happiness. [. . .]

---

[6] Edward VI (1537–1553) was the son of Henry VIII and Jane Seymour. Seymour died two weeks after giving birth. Edward became King of England in 1547 while still a child. A Regency Council ruled in his stead until his death in 1553.

[7] Enthusiastical: Irrational or fanatical.

[8] Addison, Hawkesworth and Johnson: All three were authors of successful and widely read English periodicals. Joseph Addison (1672–1719) coproduced the *Spectator*. Samuel Johnson (1709–1784) published the *Rambler*. When Johnson's wife died and he stopped publishing the *Rambler*, John Hawkesworth (1720–1773) started the *Adventurer* as its successor.

THIRTY-NINE

Hannah More (1745–1833)

WHILE PARTISANS OF THE AMERICAN REVOLUTION OFTEN SET ASIDE ISSUES OF GENDER *and race to achieve their nationalist agenda, we find women writers of the late eighteenth century (like the enslaved poet Phillis Wheatley, whose writing appears elsewhere in this anthology) drawing connections between different forms of unfreedom.* Slavery: A Poem *is one of the first literary evidences we have of modern feminist consciousness among white women expanding to include issues of racial injustice as well. The wide-ranging author, conversationalist, and social re- former Hannah More moved in many of the most important London religious, phil- osophical, and literary circles of her time. Born near Bristol, one of England's busiest ports and hence the home of many who owned slaves on Caribbean planta- tions, and raised by parents who ran a boarding school, More also taught school before a failed engagement freed her to leave home and pursue a writing life in Lon- don. Many of her early writings were plays, but in the 1780s she began to write on serious political subjects. Slavery was a matter of growing concern in England, which was then one of the world's leaders in slave trafficking. In 1772, Lord Somer- set in the Mansfield case had ruled that a slave who traveled to England from the British colonies could not be compelled to remain a slave, establishing England as a sort of refuge for slaves within the Empire; Phillis Wheatley took advantage of the Mansfield ruling to secure her manumission in 1773. During the 1770s, the Society of Friends, or Quakers, resolved that slavery was inconsistent with its theology and called upon Friends worldwide to emancipate their slaves. This along with the organizing and advocacy of enslaved and free Blacks set off a wave of antislave trade and antislavery activism in Great Britain. Antislavery societies formed, and Afro-Britons like Olaudah Equiano published their own autobiographies to publicize the horrors of the slave trade.*

Many of the early feminist authors included in this anthology had described the situation of women as enslavement, and some had commented favorably or unfavorably on the situation of women in other cultures and other regions of the globe. Hannah More boldly challenges the proslavery rationale that human beings on one continent were endowed with greater intelligence or humanity than others: appealing to a timely notion of universal human rights, she demands, "Does th' immortal principle within/Change with the casual colour of a skin?" She also cites the example of the enslaved African royal Oroonoko, a fictitious character created by Aphra Behn (and recreated by Thomas Southerne in his 1696 play adaptation), and uses her own imagination to depict the pains of African families sundered by slavery. More declares that agents of conquest and the slave trade are not Christians but "white savage[s]" and criticizes the incompatibility of British values of freedom and its involvement in the slave trade.

SLAVERY: A POEM (1788)

IF heaven has into being deign'd to call
Thy light, O Liberty! to shine on all;
Bright intellectual Sun! why does thy ray
To earth distribute only partial day?
Since no resisting cause from spirit flows
Thy penetrating essence to op[p]ose;
No obstacles by Nature's hand imprest,
Thy subtle and ethereal beams arrest;
Nor motion's laws can speed thy active course,
Nor strong repulsion's pow'rs obstruct thy force;
Since there is no convexity in MIND,
Why are thy genial beams to parts confin'd?
While the chill North with thy bright ray is blest,
Why should fell darkness half the South invest?
Was it decreed, fair Freedom! at thy birth,
That thou shou'd'st ne'er irradiate *all* the earth?
While Britain basks in thy full blaze of light,
Why lies sad Afric quench'd in total night?

    Thee only, sober Goddess! I attest,
In smiles chastis'd, and decent graces drest,
Not that unlicens'd monster of the crowd,
Whose roar terrific bursts in peals so loud,

Deaf'ning the ear of Peace: fierce Faction's tool;

Of rash Sedition born, and mad Misrule;

Whose stubborn mouth, rejecting Reason's rein,

No strength can govern, and no skill restrain;

Whose magic cries the frantic vulgar draw

To spurn at Order, and to outrage Law;

To tread on grave Authority and Pow'r,

And shake the work of ages in an hour:

Convuls'd her voice, and pestilent her breath,

She raves of mercy, while she deals out death:

Each blast is fate; she darts from either hand

Red conflagration o'er th' astonish'd land;

Clamouring for peace, she rends the air with noise,

And to reform a part, the whole destroys.

O, plaintive Southerne![1] whose impassion'd strain

So oft has wak'd my languid Muse in vain!

Now, when congenial themes her cares engage,

She burns to emulate thy glowing page;

Her failing efforts mock her fond desires,

She shares thy feelings, not partakes thy fires.

Strange pow'r of song! the strain that warms the heart

Seems the same inspiration to impart;

Touch'd by the kindling energy alone,

We think the flame which melts us is our own;

Deceiv'd, for genius we mistake delight,

Charm'd as we read, we fancy we can write.

Tho' not to me, sweet Bard, thy pow'rs belong

Fair Truth, a hallow'd guide! inspires my song.

Here Art wou'd weave her gayest flow'rs in vain,

For Truth the bright invention wou'd disdain.

For no fictitious ills these numbers flow,

But living anguish, and substantial woe;

No individual griefs my bosom melt,

For millions feel what Oronoko[2] felt:

---

[1] Thomas Southerne (1660–1746): Irish playwright, author of *Oroonoko* (1696), an antislavery play based on the novella of the same title by Aphra Behn.

[2] Oronoko: Enslaved African prince, hero of the novel *Oroonoko* (1688) by Aphra Behn and the play *Oroonoko* (1696) by Thomas Southerne.

Fir'd by no single wrongs, the countless host
I mourn, by rapine dragg'd from Afric's coast.
    Perish th'illiberal thought which wou'd debase
The native genius of the sable race!
Perish the proud philosophy, which sought
To rob them of the pow'rs of equal thought!
Does then th' immortal principle within
Change with the casual colour of a skin?
Does matter govern spirit? or is mind
Degraded by the form to which 'tis join'd?
    No: they have heads to think, and hearts to feel,
And souls to act, with firm, tho' erring, zeal;[3]
For they have keen affections, kind desires,
Love strong as death, and active patriot fires;
All the rude energy, the fervid flame,
Of high-soul'd passion, and ingenuous shame:
Strong, but luxuriant virtues boldly shoot
From the wild vigour of a savage root.
Nor weak their sense of honour's proud control,
For pride is virtue in a Pagan soul;
A sense of worth, a conscience of desert,
A high, unbroken haughtiness of heart:
That self-same stuff which erst proud empires sway'd,
Of which the conquerers of the world were made.
Capricious fate of man! that very pride
In Afric scourg'd, in Rome was deify'd.
    No Muse, O Quashi![4] shall thy deeds relate,
No statue snatch thee from oblivious fate!

---

[3] Firm, tho' erring, zeal: Strong but mistaken religious beliefs, a reference to the fact that most Africans were not Christians, although some, like Phillis Wheatley, converted in America.

[4] More's note: "It is a point of honour among negroes of a high spirit to die rather than to suffer their glossy skin to bear the mark of the whip. Qua-shi had somehow offended his master, a young planter with whom he had been bred up in the endearing intimacy of a play-fellow. His services had been faithful; his attachment affectionate. The master resolved to punish him, and persued him for that purpose. In trying to escape Qua-shi stumbled and fell; the master fell upon him; they wrestled long with doubtful victory; at length Qua-shi got uppermost, and, being firmly seated on his master's breast, he secured his legs with one hand, and with the other drew a sharp knife; then said, "Master, I have been bred up with you from a child; I have loved you as myself: in return, you have condemned me to a punishment of which I must ever have borne the marks: thus only can I avoid them;" so saying, he drew the knife with all his strength across his own throat, and fell down

For thou wast born where never gentle Muse
On Valour's grave the flow'rs of Genius strews;
And thou wast born where no recording page
Plucks the fair deed from Time's devouring rage.
Had Fortune plac'd thee on some happier coast,
Where polish'd souls heroic virtue boast,
To thee, who sought'st a voluntary grave,
Th' uninjur'd honours of thy name to save,
Whose generous arm thy barbarous Master spar'd,
Altars had smok'd, and temples had been rear'd.
　　Whene'er to Afric's shores I turn my eyes,
Horrors of deepest, deadliest guilt arise;
I see, by more than Fancy's mirror shewn,
The burning village, and the blazing town:
See the dire victim torn from social life,
The shrieking babe, the agonizing wife!
She, wretch forlorn! is dragg'd by hostile hands,
To distant tyrants sold, in distant lands!
Transmitted miseries, and successive chains,
The sole sad heritage her child obtains!
Ev'n this last wretched boon their foes deny,
To weep together, or together die.
By felon hands, by one relentless stroke,
See the fond links of feeling nature broke!
The fibres twisting round a parent's heart,
Torn from their grasp, and bleeding as they part.
　　Hold, murderers, hold! not aggravate distress;
Respect the passions you yourselves possess;
Ev'n you, of ruffian heart, and ruthless hand,
Love your own offspring, love your native land.
Ah! leave them holy Freedom's cheering smile,
The heav'n-taught fondness for the parent soil;
Revere affections mingled with our frame,

---

dead, without a groan, on his master's body. Ramsay's *Essay on the Treatment of African Slaves*."
James Ramsay (1733–1789) was an English abolitionist, ship's surgeon, and Anglican priest who
had served Black and white parishioners in the Caribbean; his *Essay on the Treatment and Conversion of African Slaves in the British Sugar Colonies* was published in 1784.

In every nature, every clime the same;

In all, these feelings equal sway maintain;

In all the love of HOME and FREEDOM reign:

And Tempe's vale,[5] and parch'd Angola's[6] sand,

One equal fondness of their sons command.

Th' unconquer'd Savage laughs at pain and toil,

Basking in Freedom's beams which gild his native soil.

    Does thirst of empire, does desire of fame,

(For these are specious crimes) our rage inflame?

No: sordid lust of gold their fate controls,

The basest appetite of basest souls;

Gold, better gain'd, by what their ripening sky,

Their fertile fields, their arts[7] and mines supply.

    What wrongs, what injuries does Opression plead

To smooth the horror of th' unnatural deed?

What strange offence, what aggravated sin?

They stand convicted—of a darker skin!

Barbarians, hold! th' opprobious commerce spare,

Respect *his* sacred image which they bear:

Tho' dark and savage, ignorant and blind,

They claim the common privilege of kind;

Let Malice strip them of each other plea,

They still are men, and men shou'd still be free.

Insulted Reason, loaths th' inverted trade—

Dire change! the agent is the purchase made!

Perplex'd, the baffled Muse involves the tale;

Nature confounded, well may language fail!

The outrag'd Goddess with abhorrent eyes

Sees MAN the traffic, SOULS the merchandize!

    Plead not, in reason's palpable abuse,

Their sense of feeling[8] callous and obtuse:

---

[5] Tempe's vale: The vale of Tempe is a rugged valley at the foot of Mount Olympus in northeastern Greece, reputed to be the home of Artemis and other Greek gods.

[6] Angola: Southern-central African country, a former Portuguese colony.

[7] More's note: "Besides many valuable productions of the soil, cloths and carpets of exquisite manufacture are brought from the coast of Guinea." Guinea is a coastal West African country, a former French colony.

[8] More's note: "Nothing is more frequent than this cruel and stupid argument, that they do not *feel* the miseries inflicted on them as Europeans would do."

From heads to hearts lies Nature's plain appeal,
Tho' few can reason, all mankind can feel.
Tho' wit may boast a livelier dread of shame,
A loftier sense of wrong refinement claim;
Tho' polished manners may fresh wants invent,
And nice distinctions nicer souls torment;
Tho' these on finer spirits heavier fall,
Yet natural evils are the same to all.
Tho' wounds there are which reason's force may heal,
There needs no logic sure to make us feel.
The nerve, howe'er untutor'd, can sustain
A sharp, unutterable sense of pain;
As exquisitely fashion'd in a slave,
As where unequal fate a sceptre gave.
Sense is as keen where Congo's[9] sons preside,
As where proud Tiber[10] rolls his classic tide.
Rhetoric or verse may point the feeling line,
They do not whet sensation, but define.
Did ever slave less feel the galling chain,
When Zeno[11] prov'd there was no ill in pain?
Their miseries philosophic quirks deride,
Slaves groan in pangs disown'd by Stoic pride.

    When the fierce Sun darts vertical his beams,
And thirst and hunger mix their wild extremes;
When the sharp iron[12] wounds his inmost soul,
And his strain'd eyes in burning anguish roll;
Will the parch'd negro find, ere he expire,
No pain in hunger, and no heat in fire?
    For him, when fate his tortur'd frame destroys,
What hope of present fame, or future joys?
For *this*, have heroes shorten'd nature's date;
For *that*, have martyrs gladly met their fate;

---

[9] Congo: Central African country, a former French colony.
[10] Tiber: Legendary Italian river.
[11] Zeno of Elea (490 BC?–430 BC?), Stoic philosopher who argued that pain, while unpleasant, was not evil.
[12] More's note: "This is not said figuratively. The writer of these lines has seen a complete set of chains, fitted to every separate limb of these unhappy, innocent men; together with instruments for wrenching open the jaws, contrived with such ingenious cruelty as would shock the humanity of an inquisitor."

But him, forlorn, no hero's pride sustains,
No martyr's blissful visions sooth his pains;
Sullen, he mingles with his kindred dust,
For he has learn'd to dread the Christian's trust;
To him what mercy can that Pow'r display,
Whose servants murder, and whose sons betray?
Savage! thy venial error I deplore,
They are *not* Christians who infest thy shore.
    O thou sad spirit, whose preposterous yoke
The great deliver Death, at length, has broke!
Releas'd from misery, and escap'd from care,
Go meet that mercy man deny'd thee here.
In thy dark home, sure refuge of th' opress'd,
The wicked vex not, and the weary rest.
And, if some notions, vague and undefin'd,
Of future terrors have assail'd thy mind;
If such thy masters have presum'd to teach,
As terrors only they are prone to preach;
(For shou'd they paint eternal Mercy's reign,
Where were th' oppressor's rod, the captive's chain?)
If, then, thy troubled soul has learn'd to dread
The dark unknown thy trembling footsteps tread;
On HIM, who made thee what thou art, depend;
HE, who withholds the means, accepts the end.
Not *thine* the reckoning dire of LIGHT abus'd,
KNOWLEDGE disgrac'd, and LIBERTY misus'd;
On *thee* no awful judge incens'd shall sit
For parts perverted, and dishonour'd wit.
Where ignorance will be found the surest plea,
How many learn'd and wise shall envy *thee*!
    And thou, WHITE SAVAGE! whether lust of gold,
Or lust of conquest, rule thee uncontrol'd!
Hero, or robber!—by whatever name
Thou plead thy impious claim to wealth or fame;
Whether inferior mischiefs be thy boast,
A petty tyrant rifling Gambia's[13] coast:

---

[13] Gambia: West African nation, a former British colony.

Or bolder carnage track thy crimson way,
Kings disposses'd, and Provinces thy prey;
Panting to tame wide earth's remotest bound;
All Cortez[14] murder'd, all Columbus[15] found;
O'er plunder'd realms to reign, detested Lord,
Make millions wretched, and thyself abhorr'd;—
In Reason's eye, in Wisdom's fair account,
Your sum of glory boasts a like amount;
The means may differ, but the end's the same;
Conquest is pillage with a nobler name.
Who makes the sum of human blessings less,
Or sinks the stock of general happiness,
No solid fame shall grace, no true renown,
His life shall blazon, or his memory crown.

   Had those advent'rous spirits who explore
Thro' ocean's trackless wastes, the far-sought shore;
Whether of wealth insatiate, or of pow'r,
Conquerors who waste, or ruffians who devour:
Had these possess'd, O COOK![16] thy gentle mind,
Thy love of arts, thy love of humankind;
Had these pursued thy mild and liberal plan,
DISCOVERERS had not been a curse to man!
The[n], bless'd Philanthropy! thy social hands
Had link'd dissever'd worlds in brothers bands;
Careless, if colour, or if clime divide;
Then, lov'd, and loving, man had liv'd, and died.

   The purest wreaths which hang on glory's shrine,
For empires founded, peaceful PENN![17] are thine;
No blood-stain'd laurels crown'd thy virtuous toil,
No slaughter'd natives drench'd thy fair-earn'd soil.

---

[14] Hernan Cortes (1485–1547): Spanish conquistador credited with the conquest of the Aztec Empire in Mexico.

[15] Christopher Columbus (1451–1506): Italian-born explorer and colonizer credited with initiating Spanish colonization in the Americas after his landing in Hispaniola in 1492.

[16] James Cook (1728–1779): English explorer and cartographer best known for his exploration of the South Pacific, Australia, and the northwestern coast of North America.

[17] William Penn (1644–1718): English colonist, founder of Pennsylvania. A member of the Society of Friends, or Quakers, Penn was a pacifist.

Still thy meek spirit in thy[18] flock survives,
Consistent still, *their* doctrines rule their lives;
Thy followers only have effac'd the shame
Inscrib'd by SLAVERY on the Christian name.

    Shall Britain, where the soul of freedom reigns,
Forge chains for others she herself disdains?
Forbid it, Heaven! O let the nations know
The liberty she loves she will bestow;
Not to herself the glorious gift confin'd,
She spreads the blessing wide as humankind;
And, scorning narrow views of time and place,
Bids all be free in earth's extended space.

    What page of human annals can record
A deed so bright as human rights restor'd?
O may that god-like deed, that shining page,
Redeem OUR fame, and consecrate OUR age!

    And see, the cherub Mercy from above,
Descending softly, quits the sphere of love!
On feeling hearts she sheds celestial dew,
And breathes her spirit o'er th' enlighten'd few;
From soul to soul the spreading influence steals,
Till every breast the soft contagion feels.
She bears, exulting, to the burning shore
The loveliest office Angel ever bore;
To vindicate the pow'r in Heaven ador'd,
To still the clank of chains, and sheathe the sword;
To cheer the mourner, and with soothing hands
From bursting hearts unbind th' Oppressor's bands;
To raise the lustre of the Christian name,
And clear the foulest blot that dims its fame.

    As the mild Spirit hovers o'er the coast,
A fresher hue the wither'd landscapes boast;
Her healing smiles the ruin'd scenes repair,

---

[18] More's note: "The Quakers have emancipated all their slaves throughout America." Concerns about slaveholding were articulated by Quakers from founding of the faith in the seventeenth century. Quaker antislavery gained momentum in the 1750s, and the world's first antislavery society was founded by Quakers in Philadelphia in 1775.

And blasted Nature wears a joyous air.

She spreads her blest commission from above,

Stamp'd with the sacred characters of love;

She tears the banner stain'd with blood and tears,

And, LIBERTY! thy shining standard rears!

As the bright ensign's glory she displays,

See pale OPPRESSION faints beneath the blaze!

The giant dies! no more his frown appals,

The chain untouch'd, drops off; the fetter falls.

Astonish'd echo tells the vocal shore,

Opression's fall'n, and Slavery is no more!

The dusky myriads crowd the sultry plain,

And hail that mercy long invok'd in vain.

Victorious Pow'r! she bursts their two-fold bands,

And FAITH and FREEDOM spring from Mercy's hands.

FINIS.

FORTY

Anonymous

ONE OF THE DEFINING EVENTS OF THE AGE OF REVOLUTIONS WAS THE FRENCH *Revolution (1789–1799), a period of radical transformation and moderni-zation of France's once monarchical, aristocratic, and feudal society. It began in May 1789 with the Convocation of the Estates-General, a meeting between rep-resentatives of the different estates, or classes, in French society and King Louis XVI. (Louiss' indifference to the demands of the people at the Convocation was one of the proximate causes of the storming of the Bastille on July 14, 1789.) Prerevolutionary France (and much of Europe) recognized three estates: the clergy (the first estate), the nobility (the second estate), and commoners (the third estate), who were supported by their own labor rather than by inherited wealth. Peasants in the countryside, though excluded from wealth by the siegneural system of land tenure, could sometimes hope to grow their own food, but the urban working poor depended on affordable bread to survive. Poor crops led to widespread hunger during the revolutionary years, and women were especially vulnerable. Because their work as seamstresses, embroiderers, and clothing sellers took women of the third estate into the marketplace, they were often regarded in the same light as prostitutes, as women who sold their labor publicly for subsistence. Indeed, during times of hardship many women were forced into prostitution to obtain food for themselves or their children. Many revolutionary leaders (such as Pauline Léon and Olympe de Gouges) came from the third estate.*

Women participated in the Convocation by drafting this petition, using an important genre of modern political writing to express their grievances. Here, the women ask the King, still society's highest authority in this prerevolutionary moment, to make education available to working women so that they can better support themselves, and to protect their traditional professions from men. In the period leading up to the Revolution, women did not have the right to meet as a group, draft grievances, or vote in the elections of estate representatives, yet these women met and put their concerns on paper in a gesture of revolutionary hopefulness.

PETITION OF WOMEN OF THE THIRD ESTATE
TO THE KING (1789)[1]

Sire,

At a time when the various orders of the state are busy with their interests, when everyone is trying to assert his titles and his rights, when some people are worrying about recalling centuries of servitude and anarchy, when others are making every effort to shake off the last links which still bind them to the imperious remains of the feudal system, women—continual objects of the admiration and scorn of men—women, wouldn't it be possible for them also to make their voice heard amidst this general agitation?

Excluded from the national assemblies by laws too well consolidated for them to hope to break, they do not ask, Sire, for your permission to send their deputies to the Estates General; they know too well how great a role interest[2] would play in an election and how easy it would be for the representatives [*les élus*] to impede the freedom of the votes.

We prefer, Sire, to place our cause at your feet; not wishing to obtain anything except from your heart, we address our complaints and confide our miseries to it.

The women of the Third Estate are almost all born without fortune; their education is very neglected or very defective: it consists in their being sent to schools at the house of a teacher who himself does not know the first word of the language he is teaching. They continue going there until they are able to read the service of the Mass in French and Vespers in Latin.[3] Having fulfilled the first duties of religion, they are taught to work; having reached the age of fifteen or sixteen, they can make five or six *sous* a day. If nature has refused them beauty, they get married without dowry to unfortunate artisans, lead aimless, difficult lives stuck away in the provinces,

---

[1] From *Women in Revolutionary Paris, 1789–1795: Selected Documents Translated with Notes and Commentary.* Translated with notes and commentary by Darline Gay Levy, Harriet Branson Applewhite, and Mary Durham Johnson. Copyright 1979 by the Board of Trustees of the University of Illinois. Used with permission of the editors and the University of Illinois Press.

[2] Interest: Political partisanship.

[3] Mass, Vespers: Roman Catholic religious rituals.

and give birth to children they are incapable of raising. If, on the contrary, they are born pretty, without culture, without principles, without any idea of morals, they become the prey of the first seducer, commit a first sin, come to Paris to bury their shame, end by losing it altogether, and die victims of licentious ways.

Today, when the difficulty of subsisting forces thousands of them to put themselves up for auction, when men find it easier to buy them for a spell than to win them forever, those whom a happy penchant inclines to virtue, who are consumed by the desire to learn, who feel themselves led by a natural taste, who have overcome the deficiencies of their education and know a little of everything without having learned anything, those, to conclude, whom a haughty soul, a noble heart, a pride of sentiment cause to be called *prudish*, are forced to throw themselves into cloisters where only a modest dowry is required, or forced to hire themselves out when they do not have enough courage, enough heroism, to share the generous devotion of the daughters of Vincent de Paul.

Also, several, solely because they are born girls, are disdained by their parents, who refuse to set them up, preferring to concentrate their fortune on the head of a son whom they designate to carry on their name in the capital; for it is good that Your Majesty understands that we also have names to keep up. Or, if old age finds them spinsters, they spend it in tears and see themselves the object of the scorn of their nearest relatives.

To prevent so many ills, Sire, we ask that men not be allowed, under any pretext, to exercise trades that are the prerogative of women—such as seamstress, embroiderer, *marchande de mode*, etc., etc.;[4] if we are left at least with the needle and the spindle, we promise never to handle the compass or the square.

We ask, Sire, that your benevolence provide us with the means of putting to use the talents with which nature will have furnished us, notwithstanding the impediments which are forever being placed on our education.

May you assign us positions, which we alone will be able to fill, which we will occupy only after having passed a strict examination, after trustworthy inquiries concerning the purity of our morals.

We ask to be enlightened, to have work, not in order to usurp men's authority, but in order to be better esteemed by them, so that we might have the means of living out of the way of misfortune and so that poverty does not force the weakest among us, who are blinded by luxury and swept along by example, to join the crowd of unfortunate beings who overpopulate the streets and whose debauched audacity is a disgrace to our sex and to the men who keep them company.

---

[4] *Marchande de mode*: Clothing seller.

We would want this class of women to wear a mark of identification. Today, when they go so far as to adopt the modesty of our dress, when they mingle everywhere in all kinds of clothing, we often find ourselves taken for them; some men are mistaken and make us blush because of their scorn. It would be necessary that under pain of having to work in the public workshops for the benefit of the poor (it is known that work is the greatest punishment that can be inflicted on them), they never be able to remove this mark. . . . . . . [sic] However, it occurs to us that the empire of fashion would be destroyed and one would run the risk of seeing many too many women dressed in the same color.

We implore you, Sire, to set up free schools where we could learn our language on the basis of principles [and] religion and ethics. May one and the other be offered to us in all their grandeur, entirely stripped of the petty applications which attenuate their majesty; may our hearts be formed there; may we be taught above all to practice the virtues of our sex: gentleness, modesty, patience, charity; as for the arts that please, women learn them without teachers. Sciences? . . . they serve only to inspire us with a stupid pride, lead us to pedantry, go against the desires of nature, make of us mixed beings who are rarely faithful wives and still more rarely good mothers of families.

We ask to come out of the state of ignorance, to be able to give our children a sound and reasonable education so as to make of them subjects worthy of serving you. We will teach them to cherish the beautiful name of Frenchmen; we will transmit to them the love we have for Your Majesty, for we are willing to leave valor and genius to men, but we will challenge them over the dangerous and precious gift of sensitivity; we defy them to love you better than we; they run to Versailles.[5] most of them for their interests, and when we, Sire, see you there, with difficulty and with pounding hearts, and are able to gaze for an instant upon your August Person, tears flow from our eyes. The idea of Majesty, of Sovereign, vanishes, and we see in you only a tender Father, for whom we would sacrifice our lives a thousand times.

---

[5] *Versailles*: The royal residence.

FORTY-ONE

Gilbert du Motier, Marquis de Lafayette (1757–1834)

*L*AFAYETTE, *AN ARISTOCRAT FROM AUVERGNE IN SOUTH CENTRAL FRANCE, COMPOSED THIS*
fundamental document of the French Revolution in consultation with Thomas
Jefferson. Lafayette had traveled to the North American colonies at the age of 19,
where he met both Jefferson and Washington. He received a commission of Major
General in the United States Revolutionary Army and was instrumental in the defeat
of the British. He then returned to France to support the revolution there, serving as
a leader of the Garde Nationale, a system of militias set up to ensure order and
defend the Constitution in the wake of the storming of the Bastille in 1789.

Adopted in August 1789, the document below was a foundational instrument for
writing the constitution of France and later international human rights agreements
because of its articulation of the Enlightenment philosophy of "natural rights," the
idea that human beings are endowed with certain universal rights regardless of the
laws or customs of any particular culture or country. Although the document fails to
address either the end of slavery or the enfranchisement of women, it was often cited
in arguments for abolition and women's suffrage. The slave trade ended in France in
1832; women won the vote in 1944.

DECLARATION OF THE RIGHTS OF MAN AND CITIZEN (1789)

PREAMBLE

THE representatives of the French people, constituted as a national assembly, believing that the ignorance, neglect, or contempt of the rights of man are the sole causes of public troubles and of the corruption of governments, have resolved to set forth, in a solemn declaration, the natural, unalienable and sacred rights of man, in order that this declaration, being constantly before all the members of the social body, shall remind them continually of their rights and duties; in order that acts of legislative power, and those of executive power, may be compared at any moment with the aims of any political institution, and be more respected; in order that the grievances of the citizens, based henceforth upon simple and incontestable principles, shall tend always to the maintenance of the constitution and to the happiness of all.

CONSEQUENTLY, the national assembly recognizes and declares, in the presence and under the auspices of the supreme Being, the following rights of man and of citizen:

FIRST ARTICLE.

MEN are born and live free and equal in rights. Social distinctions can be based only on the common utility.

II.

THE purpose of any political association is the conservation of the natural and imprescriptible rights of man: these rights are liberty, property, security, and resistance to oppression.[1]

III.

THE principle of all sovereignty rests essentially with the nation. No body and no individual can exercise any authority which does not come expressly from it.

IV.

LIBERTY consists of the ability to do anything that does not harm others; thus, the only limits on the exercise of the natural rights of each man are those which assure the other members of society the enjoyment of the same rights; these limits can only be determined by law.

V.

LAW can only proscribe those acts harmful to society. Everything which is not prohibited by law cannot be prevented, and no one can be constrained to do what they do not command.

VI.

LAW is the expression of the general will. All citizens have a right to contribute either personally, or through their representatives, to its formation; it must be the

---

[1] Imprescriptible: Not to be proscribed or limited.

same for all, whether it protects, whether it punishes. All citizens being equal in the eyes of the law are equally admitted to all honors, positions, and public employment, according to their capacity, and without other distinctions besides those of their virtues and talents.

VII.

NO person shall be accused, arrested, or detained except in cases determined by law, and according to the forms it prescribes, those who solicit, transmit, execute, or cause to be executed, any arbitrary order, must be punished; but any citizen summoned or seized by virtue of the law must obey without delay: he renders himself guilty through resistance.

VIII.

LAW must establish only those penalties that are strictly and obviously necessary, and no one can be punished except by virtue of a law established and promulgated prior to the crime, and legally applicable.

IX.

EVERY man being presumed innocent until he has been declared guilty, if it is judged indispensable to arrest him, any severity [*rigueur*] not essential for assuring his person must be severely repressed by law.

X.

NO one is to be disquieted for his opinions, including religious ones, provided that their demonstration does not disturb the legally established public order.

XI.

THE free communication of thoughts and opinions is one of the most precious rights of man: every citizen thus may speak [*parler*], write, print freely, but shall be responsible for the abuse of this liberty in cases determined by law.

XII.

THE guarantee of the rights of man and of citizen implies a public force: this force is thus instituted for the advantage of all, and not for the particular benefit of those to whom it is entrusted.

XIII.

FOR the support of the public force, and the expenses of administration, a common contribution is essential: it must be equally distributed among all citizens, in proportion to their means.

XIV.

ALL citizens have the right to verify, either by themselves or through their representatives, the necessity of the public contribution, to consent to it freely, to monitor its use, and to determine its proportion, base, collection, and duration.

XV.

SOCIETY has the right to demand an accounting of his administration from any public agent.

XVI.

NO society has a constitution without the guarantee of rights and the separation of powers.

XVII.

AS property is an inviolable and sacred right, no one shall be deprived of it, unless the legally determined public need obviously dictates it, and then only with a just and prior indemnity.

FORTY-TWO

Catharine Sawbridge Macaulay Graham (1731–1791)

W OMEN AROUND THE REVOLUTIONARY ATLANTIC WORLD LOOKED TO THE ENGLISH HIS-
*torian Catharine Macaulay as an example of female intellectual accom-
plishment. Between 1763 and 1783, Macaulay, who had been born near Wye in
Kent, England, and privately educated,* wrote a hefty eight-volume History of
England from the Accession of James 1 to the Elevation of the House of Hanover, *a
work of more than three thousand pages that was esteemed by her learned contemporaries as the best history of England ever produced. Her intellectual work and
political republicanism won Macaulay friends around the Atlantic world, including
Benjamin Franklin, whom she met in Paris in 1775; George Washington, whom she
visited at Mount Vernon in 1785; and the American republican and feminist
Mercy Otis Warren (also included in this volume), with whom she maintained a
twenty-year correspondence.*

Macaulay's Letters on Education (1790) *covered a wide range of subjects from
the care and feeding of infants and children—Macaulay advocated vegetarianism—
to adult sexual and social conduct. For feminists one of the* Letters' *most important
contributions was to the ongoing philosophical conversation about differences
between the sexes: the philosopher Jean-Jacques Rousseau (1712–1778) had argued
a view of men and women as "complementary and different" both in the designs of
their anatomy and in their moral natures as well. Macaulay rejected Rousseau's
views, insisting that differences between the sexes were not rooted in biology but in
"the situation and education of women." She continued the campaign for equal
education begun by her English foremothers Bathsua Makin and Mary Astell and
shared by her American contemporaries Susanna Wright and Judith Sargent Murray.*

Like Murray (whose writings appear elsewhere in this volume), Macaulay also warned women against fashioning themselves as mindless "coquettes" and leaving themselves at the mercy of "rakes" who would exploit them, a theme that animated popular romance novels of the time like Charlotte Temple *(1791) and* The Coquette *(1797).*

Published just after the onset of the French Revolution, the Letters *did not initially make a great splash: the reading public was more interested in more radical happenings in France than in a pragmatic, moderate take on educational reform. But Macaulay's cool insistence that sex differences were the result of custom and education rather than nature and that "there is but one rule of right for the conduct of all human beings" proved highly influential for later feminists such as Mary Wollstonecraft, who wrote in the* Vindication of the Rights of Woman *(1795) that she "anticipated Mrs. Macaulay's approbation."*

FROM *LETTERS ON EDUCATION* (1790)

LETTER XXI.

Morals must be taught on immutable Principles.

It is one thing, Hortensia,[1] to educate a citizen, and another to educate a philosopher. The mere citizen will have learnt to obey the laws of his country, but he will never understand those principles on which all laws ought to be established; and without such an understanding, he can never be religious on rational principles, or truly moral; nor will he ever have any of that active wisdom which is necessary for co-operating in any plan of reformation. But to teach morals on an immutable fitness, has never been the practice in any system of education yet extant. Hence all our notions of right and wrong are loose, unconnected, and inconsistent. Hence the murderer, in one situation, is extolled to the skies; and, in another, is followed with reproach even beyond the grave. For it is not only the man of the world who idolises power, though in the garb of villainy, and persecutes dishonesty when united to weakness, but even those who bear the specious title of philosophers are apt to be

---

[1] Hortensia: Following eighteenth-century epistolary style, Macaulay addresses her letters to a fictional correspondent she names Hortensia after a well-known female orator of the Roman Republic who in 42 BC defended the rights and interests of wealthy Roman women against a tax levied upon them to finance imperial wars.

dazzled with the brilliancy of success, and to treat qualities and characters differently, according to the smiles or frowns of fortune.

[. . . .]

In order to take from public sentiment a reproach which leaves a deep stain on the human character, and to correct many irregularities, and even enormities, which arise from incorrect systems of ethics, it ought to be the first care of education to teach virtue on immutable principles, and to avoid that confusion which must arise from confounding the laws and customs of society with those obligations which are founded on correct principles of equity. But as you have had patience to go through my whole plan of education, from infancy to manhood, it is but fair that I should attend to your objections, and examine whether my plan is founded on error, or on the principles of reason and truth. Know then, good Hortensia, that I have given similar rules for male and female education, on the following grounds of reasoning.

First, That there is but one rule of right for the conduct of all rational beings; consequently that true virtue in one sex must be equally so in the other, whenever a proper opportunity calls for its exertion; and, *vice versa*, what is vice in one sex, cannot have a different property when found in the other.

Secondly, That true wisdom, which is never found at variance with rectitude, is as useful to women as to men; because it is necessary to the highest degree of happiness, which can never exist with ignorance.

Lastly, That as on our first entrance into another world, our state of happiness may possibly depend on the degree of perfection we have attained in this, we cannot justly lessen, in one sex or the other, the means by which perfection, that is another word for wisdom, is acquired.

It would be paying you a bad compliment, Hortensia, were I to answer all the frivolous objections which prejudice has framed against the giving a learned education to women; for I know of no learning, worth having, that does not tend to free the mind from error, and enlarge our stock of useful knowledge. Thus much it may be proper to observe, that those hours which are spent in studious retirement by learned women, will not in all probability intrude so much on the time for useful avocation, as the wild and spreading dissipations of the present day; that levity and ignorance will always be found in opposition to what is useful and graceful in life; and that the contrary may be expected from a truly enlightened understanding. However, Hortensia, to throw some illustration on what I have advanced on this subject, it may be necessary to shew you, that all those vices and imperfections which have been generally regarded as inseparable from the female character, do not in any manner proceed from sexual causes, but are entirely the effects of situation and education. But these observations must be left to farther discussion.

LETTER XXII.

No characteristic Difference in Sex.

The great difference that is observable in the characters of the sexes, Hortensia, as they display themselves in the scenes of social life, has given rise to much false speculation on the natural qualities of the female mind.—For though the doctrine of innate ideas, and innate affections, are in a great measure exploded by the learned, yet few persons reason so closely and so accurately on abstract subjects as, through a long chain of deductions, to bring forth a conclusion which in no respect militates with their premises.

It is a long time before the crowd give up opinions they have been taught to look upon with respect; and I know many persons who will follow you willingly through the course of your argument, till they perceive it tends to the overthrow of some fond prejudice; and then they will either sound a retreat, or begin a contest in which the contender for truth, though he cannot be overcome, is effectually silenced, from the mere weariness of answering positive assertions, reiterated without end. It is from such causes that the notion of a sexual difference in the human character has, with a very few exceptions, universally prevailed from the earliest times, and the pride of one sex, and the ignorance and vanity of the other, have helped to support an opinion which a close observation of Nature, and a more accurate way of reasoning, would disprove.

It must be confessed, that the virtues of the males among the human species, though mixed and blended with a variety of vices and errors, have displayed a bolder and a more consistent picture of excellence than female nature has hitherto done. It is on these reasons that, when we compliment the appearance of a more than ordinary energy in the female mind, we call it masculine; and hence it is, that Pope has elegantly said *a perfect woman's but a softer man.* And if we take in the consideration, that there can be but one rule of moral excellence for beings made of the same materials, organized after the same manner, and subjected to similar laws of Nature, we must either agree with Mr. Pope, or we must reverse the proposition, and say, that *a perfect man is a woman formed after a coarser mold.* The difference that actually does subsist between the sexes, is too flattering for men to be willingly imputed to accident; for what accident occasions, wisdom might correct; and it is better, says Pride, to give up the advantages we might derive from the perfection of our fellow associates, than to own that Nature has been just in the equal distribution of her favours. These are the sentiments of the men; but mark how readily they are yielded to by the women; not from humility I assure you, but merely to preserve with character those fond vanities on which they set their hearts. No; suffer them to idolize their persons, to throw away their life in the pursuit of trifles, and to indulge in the gratification of the meaner passions, and they will heartily join in the sentence of their degradation.

Among the most strenuous asserters of a sexual difference in character, Rousseau[2] is the most conspicuous, both on account of that warmth of sentiment which distinguishes all his writings, and the eloquence of his compositions: but never did enthusiasm and the love of paradox, those enemies to philosophical disquisition, appear in more strong opposition to plain sense than in Rousseau's definition of this difference. He sets out with a supposition, that Nature intended the subjection of the one sex to the other; that consequently there must be an inferiority of intellect in the subjected party; but as man is a very imperfect being, and apt to play the capricious tyrant, Nature, to bring things nearer to an equality, bestowed on the woman such attractive graces, and such an insinuating address, as to turn the balance on the other scale. Thus Nature, in a giddy mood, recedes from her purposes, and subjects prerogative to an influence which must produce confusion and disorder in the system of human affairs. Rousseau saw this objection; and in order to obviate it, he has made up a moral person of the union of the two sexes, which, for contradiction and absurdity, outdoes every metaphysical riddle that was ever formed in the schools. In short, it is not reason, it is not wit; it is pride and sensuality that speak in Rousseau, and, in this instance, has lowered the man of genius to the licentious pedant.

But whatever might be the wise purpose intended by Providence in such a disposition of things, certain it is, that some degree of inferiority, in point of corporal strength, seems always to have existed between the two sexes; and this advantage, in the barbarous ages of mankind, was abused to such a degree, as to destroy all the natural rights of the female species, and reduce them to a state of abject slavery. What accidents have contributed in Europe to better their condition, would not be to my purpose to relate; for I do not intend to give you a history of women; I mean only to trace the sources of their peculiar foibles and vices; and these I firmly believe to originate in situation and education only: for so little did a wise and just Providence

---

[2] Rousseau: Jean-Jacques Rousseau (1712–1778), the French philosopher, composer, and novelist who propounded a view of the sexes as "complementary and different." Rousseau's influential philosophical narrative *Emile: or, On Education* (1762), which describes the intellectual and moral education of a young boy to become a rational man and self-governing adult citizen. By contrast, the education of Emile's female counterpart Sophie as imagined by Rousseau prepares her to be governed by her husband and to remain within the domestic and private sphere, in accordance with what Rousseau believed to be a natural and necessary hierarchy of the sexes.

intend to make the condition of slavery an unalterable law of female nature, that in the same proportion as the male sex have consulted the interest of their own happiness, they have relaxed in their tyranny over women; and such is their use in the system of mundane creation, and such their natural influence over the male mind, that were these advantages properly exerted, they might carry every point of any importance to their honour and happiness. However, till that period arrives in which women will act wisely, we will amuse ourselves in talking of their follies.

The situation and education of women, Hortensia, is precisely that which must necessarily tend to corrupt and debilitate both the powers of mind and body. From a false notion of beauty and delicacy, their system of nerves is depraved before they come out of their nursery; and this kind of depravity has more influence over the mind, and consequently over morals, than is commonly apprehended. But it would be well if such causes only acted towards the debasement of the sex; their moral education is, if possible, more absurd than their physical. The principles and nature of virtue, which is never properly explained to boys, is kept quite a mystery to girls. They are told indeed, that they must abstain from those vices which are contrary to their personal happiness, or they will be regarded as criminals, both by God and man; but all the higher parts of rectitude, every thing that ennobles our being, and that renders us both innoxious and useful, is either not taught, or is taught in such a manner as to leave no proper impression on the mind. This is so obvious a truth, that the defects of female education have ever been a fruitful topic of declamation for the moralist; but not one of this class of writers have laid down any judicious rules for amendment. Whilst we still retain the absurd notion of a sexual excellence, it will militate against the perfecting a plan of education for either sex. The judicious Addison[3] animadverts on the absurdity of bringing a young lady up with no higher idea of the end of education than to make her agreeable to a husband, and confining the necessary excellence for this happy acquisition to the mere graces of person.

Every parent and tutor may not express himself in the same manner as is marked out by Addison; yet certain it is, that the admiration of the other sex is held out to women as the highest honour they can attain; and whilst this is considered as their *summum bonum*,[4] and the beauty of their persons the chief *desideratum*[5] of men, Vanity, and its companion Envy, must taint, in their characters, every native and every acquired excellence. Nor can you, Hortensia, deny, that these qualities, when

---

[3] Addison: Joseph Addison (1672–1719), an English essayist, author of the influential tragedy *Cato* (1712), and cofounder of the *Spectator* magazine.

[4] *Summum bonum*: Latin phrase meaning "the highest good."

[5] *Desideratum*: Latin word meaning "something considered necessary or desirable."

united to ignorance, are fully equal to the engendering and rivetting all those vices and foibles which are peculiar to the female sex; vices and foibles which have caused them to be considered, in ancient times, as beneath cultivation, and in modern days have subjected them to the censure and ridicule of writers of all descriptions, from the deep thinking philosopher to the man of ton[6] and gallantry, who, by the bye, sometimes distinguishes himself by qualities which are not greatly superior to those he despises in women. Nor can I better illustrate the truth of this observation than by the following picture, to be found in the polite and gallant Chesterfield.[7] "Women," says his Lordship, "are only children of a larger growth. They have an entertaining tattle, sometimes wit; but for solid reasoning, and good sense, I never in my life knew one that had it, or who acted or reasoned in consequence of it for four and twenty hours together. A man of sense only trifles with them, plays with them, humours and flatters them, as he does an engaging child; but he neither consults them, nor trusts them in serious matters."

LETTER XXIII.

Coquettry.

Though the situation of women in modern Europe, Hortensia, when compared with that condition of abject slavery in which they have always been held in the east,[8] may be considered as brilliant; yet if we withhold comparison, and take the matter in a positive sense, we shall have no great reason to boast of our privileges, or of the candour and indulgence of the men towards us. For with a total and absolute exclusion of every political right to the sex in general, married women, whose situation demand a particular indulgence, have hardly a civil right to save them from the grossest injuries; and though the gallantry of some of the European societies have necessarily produced indulgence, yet in others the faults of women are treated with a severity and rancour which militates against every principle of religion and common sense. Faults, my friend, I hear you say; you take the matter in too general a sense; you know there is but one fault which a woman of honour may not commit with impunity; let her only take care that she is not caught in a love intrigue, and she may lie,

---

[6] Ton: Good taste; a word adopted in England during the middle eighteenth century from the French *ton*, meaning "manners."

[7] Chesterfield: Phillip Dormer Stanhope, Fourth Earl of Chesterfield (1694–1773), British politician, statesman, orator, writer, and wit.

[8] Macaulay here reiterates a familiar Orientalist or Islamophobic stereotype of women from Asia and the Middle East as drudges and harem inmates.

she may deceive, she may defame, she may ruin her own family with gaming, and the peace of twenty others with her coquettry, and yet preserve both her reputation and her peace. These are glorious privileges indeed, Hortensia; but whilst plays and novels are the favourite study of the fair, whilst the admiration of men continues to be set forth as the chief honour of woman, whilst power is only acquired by personal charms, whilst continual dissipation banishes the hour of reflection, Nature and flattery will too often prevail; and when this is the case, self preservation will suggest to conscious weakness those methods which are the most likely to conceal the ruinous trespass, however base and criminal they may be in their nature. The crimes that women have committed, both to conceal and to indulge their natural failings, shock the feelings of moral sense; but indeed every love intrigue, though it does not terminate in such horrid catastrophes, must naturally tend to debase the female mind, from its violence to educational impressions, from the secrecy with which it must be conducted, and the debasing dependancy to which the intriguer, if she is a woman of reputation, is subjected. Lying, flattery, hypocrisy, bribery, and a long catalogue of the meanest of human vices, must all be employed to preserve necessary appearances. Hence delicacy of sentiment gradually decreases; the warnings of virtue are no longer felt; the mind becomes corrupted, and lies open to every solicitation which appetite or passion presents. This must be the natural course of things in every being formed after the human plan; but it gives rise to the trite and foolish observation, that the first fault against chastity in woman has a radical power to deprave the character. But no such frail beings come out of the hands of Nature. The human mind is built of nobler materials than to be so easily corrupted; and with all the disadvantages of situation and education, women seldom become entirely abandoned till they are thrown into a state of desperation by the venomous rancour of their own sex.

The superiority of address peculiar to the female sex, says Rousseau, is a very equitable indemnification for their inferiority in point of strength. Without this, woman would not be the companion of man, but his slave; it is by her superior art and ingenuity that she preserves her equality, and governs him, whilst she affects to obey. Woman has every thing against her; as well our faults, as her own timidity and weakness. She has nothing in her favor but her subtlety and her beauty; is it not very reasonable therefore that she should cultivate both?

I am persuaded that Rousseau's understanding was too good to have led him into this error, had he not been blinded by his pride and his sensuality. The first was soothed by the opinion of superiority, lulled into acquiescence by cajolement; and the second was attracted by the idea of women playing off all the arts of coquettry to raise the passions of the sex. Indeed the author fully avows his sentiments, by acknowledging that he would have a young French woman cultivate her agreeable talents, in order to please her future husband, with as much care and assiduity as a young Circassian cultivates hers to fit her for the harem of an eastern bashaw.[9]

These agreeable talents, as the author expresses it, are played off to great advantage by women in all the courts of Europe; who, for the arts of female allurement, do not give place to the Circassian. But it is the practice of these very arts, directed to enthral the men, which act in a peculiar manner to corrupting the female mind. Envy, malice, jealousy, a cruel delight in inspiring sentiments which at first perhaps were never intended to be reciprocal, are leading features in the character of the coquet, whose aim is to subject the whole world to her own humour; but in this vain attempt she commonly sacrifices both her decency and her virtue.

By the intrigues of women, and their rage for personal power and importance, the whole world has been filled with violence and injury; and their levity and influence have proved so hostile to the existence or permanence of rational manners, that it fully justifies the keenness of Mr. Pope's satire on the sex.[10]

But I hear my Hortensia say, whither will this fit of moral anger carry you? I expected an apology, instead of a libel, on women; according to your description of the sex, the philosopher has more reason to regret the indulgence, than what you have sometimes termed the injustice of the men; and to look with greater complacency on the surly manners of the ancient Greeks, and the selfishness of Asiatic luxury, than on the gallantry of modern Europe.

Though you have often heard me express myself with warmth in the vindication of female nature, Hortensia, yet I never was an apologist for the conduct of women. But I cannot think the surliness of the Greek manners, or the selfishness of Asiatic luxury, a proper remedy to apply to the evil. If we could inspect narrowly into the domestic concerns of ancient and modern Asia, I dare say we should perceive that the first springs of the vast machine of society were set a going by women; and as to the Greeks, though it might be supposed that the peculiarity of their manners would have rendered them indifferent to the sex, yet they were avowedly governed by them. They only transferred that confidence which they ought to have given their wives, to their courtezans,[11] in the same manner as our English husbands do their tenderness and their complaisance. They will sacrifice a wife of fortune and family to resentment, or

---

[9] Circassian . . .bashaw: A *Circassian* was a common name for ethnic Turkish people; *bashaw* is an Anglicization of the Turkish word *pasha*, meaning a civic or military leader.

[10] Pope: Alexander Pope (1688–1744), famed English poet and essayist, author of *The Rape of the Lock* (1712) and the *Dunciad* (1728).

[11] Courtezan: A female courtier, often understood to be a partner in illicit sexual affairs with royalty and other gentlemen of the court.

the love of change, provided she give them opportunity, and bear with much Christian patience to be supplanted by their footman in the person of their mistress.

No; as Rousseau observes, it was ordained by Providence that women should govern some way or another; and all that reformation can do, is to take power out of the hands of vice and folly, and place it where it will not be liable to be abused.

To do the sex justice, it must be confessed that history does not set forth more instances of positive power abused by women, than by men; and when the sex have been taught wisdom by education, they will be glad to give up indirect influence for rational privileges; and the precarious sovereignty of an hour enjoyed with the meanest and most infamous of the species, for those established rights which, independent of accidental circumstances, may afford protection to the whole sex.

LETTER XXIV.

Flattery–Chastity–Male Rakes.

After all that has been advanced, Hortensia, the happiness and perfection of the two sexes are so reciprocally dependant on one another that, till both are reformed, there is no expecting excellence in either. The candid Addison has confessed, that in order to embellish the mistress, you must give a new education to the lover, and teach the men not to be any longer dazzled by false charms and unreal beauty. Till this is the case, we must endeavour to palliate the evil we cannot remedy; and, in the education of our females, raise as many barriers to the corruptions of the world, as our understanding and sense of things will permit.

As I give no credit to the opinion of a sexual excellence, I have made no variation in the fundamental principles of the education of the two sexes; but it will be necessary to admit of such a difference in the plan as shall in some degree form the female mind to the particularity of its situation.

The fruits of true philosophy are modesty and humility; for as we advance in knowledge, our deficiencies become more conspicuous; and by learning to set a just estimate on what we possess, we find little gratification for the passion of pride. This is so just an observation, that we may venture to pronounce, without any exception to the rule, that a vain or proud man is, in a positive sense, an ignorant man. However if it should be our lot to have one of the fair sex, distinguished for any eminent degree of personal charms, committed to our care, we must not attempt by a premature cultivation to gather the fruits of philosophy before their season, nor expect to find the qualities of true modesty and humility make their appearance till the blaze of beauty has in some measure been subdued by time. For should we exhaust all the powers of oratory, and all the strength of sound argument, in the endeavour to convince our pupil that beauty is of small weight in the scale of real excellence, the enflamed praises she will continually hear bestowed on this quality will fix her in the opinion, that we *mean* to keep her in ignorance of her true worth. She will think herself deceived, and she will resent the injury by giving little credit to our precepts, and placing her confidence in those who tickle her ears with lavish panegyric on the captivating graces of her person.

Thus vanity steals on the mind, and thus a daughter, kept under by the ill exerted power of parental authority, gives a full ear to the flattery of a coxcomb.[12] Happy would it be for the sex did the mischief end here; but the footings of flattery never fail to operate on the affections of the heart; and when love creeps into the bosom, the empire of reason is at an end. To prevent our fair pupils therefore from becoming the prey of coxcombs, and serving either to swell their triumph, or repair their ruined fortunes, it will be necessary to give them a full idea of the magnitude of their beauty, and the power this quality has over the frail mind of man. Nor have we in this case so much to fear from the intimations of a judicious friend, as from the insiduous adulation of a designing admirer. The haughty beauty is too proud to regard the admiration of fops and triflers; she will never condescend to the base, the treacherous, the dangerous arts of coquettry; and by keeping her heart free from the snares of love, she will have time to cultivate that philosophy which, if well understood, is a never failing remedy to human pride.

But the most difficult part of female education, is to give girls such an idea of chastity, as shall arm their reason and their sentiments on the side of this useful virtue. For I believe there are more women of understanding led into acts of imprudence by the ignorance, the prejudices, and the false craft of those by whom they are educated, than from any other cause founded either in nature or in chance. You may train up a docile idiot to any mode of thinking or acting, as may best suit the intended purpose; but a reasoning being will scan over your propositions, and if they find them grounded in falsehood, they will reject them with disdain. When you tell a girl of spirit and reflection that chastity is a sexual virtue, and the want of it a sexual vice, she will be apt to examine into the principles of religion, morals, and the reason of things, in order to satisfy herself on the truth of your proposition. And when, after the strictest inquiries, she finds nothing that will warrant the confining the proposition to a particular sense, she will entertain doubts either of your wisdom or your sincerity; and regarding you either as a deceiver or a fool, she will transfer her confidence to the companion of the easy vacant hour, whose compliance with her opinions can

---

[12] Coxcomb: A conceited, foolish man.

flatter her vanity. Thus left to Nature, with an unfortunate biass on her mind, she will fall a victim to the first plausible being who has formed a design on her person. Rousseau is so sensible of this truth, that he quarrels with human reason, and would put her out of the question in all considerations of duty. But this is being as great a fanatic in morals, as some are in religion; and I should much doubt the reality of that duty which would not stand the test of fair enquiry; beside, as I intend to breed my pupils up to act a rational part in the world, and not to fill up a niche in the seraglio of a sultan, I shall certainly give them leave to use their reason in all matters which concern their duty and happiness, and shall spare no pains in the cultivation of this only sure guide to virtue. I shall inform them of the great utility of chastity and continence; that the one preserves the body in health and vigor, and the other, the purity and independence of the mind, without which it is impossible to possess virtue or happiness. I shall intimate, that the great difference now beheld in the external consequences which follow the deviations from chastity in the two sexes, did in all probability arise from women having been considered as the mere property of the men; and, on this account had no right to dispose of their own persons: that policy adopted this difference, when the plea of property had been given up; and it was still preserved in society from the unruly licentiousness of the men, who, finding no obstacles in the delicacy of the other sex, continue to set at defiance both divine and moral law, and by mutual support and general opinion to use their natural freedom with impunity. I shall observe, that this state of things renders the situation of females, in their individual capacity very precarious; for the strength which Nature has given to the passion of love, in order to serve her purposes, has made it the most ungovernal propensity of any which attends us. The snares therefore, that are continually laid for women, by persons who run no risk in compassing their seduction, exposes them to continual danger; whilst the implacability of their own sex, who fear to give up any advantages which a superior prudence, or even its appearances, give them, renders one false step an irretrievable misfortune. That, for these reasons, coquettry in women is as dangerous as it is dishonorable. That a coquet commonly finds her own perdition, in the very flames which she raises to consume others; and that if any thing can excuse the baseness of female seduction, it is the baits which are flung out by women to entangle the affections, and excite the passions of men.

I know not what you may think of my method, Hortensia, which I must acknowledge to carry the stamp of singularity; but for my part, I am sanguine enough to expect to turn out of my hands a careless, modest beauty, grave, manly, noble, full of strength and majesty; and carrying about her an aegis sufficiently powerful to defend her against the sharpest arrow that ever was shot from Cupid's bow. A woman, whose virtue will not be of the kind to wrankle into an inveterate malignity against her own sex for faults which she even encourages in the men, but who, understanding the principles of true religion and morality, will regard chastity and truth as indispensible qualities in virtuous characters of either sex; whose justice will incline her to extend her benevolence to the frailties of the fair as circumstances invite, and to manifest her resentment against the underminers of female happiness; in short, a woman who will not take a male rake either for a husband or a friend. And let me tell you, Hortensia, if women had as much regard for the virtue of chastity as in some cases they pretend to have, a reformation would long since have taken place in the world; but whilst they continue to cherish immodesty in the men, their bitter persecution of their own sex will not save them from the imputation of those concealed propensities with which they are accused by Pope, and other severe satirists on the sex.

FORTY-THREE

Pauline Léon (1758–?)

*T*HE WOMEN OF REVOLUTIONARY PARIS DEMANDED LEGAL EQUALITY IN MARRIAGE; EDUCA-
*tion for girls; licensing of midwives; an end to the exclusion of women from the
professions; and the right to bear arms. Like Olympe de Gouges and the women who
petitioned the king (all included in this volume), Pauline Léon was not an aristocrat
but a member of the Parisian artisan class or third estate, a chocolate maker. She
worked to fulfill the Revolution's promises to the poor and to women. After the death
of her father when Léon was 16, she remained at home to help her mother take care
of her five younger siblings. She became a member of the Club des Cordeliers and
other revolutionary organizations, and in 1787 married Jean-Théophile Leclerc,
leader of the Enragés, a group that advocated price controls and other economic
reforms to address starvation among the poor. The two were arrested and imprisoned
in Luxembourg in 1794. With Claire Lacombe, an actor, Léon founded a women's
revolutionary organization, Société des Républicaines Révolutionnaires, and became
its president on July 9, 1793. Later that year she became a leader of the Femmes
Sans-Culottes, who also advocated subsistence for the starving populace. Léon later
became a schoolteacher and lived with her sister in Paris until her death in 1838.*

Like Lafayette in the Declaration of the Rights of Man and Citizen *(above) to
which she appeals for authority, Léon cites "the right nature gives us," a natural
right to equality with men, to argue that women need arms both to participate in the
revolutionary struggle and to protect themselves against assault in the chaos of a
war-torn city. Léon appeared before the National Assembly of France on March 6,
1791, and read this address.*

PETITION TO THE NATIONAL ASSEMBLY ON WOMEN'S RIGHTS TO BEAR ARMS (1791)[1]

Legislators:

Patriotic women come before you to claim the right which any individual has to defend his life and liberty.

Everyone predicts that a violent shock is coming; our fathers, husbands, and brothers may be the victims of the fury of our enemies. Could we be denied the joy of avenging them or of dying at their sides? We are *citoyennes,* and we cannot be indifferent to the fate of the fatherland.[2]

Your predecessors deposited the Constitution as much in our hands as in yours. Oh, how to save it, if we have no arms to defend it from the attacks of its enemies?

Yes, Gentlemen, we need arms, and we come to ask your permission to procure them. May our weakness be no obstacle; courage and intrepidity will supplant it, and the love of the fatherland and hatred of tyrants will allow us to brave all dangers with ease. Do not believe, however, that our plan is to abandon the care of our families and home, always dear to our hearts, to run to meet the enemy.

No, Gentlemen. We wish only to defend ourselves the same as you; you cannot refuse us, and society cannot deny the right nature gives us, unless you pretend the Declaration of Rights does not apply to women, and that they should let their throats be cut like lambs, without the right to defend themselves. For can you believe the tyrants would spare us? No, no—they remember October 5 and 6, 1789 . . . [in text].[3] But, you say, men are armed for your defense. Of course, but we reply, why deprive us of the right to join that defense, and of the pleasure of saving their days by using ours? Do they know the number and strength of our hidden enemies? Have they but one fight to fight? Is our life dearer than theirs? Are our children not orphaned by the loss of their fathers as much as their mothers? Why then not terrorize aristocracy and tyranny with all the resources of civic effort [*civisme*] and the purest zeal, zeal which cold men can well call fanaticism and exaggeration, but which is only the natural result of a heart burning with love for the public weal?[4]

---

[1] From *Women in Revolutionary Paris, 1789–1795: Selected Documents Translated with Notes and Commentary.* Translated with notes and commentary by Darline Gay Levy, Harriet Branson Applewhite, and Mary Durham Johnson. Copyright 1979 by the Board of Trustees of the University of Illinois. Used with permission of the editors and the University of Illinois Press.

[2] *Citoyennes*: The female form of the French word for "citizen."

[3] October 5 and 6, 1789: On these dates women led a delegation to the king, demanding bread. He did not provide it or otherwise acknowledge their actions.

[4] *Civisme*: Support for the French Revolution; later, proper civic pride.

Without doubt, Gentlemen, the most joyous success will crown the justice of our cause. Well then, we shall have the pleasure of having contributed to the victory. But if, by the wiles of our enemies or the treachery of some on our side, the evil ones win victory, then is it not cruel to condemn us to await in our homes a shameful death and all the horrors which will precede it? Or—an even worse misfortune——to survive the loss of what we hold most dear, our families and our liberty?

No, Gentlemen, do not imagine it. If, for reasons we cannot guess, you refuse our just demands, these women you have raised to the ranks of *citoyennes* by granting that title to their husbands, these women who have sampled the promises of liberty, who have conceived the hope of placing free men in the world, and who have sworn to live free or die—such women, I say, will never consent to concede the day to slaves; they will die first. They will uphold their oath, and a dagger aimed at their breasts will deliver them from the misfortunes of slavery! They will die, regretting not life, but the uselessness of their death; regretting moreover, not having been able to drench their hands in the impure blood of the enemies of the fatherland and to avenge some of their own!

But, Gentlemen, let us cast our eyes away from these cruel extremes. Whatever the rages and plots of aristocrats, they will not succeed in vanquishing a whole people of united brothers armed to defend their rights. We also demand only the honor of sharing their exhaustion and glorious labors and of making tyrants see that women also have blood to shed for the service of the fatherland in danger.

Gentlemen, here is what we hope to obtain from your justice and equity:

1. Permission to procure pikes, pistols, and sabres (even muskets for those who are strong enough to use them), within police regulations.
2. Permission to assemble on festival days and Sundays on the Champ de la Fédération,[5] or in other suitable places, to practice maneuvers with these arms.
3. Permission to name the former French Guards to command us, always in conformity with the rules which the mayor's wisdom prescribes for good order and public calm.

Signed,
Léon, *fille,* etc.
Something more than three hundred signatures follow.

---

[5] Champ de la Fédération: On July 14, 1790, the citizens of Paris transformed the Champ de Mars (a field then far outside Paris, now just in front of the Eiffel Tower) into a site for a festive celebration of what they considered the end of the Revolution: the establishment of a constitutional monarchy. A meal was offered to 22,000 people. July 14 is still celebrated as the anniversary of the French nation, although it was to go through several subsequent forms of government after 1790.

FORTY-FOUR

Olympe de Gouges (1748–1793)

*B*ORN MARIE GOUZE IN *1748*, THE DAUGHTER OF A BUTCHER AND A CLOTH-MAKER, MARIE-*Olympe de Gouges was a French political philosopher and woman of letters, best known as the author of the treatise* The Declaration of the Rights of Woman and Citizen. *She was married against her will at 16 but her husband died shortly afterwards. She never remarried, referring to the institution as "the tomb of trust and love." She then moved to Paris, taking her young son with her to live with her sister. There, she met the wealthy Jacques Biétrix de Rozières. She refused his offer of marriage, but remained close to him throughout the revolutionary years. The bourgeois education her mother made sure she received in her home town of Montauban allowed de Gouges, with the support of de Rozières, to embark upon a life of writing and revolutionary politics in Paris. She started her own theater company, making her name with the drama* l'Esclavage des Noirs *(Black Slavery), performed at the famous Comédie-Française in 1785 and published in 1792. De Gouges was the target of harassment and threats as a result of her activism and writing critical of slavery in the French colonies. Like many, she greeted the advent of the Revolution with joy, hoping that it would usher in a new era of full human rights for all. Affiliated with the more moderate Girondins, de Gouges favored a constitutional monarchy rather than a fully republican state, and opposed the execution of Louis XVI. By 1793, she had become increasingly suspicious of the ascension of Robespierre's Montagnard faction, publishing pamphlets criticizing their violence and practice of summary assassination. She was executed in November of that year and was condemned by the Commune of Paris in the following words, evidently intended to menace all French women: "virago, woman-man, the impudent Olympe de Gouges who congregated with other women, abandoned her household responsibilities, and became a political criminal . . . Would you like to imitate her? No! . . . We want women to be respected, which is why we force them to respect themselves."*

De Gouges's Declaration *intentionally echoes the 1789* Declaration of the Rights of Man and Citizen *(at times word for word as in the seventeen Articles), marshalling the same Enlightenment reasoning used to establish the French republic in order to argue for the full enfranchisement of its women. Her language is direct and imperative, and she assumes an audience of women, demanding "Woman, wake up! . . . What advantage have you received from the Revolution?" She argues that religious marriage has no place in a republic and is contrary to the interests of women, making the very modern argument for civil unions instead. Indeed, divorce is the one right that was granted to French women in the early years of the Republic, adopted by the Girondins a few months after the publication of de Gouges's* Declaration. *De Gouges's treatise is probably the boldest claim made in print in the period for full human rights for women: "male and female citizens, being equal in the eyes of the law, must be equally admitted to all honors, positions, and public employment according to their capacity." But in addition to this universalist argument, she also argues from difference, claiming a sex-specific version of free speech: women must be able to "say freely, I am the mother of a child which belongs to you, without being forced by a barbarous prejudice to hide the truth." And like the Cherokee orator Nancy Ward a few years earlier, de Gouges refers to women's "courage during the sufferings of maternity" as one way women are "superior." This document remains an inspiration to women around the world; its demands have yet to be fully met.*

DECLARATION OF THE RIGHTS OF WOMAN AND CITIZEN (1791)[1]

To the Queen: Madame,[2]

Little suited to the language one holds to with kings, I will not use the adulation of courtiers to pay you homage with this singular production. My purpose, Madame, is to speak frankly to you; I have not awaited the epoch of liberty to thus explain myself; I bestirred myself as energetically in a time when the blindness of despots punished such noble audacity.

When the whole empire accused you and held you responsible for its calamities, I alone in a time of trouble and storm, I alone had the strength to take up your

---

[1] From *Women in Revolutionary Paris, 1789–1795: Selected Documents Translated with Notes and Commentary*. Translated with notes and commentary by Darline Gay Levy, Harriet Branson Applewhite, and Mary Durham Johnson. Copyright 1979 by the Board of Trustees of the University of Illinois. Used with permission of the editors and the University of Illinois Press.

[2] Madame: Marie-Antoinette of Austria (1755–1793), wife of Louis XVI, who ascended the throne with her husband to become Queen of France in 1774. Anti-monarchists accused the queen of many moral crimes, including lesbianism and sexual relations with her own son.

defense. I could never convince myself that a princess, raised in the midst of grandeur, had all the vices of baseness.

Yes, Madame, when I saw the sword raised against you, I threw my observations between that sword and you, but today when I see who is observed near the crowd of useless hirelings, and [when I see] that she is restrained by fear of the laws, I will tell you, Madame, what I did not say then.

If the foreigner bears arms into France, you are no longer in my eyes this falsely accused Queen, this attractive Queen, but an implacable enemy of the French. Oh, Madame, bear in mind that you are mother and wife; employ all your credit for the return of the Princes. This credit, if wisely applied, strengthens the father's crown, saves it for the son, and reconciles you to the love of the French. This worthy negotiation is the true duty of a queen. Intrigue, cabals, bloody projects will precipitate your fall, if it is possible to suspect that you are capable of such plot.[3]

Madame, may a nobler function characterize you, excite your ambition, and fix your attentions. Only one whom chance has elevated to an eminent position can assume the task of lending weight to the progress of the Rights of Woman and of hastening its success. If you were less well informed, Madame, I might fear that your individual interests would outweigh those of your sex. You love glory; think, Madame, the greatest crimes immortalize one as much as the greatest virtues, but what a different fame in the annals of history! The one is ceaselessly taken as an example, and the other is eternally the execration of the human race.

It will never be a crime for you to work for the restoration of customs, to give your sex all the firmness of which it is capable. This is not the work of one day, unfortunately for the new regime. This revolution will happen only when all women are aware of their deplorable fate, and of the rights they have lost in society. Madame, support such a beautiful cause, defend this unfortunate sex, and soon you will have half the realm on your side, and at least one-third of the other half.

Those, Madame, are the feats by which you should show and use your credit. Believe me, Madame, our life is a pretty small thing, especially for a Queen, when it is not embellished by people's affection and by the eternal delights of good deeds.

If it is true that the French arm all the powers against their own Fatherland, why? For frivolous prerogatives, for chimeras. Believe, Madame, if I judge by what I

---

[3] Marie-Antoinette was born Archduchess of Austria. After Louis XVI was deposed and his family (including his wife) imprisoned, she maintained contact with her Austrian family, attempting to arrange a safe haven for herself, her husband, and her children. France declared war on Austria in 1792, so many in France saw the queen's communications with the Austrian monarch, her brother, as treasonous duplicity.

feel——the monarchical party will be destroyed by itself, it will abandon all tyrants, and all hearts will rally around the fatherland to defend it.

There are my principles, Madame. In speaking to you of my fatherland, I lose sight of the purpose of this dedication. Thus, any good citizen sacrifices his glory and his interests when he has none other than those of his country.

I am with the most profound respect, Madame,

Your most humble and most obedient servant,

de Gouges

The Rights of Woman

Man, are you capable of being just? It is a woman who poses the question; you will not deprive her of that right at least. Tell me, what gives you sovereign empire to oppress my sex? Your strength? Your talents? Observe the Creator in his wisdom; survey in all her grandeur that nature with whom you seem to want to be in harmony, and give me, if you dare, an example of this tyrannical empire. Go back to animals, consult the elements, study plants, finally glance at all the modifications of organic matter, and surrender to the evidence when I offer you the means; search, probe, and distinguish, if you can, the sexes in the administration of nature. Everywhere you will find them mingled; everywhere they cooperate in harmonious togetherness in this immortal masterpiece.

Man alone has raised his exceptional circumstances to a principle. Bizarre, blind, bloated with science and degenerated—in a century of enlightenment and wisdom—into the crassest ignorance, he wants to command as a despot a sex which is in full possession of its intellectual faculties; he pretends to enjoy the Revolution and to claim his rights to equality in order to say nothing more about it.

Declaration of the Rights of Woman and the Female Citizen

For the National Assembly to decree in its last sessions, or in those of the next legislature:

Preamble

Mothers, daughters, sisters [and] representatives of the nation demand to be constituted into a national assembly. Believing that ignorance, omission, or scorn for the rights of woman are the only causes of public misfortunes and of the corruption of governments, [the women] have resolved to set forth in a solemn declaration the natural, inalienable, and sacred rights of woman in order that this declaration, constantly exposed before all members of the society, will ceaselessly remind them of their rights and duties; in order that the authoritative acts of women and the authoritative acts of men may be at any moment compared with and respectful of the purpose of all political institutions; and in order that citizens' demands, henceforth based on simple and incontestable principles, will always support the constitution, good morals, and the happiness of all.

Consequently, the sex that is as superior in beauty as it is in courage during the sufferings of maternity recognizes and declares in the presence and under the auspices of the Supreme Being, the following Rights of Woman and of Female Citizens.

Article I

Woman is born free and lives equal to man in her rights. Social distinctions can be based only on the common utility.

Article II

The purpose of any political association is the conservation of the natural and impresciptible rights of woman and man; these rights are liberty, property, security, and especially resistance to oppression.[4]

Article III

The principle of all sovereignty rests essentially with the nation, which is nothing but the union of woman and man; no body and no individual can exercise any authority which does not come expressly from it (the nation).

Article IV

Liberty and justice consist of restoring all that belongs to others; thus, the only limits on the exercise of the natural rights of woman are perpetual male tyranny; these limits are to be reformed by the laws of nature and reason.

---

[4] Imprescriptible: That cannot rightfully be taken away or proscribed; inviolable.

Article V

Laws of nature and reason proscribe all acts harmful to society; everything which is not prohibited by these wise and divine laws cannot be prevented, and no one can be constrained to do what they do not command.

Article VI

The law must be the expression of the general will; all female and male citizens must contribute either personally or through their representatives to its formation; it must be the same for all: male and female citizens, being equal in the eyes of the law, must be equally admitted to all honors, positions, and public employment according to their capacity and without other distinctions besides those of their virtues and talents.

Article VII

No woman is an exception; she is accused, arrested, and detained in cases determined by law. Women, like men, obey this rigorous law.

Article VIII

The law must establish only those penalties that are strictly and obviously necessary, and no one can be punished except by virtue of a law established and promulgated prior to the crime and legally applicable to women.

Article IX

Once any woman is declared guilty, complete rigor is [to be] exercised by law.

Article X

No one is to be disquieted for his very basic opinions; woman has the right to mount the scaffold; she must equally have the right to mount the rostrum, provided that her demonstrations do not disturb the legally established public order.

Article XI

The free communication of thoughts and opinions is one of the most precious rights of woman, since that liberty assures recognition of children by their fathers. Any female citizen thus may say [*dire*] freely, I am the mother of a child which belongs to you, without being forced by a barbarous prejudice to hide the truth; [an exception may be made] to respond to the abuse of this liberty in cases determined by law.

Article XII

The guarantee of the rights of woman and the female citizen implies a major benefit; this guarantee must be instituted for the advantage of all, and not for the particular benefit of those to whom it is entrusted.

Article XIII

For the support of the public force and the expenses of administration, the contributions of woman and man are equal; she shares all the duties [*corvées*] and all the painful tasks; therefore, she must have the same share in the distribution of positions, employment, offices, honors, and jobs [*industrie*].

Article XIV

Female and male citizens have the right to verify, either by themselves or through their representatives, the necessity of the public contribution. This can only apply to women if they are granted an equal share, not only of wealth, but also of public administration, and in the determination of the proportion, the base, the collection, and the duration of the tax.

Article XV

The collectivity of women, joined for tax purposes to the aggregate of men, has the right to demand an accounting of his administration from any public agent.

Article XVI

No society has a constitution without the guarantee of rights and the separation of powers; the constitution is null if the majority of individuals comprising the nation have not cooperated in drafting it.

Article XVII

Property belongs to both sexes whether united or separate; for each it is an inviolable and sacred right; no one can be deprived of it, since it is the true patrimony of nature, unless the legally determined public need obviously dictates it, and then only with a just and prior indemnity.

Postscript

Woman, wake up; the tocsin of reason is being heard throughout the whole universe; discover your rights.[5] The powerful empire of nature is no longer surrounded by prejudice, fanaticism, superstition, and lies. The flame of truth has dispersed all the clouds of folly and usurpation. Enslaved man has multiplied his strength and needs recourse to yours to break his chains. Having become free, he has become unjust to his companion. Oh, women, women! When will you cease to be blind? What advantage have you received from the Revolution? A more pronounced scorn, a more marked disdain. In the centuries of corruption you ruled only over the weakness of men. The reclamation of your patrimony, based on the wise decrees of nature—what have you to dread from such a fine undertaking? The *bon mot* of the legislator of the marriage of Cana? Do you fear that our French legislators, correctors of that morality, long ensnared by political practices now out of date, will only say again to you: women, what is there in common between you and us? Everything, you will have to answer. If they persist in their weakness in putting this non sequitur in contradiction to their principles, courageously oppose the force of reason to the empty pretentions of superiority; unite yourselves beneath the standards of philosophy; deploy all the energy of your character, and you will soon see these haughty men, not groveling at your feet as servile adorers, but proud to share with you the treasures of the Supreme Being.[6] Regardless of what barriers confront you, it is in your power to free yourselves; you have only to want to. Let us pass now to the shocking tableau of what you have been in society; and since the national education is in question at this moment, let us see whether our wise legislators will think judiciously about the education of women.

Women have done more harm than good. Constraint and dissimulation have been their lot. What force has robbed them of, ruse returned to them; they had recourse to

---

[5] Tocsin: An alarm bell or signal.

[6] *Non sequitur*: Latin for "it does not follow," a logical fallacy in which the conclusion in an argument does not follow from the stated premise.

all the resources of their charms, and the most irreproachable person did not resist them. Poison and the sword were both subject to them; they commanded in crime as in fortune. The French government, especially, depended throughout the centuries on the nocturnal administration of women; the cabinet kept no secret from their indiscretion; ambassadorial post, command, ministry, presidency, pontificate, college of cardinals; finally, anything which characterizes the folly of men, profane and sacred, all have been subject to the cupidity and ambition of this sex, formerly contemptible and respected, and since the revolution, respectable and scorned.

In this sort of contradictory situation, what remarks could I not make! I have but a moment to make them, but this moment will fix the attention of the remotest posterity. Under the Old Regime, all was vicious, all was guilty; but could not the amelioration of conditions be perceived even in the substance of vices? A woman only had to be beautiful or amiable; when she possessed these two advantages, she saw a hundred fortunes at her feet. If she did not profit from them, she had a bizarre character or a rare philosophy which made her scorn wealth; then she was deemed to be like a crazy woman; the most indecent made herself respected with gold; commerce in women was a kind of industry in the first class [of society], which, henceforth, will have no more credit. If it still had it, the revolution would be lost, and under the new relationships we would always be corrupted; however, reason can always be deceived [into believing] that any other road to fortune is closed to the woman whom a man buys, like the slave on the African coasts. The difference is great; that is known. The slave is commanded by the master; but if the master gives her liberty without recompense, and at an age when the slave has lost all her charms, what will become of this unfortunate woman? The victim of scorn, even the doors of charity are closed to her; she is poor and old, they say; why did she not know how to make her fortune? Reason finds other examples that are even more touching. A young, inexperienced woman, seduced by a man whom she loves, will abandon her parents to follow him; the ingrate will leave her after a few years, and the older she has become with him, the more inhuman is his inconstancy; if she has children, he will likewise abandon them. If he is rich, he will consider himself excused from sharing his fortune with his noble victims. If some involvement binds him to his duties, he will deny them, trusting that the laws will support him. If he is married, any other obligation loses its rights. Then what laws remain to extirpate vice all the way to its root? The law of dividing wealth and public administration between men and women. It can easily be seen that one who is born into a rich family gains very much from such equal sharing. But the one born into a poor family with merit and virtue—what is her lot? Poverty and opprobrium. If she does not precisely excel in music or painting, she cannot be admitted to any public function when she has all the capacity for it. I do not want to give only a sketch of things; I will go more deeply into this in the new edition of all my political writings, with notes, which I propose to give to the public in a few days.

I take up my text again on the subject of morals. Marriage is the tomb of trust and love. The married woman can with impunity give bastards to her husband, and also give them the wealth which does not belong to them. The woman who is unmarried has only one feeble right; ancient and inhuman laws refuse to her for her children the right to the name and the wealth of their father; no new laws have been made in this matter. If it is considered a paradox and an impossibility on my part to try to give my sex an honorable and just consistency, I leave it to men to attain glory for dealing with this matter; but while we wait, the way can be prepared through national education, the restoration of morals, and conjugal conventions.

Form for a Social Contract Between Man and Woman

We, _____ and _____, moved by our own will, unite ourselves for the duration of our lives, and for the duration of our mutual inclinations, under the following conditions: We intend and wish to make our wealth communal, meanwhile reserving to ourselves the right to divide it in favor of our children and of those toward whom we might have a particular inclination, mutually recognizing that our property belongs directly to our children, from whatever bed they come, and that all of them without distinction have the right to bear the name of the fathers and mothers who have acknowledged them, and we are charged to subscribe to the law which punishes the renunciation of one's own blood. We likewise obligate ourselves, in case of separation, to divide our wealth and to set aside in advance the portion the law indicates for our children, and in the event of a perfect union, the one who dies will divest himself of half his property in his children's favor, and if one dies childless, the survivor will inherit by right, unless the dying person has disposed of half the common property in favor of one whom he judged deserving.

That is approximately the formula for the marriage act I propose for execution. Upon reading this strange document, I see rising up against me the hypocrites, the prudes, the clergy, and the whole infernal sequence. But how it [my proposal] offers to the wise the moral means of achieving the perfection of a happy government! I am going to give in a few words the physical proof of it. The rich, childless Epicurean finds it very good to go to his poor neighbor to augment his family. When there is a law authorizing a poor man's wife to have a rich one adopt their children, the bonds of society will be strengthened and morals will be purer. This law will perhaps save the community's wealth and hold back the disorder which drives so many victims to the almshouses of shame, to a low station, and into degenerate human principles where nature has groaned for so long. May the detractors of wise philosophy then cease to cry out against primitive morals, or may they lose their point in the source of their citations.[7]

Moreover, I would like a law which would assist widows and young girls deceived by the false promises of a man to whom they were attached; I would like, I say, this law to force an inconstant man to hold to his obligations or at least [to pay] an indemnity equal to his wealth. Again, I would like this law to be rigorous against women, at least those who have the effrontery to have recourse to a law which they themselves had violated by their misconduct, if proof of that were given. At the same time, as I showed in *Le Bonheur primitif de l'homme*, in 1788, that prostitutes should be placed in designated quarters.[8] It is not prostitutes who contribute the most to the depravity of morals, it is the women of society.[9] In regenerating the latter, the former are changed. This link of fraternal union will first bring disorder, but in consequence it will produce at the end a perfect harmony.

I offer a foolproof way to elevate the soul of women; it is to join them to all the activities of man; if man persists in finding this way impractical, let him share his fortune with woman, not at his caprice, but by the wisdom of laws. Prejudice falls, morals are purified, and nature regains all her rights. Add to this the marriage of priests and the strengthening of the king on his throne, and the French government cannot fail.

It would be very necessary to say a few words on the troubles which are said to be caused by the decree in favor of colored men in our islands. There is where nature shudders with horror; there is where reason and humanity have still not touched callous souls; there, especially, is where division and discord stir up their inhabitants. It is not difficult to divine the instigators of these incendiary fermentations; they are even in the midst of the National Assembly; they ignite the fire in Europe which must inflame America. Colonists make a claim to reign as despots over the men whose fathers and brothers they are; and, disowning the rights of nature, they trace the source of [their rule] to the scantiest tint of their blood. These inhuman colonists say: our blood flows in their veins, but we will shed it all if necessary to glut our greed or our blind ambition. It is in these places nearest to nature where the father scorns the son; deaf to the cries of blood, they stifle all its attraction; what can be hoped from

---

[7] Original footnote: "Abraham had some very legitimate children by Agar, the servant of his wife."

[8] *Le Bonheur primitif de l'homme*: *The Primitive Happiness of Man*, a philosophical pamphlet.

[9] Women of society: Women considered well-born and respectable.

the resistance opposed to them? To constrain [blood] violently is to render it terrible; to leave [blood] still enchained is to direct all calamities towards America. A divine hand seems to spread liberty abroad throughout the realms of man; only the law has the right to curb this liberty if it degenerates into license, but it must be equal for all; liberty must hold the National Assembly to its decree dictated by prudence and justice. May it act the same way for the state of France and render her as attentive to new abuses as she was to the ancient ones which each day become more dreadful. My opinion would be to reconcile the executive and legislative power, for it seems to me that the one is everything and the other is nothing—whence comes, unfortunately perhaps, the loss of the French Empire. I think that these two powers, like man and woman, should be united but equal in force and virtue to make a good household. . . .

.

FORTY-FIVE

Margaretta Bleecker Faugeres (1771–1801)

NEWS FROM THE FRENCH REVOLUTION CIRCULATED QUICKLY AROUND THE REVOLUTIONARY
*Atlantic world, firing the imagination of political radicals and lovers of free-
dom. Among those inspired to take up the pen was a Dutch-American poet and survivor of the American Revolution named Margaretta Bleecker. At 6 years old, with
invading British forces advancing on the family on the New York frontier, Margaretta
and her family were forced to flee for Albany. Her infant sister Abella did not survive
the journey. The Revolutionary War and its stresses sent her mother, the poet Eliza Ann
Bleecker (1752–1783), into a deep depression that shadowed most of Margaretta's
childhood; she died when Margaretta was 12. As she grew older, Margaretta developed a radical political outlook and a writing career of her own. Under the pen name
"Ella," an adaptation of her deceased sister Abella's name, she published poems and
antislavery essays in the* New York Magazine. *On Bastille Day, July 14, 1792, Margaretta Bleecker entered into what would be an unhappy marriage to Peter Faugeres,
a French doctor who shared her political ideals. In 1793, Faugeres published* The
Posthumous Works of Ann Eliza Bleecker, *a collection of her mother's poetry that
also included a section of her own poetry and essays.*

*Her poem "On seeing a Print, exhibiting the Ruins of the Bastille," commemo-
rates the storming of the Bastille prison by the people of Paris on July 14, 1789, a
culminating symbolic event of the French Revolution. The Bastille served as the ar-
mory for the absolutist monarchic government and a prison for political dissidents.
Within weeks of the attack, the French abolished feudalism and issued the Declaration of the Rights of Man, a document that proclaimed universal human rights and
popular sovereignty. In this poem, published in the* New York Magazine *in November
1792, Faugeres offers a sensuously vivid reminiscence of the French Revolution,
recognizing its deep connections to the "small flame" of revolution that started in*

North America, and looking forward to its progress "envelop[ing] neighbouring empires in the blaze." Other feminist writers such as Mary Wollstonecraft would use the word "Bastille" as a verb for the repression of women: "he bastille'd me," Wollstonecraft wrote in her novel Maria, or the Wrongs of Woman. *Despite tremendous personal sadness, Margaretta Bleecker Faugeres found hope in the far-reaching potential of the Age of Revolutions.*

"ON SEEING A PRINT, EXHIBITING THE RUINS OF THE BASTILLE" (1792)

At each return of the auspicious day
Which laid this mighty fabric in the dust,
Let joy inspire each patriotic breast
To bless and venerate its august ray,
Let *Gallia's*[1] sons attune the harp of joy,
And teach the trump its boldest notes t'employ;
Let clarions shrill the deed declare,
And blow their son'rous notes afar;
Let music rife from ev'ry plain,
Each vine-clad mount or daisied dell;
And let *Zephyrus*[2] float the strain
Across old Ocean's ample swell.
Ah! see the *Bastille's* iron walls thrown down,
That bulwark strong of *Tyranny*;
See her proud turrets smoke along the ground,
Crush'd by the giant arm of *Liberty*!
Her gloomy tow'rs—her *vaults* impure,
Which once could boast eternal night;
Her *dungeons* deep, her *dens* obscure,
Are urg'd unwilling to the light.
Oft in these dreary cells, the *captive's* moan
Broke the dead silence of the midnight watch;
When *Memory*, pointing to the days long gone,
To wasting sorrows woke the feeling wretch.
Here everlasting darkness spread

---

[1] Gallia: France.
[2] Zephyrus: In Greek mythology, ruler of the winds.

Her veil o'er scenes of misery,
Where *Sickness* heav'd an anguish'd head,
And roll'd a hopeless eye.
here drown'd in tears, pale *Agony*
Spread her clasp'd hands toward the sky,
While all convuls'd *extreme Despair*
Swallow'd the earth in speechless rage,
Or phrenzied gnaw'd his *iron cage*,
Tore off his flesh, and rent his hair.
Such were thy glories, O Bastille!
Such the rich blessings of *despotic pow'r*,
Whose horrid damon quaff'd his fill,
Daily of bitter tears and human gore:
But now 'tis o'er—thy long—long reign is o'er,
Thy thunders fright the trembling hosts no more;
Thy shafts are spent—thy sons no more engage
To add new triumphs to thy train,
To bind new victims to thy chain;
For thy most valiant sons are slain
By the fierce strokes of kindled patriot rage.
Roll'd in the dust, behold thine honours lie,
The sport—the scorn of each exploring eye.
Hail gallant Gauls![3] heroic people hail!
Who spurn the ills that Virtue's sons assail,
Whose hearts benevolent, with ardour bound
The hard-got blessing to diffuse around:
Oh! be your struggles blest, and may you see
Your labours rivall'd by posterity;
'Till the small *flame* (which first was seen to rise,
'Midst threat'ning blasts, beneath *Columbian* skies,
Which, as it taught its splendours to expand,
Arose indignant from Oppression's hand,
And blaz'd effulgent o'er the mighty plain)
Luring your heroes o'er the stormy main,
'Till this small flame, fed by their nurturing hand,
Not only canopies your native land,

---

[3] Gauls: Ancient name of the French people.

But far extending its prolific rays,

Envelopes neighbouring empires in the blaze.

And thou, FAYETTE![4] whom distant lands deplore,

As now *self-banish'd* from thy native shore;

Tho' *zeal mistaken*, may a shadow throw

Athwart the laurels which adorn thy brow;

Yet shall they bloom—for in thy generous breast

No foul like *Coriolanus*[5] is confess'd:

To Gallia still thy warmest wishes tend,

And tho' an *injured exile*, still a friend!

When grateful nations tell thine acts to *Fame*,

America shall urge her oldest claim,

Point to the *worthies* whom her sons revere,

And place FAYETTE with those she holds most dear.

---

[4] Fayette: Marie-Joseph Paul Yves Roch Gilbert du Motier, Marquis de Lafayette (1757–1834), an aristocratic French military officer who volunteered for the Patriot side during the American Revolution, then returned to France where he played a significant role as a moderate pro-revolutionary political and military leader, and was subsequently declared a traitor and effectively exiled by more radical Jacobin factions. Lafayette, who supported religious tolerance, freedom of the press, trial by jury, and slave emancipation, was one of the authors of the *Declaration of the Rights of Man and the Citizen* (1790).

[5] Coriolanus: Gaius Marcus Coriolanus, a legendary fifth-century Roman general, whose antidemocratic career was commemorated by William Shakespeare in the play *Coriolanus* (1623).

FORTY-SIX

Mary Wollstonecraft (1759–1797)

A FEMINIST PHILOSOPHER, NOVELIST, HISTORIAN, REVOLUTIONARY SYMPATHIZER, MOTHER, *and lover, Mary Wollstonecraft was born into an impoverished middle-class London family. Wollstonecraft confronted with tremendous courage and intellectual fortitude the twisted tyrannies of sex that she encountered throughout her life. When she was a teenager, she protected her sisters and mother from the drunken rages of her father, lying across the doorstep of her mother's bedroom at night. She formed crucial friendships with other women who could expand her access to the world of ideas and dreamed as did many Anglophone feminists in the Age of Revolutions of establishing a utopian community for women. After working as a governess and observing the sufferings of her women friends and family from the heavy (sometimes mortal) personal costs of marriage, childbirth, and childrearing, Wollstonecraft moved to London in 1787 to live independently and begin her career as a writer. In London, she found her way to influential political circles, befriending radical philosophers such as Thomas Paine and the anarchist William Godwin. In 1790, she wrote* A Vindication of the Rights of Men, *a defense of the French Revolution; the work was received with acclaim and secured Wollstonecraft fame and esteem in the revolutionary Atlantic world. In 1792, she applied the revolutionary ideals she celebrated in* Rights of Men *to the situation of women, producing* A Vindication of the Rights of Woman, *which would become one of the most powerful and celebrated books in the history of feminist thought.*

A forceful and moving argument for the equality of the sexes and the liberation of humankind from sexual hierarchy, A Vindication of the Rights of Woman *demands that the most progressive ideals of the revolutionary age—the essential equality and capacity for self-governance of all human beings, the abolition of political relations of despotism and dependence, the triumph of reason over custom—be applied to women as well. Wollstonecraft enlarges the feminist case against innate sexual difference by showing how a systematic denial of education to women has created the appearance of essential difference in character and intellect. She demolishes educational philosophies propounded by the influential Jean-Jacques Rousseau who had claimed the object of a man's education should be to prepare him for independent, rational, moral thought and action but that the education of women should prepare them only for a lifetime of dependence on the governance of fathers and husbands, in accordance with an imagined "natural" hierarchy between the sexes. Such thinking, Wollstonecraft argued, was dehumanizing to men and women both, injurious to their intimate relationships, damaging to children, and incompatible with the ideals of a just and reasonable society. Her call for a "REVOLUTION in female manners" was received with scorn and vitriol by conservative readers, but revolutionary men and women around the Atlantic world embraced the book, which was immediately reprinted in Boston and Philadelphia, and went through four more American editions before the end of the eighteenth century.*

After writing Rights of Woman, *Wollstonecraft moved to Paris in December 1792, to witness firsthand and take part in the excitement of the French Revolution. There, she met and fell in love with the American merchant-adventurer Gilbert Imlay, and together the couple had a child named Fanny in 1794. Imlay soon abandoned Wollstonecraft and Fanny, and when the political situation in France became dangerous for British citizens, Wollstonecraft returned to London in 1795. Deeply depressed, she eventually resumed her place among liberal political and literary circles and began an affair with the anarchist William Godwin. She became pregnant by Godwin and gave birth to her daughter Mary (who would grow up to become Mary Shelley, author of* Frankenstein) *on August 30, 1797. Wollstonecraft died ten days later of complications from childbirth. The power and truthfulness of* Rights of Woman *resonates to this day.*

FROM *A VINDICATION OF THE RIGHTS OF WOMAN* (1792)

Introduction

After considering the historic page, and viewing the living world with anxious solicitude, the most melancholy emotions of sorrowful indignation have depressed my spirits, and I have sighed when obliged to confess, that either nature has made a great difference between man and man, or that the civilization which has hitherto taken place in the world has been very partial. I have turned over various books written on the subject of education, and patiently observed the conduct of parents and the management of schools; but what has been the result?—a profound conviction that the neglected education of my fellow-creatures is the grand source of the misery I deplore; and that women, in particular, are rendered weak and wretched by a variety of concurring causes, originating from one hasty conclusion. The conduct and manners of women, in fact, evidently prove that their minds are not in a healthy state; for, like the flowers which are planted in too rich a soil, strength and usefulness are sacrificed to beauty; and the flaunting leaves, after having pleased a fastidious eye, fade, disregarded on the stalk, long before the season when they ought to have arrived at maturity.—One cause of this barren blooming I attribute to a false system of education, gathered from the books written on this subject by men who, considering females rather as women than human creatures, have been more anxious to make them alluring mistresses than affectionate wives and rational mothers; and the understanding of the sex has been so bubbled by this specious homage, that the civilized women of the present century, with a few exceptions, are only anxious to inspire love, when they ought to cherish a nobler ambition, and by their abilities and virtues exact respect.

In a treatise, therefore, on female rights and manners, the works which have been particularly written for their improvement must not be overlooked; especially when it is asserted, in direct terms, that the minds of women are enfeebled by false refinement; that the books of instruction, written by men of genius, have had the same tendency as more frivolous productions; and that, in the true style of Mahometanism,[1] they are treated as a kind of subordinate beings, and not as a part of the human species, when improveable reason is allowed to be the dignified distinction which raises men above the brute creation, and puts a natural sceptre in a feeble hand.

Yet, because I am a woman, I would not lead my readers to suppose that I mean violently to agitate the contested question respecting the equality or inferiority of the sex; but as the subject lies in my way, and I cannot pass it over without subjecting the main tendency of my reasoning to misconstruction, I shall stop a moment to deliver, in a few words, my opinion.—In the government of the physical world it is observable that the female in point of strength is, in general, inferior to the male. This is the

---

[1] Mahometanism: Islam. Wollstonecraft's condemnation of Islam here and throughout *Rights of Woman* reveals that Orientalism—defined by the scholar Edward Said as a tradition of prejudicial and deprecatory depictions of Middle Eastern and Asian cultures—was firmly in place in the late eighteenth century.

law of nature; and it does not appear to be suspended or abrogated in favour of woman. A degree of physical superiority cannot, therefore, be denied—and it is a noble prerogative! But not content with this natural pre-eminence, men endeavour to sink us still lower, merely to render us alluring objects for a moment; and women, intoxicated by the adoration which men, under the influence of their senses, pay them, do not seek to obtain a durable interest in their hearts, or to become the friends of the fellow creatures who find amusement in their society. . . .

My own sex, I hope, will excuse me, if I treat them like rational creatures, instead of flattering their *fascinating* graces, and viewing them as if they were in a state of perpetual childhood, unable to stand alone. I earnestly wish to point out in what true dignity and human happiness consists—I wish to persuade women to endeavour to acquire strength, both of mind and body, and to convince them that the soft phrases, susceptibility of heart, delicacy of sentiment, and refinement of taste, are almost synonymous with epithets of weakness, and that those beings who are only the objects of pity and that kind of love, which has been termed its sister, will soon become objects of contempt.

Dismissing then those pretty feminine phrases, which the men condescendingly use to soften our slavish dependence, and despising that weak elegancy of mind, exquisite sensibility, and sweet docility of manners, supposed to be the sexual characteristics of the weaker vessel, I wish to shew that elegance is inferior to virtue, that the first object of laudable ambition is to obtain a character as a human being, regardless of the distinction of sex; and that secondary views should be brought to this simple touchstone.

This is a rough sketch of my plan; and should I express my conviction with the energetic emotions that I feel whenever I think of the subject, the dictates of experience and reflection will be felt by some of my readers. Animated by this important object, I shall disdain to cull my phrases or polish my style;—I aim at being useful, and sincerity will render me unaffected; for, wishing rather to persuade by the force of my arguments, than dazzle by the elegance of my language, I shall not waste my time in rounding periods, or in fabricating the turgid bombast of artificial feelings, which, coming from the head, never reach the heart.—I shall be employed about things, not words!—and, anxious to render my sex more respectable members of society, I shall try to avoid that flowery diction which has slided from essays into novels, and from novels into familiar letters and conversation. . . .

The education of women has, of late, been more attended to than formerly; yet they are still reckoned a frivolous sex, and ridiculed or pitied by the writers who endeavour by satire or instruction to improve them. It is acknowledged that they spend many of the first years of their lives in acquiring a smattering of accomplishments; meanwhile strength of body and mind are sacrificed to libertine notions of beauty, to the desire of establishing themselves,—the only way women can rise in the world,—by marriage. And this desire making mere animals of them, when they marry they act as such children may be expected to act:—they dress; they paint, and nickname God's creatures.— Surely these weak beings are only fit for a seraglio![2]—Can they be expected to govern a family with judgment, or take care of the poor babes whom they bring into the world? . . .

Women are, in fact, so much degraded by mistaken notions of female excellence, that I do not mean to add a paradox when I assert, that this artificial weakness produces a propensity to tyrannize, and gives birth to cunning, the natural opponent of strength, which leads them to play off those contemptible infantine airs that undermine esteem even whilst they excite desire. Let men become more chaste and modest, and if women do not grow wiser in the same ratio, it will be clear that they have weaker understandings. It seems scarcely necessary to say, that I now speak of the sex in general. Many individuals have more sense than their male relatives; and, as nothing preponderates where there is a constant struggle for an equilibrium, without it has naturally more gravity, some women govern their husbands without degrading themselves, because intellect will always govern . . .

Chapter 2: The Prevailing Opinion of a Sexual Character Discussed.

To account for, and excuse the tyranny of man, many ingenious arguments have been brought forward to prove, that the two sexes, in the acquirement of virtue, ought to aim at attaining a very different character: or, to speak explicitly, women are not allowed to have sufficient strength of mind to acquire what really deserves the name of virtue. Yet it should seem, allowing them to have souls, that there is but one way appointed by Providence to lead *mankind* to either virtue or happiness.

If then women are not a swarm of ephemeron[3] triflers, why should they be kept in ignorance under the specious name of innocence? Men complain, and with reason, of the follies and caprices of our sex, when they do not keenly satirize our headstrong passions and groveling vices.—Behold, I should answer, the natural effect of ignorance! The mind will ever be unstable that has only prejudices to rest on, and the current will run with destructive fury when there are no barriers to break its force.

---

[2] See p. 157, note 4.
[3] Ephemeron: Short-lived.

Women are told from their infancy, and taught by the example of their mothers, that a little knowledge of human weakness, justly termed cunning, softness of temper, outward obedience, and a scrupulous attention to a puerile kind of propriety, will obtain for them the protection of man; and should they be beautiful, every thing else is needless, for, at least, twenty years of their lives.

Thus Milton describes our first frail mother; though when he tells us that women are formed for softness and sweet attractive grace,[4] I cannot comprehend his meaning, unless, in the true Mahometan strain, he meant to deprive us of souls, and insinuate that we were beings only designed by sweet attractive grace, and docile blind obedience, to gratify the senses of man when he can no longer soar on the wing of contemplation.

How grossly do they insult us who thus advise us only to render ourselves gentle, domestic brutes! For instance, the winning softness so warmly, and frequently, recommended, that governs by obeying. What childish expressions, and how insignificant is the being—can it be an immortal one? who will condescend to govern by such sinister methods! 'Certainly,' says Lord Bacon, 'man is of kin to the beasts by his body; and if he be not of kin to God by his spirit, he is a base and ignoble creature!'[5] Men, indeed, appear to me to act in a very unphilosophical manner when they try to secure the good conduct of women by attempting to keep them always in a state of childhood. Rousseau was more consistent when he wished to stop the progress of reason in both sexes, for if men eat of the tree of knowledge, women will come in for a taste; but, from the imperfect cultivation which their understandings now receive, they only attain a knowledge of evil.[6]

Children, I grant, should be innocent; but when the epithet is applied to men, or women, it is but a civil term for weakness. For if it be allowed that women were destined by Providence to acquire human virtues, and by the exercise of their understandings, that stability of character which is the firmest ground to rest our future hopes upon, they must be permitted to turn to the fountain of light, and not forced to shape their course by the twinkling of a mere satellite. . . .

Consequently, the most perfect education, in my opinion, is such an exercise of the understanding as is best calculated to strengthen the body and form the heart. Or,

---

[4] Wollstonecraft refers to John Milton's depiction of Eve in *Paradise Lost* (1667). In Book IV, Milton describes Adam and Eve: "Not equal, as thir sex not equal seemd; / For contemplation hee and valour formd, / For softness shee and sweet attractive Grace, / Hee for God only, shee for God in him."

[5] Lord Bacon: Francis Bacon, Baron Verulam (1561–1626); English philosopher and statesman. These lines are from Bacon's essay "Of Atheism."

[6] Rousseau: Jean-Jacques Rousseau (1712–1778); French philosopher, composer, and novelist.

in other words, to enable the individual to attain such habits of virtue as will render it independent. In fact, it is a farce to call any being virtuous whose virtues do not result from the exercise of its own reason. This was Rousseau's opinion respecting men: I extend it to women, and confidently assert that they have been drawn out of their sphere by false refinement, and not by an endeavour to acquire masculine qualities. Still the regal homage which they receive is so intoxicating, that till the manners of the times are changed, and formed on more reasonable principles, it may be impossible to convince them that the illegitimate power, which they obtain, by degrading themselves, is a curse, and that they must return to nature and equality, if they wish to secure the placid satisfaction that unsophisticated affections impart. But for this epoch we must wait—wait, perhaps, till kings and nobles, enlightened by reason, and, preferring the real dignity of man to childish state, throw off their gaudy hereditary trappings: and if then women do not resign the arbitrary power of beauty— they will prove that they have *less* mind than man. . . .

Many are the causes that, in the present corrupt state of society, contribute to enslave women by cramping their understandings and sharpening their senses. One, perhaps, that silently does more mischief than all the rest, is their disregard of order.

To do every thing in an orderly manner, is a most important precept, which women, who, generally speaking, receive only a disorderly kind of education, seldom attend to with that degree of exactness that men, who from their infancy are broken into method, observe. This negligent kind of guess-work, for what other epithet can be used to point out the random exertions of a sort of instinctive common sense, never brought to the test of reason? prevents their generalizing matters of fact—so they do to-day, what they did yesterday, merely because they did it yesterday.

This contempt of the understanding in early life has more baneful consequences than is commonly supposed; for the little knowledge which women of strong minds attain, is, from various circumstances, of a more desultory kind than the knowledge of men, and it is acquired more by sheer observations on real life, than from comparing what has been individually observed with the results of experience generalized by speculation. Led by their dependent situation and domestic employments more into society, what they learn is rather by snatches; and as learning is with them, in general, only a secondary thing, they do not pursue any one branch with that persevering ardour necessary to give vigour to the faculties, and clearness to the judgment. In the present state of society, a little learning is required to support the character of a gentleman; and boys are obliged to submit to a few years of discipline. But in the education of women, the cultivation of the understanding is always subordinate to the acquirement of some corporeal accomplishment; even while enervated by confinement and false notions of modesty, the body is prevented from attaining that grace and beauty which relaxed half-formed limbs never exhibit. Besides, in youth their faculties are not brought forward by emulation; and having no serious scientific study, if they have natural sagacity it is turned too soon on life and manners. They dwell on effects, and modifications, without tracing them back to causes; and complicated rules to adjust behaviour are a weak substitute for simple principles. . . .

Riches and hereditary honours have made cyphers of women to give consequence to the numerical figure; and idleness has produced a mixture of gallantry and despotism into society, which leads the very men who are the slaves of their mistresses to tyrannize over their sisters, wives, and daughters. This is only keeping them in rank and file, it is true. Strengthen the female mind by enlarging it, and there will be an end to blind obedience; but, as blind obedience is ever sought for by power, tyrants and sensualists are in the right when they endeavour to keep women in the dark, because the former only want slaves, and the latter a play-thing. The sensualist, indeed, has been the most dangerous of tyrants, and women have been duped by their lovers, as princes by their ministers, whilst dreaming that they reigned over them.

I now principally allude to Rousseau, for his character of Sophia is, undoubtedly, a captivating one, though it appears to me grossly unnatural;[7] however it is not the superstructure, but the foundation of her character, the principles on which her education was built, that I mean to attack; nay, warmly as I admire the genius of that able writer, whose opinions I shall often have occasion to cite, indignation always takes place of admiration, and the rigid frown of insulted virtue effaces the smile of complacency which his eloquent periods are wont to raise, when I read his voluptuous reveries. Is this the man, who, in his ardour for virtue, would banish all the soft arts of peace, and almost carry us back to Spartan discipline? Is this the man who delights to paint the useful struggles of passion, the triumphs of good dispositions, and the heroic flights which carry the glowing soul out of itself?—How are these mighty sentiments lowered when he describes the pretty foot and enticing airs of his little favourite! But, for the present, I wave the subject, and, instead of severely reprehending the transient effusions of overweening sensibility, I shall only observe, that whoever has cast a benevolent eye on society, must often have been gratified by the sight

---

[7] Throughout *Rights of Woman*, Wollstonecraft critiques Rousseau's influential philosophical narrative *Emile: or, On Education* (1762), which describes the intellectual and moral education of a young boy to become a rational man and self-governing adult citizen. By contrast, the education of Emile's female counterpart Sophie as imagined by Rousseau prepares her to be governed by her husband and to remain within the domestic and private sphere, in accordance with what Rousseau believed to be a natural and necessary hierarchy of the sexes.

of a humble mutual love, not dignified by sentiment, or strengthened by a union in intellectual pursuits. The domestic trifles of the day have afforded matters for cheerful converse, and innocent caresses have softened toils which did not require great exercise of mind or stretch of thought: yet, has not the sight of this moderate felicity excited more tenderness than respect? An emotion similar to what we feel when children are playing, or animals sporting,[8] whilst the contemplation of the noble struggles of suffering merit has raised admiration, and carried our thoughts to that world where sensation will give place to reason.

Women are, therefore, to be considered either as moral beings, or so weak that they must be entirely subjected to the superior faculties of men.

Let us examine this question. Rousseau declares that a woman should never, for a moment, feel herself independent, that she should be governed by fear to exercise her *natural* cunning, and made a coquetish slave in order to render her a more alluring object of desire, a *sweeter* companion to man, whenever he chooses to relax himself. He carries the arguments, which he pretends to draw from the indications of nature, still further, and insinuates that truth and fortitude, the corner stones of all human virtue, should be cultivated with certain restrictions, because, with respect to the female character, obedience is the grand lesson which ought to be impressed with unrelenting rigour.

What nonsense! When will a great man arise with sufficient strength of mind to puff away the fumes which pride and sensuality have thus spread over the subject! If women are by nature inferior to men, their virtues must be the same in quality, if not in degree, or virtue is a relative idea; consequently, their conduct should be founded on the same principles, and have the same aim.

Connected with man as daughters, wives, and mothers, their moral character may be estimated by their manner of fulfilling those simple duties; but the end, the grand end of their exertions should be to unfold their own faculties and acquire the dignity of conscious virtue. They may try to render their road pleasant; but ought never to forget, in common with man, that life yields not the felicity which can satisfy an immortal soul. . . .

---

[8] Wollstonecraft's note: "Similar feelings has Milton's pleasing picture of paradisiacal happiness ever raised in my mind; yet, instead of envying the lovely pair, I have, with conscious dignity, or Satanic pride, turned to hell for sublimer objects. In the same style, when viewing some noble monument of human art, I have traced the emanation of the Deity in the order I admired, till, descending from that giddy height, I have caught myself contemplating the grandest of all human sights;—for fancy quickly placed, in some solitary recess, an outcast of fortune, rising superior to passion and discontent."

But Rousseau, and most of the male writers who have followed his steps, have warmly inculcated that the whole tendency of female education ought to be directed to one point:—to render them pleasing.

Let me reason with the supporters of this opinion who have any knowledge of human nature, do they imagine that marriage can eradicate the habitude of life? The woman who has only been taught to please will soon find that her charms are oblique sunbeams, and that they cannot have much effect on her husband's heart when they are seen every day, when the summer is passed and gone. Will she then have sufficient native energy to look into herself for comfort, and cultivate her dormant faculties? or, is it not more rational to expect that she will try to please other men; and, in the emotions raised by the expectation of new conquests, endeavour to forget the mortification her love or pride has received? When the husband ceases to be a lover— and the time will inevitably come, her desire of pleasing will then grow languid, or become a spring of bitterness; and love, perhaps, the most evanescent of all passions, gives place to jealousy or vanity.

I now speak of women who are restrained by principle or prejudice; such women, though they would shrink from an intrigue with real abhorrence, yet, nevertheless, wish to be convinced by the homage of gallantry that they are cruelly neglected by their husbands; or, days and weeks are spent in dreaming of the happiness enjoyed by congenial souls till their health is undermined and their spirits broken by discontent. How then can the great art of pleasing be such a necessary study? it is only useful to a mistress; the chaste wife, and serious mother, should only consider her power to please as the polish of her virtues, and the affection of her husband as one of the comforts that render her task less difficult and her life happier.—But, whether she be loved or neglected, her first wish should be to make herself respectable, and not to rely for all her happiness on a being subject to like infirmities with herself.

The worthy Dr. Gregory fell into a similar error. I respect his heart; but entirely disapprove of his celebrated *Legacy to his Daughters*.[9]

He advises them to cultivate a fondness for dress, because a fondness for dress, he asserts, is natural to them. I am unable to comprehend what either he or Rousseau mean, when they frequently use this indefinite term. If they told us that in a pre-existent state the soul was fond of dress, and brought this inclination with it into a new body, I should listen to them with a half smile, as I often do when I hear a rant

---

[9] Dr. Gregory: John Gregory (1724–1773); Scottish philosopher and physician; author of *A Father's Legacy to his Daughters* (1761), which argues that women should not reveal the extent of their intellect or learning lest they deter potential marriage partners.

about innate elegance.—But if he only meant to say that the exercise of the faculties will produce this fondness—I deny it.—It is not natural; but arises, like false ambition in men, from a love of power.

Dr. Gregory goes much further; he actually recommends dissimulation, and advises an innocent girl to give the lie to her feelings, and not dance with spirit, when gaiety of heart would make her feel eloquent without making her gestures immodest. In the name of truth and common sense, why should not one woman acknowledge that she can take more exercise than another? or, in other words, that she has a sound constitution; and why, to damp innocent vivacity, is she darkly to be told that men will draw conclusions which she little thinks of?—Let the libertine draw what inference he pleases; but, I hope, that no sensible mother will restrain the natural frankness of youth by instilling such indecent cautions. Out of the abundance of the heart the mouth speaketh;[10] and a wiser than Solomon hath said,[11] that the heart should be made clean, and not trivial ceremonies observed, which it is not very difficult to fulfill with scrupulous exactness when vice reigns in the heart.[12]

Women ought to endeavour to purify their heart; but can they do so when their uncultivated understandings make them entirely dependent on their senses for employment and amusement, when no noble pursuit sets them above the little vanities of the day, or enables them to curb the wild emotions that agitate a reed over which every passing breeze has power? To gain the affections of a virtuous man is affectation necessary? Nature has given woman a weaker frame than man; but, to ensure her husband's affections, must a wife, who by the exercise of her mind and body whilst she was discharging the duties of a daughter, wife, and mother, has allowed her constitution to retain its natural strength, and her nerves a healthy tone, is she, I say, to condescend to use art and feign a sickly delicacy in order to secure her husband's affection? Weakness may excite tenderness, and gratify the arrogant pride of man; but the lordly caresses of a protector will not gratify a noble mind that pants for, and deserves to be respected. Fondness is a poor substitute for friendship!

In a seraglio, I grant, that all these arts are necessary; the epicure must have his palate tickled, or he will sink into apathy; but have women so little ambition as to be satisfied with such a condition? Can they supinely dream life away in the lap of pleasure, or the languor of weariness, rather than assert their claim to pursue reasonable pleasures and render themselves conspicuous by practising the virtues which dignify

---

[10] See Matthew 12:34, Luke 6:45.
[11] A wiser than Solomon: Jesus.
[12] See Matthew 23:25–28, Luke 11:37–41.

mankind? Surely she has not an immortal soul who can loiter life away merely employed to adorn her person, that she may amuse the languid hours, and soften the cares of a fellow-creature who is willing to be enlivened by her smiles and tricks, when the serious business of life is over.

Besides, the woman who strengthens her body and exercises her mind will, by managing her family and practising various virtues, become the friend, and not the humble dependent of her husband; and if she, by possessing such substantial qualities, merit his regard, she will not find it necessary to conceal her affection, nor to pretend to an unnatural coldness of constitution to excite her husband's passions. In fact, if we revert to history, we shall find that the women who have distinguished themselves have neither been the most beautiful nor the most gentle of their sex. . . .

Supposing, for a moment, that the soul is not immortal, and that man was only created for the present scene,—I think we should have reason to complain that love, infantine fondness, ever grew insipid and palled upon the sense. Let us eat, drink, and love, for to-morrow we die,[13] would be, in fact, the language of reason, the morality of life; and who but a fool would part with a reality for a fleeting shadow? But, if awed by observing the improbable powers of the mind, we disdain to confine our wishes or thoughts to such a comparatively mean field of action; that only appears grand and important, as it is connected with a boundless prospect and sublime hopes, what necessity is there for falsehood in conduct, and why must the sacred majesty of truth be violated to detain a deceitful good that saps the very foundation of virtue? Why must the female mind be tainted by coquetish arts to gratify the sensualist, and prevent love from subsiding into friendship, or compassionate tenderness, when there are not qualities on which friendship can be built? Let the honest heart shew itself, and *reason* teach passion to submit to necessity; or, let the dignified pursuit of virtue and knowledge raise the mind above those emotions which rather imbitter than sweeten the cup of life, when they are not restrained within due bounds. . . .

But to view the subject in another point of view. Do passive indolent women make the best wives? Confining our discussion to the present moment of existence, let us see how such weak creatures perform their part? Do the women who, by the attainment of a few superficial accomplishments, have strengthened the prevailing prejudice, merely contribute to the happiness of their husbands? Do they display their charms merely to amuse them? And have women, who have early imbibed notions of passive obedience, sufficient character to manage a family or educate children? So far from it, that, after surveying the history of woman, I cannot help, agreeing with

---

[13] See Isaiah 22:13, 1 Corinthians 15:32.

the severest satirist, considering the sex as the weakest as well as the most oppressed half of the species. What does history disclose but marks of inferiority, and how few women have emancipated themselves from the galling yoke of sovereign man?—So few, that the exceptions remind me of an ingenious conjecture respecting Newton: that he was probably a being of a superior order, accidentally caged in a human body.[14] Following the same train of thinking, I have been led to imagine that the few extraordinary women who have rushed in eccentrical directions out of the orbit prescribed to their sex, were male spirits, confined by mistake in female frames. But if it be not philosophical to think of sex when the soul is mentioned, the inferiority must depend on the organs; or the heavenly fire, which is to ferment the clay, is not given in equal portions.

But avoiding, as I have hitherto done, any direct comparison of the two sexes collectively, or frankly acknowledging the inferiority of woman, according to the present appearance of things, I shall only insist that men have increased that inferiority till women are almost sunk below the standard of rational creatures. Let their faculties have room to unfold, and their virtues to gain strength, and then determine where the whole sex must stand in the intellectual scale. Yet let it be remembered, that for a small number of distinguished women I do not ask a place.

It is difficult for us purblind mortals to say to what height human discoveries and improvements may arrive when the gloom of despotism subsides, which makes us stumble at every step; but, when morality shall be settled on a more solid basis, then, without being gifted with a prophetic spirit, I will venture to predict that woman will be either the friend or slave of man. We shall not, as at present, doubt whether she is a moral agent, or the link which unites man with brutes. But, should it then appear, that like the brutes they were principally created for the use of man, he will let them patiently bite the bridle, and not mock them with empty praise; or, should their rationality be proved, he will not impede their improvement merely to gratify his sensual appetites. He will not, with all the graces of rhetoric, advise them to submit implicitly their understanding to the guidance of man. He will not, when he treats of the education of women, assert that they ought never to have the free use of reason, nor would he recommend cunning and dissimulation to beings who are acquiring, in like manner as himself, the virtues of humanity . . .

If, I say, for I would not impress by declamation when Reason offers her sober light, if they be really capable of acting like rational creatures, let them not be treated like slaves; or, like the brutes who are dependent on the reason of man, when they

---

[14] Newton: Sir Isaac Newton (1643–1727); English scientist and philosopher.

associate with him; but cultivate their minds, give them the salutary, sublime curb of principle, and let them attain conscious dignity by feeling themselves only dependent on God. Teach them, in common with man, to submit to necessity instead of giving, to render them more pleasing, a sex to morals.

Further, should experience prove that they cannot attain the same degree of strength of mind, perseverance, and fortitude, let their virtues be the same in kind, though they may vainly struggle for the same degree; and the superiority of man will be equally clear, if not clearer; and truth, as it is a simple principle, which admits of no modification, would be common to both. Nay, the order of society as it is at present regulated would not be inverted, for woman would then only have the rank that reason assigned her, and arts could not be practised to bring the balance even, much less to turn it.

These may be termed Utopian dreams.—Thanks to that Being who impressed them on my soul, and gave me sufficient strength of mind to dare to exert my own reason, till, becoming dependent only on him for the support of my virtue, I view, with indignation, the mistaken notions that enslave my sex.

I love man as my fellow; but his scepter, real, or usurped, extends not to me, unless the reason of an individual demands my homage; and even then the submission is to reason, and not to man. In fact, the conduct of an accountable being must be regulated by the operations of its own reason; or on what foundation rests the throne of God?

It appears to me necessary to dwell on these obvious truths, because females have been insulated, as it were; and, while they have been stripped of the virtues that should clothe humanity, they have been decked with artificial graces that enable them to exercise a short-lived tyranny. Love, in their bosoms, taking place of every nobler passion, their sole ambition is to be fair, to raise emotion instead of inspiring respect; and this ignoble desire, like the servility in absolute monarchies, destroys all strength of character. Liberty is the mother of virtue, and if women be, by their very constitution, slaves, and not allowed to breathe the sharp invigorating air of freedom, they must ever languish like exotics, and be reckoned beautiful flaws in nature.

As to the argument respecting the subjection in which the sex has ever been held, it retorts on man. The many have always been enthralled by the few; and monsters, who scarcely have shewn any discernment of human excellence, have tyrannized over thousands of their fellow-creatures. Why have men of superiour endowments submitted to such degradation? For, is it not universally acknowledged that kings, viewed collectively, have ever been inferior, in abilities and virtue, to the same number of men taken from the common mass of mankind—yet, have they not, and are they not still treated with a degree of reverence that is an insult to reason? China is not the only country where a living man has been made a God.[15] Men have submitted to su-perior strength to enjoy with impunity the pleasure of the moment—women have only done the same, and therefore till it is proved that the courtier, who servilely resigns the birthright of a man, is not a moral agent, it cannot be demonstrated that woman is essentially inferior to man because she has always been subjugated.

Brutal force has hitherto governed the world, and that the science of politics is in its infancy, is evident from philosophers scrupling to give the knowledge most useful to man that determinate distinction.

I shall not pursue this argument any further than to establish an obvious infer-ence, that as sound politics diffuse liberty, mankind, including woman, will become more wise and virtuous. . . .

Chapter 13: Some Instances of the Folly Which the Ignorance of Women Generates; with Concluding Reflections on the Moral Improvement That a Revolution in Female Manners Might Naturally Be Expected to Produce.

Another instance of that feminine weakness of character, often produced by a con-fined education, is a romantic twist of the mind, which has been very properly termed *sentimental*.

Women subjected by ignorance to their sensations, and only taught to look for happiness in love, refine on sensual feelings, and adopt metaphysical notions re-specting that passion, which lead them shamefully to neglect the duties of life, and frequently in the midst of these sublime refinements they plump into actual vice.

These are the women who are amused by the reveries of the stupid novelists, who, knowing little of human nature, work up stale tales, and describe meretricious scenes, all retailed in a sentimental jargon, which equally tend to corrupt the taste, and draw the heart aside from its daily duties. I do not mention the understanding, because never having been exercised, its slumbering energies rest inactive, like the lurking particles of fire which are supposed universally to pervade matter.

Females, in fact, denied all political privileges, and not allowed, as married women, excepting in criminal cases, a civil existence, have their attention naturally drawn from the interest of the whole community to that of the minute parts, though the private duty of any member of society must be very imperfectly performed when not connected with the general good. The mighty business of female life is to please,

---

[15] Wollstonecraft refers critically to the Imperial Chinese tradition of regarding the ruling Emperor as a "Son of Heaven."

and restrained from entering into more important concerns by political and civil oppression, sentiments become events, and reflection deepens what it should, and
would have effaced, if the understanding had been allowed to take a wider range.

But, confined to trifling employments, they naturally imbibe opinions which the
only kind of reading calculated to interest an innocent frivolous mind, inspires. Unable to grasp any thing great, is it surprising that they find the reading of history a
very dry task, and disquisitions addressed to the understanding intolerably tedious,
and almost unintelligible? Thus are they necessarily dependent on the novelist for
amusement. Yet, when I exclaim against novels, I mean when contrasted with those
works which exercise the understanding and regulate the imagination.—For any
kind of reading I think better than leaving a blank still a blank, because the mind
must receive a degree of enlargement and obtain a little strength by a slight exertion
of its thinking powers; besides, even the productions that are only addressed to the
imagination, raise the reader a little above the gross gratification of appetites, to
which the mind has not given a shade of delicacy. . . .

I recollect many other women who, not led by degrees to proper studies, and not
permitted to choose for themselves, have indeed been overgrown children; or have
obtained, by mixing in the world, a little of what is termed common sense: that is, a
distinct manner of seeing common occurrences, as they stand detached: but what
deserves the name of intellect, the power of gaining general or abstract ideas, or even
intermediate ones, was out of the question. Their minds were quiescent, and when
they were not roused by sensible objects and employments of that kind, they were
low-spirited, would cry, or go to sleep.

When, therefore, I advise my sex not to read such flimsy works, it is to induce
them to read something superiour. . . .

In fact the female mind has been so totally neglected, that knowledge was only to
be acquired from this muddy source, till from reading novels some women of superiour talents learned to despise them.

The best method, I believe, that can be adopted to correct a fondness for novels
is to ridicule them: not indiscriminately, for then it would have little effect; but, if a
judicious person, with some turn for humour, would read several to a young girl, and
point out both by tones, and apt comparisons with pathetic incidents and heroic characters in history, how foolishly and ridiculously they caricatured human nature, just
opinions might be substituted instead of romantic sentiments. . . .

Ignorance and the mistaken cunning that nature sharpens in weak heads as a principle of self-preservation, render women very fond of dress, and produce all the
vanity which such a fondness may naturally be expected to generate, to the exclusion
of emulation and magnanimity.

I agree with Rousseau that the physical part of the art of pleasing consists in ornaments, and for that very reason I should guard girls against the contagious fondness for dress so common to weak women, that they may not rest in the physical part. Yet, weak are the women who imagine that they can long please without the aid of the mind, or, in other words, without the moral art of pleasing. But the moral art, if it be not a profanation to use the word art, when alluding to the grace which is an effect of virtue, and not the motive of action, is never to be found with ignorance; the sportiveness of innocence, so pleasing to refined libertines of both sexes, is widely different in its essence from this superiour gracefulness.

A strong inclination for external ornaments ever appears in barbarous states, only the men not the women adorn themselves; for where women are allowed to be so far on a level with men, society has advanced, at least, one step in civilization.

The attention to dress, therefore, which has been thought a sexual propensity, I think natural to mankind. But I ought to express myself with more precision. When the mind is not sufficiently opened to take pleasure in reflection, the body will be adorned with sedulous care; and ambition will appear in tattooing or painting it.

So far is this first inclination carried, that even the hellish yoke of slavery cannot stifle the savage desire of admiration which the black heroes inherit from both their parents, for all the hardly earned savings of a slave are commonly expended in a little tawdry finery. And I have seldom known a good male or female servant that was not particularly fond of dress.[16] Their clothes were their riches; and, I argue from analogy, that the fondness for dress, so extravagant in females, arises from the same cause— want of cultivation of mind. When men meet they converse about business, politics, or literature; but, says Swift, 'how naturally do women apply their hands to each others lappets and ruffles.'[17] And very natural is it—for they have not any business to interest them, have not a taste for literature, and they find politics dry, because they have not acquired a love for mankind by turning their thoughts to the grand pursuits that exalt the human race, and promote general happiness.

Besides, various are the paths to power and fame which by accident or choice men pursue, and though they jostle against each other, for men of the same profession are seldom friends, yet there is a much greater number of their fellow-creatures with whom they never clash. But women are very differently situated with respect to each other—for they are all rivals.

---

[16] Here Wollstonecraft reflects common eighteenth-century racial and class stereotypes.
[17] Swift: Jonathan Swift (1667–1745); Anglo-Irish novelist, essayist, and satirist; these lines are from his "Letter to a Young Lady on Her Marriage" (1727).

Before marriage it is their business to please men; and after, with a few exceptions, they follow the same scent with all the persevering pertinacity of instinct. Even virtuous women never forget their sex in company, for they are for ever trying to make themselves *agreeable*. A female beauty, and a male wit, appear to be equally anxious to draw the attention of the company to themselves; and the animosity of contemporary wits is proverbial.

Is it then surprising that when the sole ambition of woman centres in beauty, and interest gives vanity additional force, perpetual rivalships should ensue? They are all running the same race, and would rise above the virtue of mortals, if they did not view each other with a suspicious and even envious eye.

An immoderate fondness for dress, for pleasure, and for sway, are the passions of savages; the passions that occupy those uncivilized beings who have not yet extended the dominion of the mind, or even learned to think with the energy necessary to concatenate that abstract train of thought which produces principles. And that women from their education and the present state of civilized life, are in the same condition, cannot, I think, be controverted. To laugh at them then, or satirize the follies of a being who is never to be allowed to act freely from the light of her own reason, is as absurd as cruel; for, that they who are taught blindly to obey authority, will endeavour cunningly to elude it, is most natural and certain. . . .

Women are supposed to possess more sensibility, and even humanity, than men, and their strong attachments and instantaneous emotions of compassion are given as proofs; but the clinging affection of ignorance has seldom any thing noble in it, and may mostly be resolved into selfishness, as well as the affection of children and brutes. I have known many weak women whose sensibility was entirely engrossed by their husbands; and as for their humanity, it was very faint indeed, or rather it was only a transient emotion of compassion. Humanity does not consist 'in a squeamish ear,' says an eminent orator. 'It belongs to the mind as well as the nerves.'[18] . . .

I know that a little sensibility, and great weakness, will produce a strong sexual attachment, and that reason must cement friendship; consequently, I allow that more friendship is to be found in the male than the female world, and that men have a higher sense of justice. The exclusive affections of women seem indeed to resemble Cato's most unjust love for his country. He wished to crush Carthage, not to save

---

[18] Charles James Fox (1749–1806), a British politician, reportedly spoke these words during a speech before the Commons, when his audience became discomfited by an impassioned and graphic speech to end the slave trade.

Rome, but to promote its vain-glory;[19] and, in general, it is to similar principles that humanity is sacrificed, for genuine duties support each other.

Besides, how can women be just or generous, when they are the slaves of injustice?

As the rearing of children, that is, the laying a foundation of sound health both of body and mind in the rising generation, has justly been insisted on as the peculiar destination of woman, the ignorance that incapacitates them must be contrary to the order of things. And I contend that their minds can take in much more, and ought to do so, or they will never become sensible mothers. Many men attend to the breeding of horses, and overlook the management of the stable, who would, strange want of sense and feeling! think themselves degraded by paying any attention to the nursery; yet, how many children are absolutely murdered by the ignorance of women! But when they escape, and are destroyed neither by unnatural negligence nor blind fondness, how few are managed properly with respect to the infant mind! So that to break the spirit, allowed to become vicious at home, a child is sent to school; and the methods taken there, which must be taken to keep a number of children in order, scatter the seeds of almost every vice in the soil thus forcibly torn up. . . .

One striking instance of the folly of women must not be omitted.—The manner in which they treat servants in the presence of children, permitting them to suppose that they ought to wait on them, and bear their humours. A child should always be made to receive assistance from a man or woman as a favour; and, as the first lesson of independence, they should practically be taught, by the example of their mother, not to require that personal attendance, which it is an insult to humanity to require, when in health; and instead of being led to assume airs of consequence, a sense of their own weakness should first make them feel the natural equality of man. Yet, how frequently have I indignantly heard servants imperiously called to put children to bed, and sent away again and again, because master or miss hung about mamma, to stay a little longer. Thus made slavishly to attend the little idol, all those most disgusting humours were exhibited which characterize a spoiled child.

In short, speaking of the majority of mothers, they leave their children entirely to the care of servants; or, because they are their children, treat them as if they were little demi-gods, though I have always observed, that the women who thus idolize their children, seldom shew common humanity to servants, or feel the least tenderness for any children but their own.

---

[19] Cato: Marcus Porcius Cato (234 BC–149 BC); Roman statesman; advocated the destruction of Carthage during the Third Punic War (149–146 BC).

It is, however, these exclusive affections, and an individual manner of seeing things, produced by ignorance, which keep women for ever at a stand, with respect to improvement, and make many of them dedicate their lives to their children only to weaken their bodies and spoil their tempers, frustrating also any plan of education that a more rational father may adopt; for unless a mother concur, the father who restrains will ever be considered as a tyrant.

But, fulfilling the duties of a mother, a woman with a sound constitution, may still keep her person scrupulously neat, and assist to maintain her family, if necessary, or by reading and conversations with both sexes, indiscriminately, improve her mind. For nature has so wisely ordered things, that did women suckle their children, they would preserve their own health, and there would be such an interval between the birth of each child, that we should seldom see a houseful of babes. And did they pursue a plan of conduct, and not waste their time in following the fashionable va-garies of dress, the management of their household and children need not shut them out from literature, or prevent their attaching themselves to a science, with that steady eye which strengthens the mind, or practising one of the fine arts that cultivate the taste.

But, visiting to display finery, card-playing, and balls, not to mention the idle bustle of morning trifling, draw women from their duty to render them insignificant, to render them pleasing, according to the present acceptation of the word, to every man, but their husband. For a round of pleasures in which the affections are not exer-cised, cannot be said to improve the understanding, though it be erroneously called seeing the world; yet the heart is rendered cold and averse to duty, by such a sense-less intercourse, which becomes necessary from habit even when it has ceased to amuse.

But, we shall not see women affectionate till more equality be established in so-ciety, till ranks are confounded and women freed, neither shall we see that dignified domestic happiness, the simple grandeur of which cannot be relished by ignorant or vitiated minds; nor will the important task of education ever be properly begun till the person of a woman is no longer preferred to her mind. For it would be as wise to expect corn from tares, or figs from thistles, as that a foolish ignorant woman should be a good mother. . . .

To render women truly useful members of society, I argue that they should be led, by having their understandings cultivated on a large scale, to acquire a rational affec-tion for their country, founded on knowledge, because it is obvious that we are little interested about what we do not understand. And to render this general knowledge of due importance, I have endeavoured to shew that private duties are never properly fulfilled unless the understanding enlarges the heart; and that public virtue is only an aggregate of private. But, the distinctions established in society undermine both, by beating out the solid gold of virtue, till it becomes only the tinsel-covering of vice; for whilst wealth renders a man more respectable than virtue, wealth will be sought before virtue; and, whilst women's persons are caressed, when a childish simper shews an absence of mind—the mind will lie fallow. Yet, true voluptuousness must proceed from the mind—for what can equal the sensations produced by mutual affection, supported by mutual respect? What are the cold, or feverish caresses of appetite, but sin embracing death, compared with the modest overflowings of a pure heart and exalted imagination? Yes, let me tell the libertine of fancy when he despises understanding in woman—that the mind, which he disregards, gives life to the enthusiastic affection from which rapture, short-lived as it is, alone can flow! And, that, without virtue, a sexual attachment must expire, like a tallow candle in the socket, creating intolerable disgust. To prove this, I need only observe, that men who have wasted great part of their lives with women, and with whom they have sought for pleasure with eager thirst, entertain the meanest opinion of the sex.—Virtue, true refiner of joy!—if foolish men were to fright thee from earth, in order to give loose to all their appetites without a check—some sensual wight[20] of taste would scale the heavens to invite thee back, to give a zest to pleasure!

That women at present are by ignorance rendered foolish or vicious, is, I think, not to be disputed; and, that the most salutary effects tending to improve mankind might be expected from a REVOLUTION in female manners, appears, at least, with a face of probability, to rise out of the observation. For as marriage has been termed the parent of those endearing charities which draw man from the brutal herd, the corrupting intercourse that wealth, idleness, and folly, produce between the sexes, is more universally injurious to morality than all the other vices of mankind collectively considered. To adulterous lust the most sacred duties are sacrificed, because before marriage, men, by a promiscuous intimacy with women, learned to consider love as a selfish gratification—learned to separate it not only from esteem, but from the affection merely built on habit, which mixes a little humanity with it. Justice and friendship are also set at defiance, and that purity of taste is vitiated which would naturally lead a man to relish an artless display of affection rather than affected airs. But that noble simplicity of affection, which dares to appear unadorned, has few attractions for the libertine, though it be the charm, which by cementing the matrimonial tie, secures to the pledges of a warmer passion the necessary parental attention;

---

[20] Wight: A creature or being, likely supernatural or unearthly.

for children will never be properly educated till friendship subsists between parents. Virtue flies from a house divided against itself—and a whole legion of devils take up their residence there.

The affection of husbands and wives cannot be pure when they have so few sentiments in common, and when so little confidence is established at home, as must be the case when their pursuits are so different. That intimacy from which tenderness should flow, will not, cannot subsist between the vicious.

Contending, therefore, that the sexual distinction which men have so warmly insisted upon, is arbitrary, I have dwelt on an observation, that several sensible men, with whom I have conversed on the subject, allowed to be well founded; and it is simply this, that the little chastity to be found amongst men, and consequent disregard of modesty, tend to degrade both sexes; and further, that the modesty of women, characterized as such, will often be only the artful veil of wantonness instead of being the natural reflection of purity, till modesty be universally respected.

From the tyranny of man, I firmly believe, the greater number of female follies proceed; and the cunning, which I allow makes at present a part of their character, I likewise have repeatedly endeavoured to prove, is produced by oppression. . . .

Let woman share the rights and she will emulate the virtues of man; for she must grow more perfect when emancipated, or justify the authority that chains such a weak being to her duty.—If the latter, it will be expedient to open a fresh trade with Russia for whips;[21] a present which a father should always make to his son-in-law on his wedding day, that a husband may keep his whole family in order by the same means; and without any violation of justice reign, wielding this sceptre, sole master of his house, because he is the only being in it who has reason:—the divine, indefeasible earthly sovereignty breathed into man by the Master of the universe. Allowing this position, women have not any inherent rights to claim; and, by the same rule, their duties vanish, for rights and duties are inseparable.

Be just then, O ye men of understanding! and mark not more severely what women do amiss, than the vicious tricks of the horse or the ass for whom ye provide provender—and allow her the privileges of ignorance, to whom ye deny the rights of reason, or ye will be worse than Egyptian task-masters,[22] expecting virtue where nature has not given understanding!

---

[21] Husbands in the noble households of feudal Russia were reputed to beat their wives regularly with whips as part of a religious obligation to the Eastern Orthodox Church.

[22] The Egyptians enslaved the Israelites in the Bible.

FORTY-SEVEN

Sarah Pierce (1767–1852)

WOMEN AROUND THE REVOLUTIONARY ATLANTIC SAW IN THEIR RELATIONSHIPS WITH ONE *another the possibility of freedom. One winter night in 1792 in the town of Litchfield, Connecticut, 25-year-old Sarah Pierce and her close friends the sisters Abigail and Mary Smith spent an evening together reading, drawing, and talking about their fears and hopes for the future. Sarah Pierce and Abigail Smith resolved that when Mary (who was engaged) was married, they would spend the rest of their lives together "in single blessedness." Sarah Pierce then began to plan and draw in words and pictures the home she and Abigail would share: "plain, neat, and elegant," a refuge of freedom and generosity, with a "plenteous store" for needy passersby, a landscape planted with fruiting vines and medicinal herbs, and a nearby woods for contemplation. Pierce even envisioned the place she and Abigail would be buried, together, under one stone, as "two female friends." Her "Verses, Written in the Winter of 1792, & Addressed to Abigail Smith" has been recognized as one of the first lesbian poems in American literature. Like Susanna Wright, Anna Seward, and Mary Wollstonecraft, Sarah Pierce yearned for a utopian domestic space and landscape organized around the artistic, intellectual, and political desires of women, a refuge from the tyrannies of marriage and the dangers of childbearing, where women together could pursue lives of unencumbered thought and feeling. She realized that dream in 1792 by founding a school for women in the dining room of her house in Litchfield, Connecticut. From the 1790s through the 1830s, the Litchfield Female Academy attracted more than three thousand female students (including Catherine Beecher and Harriet Beecher Stowe) from across North America to study reading, writing, history, literature, science, logic, mathematics, and geography, as well as dancing, painting, and needlework. Pierce hoped that this curriculum would "vindicate the equality of female intellect"; her use of the word "vindicate" suggests some*

familiarity with Mary Wollstonecraft's A Vindication of the Rights of Woman *(1792)*
and the overtly feminist aims of her academy. The school served as a vital point of
transition from the feminist education and sister arts movements of the eighteenth
century to the reformist movements of the nineteenth century.

"VERSES, TO ABIGAIL SMITH" (1792)[1]

On rising ground we'll rear a little dome;
    Plain, neat, and elegant, it shall appear;
No slaves shall there lament their native home,
    Or, silent, drop the unavailing tear.

Content and cheerfulness shall dwell within,
    And each domestic serve thro' love alone;
Coy Happiness we'll strive, for once, to win,
    With meek Religion there to build her throne.

And oft our friends shall bless the lonely vale,
    And, social, pass the wintry eves away;
Or, when soft Summer swells the fragrant gale,
    Delighted mark new beauties as they stray.

Pleased with the scene, by Fancy's pencil drawn,
    The various landscape rushes on my view;
The cultivated farm, the flowery lawn,
    That sucks the fragrance of the honied dew.

The fertile "meadows trim with daisies pied;"
    The garden, breathing Flora's[2] best perfumes;
And stored with herbs, whose worth, by Matrons tried,
    Dispels disease, and gives health's roseate blooms.

---

[1] Sarah Pierce's "Verses to Abigail Smith" survives in the diary of Abigail and Mary Smith's brother, the physician and writer Elihu Hubbard Smith (1771–1798). See volume 2 of his 1795 diary at Yale University's Medical Historical Library, New Haven, Connecticut.

[2] Flora: Roman goddess of flowers.

Here vines, with purple clusters bending low,
   And various fruit-trees loaded branches bear;
There roots of every kind profusely grow,
   Bespeaking plenty thro' the circling year.

See yonder hillock, where our golden corn
   Waves it's bright head to every passing breeze;
Yon fruitful fields our sportive flocks adorn,
   Our cows at rest beneath the neighboring trees.

As misty clouds from silent streams arise,
   Yon distant Town attracts the gazer's view;
Yon mount, whose lofty summit meets the skies,
   Shelters the Village on the plain below.

Behind our lot, a Wood defies the storm,
   Like those where Druids[3] wont, in days of yore,
When Superstition wore Religion's form,
   With mystic rites their unknown Gods adore.

Within this grove we'll oft retire to muse,
   Where Contemplation builds her silent seat;
Her soothing influence she will ne'er refuse
   To those who wander in this blest retreat.

A river solemn murmurs thro' the shades,
   The whispering pines, in echoes soft, reply,
Then, hoarse o'er rocks, it seeks the distant glades,
   Forming a rain-bow in the moistened sky—

Nor leaves us here—but thro' the Village winds,
   Where simple elegance, in neat array,
Might teach even pomp that, not to wealth confined,
   Genius & taste might to a cottage stray.

---

[3] Druids: Members of the learned and priestly caste in pre-Christian England, Ireland, and Western Europe.

In front, a level grass-plot smooth & green,
    Where neighboring children, pass sweet hours at play,
And Fairies oft, (if Fairies e'er have been,)
    Will featly foot the moonlight hours away.—

Our plenteous stores we'll freely give to all;
    Want ne'er shall pass, in sorrow, from our door;
With joy we'll seat the beggar in our hall,
    And learn the tale of woe that sunk his store.

But chiefly those who pine, by sickness prest;
    Whose merit, known to few, unheeded lies:
How sweet, to banish sorrow from the breast,
    And bid fair hope shine sparkling in the eyes.

Thus, humbly blest, when youthful years are flown,
    (Proud to be good, not wishing to be great,)
And swift-wing'd Time proclaimed our moments run,
    Resign'd to heaven, we'll cheerful bow to fate.

Placed in one grave, beneath a plain, smooth, stone,—
    Where oft the tear unfeign'd shall dew the face,—
The sick, the poor, shall long our fate bemoan,
    But wealth & grandeur never mark the place.

This simple Epitaph the stone adorns,—
    Which calls, from artless eyes, the frequent tear—
Matrons & maids shall often stoop to learn,
    And all the Village think it passing rare.—

The Epitaph[4]
Beneath this stone two female friends interr'd,
    Who past their lives content, in solitude;
They wish'd no ill, yet oft, through ignorance, err'd;
    Reader! depart, reflect, and be as good.

---

[4] Epitaph: Ending the poem this way is a clear reference to Thomas Gray's famous poem "Elegy Written in a Country Churchyard" (1751), which also concludes with an epitaph.

FORTY-EIGHT

Annis Boudinot Stockton (1736–1801)

*M*ARY WOLLSTONECRAFT'S A VINDICATION OF THE RIGHTS OF WOMAN *(1792) found a ready audience among the women of the revolutionary Atlantic world. In this circa 1793 letter, the American poet Annis Boudinot Stockton lays out her opinion of Wollstonecraft's* Rights of Woman. *Probably writing in 1793, only months after the book's publication in London, Stockton finds much of Wollstonecraft's argument to be common sense, especially in terms of its support for women's education and intelligence. Unlike Wollstonecraft, however, Stockton argues that men of sense desire and support women of sense; in America, moreover, she sees growing educational opportunities for women, especially those who seek them. Another disagreement with Wollstonecraft is theological. Though adamant that there is "no sex in Soul," Stockton views gender roles as divinely authorized and necessary to humanity's interdependence. Thus even as she wittily expresses her confidence in women's capabilities and critiques those who believe otherwise, she pragmatically resigns women to a conventionally feminine role in service not of men or even patriarchy, but Christian humility.*

Stockton, a published poet and a widow well known for her patriotism, wrote the letter to her daughter living in Philadelphia. Though the tone of the letter suggests an intimate privacy, she would have expected her daughter, Julia Stockton Rush, to share the letter with her husband, Dr. Benjamin Rush, and likely others, including Elizabeth Graeme Fergusson, her good friend and hostess of a distinguished literary salon that included such figures as Benjamin Franklin. In the eighteenth century, letters were often read aloud during social gatherings as a means of entertainment and spreading news as well as to inspire conversation. Thus Stockton circulated her ideas through an epistolary neighborhood alongside Wollstonecraft's Rights of Woman *and Benjamin Rush's* Thoughts Upon Female Education.

LETTER TO JULIA STOCKTON RUSH ON MARY WOLLSTONECRAFT'S *A VINDICATION OF THE RIGHTS OF WOMAN* (CA. 1793)[1]

Morven[2] 22d of March

My dear Julia

I have been engaged these two days with reading the rights of women, which I never could procure before, tho it has been much longer in the neighbourhood. I have been musing upon the subject over my solitary fire till I took up the resolution to give you my sentiments upon it tho I suppose it is an old thing with you—I wonder you never Sent me your Critique—I am much pleased with her strength of reasoning, and her sentiment in general—but think that She like many other great geniuses—establish an Hypothesis and lay such a weight upon it as to cause the superstructure to destroy the foundation.—and I am sorry to find a woman capable to write such strictures should Complement Roussaus nonesense so much as to make his Ideas of women the criterion of the rank they hold in Society.[3]—I think we need go no farther, than his Confessions,[4] to discover that he had some defect in his brain, or that he was a refined Idiot, rather than an enlightened philosopher. I have always Contended that the education of women was not made a matter of that importance, which it ought to be—but we see that error daily Correcting—and in this Country, the Empire of reason, is not monopolized by men, there is great pains taken to improve our sex, and store their minds with that knowledge best adapted, to make them useful in the situation that their creator has placed them—and we do not often see those efforts opposed by the other sex, but rather disposed to asist them by every means in their power, and men of sense generally prefer such women, as Companions thro life—The

---

[1] Mulford, Carla, ed., *Only for the Eye of a Friend: The Poems of Annis Boudinot Stockton*, pp. 304–307. © 1995 by the Rector and Visitors of the University of Virginia. The original is found under Rush I:05:08 ALsS Annis Boudinot Stockton to Julia Stockton Rush ca. 1793, Rosenbach Museum & Library, Philadelphia, Pennsylvania. Reprinted by permission of the University of Virginia Press and the Rosenbach Museum and Library.

[2] Morven: Stockton's stately home in Princeton, New Jersey. During this period, Stockton was known as the Duchess of Morven.

[3] For Wollstonecraft, Jean-Jacques Rousseau's (1712–1778) characterization of women as unintelligent and weak, suited only to seduction and a submissive domestic life, was particularly deplorable. Her disdain perhaps arose because she found much to admire in so many of his other ideas. In Chapter V of *Rights of Woman*, she devotes about fifteen pages to quoting and then countering statements he makes in *Émile, ou de L'éducation* (1762; translated that same year as *Emilius and Sophia; or, A New System of Education*), a book that is both a novel and educational treatise.

[4] Rousseau's *Confessions*, published posthumously in 1783, describes his erratic and irregular upbringing, his sexual awakening, and his profligate adulthood.

state of society may be different in Europe from what it is in America—but from the observation I have been able to make in my own Country, I do not think any of that Slavish obedience exists, that She talks so much of—I think the women have their equal right of every thing, Latin and Greek excepted.—and I believe women of the most exalted minds, and the most improved understanding, will be most likly to practice that Conciliating mode of Conduct, which She seems to Condemn, as blind Obedience, and Slavish Submission, to the Caprice of an arbitrary tyrant, which character she seems to apply to men as a sex.—but certainly exercising the virtues of moderation and forbearance—and avoiding desputes as much as possible, can easily be distinguished from Slavish fear—and must certainly tend to strengthen the mind, and give it a degree of fortitude, in accomodating ourselves to our situation, that adds dignity to the human character.—because this is necessesary, not only with a husband, that one has chosen for a Companion thro life—but with every other person, that we are obliged to be in the habits of strict intimacy—you know that it is a favourite tenet with me, that there is no sex in Soul—I believe it as firmly as I do my existance—but at the same time I do not think that the sexes were made to be independent of each other—I believe that our creator intended us for different walks in life—and that it takes equal powers of mind, and understanding, properly to fulfil the duties that he has marked out for us—as it does for the other sex, to gain a knowledge of the arts and Sciences, and if our education was the same, our improvement would be the same—but there is no occasion for exactly the same education. I think we may draw the Conclusion that there is no sex in Soul, from the following illustrations—that there are many men, that have been taught, and have *not* obtained any great degree of knowledge in the circle of the Sciences—and that there *have* been women who have excelled in every branch, when they have had an opportunity of instruction, and I have no doubt if those advantages were oftener to occur, we should see more instances.— one argument brought to prove the inferiority of the mind of a woman, is that the organs of the body are weaker than mens, and that her Constitution is not so strong—now I know a great number of women, who have much stronger organs of body, and twice the strength of Constitution, that as a great number of men, and men of genius too, can boast of—or that from their infancy, they ever did enjoy— and it does not follow, that their souls are inferior, or that they are women instead of men.

I am much pleased with her remarks upon Doctor Gregory—I have many a time drawn upon my self a sneer, for venturing to desent from that amiable man, for one of his sentiments—respecting the reserve, which a woman should treat her husband with on the Subject of her affection for him—I allway thought it a little art, and such a want of Confidence unbecoming a woman of Sense.[5] I Confess I have a nobler opinion of men than our author appears to have—I dare say there are many who answer her description—but happily for me, those that I have had an opportunity to risk my opinion on, have had as high Ideas of the rationality of women—and there equal right to the exertion of the immortal mind, as the most tenacious of our sex could be—

She has some most charming remarks on education and her observation on some of the faults of her sex are good, but her whole chapter on modesty is admirable, and has some marks of originallity. but I must Confess that not withstanding the appearance of piety in her ejaculatory addresses to the supreme being, interspersed thro the book—I am not pleased with the bold, indeed I may say, almost presumptious manner, in which She speaks of the Diety—it too much partakes of the spirit of the whole work—which I think is written in a style that does not accord with the nature of our intercourse with each other—or with the imperfection of our state.—we are all beings dependant on one another, and therefore must often expect the inconveniences that must necessarily arise from the weakness of human nature, and the imperfection of some of those with whom we are Connected. and we must make the best of it.— and some of her expressions are by far, too strong for my Ideas.—but *she* writes like a philosopher, and *I* think as a novice.—yet to sum up my poor Judgement upon this wonderful book, I do really think a great deal of instruction may be gathered from it—and I am sure that no one, can read it, but they may find something or other, that will Correct their Conduct and enlarge their Ideas.—

I am frightened at the length of my letter—and more when I look at the watch and see the hour of the night—it is past one oclock, and not a creature upon in the house but my self—but you will say, it is my custo[m] to keep the vigils of the night.

Adieu my love, may heaven bless you and yours and protect you this night, prays your ever affectionate mother

A Stockton—

---

[5] Doctor Gregory: John Gregory (1724–1773); author of *A Father's Legacy to His Daughters* (1774), a popular book read widely in England and America. While Gregory advocated companionate marriage, he thought women should conceal their good sense and intelligence. He suggests that a wise woman should always play something of the coquette, never revealing the full extent of her education or feeling, even to her husband.

FORTY-NINE

Priscilla Mason

W E MAY NOT KNOW MUCH ABOUT THE LIFE OF PRISCILLA MASON, BUT THE SPEECH SHE *delivered on graduation day, May 15, 1793, at the Young Ladies Academy of Philadelphia, gives us a sense of what it felt like to be a bold, educated young woman addressing the future, in the age of Mary Wollstonecraft and in an Age of Revolutions where the rights of women were, as she put it, "tolerated but not yet established." Around the Atlantic world, in France, in the Caribbean, in North America, colonies had revolted, monarchies had been overthrown, and yet by tyranny of sex, women were still "doomed" "to servile or frivolous employments, on purpose to degrade their minds," in Mason's words. Even as revolutionary hopes fired around the Atlantic world, especially in the new post-revolutionary United States, young women were experiencing a conservative retrenchment of gender politics. Women were denied the right to vote (except in New Jersey, where propertied women could vote until 1807). Popular romance novels represented young women as vulnerable creatures incapable of independent decision-making. Social expectations and pressures increasingly constricted women's roles to the domain of the home and family.*

The Young Ladies Academy of Philadelphia was one of the first female academies in the United States, offering a curriculum of reading, writing, arithmetic, grammar, and geography. Notable public figures like the doctor and reformer Benjamin Rush (whose writing on women's education appears in this anthology) lectured at the academy. Despite or perhaps because society at the time was hostile to learned women, a strong feminist culture flourished among the academy's students, as Mason's commencement address evidences. Taking her turn at the podium on graduation day, Mason boldly seizes on the long tradition of feminist argumentation carried forward a century earlier by Bathsua Makin and Mary Astell and more recently by Judith Sargent Murray and Mary Wollstonecraft, criticizing men for ensuring the inequality of women by withholding educational opportunity and insisting on an expanded public voice for women. The speech was published in a history of the school, The Rise and Progress of the Young Ladies' Academy *(1794).*

"ORATION" (1793)

Delivered May 15, 1793, by a member of the graduating class of the Young Ladies Academy of Philadelphia.

Venerable Trustees of this Seminary, Patrons of the improvement of the female mind; suffer us to present the first fruits of your labours as an offering to you, and cordially to salute you on this auspicious day.

Worthy Principal, tutor, friend and parent, all in one! when we recollect our obligations to you, we feel, and would speak, but delicacy forbids.

The stern republican and polish'd citizen, will certainly join e'er long, to banish the barbarous custom of offering open adulation in such a place as this.

We therefore content ourselves with simply saluting you; and wishing the events of the day may speak your praise, in language suitable to your feelings.

Respected and very respectable audience; while your presence inspires our tender bosoms with fear and anxiety, your countenances promise indulgence, and encourage us to proceed. In the name of myself and sisters, therefore, I cordially salute you, and I hope you will pardon the defects of an attempt to please you, defects arising in some measure from due respect.

A female, young and inexperienced, addressing a promiscuous assembly, is a novelty which requires an apology, as some may suppose. I, therefore, with submission, beg leave to offer a few thoughts in vindication of female eloquence.

I mean not at this early day, to become an advocate for that species of female eloquence, of which husbands so much, and so justly, stand in awe,—a species of which the famous Grecian orator, Xantippe,[1] was an illustrious example. Although the free exercise of this natural talent, is a part of the rights of woman, and must be allowed by the courtesy of Europe and America too; yet it is rather to be *tolerated* than *established*; and should rest like the sword in the scabbard, to be used only when occasion requires.—Leaving my sex in full possession of this prerogative, I claim

---

[1] Xanthippe: The wife of the Greek philosopher Socrates. In the literature of the time, Xanthippe was often depicted as a nag or a scold.

for them the further right of being heard on more public occasions—of addressing the reason as well as the fears of the other sex.

Our right to instruct and persuade cannot be disputed, if it shall appear, that we possess the talents of the orator—and have opportunities for the exercise of those talents. Is a power of speech, and volubility of expression, one of the talents of the orator? Our sex possess it in an eminent degree.

Do personal attractions give charms to eloquence, and force the orator's arguments? There is some truth mixed with the flattery we receive on this head. Do tender passions enable the orator to speak in a moving and forcible manner? This talent of the orator is confessedly ours. In all these respects the female orator stands on equal,—nay, on *superior* ground.

If therefore she should fail in the capacity for mathematical studies, or metaphysical profounditites, she has, on the whole, equal pretensions to the palm of eloquence. Granted it is, that a perfect knowledge of the subject is essential to the accomplish'd Orator. But seldom does it happen, that the abstruse sciences, become the subject of eloquence. And, as to that knowledge which is popular and practical,—that knowledge which alone is useful to the orator; who will say that the female mind is incapable?

Our high and mighty Lords (thanks to their arbitrary constitutions) have denied us the means of knowledge, and then reproached us for the want of it. Being the stronger party, they early seized the sceptre and the sword; with these they gave laws to society; they denied women the advantage of a liberal education; forbid them to exercise their talents on those great occasions, which would serve to improve them. They doom'd the sex to servile or frivolous employments, on purpose to degrade their minds, that they themselves might hold unrivall'd, the power and pre-eminence they had usurped. Happily, a more liberal way of thinking begins to prevail. The sources of knowledge are gradually opening to our sex. Some have already availed themselves of the priviledge so far, as to wipe off our reproach in some measure.

A M'Caulley, a Carter, a Moore, a Rowe,[2] and other illustrous female characters, have shown of what the sex are capable, under the cultivating hand of science. But

---

[2] M'Caulley, Carter, Moore, Rowe: Catharine Sawbridge Macaulay Graham (1731–1791): noted English historian, author of the eight-volume *History of England* (1763–1783) and *Letters on Education* (1790), excerpted in this anthology; Elizabeth Carter (1717–1806): English writer, scholar, and translator, member of the Bluestocking circle; Hannah More (1745–1833): English philanthropist and writer of plays, poems, essays, and educational treatises, also a member of the Bluestocking circle and excerpted in this anthology; Elizabeth Singer Rowe (1674–1737): English author of novels, hymns, and devotional texts.

supposing now that we possess'd all the talents of the orator, in the highest perfection; where shall we find a theatre for the display of them? The Church, the Bar, and the Senate are shut against us. Who shut them? *Man*; despotic man, first made us incapable of duty, and then forbid us the exercise. Let us by suitable education, qualify ourselves for these high departments—they will open before us. They *will*, did I say? They have done it already. Besides several Churches of less importance, a numerous and respectable Society,[3] has display'd its impartiality.—I had almost said gallantry in this respect. With *others*, women forsooth, are complimented with the wall, the right hand, the head of the table,—with a kind of mock pre-eminence in small matters: but on great occasions the sycophant changes his tune, and says, "Sit down at my feet and learn." Not so the members of the enlightened and liberal Church. They regard not the anatomical formation of the body. They look to the soul, and allow all to teach who are capable of it, be they male or female.

But Paul forbids it! Contemptible little body! The girls laughed at the deformed creature. To be revenged, he declares war against the whole sex: advises men not to marry them; and has the insolence to order them to keep silence in the Church—: afraid, I suppose, that they would say something against celibacy, or ridicule the old bachelor.[4]

With respect to the bar, citizens of either sex have an undoubted right to plead their own cause there. Instances could be given of females being admitted to plead the cause of a friend, a husband, a son; and they have done it with energy and effect. I am assured that there is nothing in our laws or constitution to prohibit the licensure of female Attornies; and sure our judges have too much gallantry, to urge *prescription* in bar of their claim. In regard to the senate, prescription is clearly in our favour. We have one or two cases exactly in point.

Heliogabalus,[5] the Roman Emperor; of blessed memory, made his grandmother a Senator of Rome. He also established a senate of women; appointed his mother President; and committed to them the important business of regulating dress and fashions. And truly methinks the dress of our country, at this day, would admit of some regulation, for it is subject to no rules at all.—It would be worthy the wisdom of Congress, to consider whether a similar institution, established at the seat of our

---

[3] The Religious Society of Friends, or Quakers, had from its beginnings a gender egalitarian theology. See the writings of Margaret Askew Fell Fox in this volume.

[4] In 1 Timothy 2:12, the Apostle Paul forbids women from teaching and commands them to "be in silence." Mason boldly attributes the unmarried Paul's antifeminism to his own romantic rejection by young women.

[5] Heliogabalus: Heliogabalus or Elagabalus (203–222); Emperor of Rome (218–222).

Federal Government, would not be a public benefit. We cannot be independent, while we receive our fashions from other countries; nor act properly, while we initiate the manners of the governments not congenial to our own. Such a Senate, composed of women most noted for wisdom, learning and taste, delegated from every part of the Union, would give dignity and independence to our manners; uniformity, and even authority to our fashions.

It would fire the female breast with the most generous ambition, prompting to illustrious actions. It would furnish the most noble Theatre for the display, the exercise and improvement of every faculty. I would call forth all that is human—all that is *divine* in the soul of woman; and having proved them equally capable with the other sex, would lead to their equal participation of honor and office.

FIFTY

Anonymous

*T*HE EVENTS OF THE FRENCH REVOLUTION INSPIRED MANY AMERICAN WOMEN—INCLUDING *the unidentified ones mentioned in this article from the July 20, 1793, issue of Charleston, South Carolina's* City Gazette and Daily Advertiser—*to articulate their support for Republican principles (if not always the war itself) through acts as well as words. Some women donned Phrygian caps, a hat worn by male and female French revolutionaries. Some decorated their clothing with cockades made from red, white, and blue ribbons, thus using colors that honored France and the United States simultaneously. Some began identifying themselves—publicly, in letters, in wedding announcements—as* citess *and* citizeness. *And, in states such as Massachusetts, North Carolina, and Pennsylvania, women marched in parades while singing French songs, drank toasts with men to the French Revolution, and adorned themselves in white outfits and took to the festival stage as representatives of Liberty and Reason.*

In this notice, we see the language of revolutionary rights utilized to critique men's "ill treatment" of their wives, often a cloaked term for marital violence. Two women "repudiate" their husbands and are then described as "widows," as if their husbands are dead to them. (Divorce was virtually impossible to obtain in most of the north Atlantic world at the time so the word "divorcée" was not in frequent use. Women without husbands were either spinsters or widows.) The tone of the notice is celebratory rather than shocked, referring several times to the "dignity" of the proceedings. The women's plan of "living together in the strictest union" is described as a "marriage," indicating that the idea of same-sex marriage may go back at least as far as the Age of Revolutions.

"ON THE MARRIAGE OF TWO CELEBRATED WIDOWS" (1793)

MARRIED. On Monday last, two celebrated widows, ladies of America and France, after having repudiated their husbands on account of their ill treatment, conceived of the design of living together in the strictest union and friendship; the said amiable ladies, in order to give a pledge of their fidelity, requested that their striped gowns[1] be pinned together, that their children should be looked upon as one family, while their mothers shewed them an equal affection. Mr. Lee[2] officiated with dignity as their proxy, and explained the reciprocal obligations these two ladies promised to confer on each other, inviting their children at the same time to imitate their mothers; Mr. Samuel Prioleau[3] acted as the sponsor of the American lady, with that dignity, which such a deserving ward required; Mr. Huger, Ramsay and Burke,[4] three of her faithful guardians, assisted at the feast given on this occasion. The brave artillery signed that contract by the fire of their guns, and all their brothers in arms by thousands of huzzas; the merry guests waited for his excellency[5] in an anxious solicitude, they lamented his absence, but they rested assured of his patriotism; the representative of the gallic[6] lady, M. A. B. Mangourit,[7] was so feelingly touched at this so noble a scene, that while his eyes overflowed with tears of joy, he only lamented the

---

[1] That the gowns were striped may symbolize the Republican fashionableness of the women or their interest in politics.

[2] The identity of Mr. Lee is unknown.

[3] Mr. Samuel Prioleau: Likely Samuel Prioleau, Jr. (1742–1813); Charleston merchant and member of a prominent French Huguenot family that had been in South Carolina since the late seventeenth century.

[4] Mr. Huger, Ramsay and Burke: Huger and Ramsay may refer to John Huger (1744–1804) and Dr. David Ramsay (1749–1815). Burke perhaps refers to Aedanus Burke (1743–1802), a South Carolinian politician and judge.

[5] His excellency: May refer to the governor of South Carolina, William Moultrie, or possibly even George Washington, then president, or Edmond-Charles Genêt, a French ambassador to the United States. Both men had previously visited South Carolina—Washington during his goodwill tour of 1791, Genêt only several months before the marriage.

[6] Gallic: French.

[7] Michel-Ange-Bernard de Mangourit (1752–1829) was the French consul for North Carolina, South Carolina, and Georgia from 1792 to 1794. Mangourit resided primarily in Charleston and, while there, he worked to align American and French Republicanism and to advocate the French side in the military conflicts that began in 1793 with Great Britain, Spain, and other European nations. Wealthy French Federalists living in Charleston disliked Mangourit and overtly opposed him, though he was successful at first in eliciting popular and military support from the South for his cause.

absence of the president and all those of his colleagues that are true friends to those ladies, to join with the French Americans, in order to celebrate the *Carmagnole*[8] and sing *Ca Ira*.[9]

---

[8] *Carmagnole*: Irreverent song and dance proclaiming the glory of the Revolution and celebrating the prosecutions of Louis XVI and Marie Antoinette. The article includes a note that describes it as "*A dance which the soldiers danced at the battle of Jemmappe*." The Battle of Jemappes took place in 1792 in Belgium. It was a victory for the infant French Republic over Austrian forces.

[9] *Ca Ira*: Another popular song from the French Revolution. It confidently asserts the impending success of the Revolution.

FIFTY-ONE

Elizabeth Hart Thwaites (1772–1833)

*T*HE HART SISTERS, ELIZABETH *(1772–1833)* AND ANNE *(1773–1834)*, SCANDALIZED *society on the British West Indian island of Antigua. Because they were daughters of a Black planter and slave holder, the rules of society deemed that they should have married within the small free Black community or even become mistresses to wealthy white men, a decision which would have been unremarkable to the island's elite planter society, even if the sisters' family had found it objectionable. Instead, while still in their mid-teens, they jointly became baptized Methodists, donned plain clothes, renounced music and other worldly activities, educated their father's enslaved workers, and publicly conveyed their abolitionist beliefs. After their defiant marriages to two white missionaries, they founded the island's first Sunday school and its Female Refuge Society, a charity that supported the orphans and children of "fallen and depraved relatives." Through it, they sought to oppose the immorality, often sexual, that they believed slavery encouraged among the enslaved. Anne Hart Gilbert worked as the Sunday school's girls' superintendent, and Elizabeth Hart Thwaites, along with her husband Charles, opened additional Sunday schools across the island as well as a primary school that daily taught two to three hundred children and adults.*

Continuing in the path of Anne Hutchinson, Margaret Fell, Magdalena, Rebecca Protten, and other women who found revolutionary potential for freedom in religion, the sisters participated in a transatlantic network that circulated letters, religious tracts, periodicals, and other texts. Through this network, they exchanged letters with other Methodists—including white Englishwomen who belonged to benevolent societies—that contained statements of encouragement and requests for prayers and financial support. They sent progress reports to other missionaries and church leaders, and read similar writings in London's Arminian Magazine. *In its pages,*

they may have seen Phillis Wheatley's last publication, "An ELEGY on Leaving"
(1784), and encountered a woman author of African descent, like themselves.

The sisters' writings insist on the powerful role of women in religious move-
ments, including black women like Mary Alley and Sophia Campbell, who led a
"praying remnant" and constructed a chapel in the absence of male missionaries
on Antigua. They also offer a trenchant critique of slavery, as seen in the 1794 letter
by Elizabeth Hart Thwaites anthologized here. Though we do not know who the
intended recipient of the letter was, it is likely that it was composed not only to be
read by a single addressee, but also to be circulated among Caribbean and English
abolitionists. Such first-person testimonies about the evils of slavery were important
tools in the abolitionist movement that began in the 1770s. As an outspoken aboli-
tionist, Hart Thwaites was exposed to public vilification as the island's planter
society witnessed multiple Caribbean slave revolts (inspired in part by the Ameri-
can and French Revolutions) and sought to avoid a similar political and social up-
heaval on Antigua. She also encountered resistance from Methodist leaders like
Thomas Coke. Whereas Coke supported gradual emancipation, in the below letter
the as-yet-unmarried Elizabeth Hart calls for slavery's immediate eradication. She
offers herself as evidence that Black persons, especially women, are not inherently
sinful or inferior; rather it is the "mercenary" system of slavery that impedes "re-
finement, useful knowledge, the sweets of social life," qualities she herself perhaps
seeks to exemplify in this letter.

LETTER FROM ELIZABETH HART TO A FRIEND (1794)[1]

Popeshead, *October* 24th, 1794[2]

Dear Sir,—

Had I not promised in my last to say something concerning slavery, I should certainly have dropped the business; for I have since thought myself a very unsuitable
person to write on controverted points; and were I equal to the task, I do not know it
will answer any end that I should take the subject in hand: however, I am (and I
believe you are likewise) on the side of truth. I have never declared my sentiments so

---

[1] The identity of the letter's recipient is unknown. Hart Thwaites wrote the letter prior to her marriage. The letter was published by the Reverend John Horsford in *A Voice from the West Indies: Being a Review of the Character and Results of Missionary Efforts in the British and Other Colonies
in the Caribbean Sea* (London: Alexander Heylin, 1856).

[2] Popeshead: Location of her father's Antiguan estate.

freely to any person (except my sister) as to you on this head. I find none disposed to receive such hard sayings; and why? Because they are not disinterested, self is concerned; and as I cannot, to please the best and wisest, lower the standard of right, or bend a straight rule to favour a crooked practice, I am, for the most part, silent.

I thank you for your kind intention to guard our minds against unnecessary solicitude at evils which we cannot remedy. In doing this, you first ask, "Is not the being so very anxious concerning it, in some measure, letting go our own work, and meddling with God's?" Undoubtedly it is, if I am very anxious. I acknowledge I am not easy about it; nor is it possible, as the matter stands, that I should feel that Christian indifference so necessary upon some other occasions. It is not the stoical, but submissive, spirit that should pervade our minds. Believe me, Sir, I do not leave my own work to meddle with God's. I do not pretend to scan His all-wise dealings with the children of men; nor am I bold to tempt the Lord, or ask Him, "What doest Thou?" Far be it from me.

I do not recollect that I ever made any objections to the merely being in a state of servitude, including much labour. This has been almost from the beginning, and perhaps subsists, more or less, in all parts of the world. Nay, were I obliged to provide for myself, I should desire no higher station than that of being servant: but Heaven forbid that I should be a slave! Nor have I said much about the shocking practice of taking the Africans from their native land, where—

> "The sable warrior, frantic with regret
> Of her he loves, and never can forget,
> Loses in tears the far receding shore,
> But not the thought that they must meet no more.
> Deprived of her and freedom at a blow,
> What has he left, that he can yet forego?
> To deepest sadness suddenly resign'd,
> He feels his body's bondage in his mind."[3]

It is not, I say, the being merely placed in a state of subordination; for this is by choice the condition of many; but it is the black train of ills which I know to be inseparably connected with *this* species of slavery: such as may you never know, if

---

[3] From "Charity," a poem by William Cowper (1731–1800). Cowper wrote several influential anti-slavery poems. In addition to making some minor alterations to the punctuation, Hart Thwaites has exchanged "sullenly" with "suddenly."

it will give you needless pain,—such as my eyes see, and my ears hear daily, and makes my heart shrink when I write. When any thing is said like compassionating persons in this situation, it is urged by some, who seem wilfully blind, that they are much better off than the poor Europeans. Now, when things are clear to a demonstration, I know not what to say of such assertions, unless, as a good man observes, "it is sometimes in morals as in optics: the eye and the object come too near to answer the end of vision."[4] I know that persons in a state of indigence, free as well as slaves, are exposed to many troubles; and are subject, especially if dependent, to every insult from those above them, who have little minds. These take every advantage of, and oppress, the poor. They have, however, laws made to redress their personal injuries. Slaves either have not, or they are never put in force; so that many of them suffer all these distresses, besides those peculiar to *their* situation. All who have their liberty, though servitude and penury may be their portion through life, have yet some of the greatest earthly joys within their reach; comforts such as give vitality to existence, and are really necessary to the being of man. They need not be deprived of those dear relatives,—

> "Whose friendly aid in every grief
> Partakes a willing share;
> In sickness yields a kind relief,
> And comfort in despair."[5]

But, alas, how is it reversed with the others! It appears to me that pains are taken to prevent, or break, the nearest alliances, often in times of sickness and distress, and sometimes from the basest views. On the neighbouring estates the sick are removed from their comfortable abodes to large, hot rooms, made for the purpose, where frequently husbands and wives, parents and children, have no intercourse but through the grates. This is to prevent their lying by longer than necessity obliges; many make their escape from these dark abodes to those blessed regions "where tyrants vex not, and the weary rest."[6] I know several who have been mothers of ten children, who never had the satisfaction to call *one* their own; and this, not from the hand of death, or separation by mutual consent, but sold, given away, or otherwise disposed of,

---

[4] Source unknown.

[5] From George Wright's "An Ode on Friendship," found in his book *The Rural Christian; or, the Pleasures of Religion* (London, 1772).

[6] From *The Grave* by the Scotsman Robert Blair (1699–1746). *The Grave* is a religious, melancholy poem that was immensely popular in the eighteenth century.

according to the will of man. Others have an only darling child, whom they wish to *see* do well, taken from them and sent to some other Island, where they would sell for the best price, no more regard being paid to the feelings of the parents than if they were cattle. I very lately saw an old lady take an only son of one of her Negroes, and with seeming pleasure declare, he would serve her to buy bread with by and by; and in a house not far from hers is a young woman who was bartered for a horse. In such cases who can tell what those feel that have not—

> "Put off their generous feelings, and, to suit
> Their tempers to their fate, assumed the brute."[7]

Christians who are not slaves, need only to be subject to the will of Heaven and of those they love; while most of those who are in bondage must either continually submit their wills to that of some irreligious, unreasonable being, or undergo a sort of martyrdom. There are likewise others, who, being endued with good natural understanding, aspire after refinement, useful knowledge, the sweets of social life, &c., &c.: were there a possibility of changing the colour of their skin, and emancipating them, with culture they would become ornaments to society. These are not permitted to emerge; they are bound down by some unenlightened, mercenary mortal, who perhaps has not a thought or wish above scraping money together. You may suppose such slaves find it a galling yoke,—

> "And oft endure, e'en while they draw their breath,
> A stroke as fatal as the scythe of death."[8]

Again, free men may enjoy the fruit of their labours; but slaves are allowed a very small portion of their earnings. Many who undoubtedly earn their masters fifteen shillings *per* week by field-work, are allowed one shilling *per* week to provide meat, drink, clothes, &c.; and those who are not very industrious, are but half-clothed and half-fed; and, if not religious, are consequently thieves. But that which pains me most is, that every contrivance is made, by the generality of those who have rule over them, to baffle their efforts for decency and virtue; sometimes punishing them for that which is highly commended in persons in the opposite situation. A fair reputation, which, a pious author observes, is one of the most laudable objects of human

---

[7] Source unknown.

[8] Also from Cowper's "Charity." Hart Thwaites has again made some minor alterations.

ambition,[9] is out of the question with them; for, in the earliest stages of their lives, every thing like modesty or rationality is crushed as it appears. I will give you one instance out of a thousand, by which you will see they are not allowed many privileges above the beasts that perish. During the Conference (District-Meeting)[10] before the last, a black woman in the Society went with her husband one evening to hear Dr. Coke preach.[11] When the meeting was over, seeing some of the noble crowding the gates with their implements of mischief, with fear and trembling she stole her husband's arm, which was no sooner observed by the gentlemen and ladies, (so called,) than she was as much ridiculed and abused for doing that which would have appeared strange in them not to do, as though she had committed a crime: the poor affrighted creature withdrew from her husband, to stop the clamour of this narrow-hearted *gentry*, and made haste out of the way. Considering all things that respect this people, I stood amazed that so much conjugal, paternal, and filial affection remains among even the irreligious part of them. Another cause of wonder to me (knowing something of the natural heart) is, that such as do not possess Christianity should display such Christian graces as subjection of the will, long-suffering, &c.; and that towards persons to whom they are bound by no other tie than that against which you would suppose the heart would continually rise; in short, adhering to St. Peter's blessed precepts to converted servants, "Being subject, with all fear, not only to the good, but to the froward, enduring grief, suffering wrongfully, being buffeted and taking it patiently," &c.[12] It is not uncommon to see old persons, who have spent their health and strength in this unreasonable service, and whose conduct merits every respect, receiving the utmost indignities at the hand of some untaught capricious little Master or Miss, who thinks nothing of lifting the hand or heel against them. Now, Sir, I have only given you a specimen of the situation of the slaves in this part of the world. It does not suit me to say the worst I know concerning it: only I assure you it comprises

---

[9] From Hannah More, *Thoughts on the Importance of the Manners of the Great to General Society* (London, 1788). This book went through six editions in the first year of publication alone. The exact quote is "A fair reputation is one of the most laudable objects of human ambition; yet even this really valuable blessing is sometimes converted into a snare, by inducing a treacherous security as soon as it is obtained."

[10] Annual conferences are part of the basic governance of the Methodist Church. Each local church belongs to an annual conference, organized regionally. Annual conferences have yearly meetings during which ministers and laity conduct business, worship, and engage in fellowship.

[11] Dr. Coke: Thomas Coke (1747–1814); Anglican clergyman and Methodist leader. The primary force behind overseas Methodist missions, Coke made four trips to the West Indies.

[12] A paraphrase of 1 Peter 2:18-20. Hart Thwaites has condensed the three lines of biblical verse into one as well as removed reference to masters. Verse 19 instructs servants to "be subject to your masters with all fear; not only to the good and gentle, but also to the froward."

a mystery of iniquity, an endless list of complicated ills, which it is not likely you will ever know. You will not, perhaps, find the sufferers disposed to complain of their case. Not many are capable of *explaining*, however keenly they may *feel*, their disadvantages. As to the opposite party, while blinded by self-interest, (and who among them are not more or less so?) they will not allow that they act unjustly. As I do not think it possible that those whose property consists in slaves can be the persons of *clean hands*, must I not think you feel something on this account? And particularly for those who are dear to me, that have been so unfortunate as to gain this wretched pre-eminence. Those of them that are any way enlightened are themselves uncomfortable, and would be extricated. They are unhappy at their deviation from the golden rule, "Whatsoever ye would that men should do unto you, even so do ye unto them."[13]

But you farther ask: "Is it not, at least, *permitted* by the all-wise Governor of the universe, and will He not do all things well? Might there not be some clue to it quite unknown to us, such as the sins of the Africans, as it was the case of the Israelites before their bondage in Babylon?"[14] I readily allow their being in a state of servitude is permitted by the Almighty, and do not question but He *may* intend bondage for this race of men; but I account the abominations that follow to be purely the will and work of corrupt, fallen man, and displeasing to God. "He doeth all things well." But we cannot take upon us to say, "This is the Lord's doing." I agree with you, that there might be some clue to it quite unknown to us; but this does not strike me as being the sins of the Africans; for, from all I can learn of them, according to their light, though barbarous and uncivilized, they are not so depraved as the generality of the Europeans, but more especially the West Indians; neither are they acquainted with so many methods of drawing down the vengeance of Heaven. England, however, has the advantage of the West Indies; not only as being a land of liberty, &c., but because there are some corners in it less corrupt than others. You will not, perhaps, find in every country the same degree of vice and extravagance; but slavery has rendered every part of the West Indies equally iniquitous. There are no asylums from the tainted throng. What I conceive to be partly the reason of this is, that the Europeans who have not independent fortunes, for the most part labour with their hands; (and I always look upon employment as being next to religion for the prevention of crime;) while most of the free people in this part of the world, of all complexions, are supported, by

---

[13] Matthew 7:12.

[14] In 2 Kings, the Israelites are carried captive to Babylon by Nebuchadnezzar. Their captivity was a result of years of sinfulness under several evil kings.

the toils of the slaves, in every degree of idleness and excess. Slavery affords them a wide field for the indulgence of every diabolical disposition, in which they "riot unscared." We do not read that the Israelites, in any of their captivities, were exposed to these miseries, though we have no doubt but *theirs* was the desert of sin.

Another thing to be observed is, that many of the slaves are not Africans; some white people sold themselves for a term of years, and shared the same fate with the blacks, being debarred their civil and religious rights; and many who now suffer as slaves, are much more nearly allied to the whites than to the others: so that I do not give full assent to your proposition at the conclusion of your queries, that the perpetrators of guilt, whether fair, black, or brown, are doing God's work. He has, and does still make use of the wicked (being most fit) as His sword to punish wickedness; but if these are *in this* case doing God's work, they have mixed so much of their own with it, as at length to be bringing the same sort of punishment upon themselves. I have thought, that when the Almighty affects a people *for sin*, they repent and are humbled before deliverance is brought near. But I believe the Africans remained in their original darkness when He raised up men in Europe to espouse their cause. Nor have we reason to suppose the Negroes in St. Domingo, Martinique, &c., are one whit better than ever they were. Concerning these we have strange accounts, many of them having taken their masters' places; and the oppressors are now the oppressed.[15] I believe, with a good man, that "present impunity is the deepest revenge."[16]

But, lastly, you inquire, "Will all our solicitude make the least change in the matter? Have we not reason to believe that a brighter scene is approaching, and that this dark night will be the precursor of a brighter morning? Should we not by all means rejoice in hope, and be thankful that we are not in bondage, either in a literal or spiritual sense?" It is certainly wrong to be solicitous about these things, it ever makes bad worse; nor do I suppose that any thing I may feel, say, or do, will make the least change in the matter, however the disposition of soul is inculcated by Him whose heart was tender; and pity is not apathy, but sensibility resigned; it is to this that I aspire, that while I feel my own and others' woes, I may recline on Heaven, and

---

[15] Slave revolt spread through the Caribbean in direct and indirect response to the French and American Revolutions. In addition to the Haitian Revolution in Saint-Domingue, there were rebellions in Martinique, Guadeloupe, Santo Domingo (which shared the island of Hispaniola with Saint-Domingue), Grenada, Dominica, and Curaçao.

[16] From William Darrell, *The Gentleman Instructed in the Conduct of a Virtuous and Happy Life* (London, 1713). Darrell writes, "[T]hose who shut the Gate of Mercy against their Brethren, mure it up against themselves; they provoke God to retaliate their Cruelty in the next World, and oftentimes in this; and if he suffers such Monsters to flourish, we may be sure he is angry, for present Impunity is the deepest Revenge, because it forebodes a future Misery."

meekly and patiently say, "Thy will be done." I think with you, we have reason to believe that a brighter scene is approaching; and agree with the sentiments of a pious writer, (who has nothing in his book respecting slavery but what follows,) when he says, "I indulge myself in moments of the most enthusiastic and delightful vision, taking encouragement from that glorious prophecy, that 'of the increase of His government there shall be no end;' a prediction which seems to be gradually accomplishing, and in no instance more, perhaps, than in the noble attempt about to be made for the abolition of the African Slave-Trade."[17] For what event can human wisdom foresee, more likely to "give His Son the heathen for His inheritance, and the uttermost parts of the earth for His possession,"[18] than the success of such an enterprise? What will restore the lustre of the Christian name, too long sullied with oppression, cruelty, and injustice? We should indeed rejoice in hope of this bright morning, be abundantly thankful that we are not in the chains of sin or *slavery*, and pray that God would hasten the time when "violence shall no more be heard in our land, neither wasting nor destruction within our borders, but our walls be salvation and our gates praise."[19] Than shall we—

"Love as He loved,—a love so unconfined
With arms extended will embrace mankind;
Self-love will cease, or be delated, when
We each behold as many *selfs* as men,
All of one family in blood allied,
His precious blood, who for our ransom died."[20]

I assure you, Sir, it is not any thing which I have read that has furnished thoughts upon the subject; I do not recollect to have seen any writing respecting it but Mr. Boucher's pamphlet,[21] (which I think you have,) and a piece on "Charity" by Cowper, from which I have quoted a few lines in the first sheet of this letter. My mind was perfectly made up before these came into my hands. I was no sooner capable of

---

[17] Also from More's anonymously published *Thoughts on the Importance of the Manners of the Great to General Society*. Here, Thwaites appears unaware that the author is More, a woman. More paraphrases Isaiah 9:7 in the above quote.

[18] Psalms 2:8.

[19] Isaiah 60:18.

[20] From "Of Divine Love" by the poet and politician Edmund Waller (1606–1687).

[21] Perhaps a reference to Jonathan Boucher's pamphlet *A View of the Causes and Consequences of the American Revolution* (1797).

thinking, than my heart shuddered at the cruelties that were presented to my sight; but more have I felt since I began to think seriously, or rather cured; this will perhaps render some of those that are without less poignant, though I do not expect that religion will deliver me from fellow-feeling, nor do I desire it should; only I wish that I (and all who are in those things like-minded) may be enabled to live–

> "Unspotted in so foul a place,
> And innocently grieve."[22]
> I am, dear Sir,
> Your Sister in Christ,
> E. H.

---

[22] From a hymn, the first line of "Saviour of Sinful Men," by Methodist founder Charles Wesley (1707–1788).

FIFTY-TWO

Anonymous

*T*HE AGE OF REVOLUTIONS PRODUCED A NEW CONCEPTION OF HUMAN RIGHTS BELONGING *universally to all human beings. Perfecting and fully implementing this revolutionary idea has been our work for centuries since. In the New York magazine the* Weekly Museum, *on April 25, 1795, an anonymous author did her part to emphasize the application of this revolutionary human rights discourse to women. Adopting the title "Rights of Woman" made famous by Mary Wollstonecraft, she wrote lyrics to match the tune of the British national anthem "God Save the King." Describing unequal gender relations in the revolutionary language of the time as a form of "slavery," and claiming Mary Wollstonecraft as a heroine, this author calls upon women to "disown" their fears, "detest" their critics, and claim the full force of the Age of the Revolutions: "Woman is Free!"*

"RIGHTS OF WOMAN" (1795)

> GOD save each Female's right,
> Show to her ravish'd sight
>   Woman is Free;
> Let Freedom's voice prevail,
> And draw aside the vail,
> Supreme Effulgence hail,
>   Sweet Liberty
> Man boasts the noble cause,
> Nor yields supine to laws
>   Tyrants ordain:

Let Woman have a share,
Nor yield to slavish fear.
Her equal rights declare,
          And well maintain.
Come forth with sense array'd,
Nor ever be dismay'd
          To meet the foe,—
Who with assuming hands
Inflict the iron bands,
To obey his rash commands,
          And vainly bow.
O let the sacred fire
Of Freedom's voice inspire
          A Female too:—
Man makes the cause his own,
And Fame his acts renown,—
Woman thy fears disown,
          Assert thy due.
Think of the cruel chain,
Endure no more the pain
          Of slavery:—
Why should a tyrant bind
A cultivated mind.
By Reason well refin'd,
          Ordained Free.
Why should a Woman lie
In base obscurity,
          Her talents hid;
Has Providence assign'd
Her soul to be confin'd.
Is not her gentle mind
          By virtue led.
With this engaging charm,
Where is so much the harm
          For her to stand,
To join the grand applause
Of truth and equal laws,
Or lend the noble cause,

Her feeble hand.
Let snarling cynics frown,
Their maxims I disown,
        Their ways detest:—
By Man, your tyrant lord,
Females no more be aw'd,
Let Freedom's sacred word,
        Inspire your breast.
Woman aloud rejoice,
Exalt thy feeble voice
        In chearful strain;
See Wolstoncraft, a friend,
Your injur'd rights defend,
Wisdom her steps attend,
        The cause maintain.
A voice re-echoing round,
With joyful accents sound,
        "Woman be Free;
Assert the noble claim,
All selfish arts disdain;"
Hark how the note proclaim,
        "Woman is Free!"

FIFTY-THREE

Helen Maria Williams (1762–1827)

*H*ELEN MARIA WILLIAMS WAS A BRITISH SALONNIÈRE AND WRITER WHO LIVED ALMOST *entirely in Paris from the early 1790s onward, thus experiencing the events of the French Revolution firsthand. A champion of Republican progressivism, she published multiple volumes about her experiences and observations, and her views influenced English and American readers alike. She praised the earliest years of the Revolution as a liberating culmination of romantic sensibility, a decidedly feminine characterization that allowed her to justify (not always successfully) her very public involvement as natural, an "affair of the heart" as she put it. She saw the Revolution's later years, once Maximilien de Robespierre (1758–1794) and the more radical Jacobins purged their Girondist opponents and initiated the Reign of Terror, as a masculinist and oppressive betrayal of its ideals, though she remained in France and advocated for a return to moderate principles.*

In her writings, Williams describes heroic Republican women and thereby publicizes the active role that women could and did take in the violent struggle for liberty. During A Sketch of the Politics of France *(1795), Williams recounts Charlotte Corday's infamous assassination of the Jacobin Jean-Paul Marat in 1793, whose speeches, essays, and newspaper writings instigated violence against "enemies of the Revolution." Her version contrasts with others' in that it depicts Corday as neither a sexless monster[1] nor an "angel of assassination" motivated by Christian wrath*

---

[1] In Paris, the Jacobins publicly declared Corday had "hurled herself completely out of her sex": "This woman being called pretty was not pretty at all; she was a *virago*, chubby rather than fresh, slovenly, as female philosophers and sharp thinkers almost always are." The Marquis de Sade exclaimed that Corday had been "vomited up from Hell to the despair of both sexes [and] directly belongs to neither."

and the (fictional) murder of a lover; instead, Williams's Corday is a rational political actor. Williams's unique approach, perhaps based upon her personal knowledge
of Corday, inspired other authors. Examples include Robert Southey, who penned a
1798 poem on Corday for The Morning Post, and Scotswoman Helen Craik, author
of Adelaide de Norbonne, with Memoirs of Charlotte de Cordet (1800). Interestingly,
in her novel Craik further advances the feminist implication of Williams's version by

**FIGURE 53.1: The heroic Charlotte la Cordé, upon her Trial, at the bar of the Revolu-
tionary Tribunal of Paris, July 17th 1793. for having rid the World of that monster of
Atheism and Murder, the Regicide MARAT, whom she Stabbed in a bath, where he had
retired on account of a Leprosy, with which Heaven had begun the punishment of his
Crimes by James Gillray (London, 1793).** *In this cartoon, Charlotte Corday stands before the
Revolutionary Tribunal with Marat's body lying between her and them. A crowd of onlookers, almost
entirely men, observes the proceedings. While the men are caricatures and often possess enlarged lips—
perhaps a play on "frog," a British epithet for a Frenchman—the figure of Corday is drawn without similar ridicule. She proclaims, "Wretches, I did not expect to appear before you—I always thought that I
should be delivered up to the rage of the people, torn in pieces, & that my head, stuck on the top of a pike,
would have preceded Marat on his state bed, to serve as a rallying point to Frenchmen, if there still are
any worthy of that name.—But happen what will, if I have the honours of the guillotine, & my clay-cold
remains are buried, they will soon have conferred upon them the honours of the Pantheon; and my
memory will be more honoured in France than that of Judith of Bethulia." The cynical artist Gillray was
known for, among other things, his ferociously anti-Jacobin drawings. Image courtesy of the Library of
Congress (reproduction number LC-DIG-ppmsca-05419).*

aligning paternal with political tyranny and by imagining Corday as a model for feminine resistance in both the public and private spheres.

FROM *LETTERS CONTAINING A SKETCH OF THE POLITICS OF FRANCE* (1795)

An event also happened at this period, which, from the calumnies to which it gave life, and the consequences it produced, proved fatal to the arrested deputies.[2] This was the assassination of Marat. In the first dawn of the conspiracy Marat became a principal instrument in the hands of the traitors, who found him well fitted for their

ASSASSINAT DE J. P. MARAT,
le 13 Juillet 1793, ou 25 Messidor, An 1er de la République.

FIGURE 53.2: *ASSASSINAT DE J. P. MARAT, le 13 Juillet, ou 25 Messidor, An 1er de la République* **by Jacques François Joseph Swebach de Fontaine (between 1793 and 1804).** *The print shows the immediate aftermath of Jean-Paul Marat's death. Charlotte Corday, knife in hand, sits next to his body while two men restrain her. Four other men and one other woman are also in the room. Image courtesy of the Library of Congress (reproduction number LC-USZ62–128497)*

---

[2] On June 2, 1793, about thirty Girondist deputies of the French National Convention were arrested at the instigation of the insurrectionary Commune of Paris. Many escaped to their respective provinces and attempted to organize forces against their opponents in Paris.

purposes; and being saved from the punishment which usually follows personal insult by the contempt which the deformity and diminutiveness of his person excited, he became the habitual retailer of all the falsehoods and calumnies which were invented by his party against every man of influence or reputation. He was the Thersites[3] of the convention, whom no one would deign to chastise; for his extravagance made his employers often disclaim him as a fool, while the general sentiment he excited was the sort of antipathy we feel for a loathsome reptile. His political sentiments often varied; for he sometimes exhorted the choice of a chief, and sometimes made declamations in favour of a limited monarchy; but what rendered him useful to the conspirators was his readiness to publish every slander which they framed, and to exhort to every horror which they mediated.——His rage for denunciation was so great that he became the dupe of the idle; and his daily paper contains the names of great criminals who existed only in the imagination of those who imposed on his credulous malignity.

After this first preacher of blood had performed the part allotted to him in the plan of evil, he was confined to his chamber by a lingering disease to which he was subject,[4] and of which he would probably soon have died. But he was assassinated in his bath by a young woman who had travelled with this intention from Caen in Normandy.[5] Charlotte Anne Marie Corday was a native of St. Saturnin in the department of the Orne.[6] She appears to have lived in a state of literary retirement with her father, and by the study of antient and modern historians to have imbibed a strong attachment to liberty.[7] She had been accustomed to assimilate certain periods of antient history with the events that were passing before her, and was probably excited by the examples of antiquity to the commission of a deed, which she believed with fond enthusiasm would deliver and save her country.

Being at Caen when the citizens of the department were enrolling themselves to march to the relief of the convention, the animation with which she saw them devoting their lives to their country, led her to execute, without delay, the project she

---

[3] Thersites: Famously ugly and low-born Greek soldier from Homer's *Iliad*. In Book 2, he addresses the Greek soldiers and insults the hero Agamemnon.

[4] Marat had a skin disease that forced him to retire from the National Convention. He continued to work from home, where he often soaked in a medicinal bath.

[5] Caen: City in northwestern France, near the English channel. Many of the Girondist deputies sought refuge in Caen after their arrest. According to Williams, Corday was inspired by their subsequent organization of forces against their opponents in Paris.

[6] St. Saturnin: Like Caen, also in northwestern France. Corday was from an aristocratic but poor family.

[7] Corday is known to have read, among other texts, Plutarch's *Lives of the Noble Greeks and Romans* and Jean-Jacques Rousseau's *Du Contrat Social* (1762).

had formed. Under pretence of going home, she came to Paris, and the third day after her arrival obtained admission to Marat. She had invented a story to deceive him; and when he promised her that all the promoters of the insurrection in the departments should be sent to the guillotine, she drew out a knife which she had purchased for the occasion, and plunged it into his breast.

She was immediately apprehended, and conducted to the Abbaye prison, from which she was transferred to the Conciergerie, and brought before the revolutionary tribunal.[8]

She acknowledged the deed, and justified it by asserting that it was a duty she owed her country and mankind to rid the world of a monster whose sanguinary doctrines were framed to involve the country in anarchy and civil war, and asserted her right to put Marat to death as a convict already condemned by the public opinion. She trusted that her example would inspire the people with that energy which had been at all times the distinguished characteristic of republicans; and which she defined to be that devotedness to our country which renders life of little comparative estimation.

Her deportment during the trial was modest and dignified. There was so engaging a softness in her countenance, that it was difficult to conceive how she could have armed herself with sufficient intrepidity to execute the deed. Her answers to the interrogatories of the court were full of point and energy. She sometimes surprised the audience by her wit, and excited their admiration by her eloquence. Her face sometimes beamed with sublimity, and was sometimes covered with smiles. At the close of her trial she took three letters from her bosom, and presented them to the judges, and requested they might be forwarded to the persons to whom they were addressed. Two were written to Barbaroux,[9] in which with great ease and spirit she relates her adventures from her leaving Caen to the morning of her trial. The other was an affectionate and solemn adieu to her father. She retired while the jury deliberated on their verdict; and when she again entered the tribunal there was a majestic solemnity in her demeanour which perfectly became her situation. She heard her sentence with attention and composure; and after conversing for a few minutes with her counsel and a friend of mine who had sat near her during the trial,[10] and whom she requested

[8] Corday was arrested at the scene. Four days later, she was tried and executed.
[9] Barbaroux: Charles Jean Marie Barbaroux (1767–1794) was among the revolutionary leaders to accuse Louis XVI of crimes and voted in favor of his execution. Later, he opposed Robespierre and the excesses of the more radical Jacobins. He was one of the deputies arrested on June 2, 1793. A transcript of the trial and Corday's letters were published in the *Times London* and the *London Chronicle* soon after her execution.
[10] This friend is probably John Hurford Stone (1763–1818), Willliams's probable lover and a staunch republican.

to discharge some trifling debts she had incurred in the prison, she left the court with the same serenity, and prepared herself for the last scene.

She had concluded her letter to her father with this verse of Corneille, "C'est le crime qui fait la honte, et non pas l'échafaud,"[11] and it is difficult to conceive the kind of heroism which she displayed in the way to execution. The women who were called furies of the guillotine,[12] and who had assembled to insult her on leaving the prison, were awed into silence by her demeanour, while some of the spectators uncovered their heads before her, and others gave loud tokens of applause. There was such an air of chastened exultation thrown over her countenance, that she inspired sentiments of love rather than sensations of pity. She ascended the scaffold with undaunted firmness, and, knowing that she had only to die, was resolved to die with dignity. She had learned from her jailor the mode of punishment, but was not instructed in the detail; and when the executioner attempted to tie her feet to the plank, she resisted, from an apprehension that he had been ordered to insult her; but on his explaining himself she submitted with a smile. When he took off her handkerchief, the moment before she bent under the fatal stroke, she blushed deeply; and her head, which was held up to the multitude the moment after, exhibited this last impression of offended modesty.

The leaders of the faction, who thought every measure good that could be made subservient to their purpose, found this event too replete with favourable circumstances to be neglected. Marat, whom they had thrown aside to die at leisure, unless perchance he should have lived to share the fate to which they afterwards condemned their other agents, was now restored to more than his antient honours, was proclaimed a martyr, and his death ordered to be lamented as an irreparable loss to the republic. The conspirators declared that no farther doubt of the federalism of the departments remained. The death of Marat was the point of conviction. Every member of the mountain was to be assassinated in his turn, and the traitors of the departments had their accomplices in Paris who had whetted their poniards to involve the city in destruction.[13] Though the Parisians were not sufficiently credulous to believe these calumnies, the faction made them the pretence

---

[11] That is, "It is the crime that brings shame, and not the scaffold." Pierre Corneille (1606–1684) was a French playwright, known for his tragedies.

[12] Furies of the guillotine: Militant Parisian women who supposedly complained that there were too few executions. Anecdotally they are said to have attended the National Convention, knitting in the galleries and urging ever more bloodthirsty acts.

[13] The mountain: *La Montagne*, or the Mountain, refers to a group of powerful Jacobin members of the National Convention. *La Montagne* and their followers, the Montagnards, were the opponents of the Girondist deputies who had escaped to the provinces. Williams writes that the Jacobins used Corday's assassination of Marat to justify their infamous Reign of Terror by casting his murder as part of a larger Girondist conspiracy to assassinate the Mountain.

to proceed to the farther commission of crimes; and while they endeavoured to amuse the people with what they called the inauguration of Marat and of Chalier,[14] they were meditating the murder of the deputies whom they had driven from the legislature.

It was impossible to contemplate without indignation and despair that glorious revolution, which had opened to mankind the brightest prospects of happiness, and which had promised the most beneficial effects to the world, become the sport of the cruel, and the prey of the rapacious; to see a people who were called to liberty, bending their necks, like the votaries of the storied assassin of the mountain, at the nod of their tyrant;[15] to see a nation which had possessed Rousseau, Mably and Voltaire,[16] prostrate in frantic enthusiasm before the shrine of Marat, like the idolaters of Montapama,[17] whose devotion rose in proportion to the hideousness of their gods.

[14] Chalier: Joseph Chalier (1747–1793) was a Jacobin and the mayor of Lyons. He was arrested by the city's National Guard along with other Jacobin municipal officers in 1793 and coincidentally guillotined on the same day as Corday.

[15] Their tyrant: Robespierre.

[16] Rousseau, Mably and Voltaire: Jean-Jacques Rousseau (1712–1778), Gabriel Bonnet de Mably (1709–1785), and Voltaire (1694–1778) were French philosophers whose writings on politics and civil liberties influenced the French and American Revolutions.

[17] Montapama: Perhaps a reference to an Aztec monarch like Montezuma, whose religion required blood sacrifices.

FIFTY-FOUR

Anna Seward (1747–1809)

*F*EMALE FRIENDSHIPS AND EDUCATION SUSTAINED FEMINIST WOMEN IN THE AGE OF REVOLU-*tions. Anna Seward was just a year old when her father, the Anglican rector Thomas Seward, published a poem entitled "The Female Right to Literature" (1748). Raised on the grounds of the Lichfield Cathedral, Seward was taught to read Shakespeare and Milton and encouraged to spend her days in the open air, reading, studying, contemplating botany, and doing needlework. Among the most important relationships of Seward's life was her close companionship with Honora Sneyd (1756–1780), a young girl adopted by the Seward family. Sneyd married Richard Lovell Edgeworth (father of the novelist Maria Edgeworth) in 1773 and died an untimely death in 1780. Seward, who never married, wrote many love poems to Sneyd. "To Honora Sneyd" (which appears below) reveals her disappointment and betrayal at Sneyd's marriage in 1773; "Elegy" (1799) mobilizes images of the seashore to reflect on the transience of their relationship. This feeling-infused literary pictorialism is a hallmark of Seward's writing.*

Relationships with women animated Seward's career as a published poet, novelist, and essayist. Lichfield, her hometown, was also the birthplace of the eminent British author, critic, and lexicographer Samuel Johnson (1709–1784), celebrated for his literary accomplishments but also criticized by Seward for his misanthropy. Seward observed that while Lichfield supported and celebrated the careers of its native sons, young women writers had to create their own opportunities and were often taken advantage of by their male mentors and peers. She developed a network of correspondences with other women writers, including the poet Mary Scott, author of a long poem The Female Advocate *(1774) that praised Seward and other women writers of the time. Seward also participated in the literary salons hosted by the poet Anna Miller at the English town of Batheaston during the 1770s and 1780s. In her later years, she developed a controversial intimate relationship with John Saville, the married vicar of Lichfield Cathedral, who became her daily companion and intellectual confidant. Moreover, she traveled to visit other famous literary women throughout Great Britain. In 1796, she paid a visit to the famed "Ladies of Llangollon," Lady Eleanor Butler and Sarah Ponsonby, two upper-class Irish Catholic women who had eloped in their youth, settled in a small cottage in north Wales, and converted their home and garden into a destination for artists and celebrities. The poems "To the Right Honourable Lady Eleanor Butler" and "To Miss Ponsonby" commemorate that visit and celebrate the long-lived love of these famed female companions "Eleonora" and "Zara" as "Angels in an Eden." Seward's writings, especially her poems, edited and published by Walter Scott in a three-volume collection in 1810, help document an important feminist aesthetic subculture of the late eighteenth-century: a lesbian "sister arts" tradition of women expressing their romantic friendships through intertwined mediums of literary writing, botanical illustration and collecting, gardening, needlework, and craft.*

"TO THE RIGHT HONOURABLE, LADY ELEANOR BUTLER" (1796)

Thou, who with firm, free step, as life arose,
Led thy loved friend where sacred Deva[1] flows,
On Wisdom's cloudless sun with thee to gaze,
And build your eyrie[2] on that rocky maze;
Ah, ELEANORA! Wilt thou gently deign
To bid these nets the tribute lines contain,
When Virtue, Genius, Rank, and Wealth, combine,
To pay ow'd homage at so pure a shrine?
And O! when kindling with the lovely theme,
The blest reality of Hope's fond dream,
Friendship, that bliss unshar'd disdains to know,
Nor sees, nor feels one unpartaken woe;
When for such worth, in each exalted mind,
Resolv'd as man, and more than woman kind,
Their warm admirers ask a length of years,

---

[1] Deva: Roman name for a Celtic river goddess associated with the River Dee in Wales and England.
[2] Eyrie: The nest of a bird of prey.

Unchill'd by terror, and unstain'd by tears,
Then may the fervent benedictions lie!
And long, long hence meet ELEANORA's eye,
While with her ZARA's it shall frequent rove
The treasur'd records of esteem, and love!

"TO MISS PONSONBY" (1796)

Seek, roseate[3] net, inchanting ZARA's hand,
And, tho' unworthy, say thy fold aspires
To guard the gentle scriptures, where expand
Deserved attachment's tributary fires!

Say, that in no charm'd spirit livelier dwells,
Than hers who wove thee, each ingenuous trace
Of the fair story this retirement tells,
The minds that sought it, and the forms that grace;

Davidean friendship,[4] emulation warm,
Coy blossoms, perishing in courtly air,
Its vain parade, restraint, and irksome form,
Cold as the ice, tho' with the comet's glare.

By firmness won, by constancy secured,
Ye nobler pleasures, be ye long their meed,
Theirs, who, each meteor vanity abjured,
The life of Angels in an Eden lead.

"TO HONORA SNEYD" (1773; PUBLISHED 1799)

HONORA, should that cruel time arrive
  When 'gainst my truth thou should'st my errors poize,[5]
  Scorning remembrance of our vanish'd joys;
  When for the love-warm looks, in which I live,

---

[3] Roseate: Rose-colored.
[4] Davidean friendship: Ideal friendship like that of David and Jonathan in the Bible.
[5] Poize: Weigh, as with a balance.

But cold respect must greet me, that shall give
    No tender glance, no kind regretful sighs;
    When thou shalt pass me with averted eyes,
    Feigning thou see'st me not, to sting, and grieve,
And sicken my sad heart, I could not bear
    Such dire eclipse of thy soul-cheering rays;
    I could not learn my struggling heart to tear
From thy loved form, that thro' my memory strays;
    Nor in the pale horizon of despair
    Endure the wintry and the darken'd days.

"ELEGY, WRITTEN AT THE SEA-SIDE" (1799)

I write, HONORA, on the sparkling sand!—
The envious waves forbid the trace to stay:
HONORA's name again adorns the strand!
Again the waters bear their prize away!

So Nature wrote her charms upon thy face,
The cheek's light bloom, the lip's envermeil'd[6] dye,
And every gay, and every witching grace,
That Youth's warm hours, and Beauty's stores supply.

But Time's stern tide, with cold Oblivion's wave,
Shall soon dissolve each fair, each fading charm;
E'en Nature's self, so powerful, cannot save
Her own rich gifts from this o'erwhelming harm.

Love and the Muse can boast superior power,
Indelible the letters they shall frame;
They yield to no inevitable hour,
But will on lasting tablets write thy name.

---

[6] Envermeil'd: Scarlet.

FIFTY-FIVE

Mary Darby Robinson (1758–1800)

*T*HE DAUGHTER OF AN ABSENTEE IRISH–CANADIAN SEA CAPTAIN AND AN ENGLISH SCHOOLMIS-*tress, Mary Robinson lived a life that exemplifies the difficulties and possibilities for women in the unstable transatlantic world of the Age of Revolutions. Born in Bristol, Mary Darby was educated for a short season at a school founded by Hannah More, whose poem "On Slavery" appears in this volume. Her education ended abruptly when, in 1768, her father, Nicholas Darby, lost the family fortune on a failed fishing venture in the Canadian territory of Labrador. Mary moved to London, where she assisted her mother, Hester Vanacott, in opening and running a school, which an embarrassed Nicholas Darby soon closed down. In London, Mary fell in love with the world of the theater but was diverted from beginning her acting career by her marriage at age 15 to Thomas Robinson, a clerk who promised her a fashionable life but whose debts soon landed the whole family, including Mary and her infant daughter Maria Elizabeth, in prison in 1775. In prison, she compiled and published a collection of poems.*

After her release, Mary Robinson embarked on what would become a celebrated acting career, performing in almost forty plays by the time she was 21 years old. Playing the role of Perdita in Shakespeare's A Winter's Tale *in 1779, she won the attention of the Prince of Wales, who solicited her to become his mistress, promising 20,000 pounds. When the prince lost interest in the affair, Robinson, again facing debt and poverty, threatened to expose his letters to the public if she were not paid 25,000 pounds. After the debacle of her affair with the prince, Mary, widely known as "Perdita" for her famous role, moved through elite social circles, developing relationships and alliances with influential men in order to secure freedom from debt and freedom to live and travel, as well as growing a reputation for her fashionable style and her many affairs. She wrote poems, plays, memoirs, and novels. She traveled to*

323

France several times in the 1780s, where she gained an appreciation for French society that won her support of the French Revolution and deeply influenced her views on gender. First published in 1799 under the pseudonym Anne Frances Randall, A Letter to the Women of England, on the Injustice of Mental Subordination *denounces gendered double standards: "What in man, is laudable; in women is deemed reprehensible, if not preposterous." She decries the situation of intellectual women in England who labor "in obscurity" and "must fly to foreign countries for celebrity, where talents are admitted to be of no sex." In France, she observes, women are the "idols of a polished society." In the indigenous South Pacific, women are brought up to delight in physical activity such as swimming. In indigenous North America, women participate fully in their societies' political councils. But women in England enjoyed none of these advantages. Thus, Robinson exhorts her "unenlightened country-women" to "shake off the trifling, glittering shackles which debase you" and to instead seek education for themselves and their daughters. Like her seventeenth-century feminist forerunner Mary Astell, Mary Robinson dreamed of starting a university for women. Like so many other English-speaking feminists around the Atlantic in her age, Robinson looked forward to the truly revolutionary day when women would have access to the intellectual resources they needed to right centuries of customary legal, political, economic, social, and religious inequality. For in her transgressive world-traveling life, as a merchant-class woman who benefited little from the spoils of mercantile imperialism, a royal mistress who benefited little from the crown, an actor, writer, mother, fashion leader, revolutionary sympathizer, and feminist, Mary Robinson, called by Samuel Taylor Coleridge "a woman of undoubted Genius," learned that the Age of Revolutions had created a turbulent new modern world that offered women few guarantees except those pleasures and powers they could win on their own.*

FROM *A LETTER TO THE WOMEN OF ENGLAND* (1799)

Custom, from the earliest periods of antiquity, has endeavoured to place the female mind in the subordinate ranks of intellectual sociability. Woman has ever been considered as a lovely and fascinating part of the creation, but her claims to mental equality have not only been questioned, by envious and interested sceptics; but, by a barbarous policy in the other sex, considerably depressed, for want of liberal and classical cultivation. I will not expatiate largely on the doctrines of certain philosophical sensualists, who have aided in this destructive oppression, because an illustrious British female, (whose death has not been sufficiently lamented, but to whose genius posterity will render justice) has already written volumes in vindication of "The Rights of Woman."[1] But I shall endeavour to prove that, under the present state of mental subordination, universal knowledge is not only benumbed and blighted, but true happiness, originating in enlightened manners, retarded in its progress. Let WOMAN once assert her proper sphere, unshackled by prejudice, and unsophisticated by vanity; and pride, (the noblest species of pride,) will establish her claims to the participation of power, both mentally and corporeally. . . .

Yet, the present era has given indisputable proofs, that woman is a thinking and an enlightened being! We have seen a Wollstonecraft, a Macaulay, a Sévigné;[2] and many others, now living, who embellish the sphere of literary splendour, with genius of the first order. The aristocracy of kingdoms will say, that it is absolutely necessary to extort obedience: if all were masters, who then would stoop to serve? By the same rule, man exclaims, if we allow the softer sex to participate in the intellectual rights and privileges we enjoy, who will arrange our domestic drudgery? who will reign (as Stephano says, while we are vice-roys over them[3]) in our household establishments? who will rear our progeny; obey our commands; be our affianced vassals; the creatures of our pleasures? I answer, women, but they will not be your slaves; they will be your associates, your equals in the extensive scale of civilized society; and in the indisputable rights of nature. . . . [4]

In what is woman inferior to man? In some instances, but not always, in corporeal strength: in activity of mind, she is his equal. Then, by this rule, if she is to endure oppression in proportion as she is deficient in muscular power, *only*, through all the stages of animation the weaker should give precedence to the stronger. Yet we should find a Lord of the Creation with a puny frame, reluctant to confess the superiority of a lusty peasant girl, whom nature had endowed with that bodily strength of which luxury had bereaved him.

---

[1] Robinson refers to Mary Wollstonecraft, *A Vindication of the Rights of Woman* (1792), excerpted in this anthology. Wollstonecraft died in 1797.

[2] Macaulay, Sévigné: Catharine Sawbridge Macaulay Graham (1731–1791), noted British historian and author of *Letters on Education* (1790), a text highly influential on later feminists such as Mary Wollstonecraft. Excerpts from her *Letters on Education* appear in this volume; Marie de Rabutin-Chantal, Marquise de Sévigné (1626–1696), a French aristocrat remembered for her accomplished and witty thirty-year correspondence with her daughter, which was published during the 1730s and 1750s.

[3] Stephano: From William Shakespeare's *The Tempest*, a drunken butler who plots the overthrow of his master.

[4] Robinson's note: "The Mahometans [i.e., Muslims] are said to be of opinion that WOMEN have no souls! Some British husbands would wish to evince that they have no SENSES, or at least not the privilege of using them: for a modern wife, I mean to say that which is denominated a *good one*, should neither hear, see, speak, nor feel, if she would wish to enjoy any tolerable portion of tranquility."

The question is simply this: Is woman persecuted and oppressed because she is the weaker creature? Supposing that to be the order of Nature; let me ask these human despots, whether a woman, of strong mental and corporeal powers, is born to yield obedience, merely because *she is a woman*, to those shadows of mankind who exhibit the effeminacy of women, united with the mischievous foolery of monkies? I remember once, to have heard one of those modern Hannibals[5] confess, that he had changed his regiments three times, because the regimentals[6] were *unbecoming*!

If woman be the *weaker* creature, why is she employed in laborious avocations? why compelled to endure the fatigue of household drudgery; to scrub, to scower, to labour, both late and early, while the powdered lacquey[7] only waits at the chair, or behind the carriage of his employer? Why are women, in many parts of the kingdom, permitted to follow the plough; to perform the laborious business of the dairy; to work in our manufactories; to wash, to brew, and to bake, while men are employed in measuring lace and ribands; folding gauzes; composing artificial bouquets; fancying feathers, and mixing cosmetics for the preservation of beauty? I have seen, and every inhabitant of the metropolis may, during the summer season, behold strong Welsh girls carrying on their heads strawberries, and other fruits from the vicinity of London to Covent-Garden market, in heavy loads which they repeat three, four, and five times, daily, for a very small pittance; while the male domesticks of our nobility are revelling in luxury, to which even their lords are strangers. Are women thus compelled to labour, because they are of the WEAKER SEX?

In my travels some years since through France and Germany, I often remember having seen stout girls, from the age of seventeen to twenty-five, employed in the most fatiguing and laborious avocations; such as husbandry, watering horses, and sweeping the public streets. Were they so devoted to toil, because they were the weaker creatures? and would not a modern petit maître[8] have fainted beneath the powerful grasp of one of these rustic or domestic amazons? [. . .]

It has lately been the fashion of the time, to laugh at the encreasing consequence of women, in the great scale of human intellect. Why? Because, by their superior lustre, the overweening and ostentatious splendour of some men, is placed in a more obscure point of view. The women of France have been by some popular, though evidently prejudiced writers, denominated little better than she-devils! And yet we have scarcely heard of

---

[5] Hannibals: Hannibal (247–183 BC); legendary Carthaginian military commander.
[6] Regimentals: Military uniform. Regiments in this era were privately sponsored by wealthy men. Each regiment had its own uniform and men of fashion vied to join the ones with the handsomest regalia.
[7] Lacquey: Lackey, personal (as opposed to household) servant.
[8] Petit maître: Fop.

one instance, excepting in the person of the vain and trifling Madame Du Barry,[9] in which the females of that country have not displayed almost a Spartan fortitude even at the moment when they ascended the scaffold. If there are political sceptics, who affect to place the genuine strength of soul to a bold but desperate temerity, rather than to a sublime effort of heroism, let them contemplate the last moments of Marie Antoinette;[10] this extraordinary WOMAN, whose days had passed in luxurious splendour; whose will had been little less than law! Behold her hurled from the most towering altitude of power and vanity; insulted, mocked, derided, stigmatized, yet *unappalled* even at the instant when she was compelled to endure an ignominious death! Let the strength of her mind, the intrepidity of her soul, put to shame the vaunted superiority of man; and at the same time place the female character in a point of view, at once favourable to nature, and worthy of example. France has, amidst its recent tumultuous scenes, exhibited WOMEN whose names will be the glory of posterity. Women who have not only faced the very front of war, but thereby sustained the heroic energies of their countrymen, by the force of *example* and the effect of *emulation*. Even the rash enthusiast, Corday,[11] whose poniard[12] annihilated the most sanguinary and atrocious monster that ever disgraced humanity, claimed our pity, (even while religion and nature shuddered), as she ascended the fatal scaffold, to expiate the deed she had accomplished. . . .

The women, the Sévignés, the Daciers, the Rolands, and the Genlis's[13] of France, were the first, of modern times, to shake off the yoke of sexual tyranny. The widow of Scarron, (afterwards Madame de Maintenon,)[14] was an ornament to her sex, till

[9] Madame du Barry: Jeanne Bécu, Comtesse du Barry (1743–1793); mistress to King Louis XV, arrested on charges of treason, and executed by guillotine during the Reign of Terror, in 1793. Du Barry was remembered for her emotional display during her walk to the guillotine.

[10] Marie Antoinette: Maria Antonia Josepha Johanna von Habsburg-Lothringen (1755–1793); Austrian-born wife of Louis XVI and Queen of France, executed for treason during the French Revolution, and remembered for her lifestyle of excess. Robinson met Marie Antoinette during her 1781 visit to France.

[11] Corday: Marie-Anne Charlotte de Corday d'Armont (1768–1793); member of the Republican Girondin faction during the French Revolution, who assassinated Jean-Paul Marat, a member of the more radical Jacobin faction, which she believed was responsible for the September Massacres (1792) and the destructively violent turn of the French Revolution. For narratives of the assassination, see Helen Maria Williams and Sarah Pogson Smith, included in this volume.

[12] Poniard: Dagger.

[13] Daciers, Rolands, Genlis's: Anne LeFevre Dacier (1654–1720), French scholar and classicist, translator of Sappho; Marie-Jeanne Philipon Roland de la Platière (1754–1793), French revolutionary and host of an important salon for the Girondin political faction, executed for her political activity; Stéphanie Félicité Ducrest de St-Aubin, Comtesse de Genlis (1746–1830), French educator, author, and revolutionary sympathizer.

[14] The widow of Scarron, (afterwards Madame de Maintenon): Francoise d'Aubigne, Madame de Maintenon (1635–1719), secret second wife of King Louis XIV, recognized for her political savvy and influence; she later founded a school for poor girls.

she became the dupe of a profligate monarch, and the instrument of bigot persecution. The freezing restraint which custom placed on the manners of other nations, and which is as far removed from true delicacy as the earth is from the heavens, in France, threw no chilling impediment on the progress of intellect. Men soon found by experience, that society was embellished, conversation enlivened, and emulation excited, by an intercourse of ideas. The younger branches of male nobility in France, were given to the care of female preceptors; and the rising generations of women, by habit, were considered as the rational associates of man. Both reason and society benefited by the change; for though the monasteries had less living victims, though monks had fewer proselytes, the republic of letters had more ornaments of genius and imagination.

Women soon became the idols of a polished people. They were admitted into the councils of statesmen, the cabinets of princes. The influence they obtained contributed greatly towards that urbanity of manners which marked the reign of Louis the Sixteenth. The tyrants of France, at the toilettes of enlightened women, were taught to shudder at the horrors of a Bastille: which was never more crowded with victims, than when bigotry and priestcraft were in their most exulting zenith.[15] I will not attempt to philosophize how far the influence of reason actuated on more recent events. That hypothesis can only be defined by posterity.

It is an indisputable fact that a woman, (excepting in some cases of supposed witchcraft) if thrown into the water, has, as Falstaff says, "a strange alacrity at sinking."[16] And yet a woman must not be taught to swim; it is not feminine! though it is perfectly masculine to let a woman drown merely because she is a woman, and denied the knowledge of preserving her existence. In this art the savages of Oreehoua and Tahoora[17] are initiated from their infancy; the females of those islands are early taught the necessary faculty of self-defence. They are familiarized to the limpid element at so early a period that a child of four years old, dropped into the sea, not only betrays no symptoms of fear, but seems to enjoy its situation. The women consider swimming as one of their favourite diversions; in which they amuse themselves when the impetuosity of the dreadful surf that breaks upon their coast, is increased to its utmost fury, in a manner equally perilous and extraordinary. And yet these courageous females are denominated of the *weaker* sex.

---

[15] Bastille: Famed Parisian prison, used to imprison political prisoners without trial, and seized by French revolutionaries on July 14, 1789; the Bastille was a symbol for repression, used by writers like Mary Wollstonecraft to symbolize the repression of women.

[16] Robinson quotes Falstaff, in William Shakespeare, *Merry Wives of Windsor*, Act III, sc. V.

[17] Oreehoua and Tahoora: Small Hawaiian islands, visited by Captain James Cook in January 1778.

A celebrated geographer[18] remarks, that "the best test of civilization, is the respect that is shewn to women."

The little regard shewn to the talents of women in this country, strongly characterizes the manners of the people. The Areopagites,[19] once put a boy to death for putting out the eyes of a bird: and they argued thus, says an elegant writer, *il ne s'agit point la d'une condamnation pour crime, mais d'un jugement de moeurs, dans une republique fondée sur les moeurs.*[20]

Heaven forbid that the criterion of this national and necessary good, should be drawn from the conduct of mankind towards British women. There is no country, at this epoch[e], on the habitable globe, which can produce so many exalted and illustrious women (I mean mentally) as England. And yet we see many of them living in obscurity; known only by their writings; neither at the tables of women of rank; nor in the studies of men of genius; we hear of no national honours, no public marks of popular applause, no rank, no tide, no liberal and splendid recompense bestowed on British literary women! They must fly to foreign countries for celebrity, where talents are admitted to be of no SEX, where genius, whether it be concealed beneath the form of a Grecian Venus,[21] or that of a Farnese Hercules,[22] is still honoured as genius, one of the best and noblest gifts of the creator.

Here, the arts and the sciences have exhibited their accomplished female votaries. We have seen the graces of poetry, painting, and sculpture, rising to unperishable fame from the pen, the pencil, and the chissel of our women. History has lent her classic lore to adorn the annals of female literature; while the manners of the age have been refined and polished by the wit, and fancy of dramatic writers. I remember hearing a man of education, an orator, a legislator, and a superficial admirer of the persecuted sex, declare, that "the greatest plague which society could meet with, was a *literary woman*!" . . .

Why are women excluded from the auditory part of the British senate? The welfare of their country, cannot fail to interest their feelings; and eloquence both exalts

---

[18] Robinson's note: "Salmon." Thomas Salmon (1679–1767), English historian and geographer.

[19] Areopagites: Members of the supreme tribunal of Athens.

[20] "It is not so much a matter of condemning a crime, but a matter of moral judgment in a republic founded on morals."

[21] Robinson's note: "Lady Hamilton, and Helen Maria Williams, are existing proofs, that an English woman, like a prophet, is never valued in her own country. In Britain they were neglected, and scarcely *known*; on the continent, they have been nearly IDOLIZED!" Emma Hart Hamilton (1761–1815) was a British actor and artist's model who won fame throughout Europe for her "Attitudes," an act in which she posed as classical figures. Helen Maria Williams (1762–1827) was a British poet, supporter of the French Revolution, and abolitionist; she lived most of her later life in France; her writing is included in this volume.

[22] Farnese Hercules: Ancient Roman statue of Hercules, noted for its large scale.

and refines the understanding.[23] Man makes woman a frivolous creature, and then condemns her for the folly he inculcates. He tells her, that beauty is her first and most powerful attraction; her second complacency of temper, and softness of manners. She therefore dedicates half her hours to the embellishment of her person; and the other half to the practice of soft, languishing, sentimental insipidity. She disdains to be strong minded, because she fears being accounted masculine; she trembles at every breeze, faints at every peril, and yields to every assailant, because it would be unwomanly to defend herself. She sees no resemblance of her own character in the Portias and Cornelias of antiquity;[24] she is content to be the epitome of her celebrated archetype, the *good woman* of St. Giles's.[25]

The embargo upon words, the enforcement of tacit submission, has been productive of consequences highly honourable to the women of the present age. Since the sex have been condemned for exercising the powers of speech, they have successfully taken up the pen: and their writings exemplify both energy of mind, and capability of acquiring the most extensive knowledge. The press will be the monuments from which the genius of British women will rise to immortal celebrity: their works will, in proportion as their educations are liberal, from year to year, challenge an equal portion of fame, with the labours of their classical *male* contemporaries.

In proportion as women are acquainted with the languages they will become citizens of the world. The laws, customs and inhabitants of different nations will be their kindred in the propinquity of nature. Prejudice will be palsied, if not receive its death blow, by the expansion of intellect: and woman being permitted to feel her own importance in the scale of society, will be tenacious of maintaining it. She will know that she was created for something beyond the mere amusement of man; that she is capable of mental energies, and worthy of the most unbounded confidence. Such a system of mental equality, would, while it stigmatized the trifling vain and pernicious

---

[23] Robinson's note: "Many of the American tribes admit women into their public councils, and allow them the privileges of giving their opinions, *first*, on every subject of deliberation. The ancient Britons allowed the female sex the same right: but in modern Britain women are scarcely allowed to express any opinions at all!" For an example of indigenous North American female leadership, see Nanye'hi/Nancy Ward in this collection.

[24] Cornelias, Portias: Cornelia is the title character of a play by the French tragedian Robert Garnier, translated into English in 1594 by Thomas Kyd (1558–1594) and reissued as *Pompey the Great, His Fair Cornelia's Tragedy* in 1595. Portia is the wife of Brutus in William Shakespeare's *Julius Caesar* (1599).

[25] Robinson's note: "This elegant and estimable female, is represented headless;—and I believe *almost* the only female in the kingdom *universally* allowed to be a *good woman*." In her edition of Robinson's *Letter* (Broadview 2003), Sharon M. Setzer posits that the woman of St. Giles "may be alluding to the shop sign of 'The Good Woman' in the London parish of St. Giles, as represented in William Hogarth's engraving 'Noon' [1738]."

race of high fashioned Messalinas,[26] produce such British women, as would equal the Portias and Arrias of antiquity.[27]

Had fortune enabled me, I would build an UNIVERSITY FOR WOMEN; where they should be politely,[28] and at the same time classically educated; the depth of their studies, should be proportioned to their mental powers; and those who were *incompetent to the labours of knowledge*, should be dismissed after a fair trial of their capabilities, and allotted to the more humble paths of life; such as *domestic and useful occupations*. The wealthy part of the community who neglected to educate their female offspring, at this seminary of learning, should pay a fine, which should be appropriated to the maintenance of the unportioned scholars. In half a century there would be a sufficient number of learned women to fill all the departments of the university, and those who excelled in an eminent degree should receive honorary medals, which they should wear as an ORDER OF LITERARY MERIT.

O! my unenlightened country-women! read, and profit, by the admonition of Reason. Shake off the trifling, glittering shackles, which debase you. Resist those fascinating spells, which, like the petrifying torpedo, fasten on your mental faculties. Be less the slaves of vanity, and more the converts of Reflection. Nature has endowed you with personal attractions: she has also given you the mind capable of expansion. Seek not the visionary triumph of universal conquest; know yourselves equal to greater, nobler, acquirements: and by prudence, temperance, firmness, and reflection, subdue that prejudice which has, for ages past, been your inveterate enemy. Let your daughters be liberally, classically, philosophically,[29] and usefully educated; let them speak and write their opinions freely; let them read and think like rational creatures; adapt their studies to their strength of intellect; expand their minds, and purify their hearts, by teaching them to feel their mental equality with their imperious rulers. By such laudable exertions, you will excite the noblest emulation; you will explode the superstitious tenets of bigotry and fanaticism; confirm the intuitive immortality of the soul, and give them that genuine glow of conscious virtue which will grace them to posterity.

---

[26] Messalinas: Messalina (ca. 22–48 BC); Roman empress known for murder and adultery; her name was used as short-hand for a devious and shameless woman.

[27] Robinson's note: "Paetus being commanded by the emperor Nero, to die by his own hands, his wife [Arria], an illustrious Roman woman, was permitted to take leave of him. She felt the impossibility of surviving him, and plunging the poniard into her bosom, exclaimed '*Paetus it is not much,*' and instantly expired. This anecdote I relate for the information of my unlearned readers." Publius Clodius Thrasea Paetus was a first-century Stoic philosopher and Roman senator who was condemned to die by suicide for opposing the reign of Emperor Nero. According to the letters of Pliny the Younger, his wife Arria seized the dagger from him and stabbed herself instead.

[28] Politely: With refinement, tastefully.

[29] Robinson's note: "By Philosophy, the writer of this Letter means rational wisdom; neither the flimsy cobwebs of pretended metaphysical and logical mysteries; nor the unbridled liberty which would lead to the boldness of licentious usurpation. A truly enlightened woman never will forget that conscious dignity of character which ennobles and sustains, but never can DEBASE her."

FIFTY-SIX

François Dominique Toussaint L'Ouverture (ca. 1743–1803)

*A*MONG THE MOST IMPORTANT ACCOMPLISHMENTS OF THE AGE OF REVOLUTIONS WAS THE *establishment of Haiti as the first Black-majority republic in the western hemisphere. Initially established as the French sugar plantation colony of Saint-Domingue in 1654, Haiti was peopled largely by African-born and African-descended slaves and ruled quite oppressively by a wealthy white French minority. White landowners used legislation to establish a rigid caste system that divided the whites or* blancs *from free blacks, "mulattoes" or* gens de couleur, *and slaves. Overwork and inadequate food, shelter, and medical care contributed to a high death among slaves and a continuing importation of new enslaved labor from Africa. The African-descended peoples of Saint-Domingue expressed their resistance to colonial domination as collectives of runaway slaves known as maroons lived in the forests of the island and mounted raids on the colony's plantations while* gens de couleur *issued written appeals to France on behalf of their own equality.*

With the advent of the French Revolution and the publication of the Declaration of the Rights of Man and Citizen *(included in this volume) in Paris in 1789, the African-descended peoples of Saint-Domingue launched their own revolutionary actions. A series of slave revolts in the 1790s led to Black control of almost one-third of the island. When Spanish and British forces invaded Saint-Domingue in 1793, French military commissioners freed many slaves to fight against the invaders. Black people consolidated these political gains at France's National Convention of 1794, which abolished slavery and granted equal rights to Black men across the French colonies.*

The National Convention's abolition of slavery in 1794 inspired a self-educated former slave and military commander named François Dominique Toussaint L'Ouverture to join the French cause with his thousands of Black troops who followed him. Within a few years, L'Ouverture became the de facto ruler of Saint-Domingue and even led the invasion of the neighboring Spanish colony of Santo Domingo to free enslaved Africans there. In 1801, L'Ouverture issued a new constitution that declared Saint-Domingue a self-governing political entity within the French empire. That constitution, excerpted here, is an important document of the Age of Revolutions and of how formerly enslaved Black people claimed the logic of the universal human rights and citizenship to achieve a measure of self-governance. It declares that slavery is "forever abolished" in Saint-Domingue and secures individual rights to security and property. But like many national constitutions created during the Age of Revolutions, the 1801 Haitian Constitution privileged men as citizens and (in article 15) as patriarchal leaders of their homes and workplaces. It also forbade divorce.

The French led by Napoleon Bonaparte did not react favorably to the 1801 Haitian Constitution, and one year after its issuance, L'Ouverture was forcibly returned to France, where he died in imprisonment in 1802. After continuing military battles between Haitian rebels and the French colonial army, the free republic of Haiti (an indigenous Arawak name for the island) was finally established by the Black leader Jean-Jacques Dessalines in 1804. Women played key roles in Haitian slave revolts and the Haitian Revolution through work stoppages, armed revolts, and by officiating in religious Voudun ceremonies to offer protection and guidance to Black rebels. The example of Toussaint L'Ouverture and the Haitian Revolution served as an inspiration to enslaved and free Blacks throughout the western hemisphere and substantially advanced the status of African-descended peoples of the Atlantic world.

CONSTITUTION OF HAITI (1801)[1]

The deputies of the departments of the Colony of St. Domingo met in Central Assembly, have decreed and laid the constitutional foundations of a system for the French colony of St. Domingo.

---

[1] This translation originally appeared in *The National Intelligencer* (Washington, DC) on August 12, 1801. It was quickly and frequently reprinted in other U.S. periodicals. Following those reprintings, we have silently corrected a few minor errors of repetition and in the spelling of Toussaint L'Ouverture's name.

TITLE I—Territory

ART. 1. St. Domingo in all its extent, and "Samana, la Tortue, la Gonave, les Cay-emites, l'ile-a-Vache, la Saone," and other adjacent islands form the territory of a single colony, which makes part of the French Empire, but which is governed by particular laws.

2. The territory of this colony is divided into departments, circles (Arrondiss-mens[2]) and parishes.

TITLE II—Of its Inhabitants.

3. Slaves are not permitted in this territory, servitude is forever abolished—All men born here, live and die freemen and Frenchmen.

4. Every man, whatever his colour may be, is eligible to all offices.

5. There exists no distinction other than that of talents and virtues, and no other superiority than that which the law confers by the exercise of some public office. The law is the same to all, either when it punishes or protects.

TITLE III—Of Religion.

6. The Catholic, Apostolic, and Roman religion, is the only one publicly pro-fessed.

7. Each parish must maintain its religious worship and its ministers. The church revenues are destined for the discharge of this expence, and the Presbyteriales (or priests houses) for the residence of the clergy.

8. The governor of the colony assigns to each pastor the limits of his spiritual administration; and these ministers can never under any pretext, form a body in the colony.[3]

TITLE IV—Morals.

9. Marriage, from its political and religious sanction, tends to purify the public morals; those who practice the virtues which this condition requires, will always be distinguished and peculiarly protected by the government.

10. Divorces are not allowed in this colony.

---

[2] Circles (Arrondissmens): Districts.

[3] This article puts priests and ministers under the direction of the government and forbids them from collectively playing a formal role in political affairs.

11. The conditions and privileges of illegitimate children shall be determined by laws, calculated to extend and to preserve the social virtues, and to encourage and cement family union.

TITLE V—Men in Society.

12. The constitution guaranties the liberty and security of each individual. No one can be arrested without orders officially expressed, proceeding from an officer to whom the law has given the power of arrestation, nor confined, in any places but such as are publicly designated for that purpose.

13. Property is sacred and inviolable—Every person either through themselves or through their representatives, shall have a free disposition and administration of whatever is known to belong to him. Whoever shall interfere with the exercise of this right, shall be considered criminal towards society and responsible to the person with those rights he has interfered.

TITLE VI—Agriculture and Commerce.

14. The colony being essentially agricultural cannot suffer the least interruption to the labours of its planters.

15. Each plantation is a manufactory which requires the union of husbandmen and workmen. It is the tranquil asylum of an industrious and orderly family, of which the proprietor of the soil or his representative, is necessarily the parent.[4]

16. Each husbandman and workman is a member of this family and a sharer of the revenues. Every change of habitation on the part of the husbandman draws with it the ruin of tillage. To repress a vice as fatal to the colony as it is contrary to public order, the governor has made all the regulations of police that circumstances required, and which were conformable to the basis of the regulations of the 20th Vendemaire, year 9 [1801],[5] and of the proclamation of the 19th Pluvoise,[6] by the general in chief Toussaint L'Ouverture.

17. The introduction of husbandmen, indispensable to the extension and re-establishment and of agriculture, shall take place in St. Domingo. The constitution

---

[4] The original French version has "le père," or father.

[5] Vendemaire: *Vendémiaire* is a month on the French Republican calendar, a calendar system proposed by revolutionaries and used by the French government from 1793 to 1805. According to this calendar, *Vendémiaire* (derived from the Latin word meaning "vintage") beginning at the fall equinox on September 22, was the first month of the year.

[6] Pluvoise: *Pluviôse* is the fifth month of the French Republican calendar year, starting January 20–22 and ending February 18–20. The name of the month comes from the Latin word for "rain."

charges the governor to take the most efficacious measures, to encourage and favor this augmentation of hands; to stipulate and balance the different interests, insure and guaranty the execution of reciprocal engagements resulting from their introduction.

18. The commerce of the colony consists only in the exchange of the commodities and productions of its own territory, consequently the introduction of the same articles is and remains prohibited. . . .

TITLE XIII—General Dispositions

63. The house of every person is an inviolable asylum. During the night no one has a right to enter it, except in cases of conflagration, inundation, or cries which proceed from within. During the day, it can be entered only for some special purpose, which shall be determined by law, or by an order proceeding from some public authority.

64. Before the act, for the arrestation of any person, can be executed, it must, 1st. formally express the reason of arrestation, & the law which decrees it, 2d. It must proceed from some public officer to whom the law has formally given the power of arrestation, 3d. A copy of the order must be given to the person arrested.

65. All such persons, who have not received from the law the power of arrestation, and shall give, sign, execute, or have executed the arrestation of any one, shall be guilty of the crime of arbitrary detention.

66. Every person has the right of addressing individual petitions to all the constituted authorities and especially to the governor.

67. There shall not be formed in the colony, incorporations or associations inimical to public order—No assembly of citizens can call themselves a popular society. All seditious assemblies shall be immediately dispersed, first by verbal command and afterwards, if necessary, by armed force.

68. Every one shall have the power of forming particular establishments for the education and instruction of youth, with the permission and under the superintendance of the municipal administrations.

69. The law will particularly superintend such occupations as affect public morals, or the security, health and fortune of citizens.

70. The law recompences the inventors of any agricultural machines, and vests in them the exclusive rights to their discoveries.

71. There shall be throughout the colony an uniformity of weights and measures.

72. Recompences shall be awarded by the governor in the name of the colony to such warriors as shall distinguish themselves in defending their country.

73. Proprietors absent from whatever cause, shall preserve all their rights to the property belonging to them, and situated in the colony. In order to obtain the removal of the sequestration, which may have been laid thereon, it will be sufficient to produce

their titles, and in the want of titles, supplimental acts, the form of which shall be determined by law. Those however, are excepted, who shall have been enlisted and who continue on the general list of French emigrants. Their property in this case will continue to be administered upon, as colonial domains, until they are erased from the list.

74. The colony proclaims, as guaranty of public faith, that all leases legally confirmed by the administration, shall continue in force, if the persons to whom the property is adjudged, do not prefer to negotiate with the proprietors or their representatives, who have obtained the removal of their sequestration.

75. It proclaims that it is upon the respect for persons and property, that the culture of the earth, all its productions, all means of labor and all social order must depend.

76. It proclaims that every citizen owes his services to the country that has given him birth, and to the soil that nourishes him, to the maintenance of liberty, and the equal division of property, whenever the law calls him to defend them.

77. The general in chief, Toussaint L'Ouverture, is charged with sending this constitution, to be presented for the sanction of the French government; nevertheless convinced of our perilous state, of our want of laws, and the necessity of the prompt re-establishment of agriculture, and listening to the unanimous wish of the inhabitants of St. Domingo, the general in chief is invited, in the name of the public welfare, to have this constitution put into execution throughout the whole extent of the colony.

Made at Port Republican, 19th Floreal, year 9[7] of the French Republic, one & indivisible. Signed, Borgella, president, Raimond, Collet, Gaston, Nogeree, La Cour, Roxas, Mugnoz, Mancebo.

Viart, Sec.[8]

After having made myself acquainted with the constitution, I give it my approbation; the invitation of the Central Assembly, I consider as a command, and in consequence thereof shall transmit it to the French government to obtain its sanction. In respect to its execution throughout the colony, the wish expressed by the Central Assembly shall be likewise fulfilled and executed.

Given at Cape Francois the 13th of Messidor year 9[9] of the French Republic, one and indivisible.

The general in Chief,

(Signed) TOUSSAINT L' OUVERTURE

---

[7] Floreal: On the French Republican calendar, *Floréal* is the eighth month of the year, beginning April 20–21 and ending May 19–20. *Floréal* is derived from the Latin word for "flower" or "blossom."

[8] This group of men was brought together by L'Ouverture expressly to write the constitution. The vast majority of the men were white, and none had ever been a slave.

[9] Messidor: On the French Republican calendar, the tenth month of the year, beginning June 19–20 and ending July 18–19. *Messidor* comes from the Latin word for "harvest."

FIFTY-SEVEN

Deborah Sampson Gannett (1760–1827)

*C*ONQUEST AND WAR DEMAND ABLE BODIES TO EXPLORE, SECURE, AND FIGHT. IN THE AGE OF *Revolutions, it was not only men who responded to such calls. Like many other women, Spaniard Catalina de Erauso, Britons Christian Davies and Hannah Snell, and American Deborah Sampson Gannett donned men's clothes and embarked upon lives of combat and adventure. These women are particularly notable because, upon discovery of their biological sex, they each published their "true" narratives of cross-dressing for fascinated audiences. Their tales directly and indirectly inspired a host of fictional memoirs of women soldiers in drag, and many eighteenth-century novels depict cross-dressing heroines, including Henry Fielding's* The Female Husband *(1746), the anonymously authored* History of Constantius and Pulchera *(1789–1790), Mary Robinson's* Walsingham; or, the Pupil of Nature *(1797), and Tabitha Tenney's* Female Quixotism *(1801).*

A range of motivations underpins the fictional heroines' decision to cross-dress, from the pursuit of a lover or an experience to the preservation of virtue or autonomy. In contrast, monetary reasons are often the most pressing in nonfictional accounts. Such was the case for Massachusetts-born Deborah Sampson Gannett. She had enlisted in the Continental Army, first in 1778 and again in 1782, at least in part to collect the signing bounty, and she began publicizing her story out of financial considerations as well. Unlike de Erauso and Snell who continued to live as men and whose memoirs hint at their romantic and sexual entanglements with women, she had returned to women's clothing after her exposure and discharge from the military. Two decades later, as an impoverished wife, mother, and farmer, Sampson Gannett needed her pension: though she had served over a year, the government had previously denied her claims on the basis of her sex. (Another New Englander, Ann Bailey, serving in the military under the name Samuel Gay, had been imprisoned when she was discovered to be a woman.) To legitimatize her case and to make money, Sampson Gannett embarked upon a lecture tour in the northeast in 1802. The government granted her a pension in 1805.

Sampson Gannett's Addr[e]ss, *published in 1802 by her biographer and probable co-author Herman Mann, is unusually introspective. Explaining why she "burst the tyrant bands, which* held [her] sex in awe," *she insists upon the American Revolution as exigent circumstances and proclaims her patriotism. In her account, the pressing need to defend natural rights transcends social strictures. Though her final words call upon American women to take up arms as republican mothers in their "kitchens" and "parlours," in actuality she concluded each speech with a military drill, thereby suggesting that women "warrior[s]" still had a legitimate public role and that citizenship, nationality, and gender are ongoing performances.*

ADDR[E]SS, DELIVERED WITH APPLAUSE, AT THE FEDERAL-STREET THEATRE, BOSTON (1802)

Not unlike the example of the patriot and philanthropist, though perhaps perfectly so in effect, do I awake from the tranquil slumbers of retirement, to active, public scenes of life, like those which now surround me. That genius which is the prompter of *curiosity,* and that spirit which is the support of *enterprize,* early drove, or, rather illured[1] me, from the corner of humble obscurity—their cheering aspect has again prevented a torpid rest.

Secondary to these are the solicitations of a number of worthy characters and friends, too persuasive and congenial with my own disposition to be answered with indifference, or to be rejected, have induced me thus to advance and bow submissive to an audience, simply and concisely to rehearse a *tale of truth;* which, though it took its rise, and finally terminated in the splendor of public life, I was determined to repeat only as the soliloquy of a hermit, or to the visionary phantoms, which hover through the glooms of solitude.

A tale—the truth of which I was ready to say, but which, perhaps, others have already said for me, ought to expel me from the enjoyment of society, from the acknowledgement of my own sex, and from the endearing friendship of the other. But this, I venture to pronounce, would be saying too much: For as I should thus not respect *myself,* should be entitled to none from *others.*

I indeed recollect it as a foible, an error and presumption, into which, perhaps, I have too inadvertently and precipitately run; but which I now retrospect with anguish

---

[1] Illured: Allured or tempted from.

and amazement—recollect it, as a THOMSON,[2] or any other moralizing naturalist, susceptible to the like fine feelings of nature, recollects the howling blasts of *winter,* at a period when *Flora* has strewed the earth with all her profusion of delicacies, and whose zephyrs are wafting their fragrance to heighten our sensations of tranquility and pleasure;—or, rather, perhaps, I ought to recollect it, as a marriner, having regained his native shore of serenity and peace, looks back on the stormy billows which, so long and so constantly had threatened to ingulph him in the bowels of the deep! And yet I must frankly confess, I recollect it with a kind of satisfaction, which no one can better conceive and enjoy than him, who, recollecting the *good intentions* of a *bad deed,* lives to see and to correct any indecorum of his life.

But without further preliminary apologies, yet with every due respect towards this brilliant and polite circle, I hasten to a review of the most conspicuous parts of that path, which led to achievements, which some have believed, but which many still doubt. Their accomplishment once seemed to me as impossible, as that I am author of them, is now incredible to the incredulous, or wounding to the ear of more refined delicacy and taste. They are a breach in the decorum of my sex, unquestionably; and, perhaps, too unfortunately ever irreconcilable with the rigid maxims of the moralist; and a sacrifice, which, while it may seem perfectly incompatible with the requirements of virtue—and which of course must ring discord in the ear, and disgust to the bosom of sensibility and refinement, I must be content to leave to time and the most scrutinizing enquiry to disclose.

Unlettered in any scholastic school of erudition, you will not expect, on this occasion, the entertainment of the soft and captivating sounds of eloquence; but rather a narration of facts in a mode as uncouth as they are unnatural. *Facts*—which, though I once experienced, and of which memory has ever been painfully retentive, I cannot now make you feel, or paint to the life.

Know then, that my juvenile mind early became inquisitive to understand—not merely whether the principles, or rather the seeds of *war* are analagous to the genuine nature of *man*—not merely to know why he should forego every trait of *humanity,* and to assume the character of a *brute;* or, in plainer language, why he should march out tranquilly, or in a paroxism of rage against his fellow-man, to butcher, or be butchered?—for these, alas! were too soon horribly verified by the massacres in our streets, in the very streets which encompass this edifice—in yonder adjacent villas,[3]

---

[2] THOMSON: James Thomson (1700–1748); Scottish poet and playwright most well known for his devotional blank-verse nature poem, *The Seasons.*

[3] Sampson Gannett's note: "Lexington, *and the adjacent towns and hamlet, when the British marched out of Boston to destroy the military forces at Concord.*" Lexington and Concord were about twenty miles from the Federal Street Theatre in Boston where Sampson Gannett delivered her address.

on yonder memorable eminence,[4] where now stand living monuments of the atrocious, the heart-distracting, mementous scenes, that followed in rapid succession!

This I am ready to affirm, though it may be deemed unnatural in my sex, is not a demoralization of human nature. The sluices, both of the blood of *freemen* and of *slaves,* were first opened here. And those hills and vallies, once the favorite resort, both of the lover and philosopher, have been drunk with their blood! A new subject was then opened to the most pathetic imagination, and to the rouzing of every latent spark of humanity, one should think, in the bosoms of the *wolves,* as well as in those of the *sheep,* for whose blood they were so thirsty.

But most of all, my mind became agitated with the enquiry—why a nation, separated from us by an ocean more than three thousand miles in extent, should endeavor to enforce on us plans of subjugation, the most unnatural in themselves, unjust, inhuman, in their operations, and unpractised even by the uncivilized savages of the wilderness? Perhaps nothing but the critical juncture of the times could have excused such a philosophical disquisition of politics in woman, notwithstanding it was a theme of universal speculation and concern to man. We indeed originated from her, as from a parent, and had, perhaps, continued to this period in subjection to her mandates, had we not discovered, that this, her romantic, avaricious and cruel disposition extended to *murder,* after having bound the *slave!*

Confirmed by this time in the justness of a defensive war on the one side, from the most aggravated one on the other—my mind ripened with my strength; and while our beds and our roses were sprinkled with the blood of indiscriminate youth, beauty, innocence, and decrepit old age, I only seemed to want the *license,* to become one of the severest *avengers* of the wrong.

For several years I looked on these scenes of havoc, rapacity and devastation, as one looks on a drowning man, on the conflagration of a city—where are not only centered his coffers of gold, but with them his choicest hopes, friends, companions, his all—without being able to extend the rescuing hand to either.

Wrought upon at length, you may say, by an enthusiasm and phrenzy, that could brook no control—I burst the tyrant bands, which *held my sex in awe,* and clandestinely, or by stealth, grasped an opportunity, which custom and the world seemed to deny, as a natural priviledge. And whilst poverty, hunger, nakedness, cold and disease had dwindled the *American Armies* to a handful—whilst universal terror and dismay

---

[4] Sampson Gannett's note: "Breed's Hill——*wrongly called* Bunker Hill." The Revolutionary War Battle of Bunker Hill (June 17, 1775) occurred about two months after the events at Lexington and Concord. Both sides suffered heavy casualties, though the British were the victors. Bunker Hill, located across the river in Charlestown, was about two miles from the theater.

ran through our country—while even WASHINGTON himself, at their head, though like a god, stood, as it were, on a pinacle tottering over the abyss of destruction, the last prelude to our falling a wretched prey to the yawning jaws of the monster aiming to devour–not merely for the sake of gratifying a fecetious curiosity, like that of my reputed Precedessor, in her romantic excursions through the garden of bliss[5]—did I throw off the soft habiliments of *my sex,* and assume those of the *warrior,* already prepared for battle.

Thus I became an actor in that important drama, with an inflexible resolution to persevere through the last scene; when we might be permitted and acknowledged to enjoy what we had so nobly declared we would possess, or lose with our lives—FREEDOM and INDEPENDENCE!—When, the philosopher might resume his researches unmolested—the statesman be disembarrassed by his distracting theme of national politics—the divine find less occasion to invoke the indignation of heaven on the usurpers and cannibals of the inherent rights and even existence of man—when the son should again be restored to the arms of his disconsolate parent, and the lover to the bosom of her, for whom indeed he is willing to jeopard his life, and for whom alone he wishes to live!

A new scene, and, as it were, a new world now opened to my view; the objects of which now seemed as important, as the transition before seemed unnatural. It would, however, here be a weakness in me to mention the tear of repentence, or of that temerity, from which the stoutest of my sex are, or ought not to be, wholly exempt on extreme emergencies, which many times involuntarily stole into my eye, and fell unheaded to the ground: And that too before I had reached the embattled field, the ramparts, which protected its internal resources—which shielded youth, beauty, and the delicacy of that sex at home, which perhaps I had forfeited in turning volunteer in their defence. *Temeritis*[6]—when reflections on my former situation, and this new kind of being, were daggers more frightful than all the implements of war—when the rustling of every leaf was an omen of danger, the whisper of each wind, a tale of woe! If then the poignancy of thought stared me thus haggardly in the face, found its way to the inmost recesses of my heart, thus forcibly, in the commencement of my career—what must I not have anticipated before its close!

The curtain is now up—a scene opens to your view; but the objects strike your attention less forcibly, and less interestingly, than they then did, not only my own eyes, but every energetic sensation of my soul. What shall I say further? Shall I not

---

[5] A reference to Eve and the Garden of Eden.
[6] *Temeritis*: Latin for temerity or rashness.

stop short, and leave to your imaginations to pourtray the tragic deeds of war? Is it not enough, that I here leave it even to unexperience to fancy the hardships, the anxieties, the dangers, even of the best life of a soldier? And were it not improper, were it not unsafe, were it not indelicate, and were I certain I should be intitled to a pardon, I would appeal to the soft bosom of my own sex to draw a parallel between the perils and sexual inconveniences of a girl in her teens, and not only in the armour, but in the capacity, at any rate, obliged to perform the duties in the field—and those who go to the camp without a masquerade, and consequently subject only to what toils and sacrifices they please: Or, will a conclusion be more natural from those, who sometimes take occasion to complain by their own domestic fire-sides, but who, indeed, are at the same time in affluence, cherished in the arms of their companions, and sheltered from the storms of war by the rougher sex in arms?

Many have seen, and many can contemplate, in the field of imagination, battles and victories amidst garments rolled in blood: but it is only one of my own sex, exposed to the storm, who can conceive of my situation.

We have all heard of, many have doubtless seen, the meteor streaming through or breaking in the horizon—the terrific glare of the comet, in its approach towards, or in its declension from us, in its excentric orbit—the howling of a tempest—the electric fluid, which darts majesty and terror through the clouds—its explosion and tremendous effects!—BOSTONIANS, and you who inhabit its environs, you who have known from experience your houses and your hills tremble from the cannonade of *Charlestown,*— your ears are yet wounded by the shrieks of her mangled and her distressed—your eyes swimming in a deluge of anguish at the sight of our butchered, expiring relatives and friends; while the conflagration of the town added the last solemnity to the scene![7]

This idea must assimulate with the progress of this horrid delusion of war. Hence you can behold the parched soil of *White-Plains* drink insatiate the blood of her most peaceful and industrious proprietors—of *freemen,* and of *slaves!*[8] I was there! The recollection makes me shudder!—A dislocated limb draws fresh anguish from my heart!

You may have heard the thunderings of a volcano—you may have contemplated, with astonishment and wonder, the burial of a city by its eruption. Your ears then are yet deafened from the thunderings of the invasion of *York Town*—your eyes dazzled, your imagination awfully sublimed, by the fire which belched from its environs, and towered,

---

[7] In 1775, while the British lay siege to Boston, American troops used the abandoned buildings of nearby Charlestown to fire on the British, who subsequently launched cannonballs and burned the town. Sampson Gannett mentions the Battle of Bunker Hill, which also took place in Charlestown, earlier in the speech.

[8] The Battle of White Plains took place in October 1776. Both sides suffered heavy casualties.

like that from an eruption of *Etna,* to the clouds![9] Your hearts yet bleed, from every principle of humanity, at the recollection of the havoc, carnage and death that reigned there!

Three successive weeks, after a long and rapid march, found me amidst this storm.[10]—But, happy for AMERICA, happy for EUROPE, perhaps for the WORLD, when, on the delivery of CORNWALLIS'S sword to the illustrious, the immortal WASHINGTON, or rather by his order, to the brave LINCOLN,[11] the sun of *Liberty* and *Independence* burst through a sable cloud, and his benign influence was, almost instantaneously, felt in our remotest corners! The phalanx of war was thus broken through, and the palladium of peace blossoming on its ruins.

I will not hence urge you to retrace with me (tranquilly you surely cannot) all the footsteps of our valient heroic LEADERS through the distraction both of elements and of war. I will not even pourtray an attempt to reinforce the brave SCHUYLER,[12] then on the borders of Canada, where, if the *war-whoop* of infernals should not strike you with dismay, the *tommahawk* would soon follow!

Nor need I point you to the death-like doors of the hospital in Philadelphia, whose avenues were crouded with the sick, the dying and the dead; though myself made one of the unhappy croud![13]

You have now but the shade of a picture; which neither time nor my abilities will permit me to show you to the life. The haggard fiend, despair, may have stared you in the face, when giving over the pursuit of a favorite, lost child: And it is only in this torture of suspense that we can rightly conceived of its situation.

Such is my experience—not that I ever mourned the loss of a child, but that I considered myself as lost! For, on the one hand, if I fell not a victim to the infuriate rabble of a mob, or of a war not yet fully terminated—a disclosure of my peculiar

---

[9] The Siege of Yorktown in Virginia (1781) ended in General Cornwallis's surrender to George Washington and thus left little doubt about American independence. The siege involved heavy bombardment, which Sampson Gannett likens to Sicily's Mount Etna, the most active volcano in Europe.

[10] Over the course of about three weeks in August and September of 1781, combined French and American forces under Generals Rochambeau and Washington marched south to Yorktown from New York.

[11] After losing the Siege of Yorktown, British commander General Cornwallis pled sickness and sent General Charles O'Hara to surrender in his place. Washington directed O'Hara to surrender to his own second-in-command, General Benjamin Lincoln.

[12] SCHUYLER: Philip John Schuyler (1733–1804); an American general who directed early campaigns against British forces along the Canadian border. The Continental Congress forced him to step down after he lost Fort Ticonderoga, though he remained invaluable for his logistical acumen and his efforts to undermine the British alliances with the region's powerful Indian nations (here referred to as "infernals").

[13] Perhaps a reference to the end of her three years of military service. According to a 1784 article in New York's *Independence Gazette*, a "violent illness, when the troops were at Philadelphia, led to the discovery of her sex."

situation seemed infinitely worse than either. And if from stratagem and perseverance, I may acquire as great knowledge in every respect as I have of myself in this, my knowledge, at least of human nature, will be as complete as it is useful.

But we will now hasten from the field, from the embattled entrenchments, built for the destruction of man, from a long, desolating war, to contemplate more desirable and delightful scenes. And notwithstanding curiosity may prompt any to retrace the climax of our revolution, the means, under a smiling, superintending providence, by which we have outrode the storms of danger and distress—what heart will forget to expand with joy and gratitude, to beat in unison, at the propitious recollection?— And I enquire, what infant tongue can ever forget or cease being taught to lisp the praises of WASHINGTON, and those of that bright constellation of WORTHIES, who swell the list of COLUMBIAN fame—those, by whose martial skill and philanthropic labors, we were first led to behold, after a long and stormy night, the smiling sun of *Peace* burst on our benighted WORLD! And while we drop a tear over the flowery turf of those patriots and sages, may she unrivalled enjoy and encrease her present bright sunshine of happiness! May agriculture and commerce, industry and manufactures, arts and sciences, virtue and decorum, union and harmony—those richest sources of our worth, and strongest pillars of our strength, become stationary, like fixed stars in the firmament, to flourish in her clime!

Hail dearest LIBERTY! thou [s]ource sublime!
What rays refulgent dart upon our clime!
For thee the direful contest has been waged,
Our hope, and all that life held dear engaged.
Thee the prime offspring which my thoughts employ,
Once fought with grief—now turns that grief to joy.
Your beatific influence extend
O'er AFRICA, whose sable race befriend.
May EUROPE, as our sister-empire, join,
To hail thee rising with your power divine.
From the lone cottage to the tyrant's throne,
May LIBERTY, ethereal guest, be known!
Be thou preserved for nations yet unborn,
Fair as the shining Star that decks the morn.

But the question again returns—*What particular inducement could she have thus to elope from the soft sphere of her own sex, to perform a deed of valor by way of sacrilege on unhallowed ground—voluntarily to face the storms both of elements and war, in the character of him, who is more fitly made to brave and endure all danger?*

And dost thou ask what fairy hand inspired
A *Nymph* to be with martial glory fired?
Or, what from art, or yet from nature's laws,
Has join'd a *Female* to her country's cause?
Why on great Mars's theatre she drew
Her *female* pourtrait, though in soldier's hue?

Then ask—why CINCINNATUS left his farm?[14]
Why science did old PLATO's bosom warm?[15]
Why HECTOR in the Trojan war should dare?
Or why should HOMER trace his actions there?[16]
Why NEWTON in philosophy has shown?[17]
Or CHARLES, for solitude, has left his throne?[18]
Why LOCKE, in metaphysics should delight—[19]
Precisian sage, to set false reason right?[20]
Why ALBION'S SONS should kindle up a war?[21]
Why JOVE or VULCAN hurried on the car?[22]
Perhaps the same propensity you use,

---

[14] CINCINNATUS: Cincinnatus (ca. 519–ca. 438 BC); statesman who left his farm to briefly rule Rome during a time of crisis. After resolving the crisis, he voluntarily returned to his farm. George Washington, who first resigned from the military after victory over the British and then stepped down after two terms in office despite his popularity, has been often referred to as the American Cincinnatus.

[15] PLATO: Plato (ca. 428–347 BC); Greek philosopher whose writings influenced a number of eighteenth-century fields including metaphysics, mathematics, and science.

[16] HECTOR, HOMER: In Homer's epic poem the *Iliad* about the Trojan War, Hector is a great Trojan hero, defeated by Achilles.

[17] NEWTON: Isaac Newton (1642–1727); mathematician and scientist whose study of gravitation revolutionized our understanding of physics.

[18] CHARLES: Perhaps a reference to the Spanish King Charles I (1500–1558) who abdicated and retired to a monastery in 1556.

[19] LOCKE: John Locke (1632–1704); English philosopher and political theorist who is regarded as a founding figure of the Enlightenment.

[20] Precisian: Rigidly precise or providing strict rules.

[21] ALBION: A poetical term for Britain.

[22] JOVE, VULCAN: Jove is another name for Jupiter, the chief god of the Roman pantheon; Vulcan is the Roman god of fire and volcanoes.

Has prompted her a martial course to choose.
Perhaps to gain refinements where she could,
This rare achievement for her country's good.
Or was some hapless *lover* from her torn—
As EMMA did her valient HAMMON mourn?[23]
Else he must tell, who would this truth attain,
Why one is form'd for pleasure—one for pain:
Or, boldly, why our MAKER made us such—
Why *here* he gives too *little*—*there* too *much!*

I would not purposely evade a pertinent answer; and yet I know not, at present, how to give a more particular one than has already been suggested.

I am indeed willing to acknowledge what I have done, an error and presumption. I will call it an *error* and *presumption,* because I swerved from the accustomed flowry paths of *female delicacy,* to walk upon the heroic precipice of feminine perdition!—I indeed left my morning pillow of roses, to prepare a couch of brambles for the night: and yet I awoke from this refreshed, to gather nought but the thorns of anguish for the next night's repose—and in the precipitancy of passion, to prepare a moment for repentance at leisure!

Had all this been achieved by the rougher hand, more properly assigned to wield the sword in duty and danger in a defensive war, the most cruel in its measure, though important in its consequences; these thorns might have been converted into wreaths of immortal glory and fame. I therefore yield every claim of honor and distinction to the hero and patriot, who met the foe in his own name; though not with more heartfelt satisfaction, with the trophies, which were most to redound to the future grandeur and importance of the country in which he lives.

But *repentance* is a sweet solace to conscience, as well as the most complete atonement to the Supreme JUDGE of our offences: not withstanding the tongue of malevolence and scurrility may be continually preparing its most poisonous ingredients for the punishment of a crime, which has already received more than half a pardon.

Yet if even this be deemed too much of an extenuation of a breach in the modesty of the *female world*—humilized and contented will I sit down inglorious, for having

---

[23] A reference to Samuel Jackson Pratt's popular epistolary novel *Emma Corbett; or, The Miseries of Civil War* (1780). It tells the story of two English lovers, Emma Corbett and Henry Hammond, on opposite sides of the American Revolution. Dressed as a boy, Emma follows Henry to America, where he fights for the British. Once there, she stains her face with berries so she can search for Henry safely disguised as an Indian "savage."

unfortunately performed an important part assigned for another—like a bewildered star traversing out of its accustomed orbit, whose twinkling beauty at most has become totally obscured in the presence of the sun.

But as the rays of the sun strike the eye with the greatest lustre when emerging from a thick fog, and as those actions which have for their objects the extended hand of charity to the indigent and wretched—to restore a bewildered traveler to light— and, to reform in ourselves any irregular and forlorn course of life; so, allowing myself to be one o[f] the greatest of these, do I still hope for some claim on the indulgence and patronage of the public; as in such case I might be conscious of the approbation of my GOD.

I cannot, contentedly, quit this subject or this place, without expressing, more emphatically, my high respect and veneration for my own SEX. The indulgence of this respectable circle supercedes my merit, as well as my most sanguine expectations. You receive at least in return my warmest gratitude. And though you can neither have, or perhaps need, from me the instructions of the sage, or the advice of the counsellor; you surely will not be wholly indifferent to my most sincere declaration of friendship for that sex, for which this checkered flight of my life may have rendered me the least ornamental example; but which, neither in adversity or prosperity, could I ever learn to forget or degrade.

I take it to be from the greatest extremes both in virtue and in vice, that the uniformly virtuous and reformed in life can derive the greatest and most salutary truths and impressions.—Who, for example, can contemplate for a moment, the *prodigal*— from the time of his revelry with harlots, to that of his eating husks with swine, and to his final return to his father—without the greatest emotions of disgust, pity and joy?[24] And is it possible to behold the effects of the unprincipled conduct of the *libertine,* the *bacchanalian,* the *debauchee,* and what is more wretched than all, of the emaciated, haggard form of a modern *baggage* in the streets, without bringing into exercise every passion of abhorrence and commisseration? And yet, happy those, who at the same time receive a monitor which fixes a resolve, never to embark on such a sea of perdition; where we see shipwreck of all that is enobling to the dignity of *man*—all that is lovely and amiable in the character of *woman!*

I cannot, indeed bring the adventures, even of the worst part of my own life, as parallels with this black catalogue of crimes. But in whatever I may be thought to have been unnatural, unwise and indelicate, it is now my most fervent desire it may

---

[24] The New Testament parable of the prodigal son (Luke 15:11–32) centers on a father and his two sons, one obedient and one wayward. When the profligate son returns home to after squandering his inheritance, the father welcomes him with open arms and chastises the dutiful one for being resentful.

have a suitable impression on you—and on me, a penitent for every wrong thought and step. The rank you hold in the scale of beings is, in many respects, superior to that of man. *Nurses* of his growth, and invariable models of his habits, he becomes a suppliant at your shrine, emulous to please, assiduous to cherish and support, to live and to die for you! *Blossoms* from your very birth, you become his admiration, his joy, his eden companions in this world.—How important then is it, that these *blossoms* bring forth such *fruit,* as will best secure your own delights and felicity, and those of him, whose every enjoyment, and even his very existence, is so peculiarly interwoven with your own!

On the whole, as we readily acquiesce in the acknowledgement, that the *field* and the *cabinet* are the proper spheres assigned for our MASTERS and our LORDS; may *we,* also, deserve the dignified title and encomium of MISTRESS and LADY, in our *kitchens* and in our *parlours.* And as an overruling providence may succeed our wishes—let us rear an offspring in every respect worthy to fill the most illustrious stations of their predecessors.

FIFTY-EIGHT

Sarah Pogson Smith (1774–1870)

*M*EN AND WOMEN AROUND THE ATLANTIC LOOKED TO FRANCE AS NOT ONLY AN INSPIRATION *but also an example of the potential excesses and dangers of revolution. Sarah Pogson Smith's* The Female Enthusiast *(1807) is a play about Charlotte Corday, the Frenchwoman who assassinated the radical Jacobin revolutionary Jean-Paul Marat in 1793. In contrast to Helen Maria Williams's reasonably factual account of the assassination, included in this collection, Pogson Smith's version is highly fictionalized. She fabricates events and characters—including a parallel plot concerning Corday's brother and the woman he secretly marries— that have the effect of creating a comparison between French and American republicanisms.*

The play suggests that while American republicanism is far more admirable, it is still vulnerable to the disruptive violence that erupted in France. An English émigré to South Carolina and a witness to the first decades of American nationhood, Pogson Smith may have been fearful of the potential tyranny of the masses as well as slave rebellion, made undeniable by Charleston's many white refugees of the Haitian Revolution. In the play, Pogson Smith includes scenes in which a mob, angered at Marat's assassination and seeking vengeance, kills Corday's father, strikes down children, and terrorizes innocents. She also creates a speech for Marat that illustrates the power of charismatic leaders who utter rousing yet manipulative sentiments. Pogson Smith's Corday, in contrast, is a passionate and patriotic woman who is willing to sacrifice her life and honor in her quest to defend the true cause of freedom while simultaneously avenging her lover's death.

Our excerpt comes from Act III. The act begins with Marat's speech before a menacingly named "motly crew" of French citizens. In the midst of his speech, he is summoned to meet with a mysterious woman who offers him information about

Jacobin enemies in Normandy. The woman, of course, is Corday, and prior to the assassination she soliloquizes about her motivations in lines that offer a parallel to Marat's more public ones. When her act is discovered, she proudly declares, "A woman's arm, when nerv'd in such a cause,/Is, as the arm of the avenging angel." The scene then changes to northern France, where a character named Duval and his daughter Estelle converse. Unaware that Estelle has already married Corday's brother Henry, Duval pushes her to marry another man. He laments that America, not France, is the only place where "Virtuous industry . . . /Is always rewarded with competence." At the conclusion of the play, Estelle and Henry abandon a chaotic France for America in order to follow this tantalizing dream of a more virtuous republic.

FROM *THE FEMALE ENTHUSIAST* (1807)

ACT III.

SCENE I. *Discovers MARAT, he is sitting meanly dress'd with his hat on; surrounded by a motly crew. CHABOT at his right hand.*[1] *Marat rises and comes forward.*

> *Marat.* Citizens! these difficulties shall cease,
> And the head of each base conspirator,
> Each foe to Liberty, and Equality
> Shall roll beneath us, an abject football.
> My countrymen, enlightened sons of France;
> Ye! ye! who comprehend *true* Freedom,
> Boldly trample on the groveling hearts
> Of those, who still adhere to kings—and priests.
> Free as the air! and equal as its surface,
> Citizens! Patriots! spill your bravest blood;
> Raise high the pile of slaughtered sycophants—
> Exterminate all those—who dare presume
> To check, this radiant dawn of liberty,
> Which soon shall blaze a full meridian sun!
> Too bright for despots, and their cringing slaves
> To look on, dazzled by its brilliancy,

---

[1] CHABOT: According to the dramatis personae, Chabot is a friend of Marat.

Unable to behold the great resplendent
Full orb'd! mighty! glorious! liberty!
Their narrow hearts will sink within their breasts
Ignobly chained to proud nobility—
To treacherous crowns—and wily priestcraft,
Not daring to complain—much less redress
The most oppressive burthens;—meanly they
Drag on existence—in debasing bonds:—
In bonds, which ye great—deserving Frenchmen
Have so gloriously burst asunder.
By yourselves—ye are emancipated.—
Live—live—to triumph in the enjoyment
Of reason. and its rights—never suffer
Those dear rights again to be invaded;
Let no ambitious—trait'rous, haughty despot,
Chain your minds or bodies more—but be free!
Frenchmen! Countrymen! My brethren! be free.
Stain your swords with the purple tide, flowing
From dying conspirators: let the foes
Of our liberty bleed—they, are vipers;
Let not bread, which should nourish true Frenchmen,
Be wasted on them! No—destroy—destroy!
Justice calls aloud destroy! well ye know,
Whose blood to spill—and whose to spare—without
The tedious mockeries of courts and judges,
Judge for yourselves—and quickly execute.

Enter a man who wispers to MARAT, Marat replies aloud.

 Mar. Tell the person, business detained me;
I received her note, and will speak with her.[2]

            [*Exit man.*

Citizens! a person waits, well informed
Of circumstances, highly important.

---

[2] Corday did in actuality gain an audience with Marat by sending him a note. She had initially intended to kill him publicly.

Delay is ever dangerous—and now

It would be culpable—therefore I go

To hear, what I trust will aid our cause;

My whole ambition is, to serve it

With all my powers of mind and body.

This arm will not spare one aristocrat.

This breast harbours eternal enmity

To each opposer of its sentiments;

The sentiments of pure Republicanism,

While ardour in its cause, gives force and tone

To all my energies—even to my steps.

I feel a Demigod—   [*Struts about.*]

How ennobled!

By the boundless confidence of such men.—

                              (*Points to them.*)

Fellow citizens! I live to serve you. [*Exit Marat.*

    Chabot, (advances.) We! to support the champion of Freedom;

And unanimous in defence of him!

We swear to stand or fall with great Marat

The people's friend.

                                        [*Exeunt all.*

Scene changes—discovers CHARLOTTE in an antichamber.

    Charl. A few short moments—and his doom is fixed.

My heart that sicken'd if an insect died;

My bosom nurs'd in softest tenderness,

Burns to destroy—feels a pow'rful impulse

Strengthening every nerve—compressing

Every thought, to one keen point.—Revenge!

Enthusiastic fervor, bears me on—

And gentler passions fly before its pow'r!

No other hand will rise:—No other eye

Will throw death's fiat on the subtle serpent.

No more shall guileless innocence be stung,

By his envenom'd tongue, and thirst of blood;

Nor shall those brave men, his savage sword condemns,

Add to the mound of butcher'd victims.

O, no! no! no! he dies.

Back Scene opens, discovers MARAT in his chamber, dressed in a loose bathing gown and slippers; at the farthest end of the room stands his bath—He comes forward.[3]

    Marat. I have too long detained thee, young woman:
Now let me have the promis'd information.
    Charl. Citizen, my errand is important.
Thy civism,[4] leads thee to destroy whate'er
Is prejudicial to *true* liberty,
And to the welfare of France. I am come
To point out, the *deadliest* foe to *both*,
And a sure way, to rid our country of him.—
              (gives a packet—he prepares to open it.)
Here in this packet, is full information,
Of a well plann'd, and deep conspiracy.
But ere thou doest examine the contents,
Suffer me to ask, what will be the fate
Of those conspirators, who fled to Normandy;[5]
And of such people, as conceal the traitors?
Adopting too, their dangerous opinions
Which threaten ruin to the noble cause
Espous'd by every true born son of freedom.
    Mar. Ha! wouldst thou, then, know what will be their fate?
I tell thee, girl—that they, and many more
Who think themselves secure—their heads quite safe,
Will feel the sharp axe of the guillotine.
              (He looks down on the packet to open it.)
    Charl. First—feel this sharper weapon—die, monster!
              (Stabs him—MARAT falls.)

---

[3] Artists and authors frequently depict Marat in his bath during the assassination. Prior to his death, Marat had stepped back from public life due to a debilitating skin disease. Confined to his rooms, he took frequent medicinal baths.

[4] Civism: A phonetic translation of the French word *civisme*, in this context meaning devotion to the cause of the French Revolution.

[5] A reference to the Girondist deputies who escaped to Caen in the northern province of Normandy after they were arrested and removed from the National Convention. They were organizing an opposition to the Jacobins back in Paris. Corday was in Caen when these deputies arrived. What she heard from them motivated her to travel to Paris and kill Marat, an act she hoped would restore what she saw as the true republican principles of the French Revolution.

There is [an] end to thy destructive course!

Thou *ignis fatuus*[6]—that deceiv'd the simple.

Murd'rer of prisoners—of priests defenceless.

Of helpess women—die!—The innocent

Shall live.—Now art thou death's prisoner.—

Mar. In sin's lowest depth, alas, I perish!

Thy friends, young woman, are too well aveng'd.

How didst thou find this courage?—O! great God!

God? Ha! that sacred name should not proceed

From my polluted lips:—I dare not pray:

My prayers would be but impious mockery.

The sighs of others never reached my ear;

Can those from my remorseless heart, e'er reach

The mightly throne omnipotent? Oh! oh! *(Groans loud:*

> *CHABOT enters: he starts: rushes up to MARAT,*
> *whom he supports.)*

    Mar. (Faintly speaks.) Is it thou, Chabot? ah! could I but live—

But no, I die—I die.—The light recedes.

My eyes are closing:—Open! open them! *(in agony.)*

O! save me from that yawning gulf! save me!

O! save me! save,——*(Springs convuls'd from the support of*

CHABOT: and dies: CHABOT seizes the poignard, and gr[a]sps an

arm of CHARLOTTE, fiercely: she looks composedly at him.)

    Chabot. Girl! what has thou done—did madness seize thee?

Tremble for the consequence of this crime.

A public expiation waits the deed;

Or my hand should now destroy, with the same

Destructive weapon, so well directed.

What instigated thee to such an act? *(Lets her go, and drops the*

    poignard.)

---

[6] *Ignis fatuus*: Also called will-o'-the-wisp. In folklore this term refers to a phosphorescent light seen
floating over unsafe marshy ground that lures fools to their death as they chase the light.

Charl. The cause of virtue. The world contained not
In all its wide circumference, so black
A traitor to its peace, and liberty,
As base Marat. My soul is satisfied.—
A woman's arm, when nerv'd in such a cause,
Is, as the arm of the avenging angel.
Think not I am a foe to liberty!
My father is a real Patriot;
My brother at this moment, joins the friends,
Soldiers of liberty! not assassins:
They, should sink beside that fall'n enemy,
To all but anarchy and cruelty; *(Points to Marat.)*
To know, that by his death, thousands are free!
Fully repays the danger I incur.
Lead me to prison—if thy conscience bids:—
But if one spark of Heav'nly liberty,
Of generous love towards thy country,
Glows within that bosom—then wilt thou say,
Depart in safety:—but I see thy purpose.
    Chab. Yes, I'll bid thee depart—ho! assistance!
                    (Enter several Men.)
To prison with her—where this heroism
Will soon be humbled, and that beautiful head
Bend lower than it designs to do at present.
Away with her!   [*Exeunt.*

Scene changes to an apartment in DUVAL'S house: DUVAL is seated, looking over the contents of a pocket-book—Enter ESTELLE. (He looks at her.)

    Duval. Still this dejected look, my dear Estelle?
I fear thy tender health will suffer, child.
Remember, while we sympathise with others,
Their sorrows must not leave too deep a trace,
Must not be made entirely our own.
But I will say no more, the subject wounds.
    Est. Alas! it does—
    Duv.   And where we cannot heal:
Discussion only gives a keener pang,

'Tis not all anguish that can be partaken.—
Yet, would thy father take thy every grief,
And bid that mouth forever wear a smile. *(embraces her.)*
    Est. My kind—my dear father!
    Duv.   Tell me, my child,
Hast thou consider'd the request I made;[7]
With deep attention weigh'd the matter well?
Thou know'st I cannot bear opposition—
Twas wrong to set thy father's will at naught—
Thou canst not disappoint his darling hope.
    Est. Disappoint thy darling hope, my father? *(In agitation.)*
    Duv. That were impossible—it was surprise,
Thou hadst not thought of leaving me, Estelle;
But, alas! I am in the vale of years;
Thy mother is no more—and heaven knows,
That thou, my child, wilt need the fost'ring care
Of one, whose love can ward off ev'ry ill.—
Single—expos'd! What—what might be thy fate?
Amidst these desolating factious times,
Sparing, nor age, nor sex.—Ah! when I'm gone,
Virtue will be thy only legacy;
And that, if unprotected—often falls
A victim to designing villainy;
Or, vainly struggling against the dark stream
Of poverty—is overwhelm'd—and sinks.
    Est. O! far, far distant be the mournful day,
That deprives me of so dear a parent.
But, my father, when it pleases *him* who gives,
And who resumes—to take thy precious life,
Paint not the future in so deep a shade;
Virtuous industry, my dearest Sir,
Is always rewarded with competence.
    Duv. There *is* a land, where such, indeed's the case;
Not *thine*, my child—it is America.—

---

[7] In a previous scene, Duval asked Estelle to marry a man named Belcour. Already secretly married to Corday's brother Henry, Estelle surprises both Duval and Belcour with her resistance to their jointly hatched plan.

There, in the conjugal or single state;
In affluence, or pale cheek'd poverty,
Each female, who respects herself, is safe:—
Each walks the path of life secure from insult
As strongly guarded by a virtuous mind,
As she, who's in a gilded chariot borne—
Surrounded by an host of glitt'ring arms.
But here, the mind adorn'd with ev'ry grace,
Compell'd to stoop, and share the body's toil,
In gloomy insolated poverty.
Too often droops—or if it makes a stand,
Its tones are blunted by adversity:
And though it springs to pierce this earthly veil,
And catch a vision of its future state,
Where virtue will surely be rewarded—
And patient merit there receive its prize:
Yet, in this life—acts an imperfect part,
Unlike the scene of wedded excellence,
Fulfilling woman's dear and sacred duties,
Scatt'ring sweets to all within its influence;
It shines the brightest gem in Nature's works.
Then, let this lovely part be thine, Estelle:
O! make thy own happiness—and Belcour's.

FIFTY-NINE

Leonora Sansay (1773–?)

*T*HE FINAL MONTHS OF THE HAITIAN REVOLUTION ARE THE BACKDROP OF LEONORA SANSAY'S Secret History; or, The Horrors of St. Domingo *(1808). Written in the epistolary form—a narrative style, quite common at the time, which unfolds via a series of letters—the novel is a combination of gothic tale, political history, and travelogue. In writing the novel, Sansay relied on firsthand experiences: an American married to a French planter from Saint-Domingue, she witnessed the same final months of the Revolution as her characters, and many of the novel's scenes may be autobiographical.*

The plot revolves around the captivating young white matron Clara and her dull husband St. Louis. Clara's sister Mary is the author of most of the letters and writes to a male friend, Aaron Burr, back home in Philadelphia. Mary describes St. Louis's inability to cultivate Clara's tender sensibility even as she recounts how that same sensibility unintentionally charms the powerful and amoral men of Saint-Domingue, thereby stoking the fires of St. Louis's jealousy; her modesty and elusiveness serve to increase her allure. As the threat of marital violence grows, the victory of the Black rebel army under Jean-Jacques Dessalines obliges Mary, Clara, and St. Louis to flee the island. Once in Cuba, Clara furtively escapes her husband and sends letters to explain her actions to Mary, who, despite her concerns about St. Louis's capacity for murder, is shocked and hurt by Clara's flight. It is at this moment that Sansay provides several letters from Clara, who counters Mary's judgmental scoldings with her own "secret history" of rape and physical abuse. A much-abbreviated version of this plot appears in an 1803 letter Sansay wrote to the real Aaron Burr, vice president of the United States and her lover. In it, Sansay appears to use the name Clara as a pseudonym for herself.

Despite Mary's frequent expressions of prim naïveté, the parallels between the social condition of women and enslaved Haitians are difficult to ignore. Yet in a way that may be troubling to the modern reader, the novel seems to use these parallels to expose men's emotional and physical tyranny over women; the brutality of slavery on Saint-Domingue—where enslaved Africans worked as much as twenty hours per day and were expected to live only seven years after arriving on the island— is mentioned only incidentally. Instead, Mary offers fascinating sketches about the many women she encounters—French, Creole, and Spanish white women as well as free mulatto and enslaved Black women. She documents their behavior within an unstable climate of brutal oppression and violent rebellion, often linking their actions to their racial and national identities. For Mary, the war gradually strips away a corrupt veneer and most women emerge at least briefly as compassionate, hardworking, and self-sacrificing even as men's cruelty becomes increasingly apparent. Even Black women who engage in wartime atrocities are depicted as noble in their fierce support for their cause. Thus the novel documents a disturbing vision of a lawless and chaotic Haitian Revolution that nonetheless offers a fleeting moment for women like Clara to claim their dignity and perhaps their freedom, too.

FROM *SECRET HISTORY; OR, THE HORRORS OF ST. DOMINGO* (1808)

Letter III

Cape Francois.[1]

. . . The place is tranquil. The arrival of General Rochambeau[2] seems to have spread terror among the negroes. I wish they were reduced to order that I might see the so much vaunted habitations where I should repose beneath the shade of orange groves; walk on carpets of rose leaves and frenchipone[3]; be fanned to sleep by silent slaves, or have my feet tickled into extacy by the soft hand of a female attendant.

Such were the pleasures of the Creole ladies whose time was divided between the bath, the table, the toilette and the lover.

---

[1] Cape Francois: Cap Français, or Le Cap (now renamed Cap Haïtien), is located on the northern coast. At the time of the Haitian Revolution, its population (including soldiers and enslaved persons) was close to 20,000, making it roughly the size of Boston. It was a dynamic cultural center, boasting a large theater, a wax museum, and bathhouses. The city served as Saint-Domingue's principal port.

[2] General Rochambeau: Donatien Marie Joseph de Vimeur de Rochambeau (1755–1813); captain-general of French forces in Saint-Domingue from January to November 1803. He was brutal in his efforts to crush the slave revolt and used man-eating dogs to hunt black revolutionaries. In the novel, Rochambeau is enamored with Clara and seeks an extramarital affair.

[3] Frenchipone: Possibly frangipani, also called plumeria, a fragrant flowering plant native to the tropical regions of the Americas and used as an ornamental shrub.

What a delightful existence! thus to pass away life in the arms of voluptuous indolence; to wander over flowery fields of unfading verdure, or through forests of majestic palm-trees, sit by a fountain bursting from a savage rock frequented by only the cooing dove, and indulge in these enchanting solitudes all the reveries of an exalted imagination.

But the moment of enjoying these pleasures is, I fear, far distant. The negroes have felt during ten years the blessing of liberty, for a blessing it certainly is, however acquired, and they will not be easily deprived of it. [T]hey have fought and vanquished the French troops, and their strength has increased from a knowledge of the weakness of their opposers, and the climate itself combats for them. Inured to a savage life they lay in the woods without being injured by the sun, the dew or the rain. A negro eats a plantain, a sour orange, the herbs and roots of the field, and requires no cloathing, whilst this mode of living is fatal to the European soldiers. The sun and the dew are equally fatal to them, and they have perished in such numbers that, if reinforcements do not arrive, it will soon be impossible to defend the town.[4]

The country is entirely in the hands of the negroes, and whilst their camp abounds in provisions, every thing in town is extremely scarce and enormously dear.

Every evening several old Creoles, who live near us, assemble at our house, and talk of their affairs. One of them, whose annual income before the revolution was fifty thousand dollars, which he always exceeded in his expenses, now lives in a miserable hut and prolongs with the greatest difficulty his wretched existence. Yet he still hopes for better days, in which hope they all join him. The distress they feel has not deprived them of their gaiety. They laugh, they sing, they join in the dance with the young girls of the neighbourhood, and seem to forget their cares in the prospect of having them speedily removed.

Letter IX

Cape Francois.

. . . A black chief and his wife were made prisoners last week, and sentenced to be shot. As they walked to the place of execution the chief seemed deeply impressed with the horror of his approaching fate: but his wife went cheerfully along, endeavoured to console him, and reproached his want of courage. When they arrived on the field, in which their grave was already dug, she refused to have her eyes bound; and turning to the soldiers who were to execute their sentence, said "Be expeditious, and don't make me linger." She received their fire without shrinking, and expired without uttering a groan. Since the commencement of the revolution she had been a very

---

[4] Much of the French army, including General Charles Victor Emmanuel Leclerc (1772–1802), succumbed to yellow fever, a disease that we now know is transmitted by mosquitoes.

devil! Her husband commanded at St. Marks,[5] and being very amorously inclined, every white lady who was unfortunate enough to attract his notice, received an order to meet him. If she refused, she was sure of being destroyed, and if she complied she was as sure of being killed by his wife's orders, which were indisputable. Jealous as a tygress, she watched all the actions of her husband; and never failed to punish the objects of his amorous approaches, often when they were entirely innocent.

How terrible was the situation of these unfortunate women, insulted by the brutal passion of a negro, and certain of perishing if they resisted or if they complied.

This same fury in female form killed with her own hand a white man who had been her husband's secretary. He offended her; she had him bound, and stabbed him with a penknife till he expired!

How often, my dear friend, do my sighs bear my wishes to your happy country; how ardently do I desire to revisit scenes hallowed by recollection, and rendered doubly dear by the peaceful security I there enjoyed, contrasted with the dangers to which we are here exposed. Yet the Creoles still hope; for

"Hope travels through, nor quits us when we die."[6]

They think it impossible that this island can ever be abandoned to the negroes. They build houses, rebuild those that were burned, and seem secure in their possession. . . .

Letter X

Cape Francois.

It is not often in the tranquility of domestic life that the poet or the historian seek their subjects! Of this I am certain, that in the calm that now surrounds us it will be difficult for me to find one for my unpoetical pen.

Clara is dull, St. Louis contented,[7] and I pass my time heavily, complaining of the fate which brought me here, and wishing to be away. We go sometimes to the concerts given by monsieur d'Or, where madame P——, a pretty little Parisian sings; and where madame A——accompanied by her daughter, presides with solemn dignity. This lady,

---

[5] St. Marks: Saint-Marc was a port city located in Saint-Domingue's Western province. In the Revolution's early years, it was the seat of the General Assembly, a republican legislature elected by and composed of rich and poor white men that opposed the more conservative and elite Provincial Assembly, located in Le Cap. Free and enslaved persons of color were excluded from both assemblies. However, *gens de couleur*, or free people of color, had previously dominated the city's politics.

[6] From *An Essay on Man*, Epistle II by Alexander Pope (1688–1744).

[7] St. Louis: Clara's mercurial, jealous, and abusive husband. Sansay's husband's first name was Louis. *L'Ordre Royal et Militaire de Saint-Louis* was also the name of a chivalric society founded and headed by French royalty. To obtain the award, a man had to be a Catholic who had served as an officer in the French military.

who is at present a most rigid censor of female conduct, and not amiable either in person or manners, lived many years with monsieur A——, who raised her from the rank of his house-keeper, to that of his mistress. But he fell in love with another lady, whom he was going to marry. The deserted fair one threw herself in despair at the feet of Toussaint,[8] with whom she had some influence, and so forcibly represented the injustice of the proceeding, that Toussaint ordered A——to be confined, saying he should not be released till he consented to marry the lady he had so long lived with. A——resisted some time, but at length yielded, and exchanged his prison for the softer one of her arms.

Before the revolution there was a convent at the Cape. The nuns in general were very rich, and devoted themselves chiefly to the education of young ladies: some of their pupils, I have heard, would have done honour to a Parisian seminary.

When religion was abolished in France,[9] the rage for abolition, as well as that of revolutionizing reached this place, and the nuns were driven from the convent by Santhonax, a name which will always fill every Frenchman's breast with horror: he caused the first destruction of the Cape. On the arrival of general Galbo, who was sent to supercede him, he said, "if Galbo reigns here, he shall reign over ashes," and actually set fire to the town.[10] The convent was not then burned; but the society was dissolved, the habit of the order laid aside; and some of the nuns, profiting by the license of the times, married. One of these became the wife of a man who, during the reign of the negroes committed crimes of the deepest die. He has not yet received the punishment due to them; but he awaits in trembling the hour of retribution. I often see her. She has been very handsome, but her charms are now in the wane; she has a great deal of vivacity, and that fluency of expression in conversing on the topics of the day, which gives to a French woman the reputation of having *beaucoup d'esprit.*[11]

---

[8] Toussaint: Toussaint L'Ouverture (1743–1803) was a former slave who became a brilliant military leader and political strategist during the Haitian Revolution. In his 1801 constitution, L'Ouverture designated himself governor general for life. Angered at such insulting audacity, Napoleon Bonaporte sent General Leclerc and fresh troops to Saint-Domingue. L'Ouverture was deposed and eventually imprisoned, and the colony briefly returned to French control before the Black army, under Jean-Jacques Dessalines, cemented Haitian independence in 1804.

[9] During the French Revolution, the legislature passed a number of antichurch acts. The government seized gold and other valuables from Catholic churches. Priests who did not swear primary allegiance to France, called nonjurors, faced imprisonment and execution. Divorce was declared legal, and the government took over administration of marriage, birth, and death registers. Various factions attempted to supplant the Catholic Church with faiths centered on rationality and reason. Such antichurch policies peaked in the mid-1790s.

[10] Santhonax, Galbo: As commissioner of Saint-Domingue in 1792, the radical French republican Léger Félicité Sonthonax (1763–1813) sought to quell unrest in the colony by granting various rights to free and enslaved Black residents. A new French governor, François-Thomas Galbaud du Fort, opposed his decisions, and violence briefly tore apart Le Cap during chaotic struggles for power in 1793 between various white and black factions.

[11] Having *beaucoup d'esprit*: Being very witty.

I know also the lady abbess, who is an excellent woman of most engaging manners. She lives in a miserable chamber, and supports herself by her industry. The greatest part of the community have perished; and general Le Clerc found it more convenient to have the convent fitted up for his own residence, than to restore it to its owners, the government house having been entirely destroyed. . . .

The mulatto women are the hated but successful rivals of the Creole ladies. Many of them are extremely beautiful; and, being destined from their birth to a life of pleasure, they are taught to heighten the power of their charms by all the aids of art, and to express in every look and gesture all the refinements of voluptuousness. It may be said of them, that their very feet speak. In this country that unfortunate class of beings, so numerous in my own,—victims of seduction, devoted to public contempt and universal scorn, is unknown. Here a false step is rarely made by an unmarried lady, and a married lady, who does not make one, is as rare; yet of both there have been instances: but the *faux pas* of a married lady is so much a matter of course, that she who has only one lover, and retains him long in her chains, is considered a model of constancy and discretion.

To the destiny of the women of colour no infamy is attached; they have inspired passions which have lasted through life, and are faithful to their lovers through every vicissitude of fortune and chance. But before the revolution their splendor, their elegance, their influence over the men, and the fortunes lavished on them by their infatuated lovers, so powerfully excited the jealousy of the white ladies, that they complained to the council of the ruin their extravagance occasioned to many families, and a decree was issued imposing restrictions on their dress. No woman of colour was to wear silk, which was then universally worn, nor to appear in public without a handkerchief on her head. They determined to oppose this tyranny, and took for that purpose a singular but effectual resolution. They shut themselves up in their houses, and appeared no more in public. The merchants soon felt the bad effects of this determination, and represented so forcibly the injury the decree did to commerce, that it was reversed, and the olive beauties triumphed.

But the rage of the white ladies still pursued them with redoubled fury, for what is so violent as female jealousy? The contest however was unequal, and the influence of their detested rivals could not be counteracted. Some of them were very rich. There is a friendliness and simplicity in their manners which is very interesting. They are the most caressing creatures in the world, and breathe nothing but affection and love. One of their most enviable privileges, and which they inherit from nature, is that their beauty is immortal——they never fade.

The French appear to understand less than any other people the delights arising from an union of hearts. They seek only the gratification of their sensual appetites. They gather the flowers, but taste not the fruits of love. They call women the *"beau sexe,"* and know them only under the enchanting form of ministers of pleasure. They may appear thus to those who have only eyes; by those who have hearts they will always be considered as sacred objects of reverence and love. A man who thinks and feels views in women the beneficent creature who nourished him with her milk, and watched over his helpless infancy; a consoling being who soothes his pains and softens his sorrows by her tenderness and even by her levity and her sports. But here female virtue is blasted in the bud by the contagious influence of example. Every girl sighs to be married to escape from the restraint in which she is held whilst single, and to enjoy the unbounded liberty she so often sees abused by her mother. A husband is necessary to give her a place in society; but is considered of so little importance to her happiness, that in the choice of one her inclination is very seldom consulted. And when her heart, in spite of custom, feels the pain of being alone, and seeks an asylum in the bosom of her husband, she too often finds it shut against her; she is assailed by those whose only desire is to add another trophy to their conquests, and is borne away by the torrent of fashion and dissipation till all traces of her native simplicity are destroyed. She joins with unblushing front, the crowd who talk of sentiments they never feel, and who indulge in the most licentious excesses without having the glow of passion to gild their errors. These reflections were suggested by a most preposterous marriage, at which I was present. A girl of fifteen was sacrificed by her grandmother to a man of sixty, of the most disagreeable appearance and forbidding manners. The soul of this unfortunate victim is all melting softness; she is of the most extraordinary beauty; she is now given to the world, and in those who surround her she will find the destroyers of her delicacy, her simplicity, and her peace.

Letter XVI

St. Jago de Cuba.[12]

We have left Barracoa, the good Father Philip, his generous sister, and the beautiful Jacinta.[13] Removed from them for ever, the recollection of their goodness will accompany me through life, and a sigh for the peaceful solitude of their retreat will often heave my breast amid the mingled scenes of pleasure and vexation in which I

---

[12] St. Jago de Cuba: Santiago, Cuba, is a port city on the southern shore, close to Saint-Domingue. In Letter XV, Mary describes her flight from Le Cap with her sister Clara and her brother-in-law St. Louis. En route to Santiago, their French vessel was commandeered by a British ship, and they were sent to the more rustic port of Baracoa, Cuba.

[13] During their brief stay in Baracoa, Cuba, Mary, Clara, and St. Louis were assisted by a priest, Father Philip, and the wife of the town's governor, Jacinta. Jacinta, a young and vivacious Spanish Creole, is enraptured with the beautiful American Clara.

shall be again engaged. Fortunate people! who, instead of rambling about the world, end their lives beneath the roofs where they first drew breath. Fortunate in knowing nothing beyond their horizon; for whom even the next town is a strange country, and who find their happiness in contributing to that of those who surround them! The wife of the governor could not separate herself from us. Taking from her neck a rosary of pearls, she put it round that of Clara, pressed her in her arms, wept on her bosom, and said she never passed a moment so painful. She is young, her soul is all tenderness and ardour, and Clara has filled her breast with feelings to which till now she has been a stranger. Her husband is a good man, but without energy or vivacity, the direct reverse of his charming wife. She can never have awakened an attachment more lively than the calmest friendship. She has no children, nor any being around her, whose soul is in unison with her own. With what devotion she would love! but if a stranger to the exquisite pleasures of that sentiment she is also ignorant of its pains! may no destructive passion ever trouble her repose.

She walked with us to the shore and waited on the beach till we embarked. She shrieked with agony when she clasped Clara for the last time to her breast, and leaning against a tree, gave unrestrained course to her tears. . . .

It is Clara's fate to inspire great passions. Nobody loves her moderately. As soon as she is known she seizes on the soul, and centres every desire in that of pleasing her. The friendship she felt for Jacinta, and the impression father Philip's goodness made on her, rendered her insensible to all around her.

The vessel was full of passengers, most of them ladies, who were astonished at beholding such grief. One of them, a native of Jeremie, was the first who attracted the attention of Clara.[14] This lady, who is very handsome, and very young, has three children of the greatest beauty, for whom she has the most impassioned fondness, and seems to view in them her own protracted existence. She has all the bloom of youth, and when surrounded by her children, no picture of Venus with the loves and graces was ever half so interesting. She is going to join her husband at St. Jago, who I hear, is a great libertine, and not sensible of her worth. An air of sadness dwells on her lovely countenance, occasioned, no doubt, by his neglect and the pain of finding a rival in every woman he meets.

There is also on board a beautiful widow whose husband was killed by the negroes, and who, without fortune or protection, is going to seek at St. Jago a subsistence, by employing her talents. There is something inconceivably interesting in these ladies. Young, beautiful, and destitute of all resource, supporting with cheerfulness their wayward fortune.

---

[14] Jeremie: Jérémie, Cuba, was located on the coast of Saint-Domingue's southwestern peninsula. For a substantial portion of the Haitian Revolution, the British occupied the town.

But the most captivating trait in their character is their fondness for their children! The Creole ladies, marrying very young, appear more like the sisters than the mothers of their daughters. Unfortunately they grow up too soon, and not unfrequently become the rivals of their mothers.

We are still on board, at the entrance of the harbour of St. Jago, which is guarded by a fort, the most picturesque object I ever saw. It is built on a rock that hangs over the sea, and the palm trees which wave their lofty heads over its ramparts, add to its beauty.

We are obliged to wait here till to-morrow; for this day being the festival of a saint, all the offices are shut. No business is transacted, and no vessel can approach the town without permission.

This delay is painful; I am on the wing to leave the vessel, though it is only four days since we left Barracoa.—I wish to know whether we shall meet as much hospitality here as in that solitary place. Yet why should I expect it? Hearts like those of father Philip and the lovely Jacinta do not abound.—How many are there who, never having witnessed such goodness, doubt its existence?

We have letters to several families here, from the governor of Barracoa and father Philip, and St. Louis has friends who have been long established at this place. Therefore, on arriving, we shall feel at home; perhaps too, we may find letters from the Cape;—God grant they may contain satisfactory intelligence.

Letter XX

St. Jago de Cuba.

The French emigrants begin to seek in their talents some resource from the frightful poverty to which they are reduced, but meet with very little encouragement. The people here are generally poor, and unaccustomed to expensive pleasures. A company of comedians are building a theatre; and some subscription balls have been given, at which the Spanish ladies were quite eclipsed by the French belles, notwithstanding their losses.

Madame D——, of Jeremie, who plays and sings divinely, gave a concert, which was very brilliant.

The French women are certainly charming creatures in society. The cheerfulness with which they bear misfortune, and the industry they employ to procure themselves a subsistence, cannot be sufficiently admired. I know ladies who from their infancy were surrounded by slaves, anticipating their slightest wishes, now working from the dawn of day till midnight to support themselves and their families. Nor do they even complain, nor vaunt their industry, nor think it surprising that they possess it. Their neatness is worthy of admiration, and their taste gives to their attire an air of fashion which the expensive, but ill-chosen, ornaments of Spanish ladies cannot attain. With one young lady I am particularly acquainted whose goodness cannot be sufficiently admired. Ah! Eliza, how shall I describe thy sweetness, thy fidelity, thy devotion to a suffering friend? Why am I not rich that I could place thee in a situation where thy virtues might be known, thy talents honoured. Alas! I never so deeply regret my own want of power as when reflecting that I am unable to be useful to you.

This amiable girl was left by her parents, who went to Charleston at the beginning of the revolution, to the care of an aunt, who was very rich, and without children. At the evacuation of Port-au-Prince, that lady embarked for this place. Her husband died on the passage; and they were robbed of every thing they possessed by an English privateer. The father of Eliza wrote for them to join him in Carolina; but the ill health of madame L—— would not suffer her to undertake the voyage, and Eliza will not hear of leaving her, but works day and night to procure for her aunt the comforts her situation requires. She is young, beautiful and accomplished. She wastes her bloom over the midnight lamp, and sacrifices her health and her rest to soothe the sufferings of her infirm relation. Her patience and mildness are angelic. Where will such virtues meet their reward? Certainly not in this country; and she is held here by the ties of gratitude and affection which, to a heart like hers, are indissoluble.

In the misfortunes of my French friends, I see clearly exemplified the advantages of a good education. Every talent, even if possessed in a slight degree of perfection, may be a resource in a reverse of fortune; and, though I liked not entirely their manner, whilst surrounded by the festivity and splendour of the Cape, I now confess that they excite my warmest admiration. They bear adversity with cheerfulness, and resist it with fortitude. In the same circumstances I fear I should be inferior to them in both. But in this country, slowly emerging from a state of barbarism, what encouragement can be found for industry or talents? The right of commerce was purchased by the Catalonians, who alone exercise it, and agriculture is destroyed in consequence of the restraints imposed on it by the government.[15] The people are poor, and therefore cannot possess talents whose acquisition is beyond their reach; but they are temperate, even to a proverb, and so hospitable that the poorest among them always find something to offer a stranger. At the same time they are said to be false, treacherous, and revengeful, to the highest degree. Certainly there are here no traces of that magnanimous spirit, which once animated the Spanish cavalier, who was considered by the whole world as a model of constancy, tenderness and heroism.[16]

---

[15] Catalonia is a northwestern region of Spain. Cuba was a Spanish colony until the United States began its occupation in 1898.

[16] Perhaps a reference to a cultural stereotype or even a reference to Don Quixote, the chivalrous, idealistic, and naïve hero created by the seventeenth-century Spanish author Miguel Cervantes.

They feel for the distressed, because they are poor; and are hospitable because they know want. In every other respect this is a degenerate race, possessing none of the qualities of the Spaniards of old except jealousy, which is often the cause of tragical events. . . .

Letter XXV

Kingston, Jamaica.[17]

The scenes of barbarity, which these girls have witnessed at the Cape, are almost incredible. The horror, however, which I felt on hearing an account of them, has been relieved by the relation of some more honourable to human nature. In the first days of the massacre, when negroes ran through the town killing all the white men they encountered, a Frenchman was dragged from the place of his concealment by a ruthless mulatto, who, drawing his sabre, bade him prepare to die. The trembling victim raised a supplicating look, and the murderer, letting fall his uplifted arm, asked if he had any money. He replied, that he had none; but that if he would conduct him to the house of an American merchant, he might probably procure any sum he might require. The mulatto consented, and when they entered the house, the Frenchman with all the energy of one pleading for his life, entreated the American to lend him a considerable sum. The gentleman he addressed was too well acquainted with the villainy of the negroes to trust to their word. He told the mulatto, that he would give the two thousand dollars demanded, but not till the Frenchman was embarked in a vessel which was going to sail in a few days for Philadelphia, and entirely out of danger. The mulatto refused. The unfortunate Frenchman wept, and the American kept firm. While they were disputing, a girl of colour, who lived with the American, entered, and having learned the story, employed all her eloquence to make the mulatto relent. She sunk at his feet, and pressed his hands which were reeking with blood. Dear brother, she said, spare for my sake this unfortunate man. He never injured you; nor will you derive any advantage from his death, and by saving him, you will acquire the sum you demand, and a claim to his gratitude. She was beautiful; she wept, and beauty in tears has seldom been resisted. Yet this unrelenting savage did resist; and swore, with bitter oaths to pursue all white men

---

[17] After Clara's flight, Mary had no reason to remain with St. Louis. She and another lady left Cuba for Jamaica. There, Mary encountered Frenchwomen she knew who then told her about the events they had witnessed or heard about back in Le Cap. After declaring victory over the French and Haitian independence, the revolutionary leader Dessalines ordered the slaughter of all the remaining French people.

with unremitting fury. The girl, however, hung to him, repeated her solicitations, and offered him, in addition to the sum proposed, all her trinkets, which were of considerable value.

The mulatto, enraged, asked if the Frenchman was anything to her? Nothing, she replied; I never saw him before; but to save the life of an innocent person how trifling would appear the sacrifice I offer. She continued her entreaties in the most caressing tone, which for some time had no effect, when softening all at once, he said, I will not deprive you of your trinkets, nor is it for the sum proposed that I relent, but for you alone, for to you I feel that I can refuse nothing. He shall be concealed, and guarded by myself till the moment of embarking; but, when he is out of danger, you must listen to me in your turn.

She heard him with horror; but, dissembling, said there would be always time enough to think of those concerns. She was then too much occupied by the object before her.

The American, who stood by and heard this proposal, made to one to whom he was extremely attached, felt disposed to knock the fellow down, but the piteous aspect of the almost expiring Frenchman withheld his hand. He gave the mulatto a note for the money he had demanded, on the conditions before mentioned, and the Frenchman was faithfully concealed till the vessel was ready to sail, and then embarked.

When he was gone, the mulatto called on the girl, and offering her the note, told her that he had accepted it as a matter of form, but that he now gave it to her; and reminded her of the promise she had made to listen to his wishes. Her lover entering at that moment told him that the vessel was then out of the harbour, and that his money was ready. He took it, and thus being in the power of the American gentleman, who had great weight with Dessalines, he probably thought it best to relinquish his projects on the charming Zuline, for she heard of him no more.

The same girl was the means of saving many others, and the accounts I have heard of her kindness and generosity oblige me to think of her with unqualified admiration.

Further Reading

Adams, Catherine, and Elizabeth H. Pleck. *Love of Freedom: Black Women in Colonial and Revolutionary New England.* New York: Oxford University Press, 2004.

Allgor, Catherine. *Parlor Politics: In Which the Ladies of Washington Help Build a City and a Government.* Richmond: University of Virginia Press, 2001.

Armstrong, Nancy. *Desire and Domestic Fiction: A Political History of the Novel.* New York: Oxford University Press, 1990.

Backscheider, Paula. *Eighteenth-Century Women Poets and Their Poetry: Inventing Agency, Inventing Genre.* Baltimore: Johns Hopkins University Press, 2007.

Baker, Samuel. *Written on the Water: British Romanticism and the Maritime Empire of Culture.* Richmond: University of Virginia Press, 2010.

Bassard, Katherine Clay. *Spiritual Interrogations: Culture, Gender, and Community in Early African American Women's Writing.* Princeton: Princeton University Press, 1999.

Basu, Amrita. *The Challenge of Global Feminisms: Women's Movements in Global Perspective.* Boulder: Westview Press, 1995.

Baucom, Ian. *Specters of the Atlantic: Finance Capital, Slavery, and the Philosophy of History.* Durham: Duke University Press, 2005.

Baym, Nina. *American Women Writers and the Work of History, 1790–1860.* New Brunswick: Rutgers University Press, 1995.

Berkin, Carol. *Revolutionary Mothers: Women in the Struggle for America's Independence.* New York: Knopf, 2005.

———, and Mary Beth Norton. *Women of America: A History.* Boston: Houghton Mifflin, 1979.

Boulukos, George. *The Grateful Slave: The Emergence of Race in Eighteenth-Century British and American Culture.* Cambridge: Cambridge University Press, 2008.

Branson, Susan. *Dangerous to Know: Women, Crime and Notoriety in the Early Republic.* Philadelphia: University of Pennsylvania Press, 2008.

———. *These Fiery, Frenchified Dames: Women and Political Culture in Early National Philadelphia.* Philadelphia: University of Pennsylvania Press, 2001.

Brooks, Joanna. *American Lazarus: Religion and the Rise of Early African American and Native American Literatures.* New York: Oxford University Press, 2003.

Bross, Kristina, and Hilary E. Wyss, eds. *Early Native Literacies in New England: A Documentary and Critical Anthology.* Amherst: University of Massachusetts Press, 2008.

Brown, Kathleen. *Good Wives, Nasty Wenches, and Anxious Patriarchs: Gender, Race, and Power in Colonial Virginia*. Chapel Hill: University of North Carolina Press, 1996.

Brown, Laura. *Ends of Empire: Women and Ideology in Early Eighteenth-Century English Literature*. Ithaca: Cornell University Press, 1993.

Butler, Marilyn. *Jane Austen and the War of Ideas*. 2nd ed. Oxford: Oxford University Press, 1987.

Carney, Virginia Moore. *Eastern Band Cherokee Women: Cultural Persistence in Their Letters and Speeches*. Knoxville: University of Tennessee Press, 2005.

Carretta, Vincent, ed. *Unchained Voices: An Anthology of Black Authors in the English-Speaking World of the Eighteenth Century*. Lexington: University Press of Kentucky, 1996.

Carroll, Lorrayne. *Rhetorical Drag: Gender Impersonation, Captivity, and the Writing of History*. Ohio: Kent State University Press, 2007.

Carruth, Mary C., ed. *Feminist Interventions in Early American Studies*. Tuscaloosa: University of Alabama Press, 2006.

Casid, Jill. *Sowing Empire: Landscape and Colonization*. Minneapolis: University of Minnesota Press, 2005.

Cohen, Matt. *The Networked Wilderness: Communication in Early New England*. Minneapolis: University of Minnesota Press, 2009.

Craciun, Adriana. *British Women Writers and the French Revolution: Citizens of the World*. London: Palgrave, 2004.

———, and Kari E. Lokke, eds. *Rebellious Hearts: British Women Writers and the French Revolution*. Albany: State University Press of New York, 2001.

Crane, Elaine Forman. *Ebb Tide in New England: Women, Seaports, and Social Change, 1630–1800*. Boston: Northeastern University Press, 1998.

Davies, Kate. *Catherine Macaulay and Mercy Otis Warren: The Revolutionary Atlantic and the Politics of Gender*. New York: Oxford University Press, 2006.

Davis, David Brion. *The Problem of Slavery in the Age of Revolution*. London: Oxford University Press, 1988.

Dillon, Elizabeth Maddock. *The Gender of Freedom: Fictions of Liberalism and the Literary Public Sphere*. Palo Alto: Stanford University Press, 2004.

Donoghue, Emma. *Passions Between Women: British Lesbian Culture, 1660–1800*. New York: Harper Perennial, 1996 (orig. 1994).

Eger, Elizabeth. *Bluestockings: Women of Reason from Enlightenment to Romanticism*. Basingstoke: Palgrave Macmillan, 2010.

Evans, Sara M. *Born for Liberty: A History of Women in America*. New York: Free Press, 1997.

Faderman, Lillian. *Surpassing the Love of Men: Romantic Friendship and Love between Women from the Renaissance to the Present*. Rev. ed. New York: Harper, 1998.

Feldman, Paula R., and Theresa M. Kelley, eds. *Romantic Women Writers: Voices and Countervoices*. Hanover, NH: University Press of New England, 1995.

Ferree, Myra, and Aili Tripp. *Global Feminism: Transnational Women's Activism, Organizing and Human Rights*. New York: New York University Press, 2006.

Ferguson, Moira, ed. *The Hart Sisters: Early African Caribbean Writers, Evangelicals, and Radicals*. Lincoln: University of Nebraska Press, 1993.

———. *Subject to Others: British Women Writers and Colonial Slavery, 1670–1834*. New York: Routledge, 1994.

Few, Martha. *Women Who Live Evil Lives: Gender, Religion, and the Politics of Power in Colonial Guatemala, 1650–1750*. Austin: University of Texas Press, 2002.

Fischer, Kirsten. *Suspect Relations: Sex, Race, and Resistance in Colonial North Carolina*. Ithaca: Cornell University Press, 2001.

Foster, Thomas, ed. *Long Before Stonewall: Histories of Same-Sex Sexuality in Early America*. New York: New York University Press, 2007.

Gaspar, David Barry, and Darlene Clark Hine, eds. *Beyond Bondage: Free Women of Color in the Americas*. Urbana: University of Illinois Press, 2004.

Gerzina, Gretchen Holbrook. *Black London: Life Before Emancipation.* New Brunswick, Rutgers University Press, 1995.

Gilroy, Paul. *The Black Atlantic: Modernity and Double Consciousness.* Cambridge: Harvard University Press, 1993.

Gomez, Michael. *Exchanging our Country Marks: The Transformation of African Identities in the Colonial and Antebellum South.* Chapel Hill: University of North Carolina Press, 1998.

Graubart, Karen. *With Our Labor and Sweat: Indigenous Women and the Formation of Colonial Society in Peru.* Palo Alto: Stanford University Press, 2007.

Gundersen, Joan. *To Be Useful to the World: Women in Revolutionary America, 1740–1790.* Rev. Ed. Chapel Hill: University of North Carolina Press, 2006.

Gutierrez, Ramon. *When Jesus Came, the Corn Mothers Went Away: Marriage, Sexuality, and Power in New Mexico, 1500–1846.* Palo Alto: Stanford University Press, 1991.

Hackel, Heidi, and Catherine Kelly. *Reading Women: Literacy, Authorship, and Culture in the Atlantic World.* Philadelphia: University of Pennsylvania Press, 2007.

Haggerty, George. *Unnatural Affections: Women and Fiction in the Later Eighteenth Century.* Bloomington: Indiana University Press, 1998.

Harris, Sharon, ed. *American Women Writers to 1800.* New York: Oxford, University Press, 1996.

———. *Executing Race: Early American Women's Narratives of Race, Society, and the Law.* Columbus: Ohio State University Press, 2005.

Hobsbawm, Eric. *The Age of Revolution, 1789–1848.* New York: Vintage, 1996 (orig. 1962).

Hoffman, Ronald, and Peter J. Albert, eds. *Women in the Age of the American Revolution.* Charlottesville: University Press of Virginia, 1989.

Hutner, Heidi. *Colonial Women: Race and Culture in Stuart Drama.* New York: Oxford University Press, 2001.

Jaffary, Nora. *False Mystics: Deviant Orthodoxy in Colonial Mexico.* Lincoln: University of Nebraska Press, 2008.

Jones, Vivien, ed. *Women in the Eighteenth Century: Constructions of Femininity.* London: Routledge, 1990.

Justice, Daniel Heath. "Katteuha (Cherokee)." *Heath Anthology of American Literature.* Vol. A. 6th ed. Ed. Paul Lauter, Richard Yarborough, et al. Boston: Houghton Mifflin, 2009. 827.

———. *Our Fire Survives the Storm: A Cherokee Literary History.* Minneapolis: University of Minnesota Press, 2006.

Kelly, Joan. *Women, History and Theory: The Essays of Joan Kelly.* Chicago: University of Chicago Press, 1986.

Kelly, Mary. *Learning to Stand and Speak: Women, Education, and Public Life.* Chapel Hill: University of North Carolina Press, 2006.

Kerber, Linda K. *No Constitutional Right to Be Ladies: Women and the Obligations of Citizenship.* New York: Hill and Wang, 1998.

———. *Women of the Republic: Intellect and Ideology in Revolutionary America.* Chapel Hill: University of North Carolina Press, 1980

Kilcup, Karen, ed. *Nineteenth-Century Native American Women Writers: An Anthology.* London: Blackwell, 1997.

Kugel, Rebecca, and Lucy Eldersveld Murphy, eds. *Native Women's History in Eastern North America before 1900: A Guide to Research and Writing.* Lincoln: University of Nebraska Press, 2007.

Landes, Joan B. *Women and the Public Sphere in the Age of the French Revolution.* Ithaca: Cornell University Press, 1988.

Langley, April C. E. *The Black Aesthetic Unbound: Theorizing the Dilemma of Eighteenth-Century African American Literature.* Columbus: Ohio State University Press, 2008.

Larson, Rebecca. *Daughters of Light: Quaker Women Preaching and Prophesying in the Colonies and Abroad, 1700–1775.* New York: Knopf, 1999.

Levy, Darline Gay, Harriet Branson Applewhite, and Mary Durham Johnson, eds. *Women in Revolutionary Paris, 1789–1795: Selected Documents Translated with Notes and Commentary.* Urbana: University of Illinois Press, 1979.

Looser, Devoney. *Women Writers and Old Age in Great Britain, 1750–1850*. Baltimore: Johns Hopkins University Press, 2008.

Lyon, Clare A. *Sex among the Rabble: An Intimate History of Gender & Power in the Age of Revolution, Philadelphia, 1730–1830*. Chapel Hill: University of North Carolina Press, 2006.

MacCubbin, Robert Purks, ed. *'Tis Nature's Fault: Unauthorized Sexuality During the Enlightenment*. Cambridge: Cambridge University Press, 1985.

Mandell, Laura. *Misogynous Economies: The Business of Literature in Eighteenth-Century Britain*. Lexington: University Press of Kentucky, 1999.

Moore, Lisa L. *Dangerous Intimacies: Toward a Sapphic History of the British Novel*. Durham: Duke University Press, 1997.

———. *Sister Arts: The Erotics of Lesbian Landscapes*. Minneapolis: University of Minnesota Press, 2011.

Norton, Mary Beth. *Founding Mothers and Fathers: Gendered Power and the Forming of American Society*. New York: Knopf, 1996.

———. *Liberty's Daughters: The Revolutionary Experience of American Women, 1750–1800*. Rev. ed. Ithaca: Cornell University Press, 1996 (orig. 1980).

———. *Separated by Their Sex: Women in Public and Private in the Colonial Atlantic World*. Ithaca: Cornell University Press, 2011.

Nussbaum, Felicity. *The Autobiographical Subject: Gender and Ideology in Eighteenth-Century England*. Baltimore: Johns Hopkins University Press, 1989.

———, ed. *The Global Eighteenth Century*. Baltimore: Johns Hopkins University Press, 2005.

———. *Rival Queens: Actresses, Performance, and the Eighteenth-Century British Theater*. Philadelphia: University of Pennsylvania Press, 2010.

———. *Torrid Zones: Maternity, Sexuality and Empire in Eighteenth-Century Narratives*. Baltimore: Johns Hopkins University Press, 1995.

———, and Laura Brown, eds. *The New Eighteenth Century: Theory, Politics, English Literature*. London and New York: Methuen, 1987.

O'Brien, Karen. *Women and Enlightenment in Eighteenth-Century Britain*. Cambridge: Cambridge University Press, 2009.

Perdue, Theda. *Cherokee Women: Gender and Culture Change, 1700–1835*. Lincoln: University of Nebraska Press, 1998.

Prior, Mary, ed. *Women in English Society 1500–1800*. London: Methuen, 1985.

Rediker, Marcus. *The Slave Ship: A Human History*. New York: Viking, 2007.

Ryan, Mary P. *Womanhood in America: From Colonial Times to the Present*. New York: Watts, 1983.

Schellenberg, Betty A. *The Professionalization of Women Authors in Eighteenth-Century Britain*. Cambridge: Cambridge University Press, 2005.

Schroeder, Susan, Stephanie Wood, and Robert Haskett, eds. *Indian Women of Early Mexico*. Norman: University of Oklahoma Press, 1997.

Schweitzer, Ivy. *Perfecting Friendship: Politics and Affiliation in Early American Literature*. Chapel Hill: University of North Carolina Press, 2006.

Sensbach, Jon. *Rebecca's Revival: Creating Black Christianity in the Atlantic World*. Cambridge: Harvard University Press, 2006.

Shockley, Ann Allen. *Afro-American Women Writers, 1746–1933*. New York: Signet, 1988.

Sidbury, James. *Becoming African in America: Race and Nation in the Early Black Atlantic*. New York: Oxford University Press, 2007.

Smallwood, Stephanie. *Saltwater Slavery: A Middle Passage from Africa to American Diaspora*. Cambridge: Harvard University Press, 2007.

Snyder, Terri. *Babbling Women: Disorderly Speech and the Law in Early Virginia*. Ithaca: Cornell University Press, 2003.

Stabile, Susan M. *Memory's Daughters: The Material Culture of Remembrance in Eighteenth-Century America*. Ithaca: Cornell University Press, 2004.

Stone, Lawrence. *The Family, Sex and Marriage in England, 1500–1800*. New York: Harper and Row, 1979.

Straub, Kristina. *Domestic Affairs: Intimacy, Eroticism, and Violence between Servants and Masters in Eighteenth-Century Britain*. Baltimore: Johns Hopkins University Press, 2008.

———. *Sexual Suspects: Eighteenth-Century Players and Sexual Ideology*. Princeton: Princeton University Press, 1991.

Summers, Claude. *Homosexuality in Renaissance and Enlightenment England: Literary Representations in Historical Context*. New York: Harrington Park Press, 1992.

Sussman, Charlotte. *Consuming Anxieties: Consumer Protest, Gender, and British Slavery, 1713–1833*. Palo Alto: Stanford University Press, 2000.

Ulrich, Laurel. *Good Wives: Image and Reality in the Lives of Women in Northern New England, 1650–1750*. New York: Knopf, 1992.

———. *A Midwife's Tale: The Life of Martha Ballard, Based on her Diary, 1785–1812*. New York: Knopf, 1990.

Woodard, Helena. *African-British Writings in the Eighteenth Century: The Politics of Race and Reason*. New York: Praeger, 1999.

Wulf, Karin A. *Not All Wives: Women of Colonial Philadelphia*. Ithaca: Cornell University Press, 2000.

Young, Alfred. *Masquerade: The Life and Times of Deborah Sampson, Continental Soldier*. New York: Vintage, 2005.

Appendix of Images

The Age of Revolutions generated a vibrant visual culture in which women often figured as emblems of national hopes and fortunes. As depicted by European and Euro-American illustrators, images of indigenous American women and women of African descent often carried the additional symbolic weight of the era's emerging conceptions of racial and national difference. In this section, we include images of women from books, broadsides, and political cartoons to be read alongside and in dialogue with the voices of women included in the anthology to provide the fullest possible sense of the significance of women in the Age of Revolutions.

FIGURE 1: *America* **(London, 1671).** *This image is the frontispiece of* America: Being the Latest, and Most Accurate Description of the New World . . . *(1671) by John Ogilby (1600–1676). Ogilby published a series of beautifully bound and illustrated volumes during the seventeenth century. Several of these, like* America, *were atlases in which he translated and compiled others' accounts. The image's focal point is the figure of America, here represented by an indigenous woman atop a cornucopia. Embodying fertility and prosperity, she tosses down gold, jewels, and a crown to the Natives and Europeans below. Image courtesy of the Harry Ransom Humanities Research Center, The University of Texas at Austin.*

FIGURE 2: *Bunkers Hill or America's Head Dress* (**London, M. Darly, 1776**). *This cartoon depicts a calm, well-dressed woman in profile. She wears an ornamental head-dress upon which soldiers under three different flags engage in combat using artillery and muskets. A sea battle occurs on the head-dress's lower portion. The cartoon's title refers to the June 1775 Battle of Bunker Hill in which the Americans battled British forces. Though the British won, it was an expensive victory: they suffered 1,000 casualties as compared to the Americans' four hundred. As a result, Americans generally felt more optimistic about their prospects for independence. Image courtesy of the Library of Congress (reproduction number LC-USZ62–54).*

FIGURE 3: *The Female Combatants, or Who Shall* (**London, 1776**). *This cartoon represents the American Revolution as two women engaged in fisticuffs. Britannia is "FOR OBEDIENCE" and declares, "I'll force you to Obedience you Rebellious Slut." Meanwhile, America responds, "Liberty Liberty for ever Mother while I exist," and punches her on the nose. The print represents America as a bare-chested Native woman who is "FOR LIBERTY." Image courtesy of The Lewis Walpole Library, Yale University.*

FIGURE 4: *America Triumphant and Britannia in Distress* **(Boston, 1782).** *This print represents America's triumph over Britain. America is depicted as the Roman goddess Minerva, usually associated with wisdom and prowess in war. The snake swallowing its tail and encircling her shield is an oroborus, an emblem of wholeness and infinity. An "EXPLANATION" at the bottom reads: "I America sitting on that quarter of the globe with the Flag of the United States displayed over her head; holding in one hand the Olive branch, inviting the ships of all nations to partake of her commerce; and in the other hand supporting the Cap of Liberty. II Fame proclaiming the joyful news to all the world. III Britannia weeping at the loss of the trade of America, attended with an evil genius. IV The British flag struck, on her strong Fortresses. V French, Spanish, Dutch &c shipping in the harbours of America. VI A view of New York wherein is exhibited the Trator Arnold, taken with remorse for selling his [country?] and Judas like hanging himself." Courtesy of the Library of Congress (reproduction number LC-DIG-ppmsca-24328)*

FIGURE 5: *The Tea-Tax-Tempest, or Old Time with His Magick-Lantern* (London: W. Humphreys, 1783). *Here, Britannia and America watch Old Time's glass lantern presentation on the American Revolution. At the presentation's center is an exploding teapot, a likely reference to the Boston Tea Party. Old Time explains the cartoon:* "There you see the little Hot Spit Fire Tea pot that has done all The Mischief—There you see the Old British Lion basking before the American Bon Fire whilst the French Cock is blowing up a storm About his Ears to Destroy him and his young Welpes—There you see see [sic] Miss America grasping at the Cap of Liberty—There you see The British Forces be yok'd and be cramp'd flying before the Congress Men—There you see the thirteen Stripes and Rattle-Snake exalted—There you see the Stamp'd Paper help to Make the Pot Boil.—There you see &. &. &." *This version was published in 1783 to commemorate the official end of the Revolution. It is an adaptation of a 1778 print by Carl Guttenberg of Nuremberg, who, in turn, had emulated a 1774 British print by John Dixon. Image courtesy of the Library of Congress (reproduction number LC-USZC4–5257).*

FIGURE 6: *Mrs. General Washington, Bestowing Thirteen Stripes on Britania* **(1783).** *In this print created for British* Rambler's Magazine, *a cross-dressing General Washington flogs Britannia using a whip with thirteen lashes to the encouragements of men representing Holland, France, and Spain. Mrs. Washington chastises Britannia, "Parents Should not behave like Tyrants to their children." Britannia responds, "Is it thus my Children treat me." Image courtesy of the Library of Congress (reproduction number LC-USZ62–45484).*

P. Rouvier inv. et del   C. Boily Sculp

SOYEZ LIBRES ET CITOYENS.

FIGURE 7: *Soyez Libre et Citoyens* by Pierre Rouvier and Charles Boily (Lyon, 1789). *"Be Free and Citizens." A group of Black men, women, and children kneels in shackles before a woman, possibly reigning Queen Marie Antoinette, who represents the French monarchy. This image is the frontispiece of Benjamin Sigismond-Frossard's* La Cause des Esclaves Negres et des Habit-ants de la Guinée . . . [The Cause of Negro Slaves and the People of Guinea]. *Sigismond-Frossard was a moderate French Protestant pastor who became a pioneering abolitionist through his contact with English evangelicals and French revolutionaries. Image courtesy of Rare Books and Special Collections, McGill University Library,*

Vive le Roi, Vive la Nation.

J'savois ben Qu'jaurions not tour.

FIGURE 8: *Vive le Roi, Vive la Nation / J'savois Ben Qu'jaurions Not Tour* (France, 1789). *On her back, a nun carries a noblewoman carrying a peasant woman. The peasant woman is well-dressed and nurses an infant. The cartoon thus visually represents the French Revolution's promised social transformation, with the Third Estate riding on top and supported by the nobility and the clergy. The title—written in ungrammatical* patois *and thus suggestive of the language of* le Peuple— *can be loosely translated as "Long Live the King, Long Live the Nation / I knew that our day would come." Image courtesy of the Library of Congress (reproduction number LC-USZC2–3575).*

Un peuple est sans honneur, et mérite ses chaînes
Quand il baisse le front sons le Sceptre des Reines .

FIGURE 9: ***Un Peuple est Sans Honneur . . .*** **(France, 1792).** *"A people is without honor, and deserves to be enchained / When it bows its head before the scepter of queens." This image is an adaptation of the frontispiece of a French book,* Les Crimes des Reines de France, depuis le Commencement de la Monarchie Jusqu'a Marie-Antoinette [Crimes of the Queens of France, since the Beginning of the Monarchy until Marie-Antoinette]. *At its center, a crowned mermaid stabs a king as two-faced Justice looks on. The bust of a satyr above the bed represents lust and licentiousness. Courtesy of the Library of Congress (reproduction number LC-DIG-ppmsca-15893).*

FIGURE 10: *The Genius of France Extirpating Despotism Tyranny & Oppression from the Face of the Earth or the Royal Warriors Defeated* **by Isaac Cruikshank (London, 1792).** *The genius of France, represented by a woman in a liberty cap, holds the reins of a donkey carrying the monarchs of Prussia, Germany, Russia, Sweden, and Brunswick. The woman beats them with a cat-o'-nine-tails and declares, "I am Determin'd to Inflict Death on all Despots & Oppressors." Between the lashes of her whip is written the charges against them: "Perverters of Public Justice," "Oppressors of the People," "The Increase of Tyranny," "The Stretch of Prerogative," "The Abuse of Power," "Despotism," "Monopolizer of Provisions to Distress the poor," "Aristocrats who screen'd by their unjust privileges rob Tradesmen of their Property," and "Religious Bigots." The donkey tramples French King Louis XVI. In the background, another donkey bucks off Turkey, Spain, China, and two other unidentified monarchs. Marie I of Portugal sits on the ground. As in this example, Cruikshank's caricatures were consistently vivid, scathing, and influential. Image courtesy of the Library of Congress (reproduction number LC-USZ62–123025).*

388   *Appendix*

THE

ANTIGALLICAN SONGSTER.

NUMBER I.

THE CONTRAST.

Religion, Morality, Loyalty, Obedience to the Laws, Independence, Personal Security, Justice, Inheritance, Protection, Property, Industry, National Prosperity, Happiness.

Atheism, Perjury, Rebellion, Treason, Anarchy, Murder, Equality, Madness, Cruelty, Injustice, Treachery, Ingratitude, Idleness, Famine, National and private Ruin, Misery.

WHICH IS BEST?

LONDON:

PRINTED FOR J. DOWNES, 240, NEAR TEMPLE-BAR, STRAND.

1793.

FIGURE 11: *The Contrast* **(London, 1793).** *Printed on the title page of* The Antigallican Songster, *a collection of songs with pro-British/anti-French lyrics, this image compares "ENGLISH LIBERTY" and "FRENCH LIBERTY." English Liberty is depicted as Minerva, the Roman goddess of wisdom, and holds the scales of justice in balance as a lion sits at her feet. Below her appear her characteristics: "Religion, Morality, Loyalty, Obedience to the Laws, Independence, Personal Security, Justice, Inheritance, Protection, Property, Industry, National Prosperity, Happiness." French Liberty resembles Medusa or a hag. She carries a head on a pike while she tramples a decapitated body. In the background, a figure hangs from a lamppost. Her characteristics are "Atheism, Perjury, Rebellion, Treason, Anarchy, Murder, Equality, Madness, Cruelty, Injustice, Treachery, Ingratitude, Idleness, Famine, National and private Ruin, Misery." Below these captions, the text facetiously asks, "WHICH IS BEST?" The songster and its accompanying image appeared in 1793, after the advent of the Reign of Terror and most Britons' condemnation of the French Revolution. This item is reproduced by permission of The Huntington Library, San Marino, California from* The Antigallican Songster, *call number 213964.*

Europe supported by Africa & America.

FIGURE 12: *Europe Supported by Africa & America by* **William Blake (London, 1796).** *This image is one of about eighty stunning illustrations created by the famed poet and engraver William Blake for John Gabriel Stedman's* Narrative, of a Five Years' Expedition, Against the Revolted Negroes of Surinam, in Guinea, on the Wild Coast of South America. *The book is a heavily edited version of the diary that Stedman kept as a military officer in the Dutch army during the campaign to suppress a Maroon rebellion in the colony of Suriname (formerly Dutch Guiana). Blake based the engravings on Stedman's own watercolors, painted while in Suriname. The above image depicts three nude women—representing Europe, Africa, and America—embracing. Europe, a white woman wearing blue beads, looks down while Africa and America, with metal armbands, gaze outward. It is the final illustration of Stedman's two-volume book, and he makes direct reference to it in the text: "[A]fter all the horrors and cruelties with which I must have hurt both the eye and the heart of the feeling reader, I will close the scene with an emblematical picture of* Europe supported by Africa and America, *accompanied by an ardent wish that in the friendly manner as they are represented, they may henceforth and to all eternity be the props of each other." Image courtesy of Rare Books and Archives, the Nettie Lee Benson Latin American Collection, The University of Texas at Austin.*

T. Stothard pinx.t   W. Grainger sculp.t

The VOYAGE of the SABLE VENUS, from ANGOLA to the WEST INDIES.

FIGURE 13: *The Voyage of the Sable Venus, from Angola to the West Indies by* Thomas Stothard **(London, 1801).** *In this sensual and fantastical image, an almost entirely nude Black woman, the Sable Venus of the title, sits on a throne while riding a scallop shell chariot pulled by two fish or dolphins. Above her, five white cherubs cheerfully serve her. In the waves below are two more cupids as well as two white men, one of whom may be Neptune, the Roman god of the seas, holding a British flag. One of the flying cherubs, probably Cupid, aims an arrow at him. The image accompanied a poem in Bryan Edwardss'* The History, Civil and Commercial, of the British Colonies in the West Indies *(3rd edition, volume 2). In the poem, "The Sable Venus: An Ode," the speaker seeks the realm of the Sable Venus, where "ready joys" and "unbought rapture meet." He compares her to the Roman Venus, and declares that the two goddesses have "no difference, no—none at night" when darkness conceals the color of their skin. Image courtesy of Rare Books and Archives, the Nettie Lee Benson Latin American Collection, The University of Texas at Austin.*

Blood Hounds attacking a Black Family in the Woods.

FIGURE 14: ***Blood Hounds Attacking a Black Family in the Woods* by J. Barlow (London, 1805).** *In* An Historical Account of the Black Empire of Hayti, *Marcus Rainsford published one of the first histories of the Haitian Revolution sympathetic to the Black revolutionaries. Many of the book's illustrations powerfully represent the wartime atrocities committed by French forces. Others depict the civility and humanity of Black Haitians. Only one illustration shows them engaged in violence. The above image depicts General Rochambeau's use of vicious dogs to terrorize the Black population. At the center of the image, a Black mother holds her infant aloft as the dogs tear at her and what are likely other members of her family. She appears to be gazing directly at the viewer. The island in the background is peaceful and idyllic. Image courtesy of the Harry Ransom Humanities Research Center, The University of Texas at Austin.*

Index

Numbers in italics indicate illustrations.

Charleston, South Carolina, 184n1, 297nn3,
7, 350
chastity, 27, 76–77, 82n12, 82–83,
239–241, 282
Cherokee General Council, 179
Cherokee Nation
role of women, 4–5, 11, 178–179,
180–182
Cherokee Women's Council, 179, 182n5
childbirth and childbearing, 21–22, 28,
261, 283
See also fertility rates; infant mortality
childhood, 23
Cholenec, Pierre, 76–77
The Life of Katherine Tegakoüita,
77–83
Christianity, 12, 35, 73, 101, 141,
213n3, 304
and Black women, 110
colonial, 11
and native people, 24, 100, 141
sacraments of, 79n5
and women, 54, 287
See also Catholic Church; Church of
England; Protestantism; *and other sects*
Christian Monthly History, The, 112
Church of England, 20, 39, 73, 68
citizenship, rights, 26, 69, 333, 339
of Black people, 333
of Native Americans, 6
and women, 9, 242–244, 243n2,
248–254, 339
City Gazette and Daily Advertiser, 296
Civil Rights Era, 6
class, 10–11, 17, 30, 32, 160, 277n16
See also laboring classes; middle class;
third estate
Claus, Daniel, 170–171
Clio, 87
See also Sansom, Martha Fowke
"Cloe to Artemisa" (Anonymous), 92–93
Coleridge, Samuel Taylor, 324
Collier, Mary, 103–104
"The Woman's Labour," 103–109
colonialism, effect on women, 25
and indigenous women, 5, 11, 114–115,
155, 179
colonies, English, 3, 13, 18, 23–24, 27, 164,
186, 291
and law, 18, 27
and literacy, 24
and slavery, 146, 210

and women, 173, 299
See also Antigua; Barbados
colonies, French, 24, 116n7, 245, 291
See also Saint-Domingue; Haiti
colonies, Spanish, 18, 116n7, 333
Columbus, Christopher, 218n15
commonplace books, 27, 28, 29
Common Sense (Paine), 3–4, 155, 261
Commune of Paris, 245, 314n2
communities
of color, 19, 22, 110, 147
of former slaves, 13, 113n2, 186
founded by women, 20–21, 29, 76,
147, 261
indigenous, 11
intellectual, 130
religious, 76, 110
See also specific groups
companionate marriage, 18, 19, 290n5
See also marriage
Constitution of Haiti, 15, 333–337, 357n8,
363n8, 366n14
Constitution of the United States, 14
Continental Army, 178, 338
Continental Congress, 4, 152n5, 153n6, 160,
344n12
"Contrast, The," *388*
conversion, to Christianity, 24, 27, 101,
140–141
Cook, James, 218n16
Coosaponakeesa, 114–115, 115nn1–3, 5,
116nn6–7, 120n18, 123n20
Memorial, 115–123
coquetry, 235–238
Corday, Charlotte, 315nn5–7
depictions of, 312n1, 312–314, *313, 314,*
316nn8–9
and Marat, assassination of, 314–318,
317n13, 327n11, 350–351, 352n2, 354n5
Cortes, Hernan, 218n14
coverture, 133–136
Cowper, William, 301n3, 303n8, 307
Craig, James Henry, 184n2
Craik, Helen, 313–314
Creek Nation, 114–115, 115n5, 116–123,
116n7, 123n20
cross-dressing, 13, 49, 338–339, 347n23, *383*
Cruikshank, Isaac
"The Genius of France Extirpating
Despotism Tyranny & Oppression from
the face of the Earth or the Royal Warriors
Defeated," *387*

Made in the USA
Middletown, DE
25 March 2020